Let Jasmine Rain Down

CHICAGO STUDIES IN ETHNOMUSICOLOGY

A SERIES EDITED BY PHILIP V. BOHLMAN AND BRUNO NETTL

Let Jasmine Rain Down

SONG AND REMEMBRANCE AMONG SYRIAN JEWS

Kay Kaufman Shelemay

THE UNIVERSITY OF CHICAGO PRESS
CHICAGO AND LONDON

Kay Kaufman Shelemay is professor of music at Harvard University. She is the author of several books, including *A Song of Longing: An Ethiopian Journey,* and is currently president of the Society for Ethnomusicology.

The University of Chicago Press, Chicago 60637
The University of Chicago Press, Ltd., London

Printed in the United States of America

07 06 05 04 03 02 01 00 99 98 5 4 3 2 1

ISBN (cloth): 0-226-75211-9
ISBN (paper): 0-226-75212-7

Library of Congress Cataloging-in-Publication Data

Shelemay, Kay Kaufman.
Let jasmine rain down : song and remembrance among Syrian Jews / Kay Kaufman Shelemay.
p. cm. — (Chicago studies in ethnomusicology)
Includes bibliographical references and index.
ISBN 0-226-75211-9. — ISBN 0-226-75212-7 (pbk.)
1. Sephardim—United States—Music—History and criticism. 2. Jews—Syria—Music—History and criticism. I. Title. II. Series
ML3776.S53 1998
782.42162'92405691—dc21 98-10938
CIP
MN

The paper used in this publication meets the minimum requirements of the American National Standard for Information Sciences—Permanence of Paper for Printed Library Materials, ANSI Z39.48-1992.

To singers—past, present, and future—of pizmonim and Arab songs

". . . And they expanded the frontier of song by raising up students: both cantors and poets. May their memory be blessed forever."

(Sheer Ushbahah Hallel Ve-Zimrah)

CONTENTS

List of Illustrations ix

Author's Note xi

Acknowledgments xiii

Jasmine: Poem on Sandpaper xvii

Introduction 1

PRELUDE: ṢUR YAH EL 15

ONE Song and Remembrance 25

PRELUDE: ATTAH EL KABBIR 54

TWO Music and Migration in a Transnational Community 64

PRELUDE: ANI ASHIR LAKH 92

THREE A Judeo-Arab Musical Tradition 104

PRELUDE: RAMAḤ EVARAI 135

FOUR Lived Musical Genres 148

PRELUDE: YEḤIDAH HITNAʿARI 172

FIVE Individual Creativity, Collective Memory 182

PRELUDE: MELEKH RAḤAMAN 207

SIX Conclusion: A Community in Song 212

Embroidered Rag: Poem on Umm Kulthum 231

Notes 233

Glossary 255

Contents of Compact Disc 258

References

Bibliography 267

Discography 277

Formal Interviews 277

Music Sessions 278

Index 279

ILLUSTRATIONS

Table

5.1 Summary of individual pizmon repertories 201

Figures

1.1 Title page, *Sheer Ushbahah Hallel Ve-Zimrah* 39
2.1 The transnational path of pizmon "Attah El Kabbir," c. 1900–1992 58
2.2 Map of Brooklyn 66
2.3 Multiple diasporas of Syrian Jews 69
2.4 Map of the Ottoman empire in 1908 76
2.5 Logo of the Sephardic Community Center 91
3.1 A summary of eight major maqāmāt prepared by David Tawil 121
5.1 Facsimile of pizmon "Yeḥidah Hitnaʿari" 175

Musical Examples

2.1 Comparison of maqām nahāwand with Western music scale 56
2.2 Transcription by A. Z. Idelsohn 57
4.1 Transcription and translation of "Al-qamḥ" ("The Wheat Song") 144
4.2 Flute theme, Tchaikovsky, *The Nutcracker* ballet, Act 2 137
4.3 "Ram Leḥasdakh" 158
4.4 "Yaḥid Ram" 164
5.1 "Ashir Na Shir Tikvah" 186
5.2 "Mifalot Elohim" 199

A gallery of photographs follows page 134

AUTHOR'S NOTE

Hebrew is transliterated according to the system presented in *Encyclopaedia Judaica,* vol. 1, col. 90. Contemporary names are transliterated or rendered as used by the person. Names and some words with an accepted English form are usually not transliterated. Arabic is transliterated according to the Library of Congress system.

Symbols Used in Musical Transcriptions

quarter tone below	𝄳
actual starting pitch	(•)
slide	♩⁄♩
microtonal ornament	〰

Transcriptions do not include instrumental parts or vocal improvisations heard before songs or within verses.

ACKNOWLEDGMENTS

This book, the outgrowth of a project that began in the autumn of 1984, has left me with debts to many. I am particularly grateful to Moses Tawil and Joseph Saff, who during that first year organized music sessions in Brooklyn that gave this project its initial impetus and who supported the research process throughout. From start to finish, Sam Catton provided invaluable information and materials about the Syrian community worldwide.

Many shared their musical tradition in performance and/or communicated its power and meaning in interviews. In New York, I acknowledge with gratitude Isaac Abadi, Rabbi Shimon Alouf, Morris Arking, Ezra Ashkenazi, Isaac Cabasso, Cantor Albert Cohen-Saban, Joseph Harari, Hyman Kaire, Meyer (Mickey) Kairey, Rabbi Ezra Labaton, Louis Massry, Moses Massry, Joseph Mosseri, Menachem Mustacchi, Cantor Yehiel Nahari, Joseph Saff, Charles Serouya, Joseph A. D. Sutton, David Tawil, Moses Tawil, Benjamin Zalta, Gabriel Zeitouni, and the late Gabriel Shrem and Albert Ashear. Sophie Kaire Cohen, Gracia Taboush Haber, Joyce Kassin, Sheila Schweky, and Sarah Tawil sat for lengthy interviews that were indispensable to my understanding of the social history and present-day status of pizmon transmission. In Israel, I thank Ezra Barnea, Yaqov Bozo, Moshe Cohen, Shaul Shemi, and Menachem Yedid. Rabbi Meir Antebi, Ramon Betech, Cantor Isaac Cain, Sadegh Harari, and Alfred Sitt enabled me to incorporate information about the Syrian community of Mexico City into this study. For their participation in various recording sessions in New York City, I thank Eli Abadi, Isaac Askov, Abraham Bavey, Edward Betesh, Joseph Catton, Al Cohen, David Cohen, Meyer Cohen, Dennis Dweck, Eddie Erani, David Esses, Joe Kassin, Meyer Levy, Michael Mizrahi, David Nizri, Morris Schweky, Ezra Setton, Joey Setton, Ralph Shasho Levy, Sam Sabin, Walter Serure, Abe Tawil, Harry Tawil, Max E. Tawil, Saul E. Tawil, and Isaac Zion.

For invitations to so many rites of passage and other special occasions in New York, Mexico City, and Israel, I sincerely thank the families Antebi,

Barnea, Betech, Cain, Cohen, Cabasso, Haber, Harary, Kaire, Massry, Shamah, Shemi, Sutton, Tawil, and Tebele. The wonderful women of the Tawil family—including Sarah Tawil, Sheila Schweky, Joyce Kassin, Judy Nasar, and Alice Tawil—played a special role throughout, offering both strong support and invaluable ethnographic information. Alice Harary facilitated many useful contacts as well as provided information concerning recent Syrian immigrants to New York City. In Mexico City, Esther Cohen Goldfein, Rachel Mintz de Fridman, Ruth Cain, Raina Betech, and Sara Betech Solomon provided an indispensable measure of assistance, information, and warm hospitality.

A number of institutions and organizations aided this project in vital ways. This project could not have been carried out without the active cooperation and collaboration of the Sephardic Archives of the Sephardic Community Center in Brooklyn. Dr. Morris Shamah and Linda Shamah, the former chair and director of the Sephardic Archives respectively, and the former coordinator Dianne O. Esses, helped to conceive, plan, and implement the initial stage of pizmon research. Over the years, Sephardic Community Center directors and staff, including Michael Witkes, Ellie Aronowitz, David Shasha, Judy Tawil, and Amir Levy, have provided advice and support. The Sephardic Community Center and the Ahi Ezer Home provided facilities in Brooklyn for interviews and recording sessions. Valuable information and materials were supplied by the Aleppo Heritage Center in Israel.

The New York University Department of Music provided substantial practical and financial resources for the initial team project, as did Wesleyan University for later stages of my own research. A generous grant from the Republic New York Corporation underwrote on-going research expenses, and along with a fellowship from the Memorial Foundation for Jewish Culture, supported fieldtrips to Mexico and Israel. This book could not have been written without a fellowship from the National Endowment for the Humanities during 1992–93, which in combination with a Harvard University sabbatical semester provided released time for research and writing. I am deeply grateful to all, without whose support I could not have seen such a complex project to completion.

Invaluable research assistance and materials have been supplied by a number of institutions or organizations. I am grateful to the National Sound Archives (Phonoteca) at The National and University Library of the Hebrew University in Jerusalem and the guidance of Ruth Freed for access to archival recordings. Similarly, the Archives of Traditional Music at Indiana University supplied historical recordings of Syrian music made in the United States. Help prior to my Mexico City fieldtrip was also extended by Dr. Judith Laikin Elkin of LAJSA.

Many of the recordings and interviews on which this book is based were gathered in collaboration with members of the New York University ethnomusicology seminar. For their hard work at the beginning of this very long road, I acknowledge Anita Clark Jaynes, Karen Bradunas, Kenneth Cohen, David Foster, Maria Garcia, Geoffrey Goldberg, Rolf Groesbeck, Amy Horowitz, Mark Horwitz, Robert Kenselaar, Kim Croft, Ingrid Monson, Emily Socolov, Sarah Weiss, and Carney Wu. Mark Kligman entered the NYU doctoral program immediately after the conclusion of the team project but continued research that has resulted in his doctoral dissertation on the Ḥalabi Sabbath morning liturgy. It has been both useful and rewarding to share materials and interpretations between our projects during the last five years.

I could not have processed the extraordinary amount of research material without the help of a series of excellent research assistants. At Wesleyan University, interview transcripts, musical transcriptions, and databases were prepared through the devoted labor of Melissa Frankel, Julija Gelazis, Miriam Gerberg, and Sara Snyder. At Harvard University, I have benefited from the assistance of Eliezer Finegold, Ruth Ochs, and Judah Cohen. For their work in translating challenging pizmon texts, I thank Geoffrey Goldberg, James Robinson, and Joshua Levisohn. The support and savvy of my Harvard Music Department assistants Galen Malicoat and Reece Michaelson made the final preparation of this manuscript a far less daunting prospect, as did the expert assistance of Liane Curtis and David Lyczkowski.

A number of colleagues across disciplines have taken the trouble to provide invaluable information, resources, introductions, and advice. I am grateful to Nabil Azzam, Arthur Berger, Judith Cohen, Virginia Danielson, Monica Devens, Stuart Feder, Gila Flam, William Graham, Ellen Harris, Jeffrey Kallberg, Ruth Katz, David King, Arthur Kleinman, David Lewin, Lewis Lockwood, Ingrid Monson, Aniruddh Patel, Anne Rasmussen, Adelaida Reyes Schramm, Daniel Schacter, Edwin Seroussi, Amnon Shiloah, Mark Slobin, Susan Sylomovics, Judith Tick, Walter Zenner, and Yael Zerubavel. To Philip V. Bohlman, Bruno Nettl, and T. David Brent, my appreciation for helpful suggestions that improved this manuscript. To copy editor Peter T. Daniels, my hearty thanks for lending an eagle eye and an extra measure of linguistic advice. Finally, I thank Matthew Howard, Siobhan Drummond, Claudia Rex, and Robert Williams, who oversaw the production process; David Ackerman, who mastered the compact disc; and Marilyn Bliss, who prepared the index.

My family, as always, has played a most important role. My parents, Raymond and Lillian Kaufman, aided my work in many ways great and small. My husband, Jack Shelemay, graciously accompanied me to many social and religious events in the Syrian community and often surprised me with his knowledge of the Arab musical tradition.

But of all my debts, the greatest is to the singers of pizmonim and Arab songs. It is to them this book is dedicated, with the further hope that a shared world of musical expression, symbolized by jasmine in the poem by Ronny Someck found in the epigraph, may indeed rain down on Jews and Arabs, awakening memories of a common past as well as mutual hopes for the future.

Jasmine

POEM ON SANDPAPER

Fairuz raises her lips
to heaven
to let jasmine rain down
on those who once met
without knowing they were in love.
I'm listening to her in Muhammad's
Fiat at noon on Ibn Gabirol St.
A Lebanese singer playing in an Italian car
that belongs to an Arab poet
from Baqa' al-Gharbiyye on a street named
after a Hebrew poet who lived in Spain.
And the jasmine?
If it falls from the sky at the end of days
it'll stay green for
just a second at
the next light.[1]

INTRODUCTION

When Jews left Aleppo, Syria, in the early twentieth century and established communities in New York and elsewhere in the Americas, they brought with them a repertory of songs called *pizmonim*. Over the years, Syrian Jews maintained and renewed this body of paraliturgical hymns, which consist primarily of Hebrew texts set to melodies borrowed from Middle Eastern Arab music. The term *pizmon,* literally meaning "adoration" or "praise," was first applied to the refrains in *piyyutim,* lyrical compositions which embellished Jewish prayers or religious ceremonies in the Middle Ages. Subsequently, piyyutim with these refrains were called pizmonim. In the modern period, the word pizmon has been used for songs in general, including, in modern Israel, popular songs (Habermann 1972: 602). Today hundreds of pizmonim are still sung, and more than five hundred of their texts are preserved in a modern edition published in Brooklyn (Shrem 1988). These songs and their significance in modern Syrian Jewish life are explored in the following pages.

This book documents and interprets the pizmon tradition for the most recent century of its history, beginning with its revitalization in late nineteenth century Aleppo, following its movement with Syrian Jews abroad, and tracing its more recent development primarily in twentieth-century Brooklyn.[1] In contrast to most ethnomusicological projects, where the unit of study slowly emerges during the course of ethnographic research, the central focus here was identified before the process of fieldwork began in consultation with members of the Syrian Jewish community in Brooklyn. The possibility of carrying out an ethnographic project among Syrian Jews first emerged in November 1983, when I accepted an invitation to a daylong seminar on Syrian-Jewish and Sephardic culture at the Sephardic Archives, an organization within the Sephardic Community Center dedicated to the documentation and preservation of Syrian cultural traditions.[2] It was a fortuitous meeting. I was casting about for a collaborative research project that would serve to bring ethnomusicology graduate students into contact with the music of an "ethnic community" in New York City at a time when the Sephardic Archives was seeking individuals with research skills to aid their community-based projects. During meetings in the spring and summer of 1984, the leaders of the Archives suggested a focus on the pizmonim, a major musical repertory that constituted a rich subject for ethnomusicological investigation as well as a contribution to community archival efforts.

The team effort resulted in a large collection of field recordings and interviews deposited in the Sephardic Archives as well as publication of a recording (Shelemay and Weiss 1985). Some of the Brooklyn research associates and student members of the research team are shown in plates 1–4.[3] However, the vitality of the music and the vigor with which it was performed soon captured my imagination. At the end of the project in December 1985, I decided to continue active research on my own within the Syrian community in New York. From 1986 through 1993, I carried out formal interviews and had many informal conversations with members of the Syrian community. I also attended numerous musical events, synagogue and domestic rituals, and other private celebrations as a participant-observer.[4] By the early 1990s I had become keenly aware of the active social and musical networks that link Syrian Jews in Brooklyn with communities of other Syrian Jews around the world. In order that ethnographic research capture the transnational dynamism of pizmon transmission and performance, I carried out two short fieldtrips for comparative purposes, one in the fall of 1992 to Mexico City, and the second in the spring of 1993 to Jerusalem.

Increasingly through the process of researching and writing this book, I found that the pizmon tradition "spoke for itself," needing only a little help from an ethnomusicologist to convey its story. Over time, it became clear that insider perspectives not only had determined the central unit of study, but had opened pathways for its interpretation as well. Thus both the theoretical and the methodological frameworks for this study in a very real way emerged from the musical materials and exegesis of its carriers. I have been guided throughout by the premise, eloquently summarized by Henry Louis Gates, Jr., in reference to his own study of African American literature, that "each [literary] tradition, at least implicitly, contains within it an argument for how it can be read" (Gates 1988:xix–xx). I firmly believe that the same holds true for the Syrian (and many other) musical tradition(s), which could not only be "read," but heard, often at a high decibel level.

Like so many aspects of human expressive culture, the pizmon is too complex to offer a single lesson, or only one unifying theme. Rather, through this musical repertory one can gain an understanding of the manner in which musical expression is implicated in an array of cultural processes, past and present. More important, the pizmon sheds light on realms of experience significant within the lives of the carriers of the music, illuminating many shadowy corners of human endeavor and social history. Through exploring the pizmon, we are able to enter into a Syrian Jewish soundworld often thought to have fallen silent. Here I follow a path in the musical domain similar to that of Ammiel Alcalay, who in *After Jews and Arabs: Remaking Levantine Culture* (1993) examines the relationship between Jews and Arabs in the domain of literary culture, exploring both "the relationship of the Jew to the Arab within him- or herself" and "the relationship of the Jew to a native space, namely the Levant" (p. 27). Alcalay reconstructs moments in Levantine literary history, beginning in the tenth century, in which one can trace "the development and erosion of the qualities of mobility, diversity, autonomy, and translatability possessed by Jews of the Levant for so long, but which for the most part no longer exist" (p. 28). However, a Judeo-Arab musical discourse does persist through the medium of the pizmonim, and its vitality is all the more striking given the ongoing tensions in the Middle East between twentieth-century Arabs and Jews.

There is no doubt that the pizmonim mean many different things to various individuals within the community that transmits them. The themes that I trace in the following pages emerged from a cross section of individuals during interviews or were underscored publicly on performance occasions. While much of the testimony quoted here is gleaned from aficionados of the pizmon tradition, virtually all are musical amateurs who have gained their musical repertories and subsidiary knowledge over the years from family members, friends, and recordings. Most are individuals to whom the pizmonim are an important aspect of daily life, both in the present and in their memories of past experience.

It is also clear that there are many in the community who do not have a rich bank of associations for these songs nor a level of expert knowledge about the musical system. However, some of the most detailed and hidden meanings of individual songs are in fact held in trust by non-specialists, individuals to whom songs were dedicated or descendants of families about whom songs were sung. Interesting insights emerged from close ethnographic investigation among non-specialists for this project. In particular, while women are not active as composers or performers, many are quite familiar with pizmonim, especially those associated with or dedicated to members of their families; women from musical families also often know the melodies of Arab songs from which such pizmonim were derived. An additional factor not generally the subject of comment is that many women within traditional Jewish communities have access to the world of male musical performance during their early childhood years, well before adolescence, when they are free to circulate among the men and even sit with their fathers in the synagogue and at domestic rituals. Many women retain strong memories of songs heard and learned during this exposure. A number of women further maintain active tape and record collections of beloved pizmonim and songs in Arabic, and while sex segregation at certain religious and domestic events restricts active participation in pizmon performance to male members of the community, some women quietly sing along in their own, separate section of the synagogue or home. Finally, and in some ways most importantly, women are heavily involved in planning and staging virtually all domestic rituals at which the pizmonim are performed and transmitted. Thus, while women may be neither seen nor heard in the context of pizmon performance, they can transmit invaluable information. Large numbers of Syrian Jews, both men and women, continue to encounter and enjoy pizmon performances during their frequent attendance at synagogue services, life cycle rituals, concerts, and social events. This book, in both its content and its form, tries to convey both the nature of articulated interpretations and the spirit that sustains pizmon performance and reception.

A recurrent theme that emerged during the research process was that of memory, of which music in general, and the pizmonim in particular, proved to be an integral part. One community leader observed,

> It's amazing how much we remember from so many years back. . . . And I think that since this is a musical group, they taught us much of our learning with tunes and with singing. And when you learn with singing it remains in your mind. . . . I find myself walking along the streets once in a while singing to myself some of the words of the Song of Songs of King Solomon, or some of the words of Proverbs. It's amazing. Music helps you remember. Of course, this is only the impression of a person who does not know music, except what little they taught me. (S. Catton, 30 October 1984)

If music is said to be an important aspect of Syrian Jewish experience, stemming at least in part from the shared heritage of Aleppo, it is further linked to memory on a number of levels within modern Syrian Jewish life.

Most immediately, melody is an integral part of historical memory, enabling an individual to recall the past:

> They have special songs for Purim. And they come back to me but I can't sing anymore. And, after all, dear, I'm an old lady now. I don't know them. I couldn't read any Hebrew. All I did was to memorize them. . . . They still sing the same songs in the synagogues every week and all melodies, they come back to me. . . . I never knew how to read, but I know them from childhood. (S. Cohen, 28 February 1985)

Since pizmon melodies remembered from childhood are for the most part borrowed from Arab songs popular at the time of their composition, they also carry memories of musical trends within both Syrian Jewish life and within the Middle Eastern community at large. Thus the performance of pizmon melodies evokes a flood of memories, familial, spatial/geographic, communal, and affective:

> They're so pretty, and when you hear them all together, . . . it makes me closer to where we came from, to my roots. I feel it, even though I was born in the United States, and my parents came [from Aleppo] at a very young age. . . . I always feel it every time I'm sitting in the shul and listening to the prayers. Maybe because I heard them ever since I can remember, since I was a young child. And the way everyone is together, and understands, and sings with one voice, that means a lot to me. It makes me feel part of a tradition that was before, is now, and probably will continue for many, many years. That won't be lost. As long as they keep it up each year, year after year after year. That's going to keep up forever, as long as there is a Hebrew nation or our people exist. I think so, from father, to son, to grandchild. This is nothing I've thought about a lot. Just a feeling you have when you're there. (R. Cain, 7 September 1992)

If melody serves to trigger a panoply of personal and shared memories, members of the community also note that it's "not just the tune that's important" (M. Kairey, 12 December 1984). The pizmon texts themselves incorporate references to a range of literary sources from prayers to psalms, as well as commemorate specific individuals and events. Thus this book also explores the manner in which a pizmon text may carry conventional cognitive memories, encoding the name of the composer (often in an acrostic), esoteric references to Jewish tradition and observance, names of the individual and family to whom the pizmon is dedicated, and veiled allusions to particular social situations.

The following pages approach the impossibly broad subject of music and memory through a close look at aspects of the musical construction of remembrance, an expressive outcome or residue of the process of remembering. Certainly the ethnomusicological literature already contains examples ripe for such an inquiry—for instance, gisalo song texts of the Kaluli people of Papua New Guinea (Feld 1990) list local places important in the life of a deceased individual. In the context of ritual performance, a gisalo song serves to remind a Kaluli individual of a recent personal loss and to memorialize the deceased. Other musical traditions are conceived as embedding remembrance and are overtly commemorative in the act of performance—for example, the laments for the dead sung in numerous societies,[5] or the Sufi qawwali rituals in Pakistan and North India (Qureshi 1986) which are performed as commemoration ceremonies for local Muslim saints. Yet despite the fact that so much of the music ethnomusicologists study is shot through with remembrance and is explicitly perceived as commemorative when performed, these important themes have remained in the background. The dearth of ethnomusicological studies explicitly treating memory is rendered even more striking given the number of recent publications related to memory and culture in a range of humanistic disciplines.[6]

Historical musicologists have given considerably more thought to the relationship of music and memory[7] and have long been concerned with music as a form of commemoration. Much of the well-studied Western musical repertory is in fact overtly commemorative, a reality often acknowledged as particularly important in the conception and composition of many works.[8] However, musical remembrance seems to have been little explored in relation to broader cultural constraints of a given time and place.

In the following pages, I seek to move ethnomusicological inquiry more directly into the domain of memory studies by drawing on admittedly heterogeneous theoretical sources. I have used the psychological literature to provide a working vocabulary and conceptual field. From this perspective, it is clear that the pizmon relates to memory in several different yet interrelated ways. Both song texts and tunes encode memories of places, people, and events past; in this manner the songs are intentionally constructed sites for long-term storage of conscious memories from the past.[9] Pizmonim, however, can also be sung, without reference to or knowledge of these historical memories embedded within them, for purposes of commemoration unrelated to their original composition. Third, and perhaps most provocative from the psychological perspective and the most difficult to access ethnographically, the process of pizmon performance necessarily draws on a largely unconscious bank of memories as it recreates sounds from the past. Thus the pizmon is located at the juncture of several domains of memory. It brings the past into the present through both its content and the act of performance, while also serving as a device through which long-forgotten aspects of the past and information unconsciously carried can be evoked, accessed, and remembered.

I have found particularly instructive the work of Daniel L. Schacter (1995a:816) concerning "explicit" [intentional, conscious] and "implicit" [unintentional, non-conscious] memory. These terms, emerging from psychological research of the last decade, refer not to two separate memory systems, but are rather concepts "primarily concerned with a person's psychological experience at the time of retrieval" (ibid.). The most prominent time of retrieval for a pizmon is of course the moment it is heard or performed. Songs can be used quite intentionally in order to remember; they are occasionally sung purposefully to commemorate events or to memorialize particular individuals. But the performance of songs can also trigger memories of people, places, and past experiences, just as the process of performing pizmonim seems to draw on what has been described as "a whole . . . world of nonconscious memory that underlies our abilities to carry out effortlessly such tasks . . . without having to direct each movement consciously every time we attempt the task" (Schacter 1996:5).

In the following pages, and most particularly in the "preludes," I explore individual pizmonim in a manner similar to that in which Schacter discusses individual artworks that expose the nature or function of memory.[10] Schacter has written that

> all art relies on memory in a general sense—every work of art is affected, directly or indirectly, by the personal experiences of the artist—but some artists have made the exploration of memory a major subject of their work. . . . Scientific research is the most powerful way to find out how memory works, but artists can illuminate the impact of memory in our day-to-day lives. (Schacter 1996:11)

Following Schacter's lead, I try to explicate the way in which the pizmon as an expressive form preserves conscious memories and provides a means for accessing unconscious memories, as well as provoking subtle changes in mood and affect that are independent of conscious recollection. However, unlike Schacter, who suggests that artists convey visually affective and experiential aspects difficult to express in words, as an ethnomusicologist working ethnographically I often use the spoken word to help lay bare the ways in which memory is situated in pizmonim. As noted above, it was the frequency and depth with which Syrian Jews *spoke* about song and memory that led me to approach their repertory from this perspective in the first place, and I used standard ethnographic methods to elicit many of the comments recorded throughout the pages of this book. Here I concur with G. Cohen, who has noted that "self-reports seem to provide a simple way of finding out how people's memories work in every day life" (1989:7). However, I did not conduct focused interviews or administer "metamemory questionnaires" (ibid. 9) explicitly on the subject of memory. Rather, it was the process of transcribing interviews and analyzing their contents that brought the subject of memory to the fore.

Here I would also note that observation of musical performance provides an additional unique perspective, one where the ethnomusicologist stands to make a contribution to understanding the moment in which a memory is constituted. If accounts of memory must "examine the environment in which retrieval occurs just as carefully as the past events to which the memory refers" (Schacter 1996:105), ethnographic observation of performance can provide insights into social and cultural factors that help shape the psychology of remembering. Rubin (1995:7) also suggests that the study of everyday human behavior, in particular the transmission of oral traditions such as poetry, epics, and ballads, provides "a more appropriate model of everyday human behavior than do psychological experiments on memory."

In the inclusion of verbal commentaries as well as the consideration of how to interpret these personal testimonies about memory in relation to the music, I have been stimulated by Stuart Feder's recent writings about the composer Charles Ives. Feder suggests that the New England composer's "childhood memories of his father are recorded in his musical works in addition to his autobiographical prose statements" (Feder 1989:310). Feder's writings, with their attention to the manner in which memories can be encoded in music and recalled in prose, and his emphasis on the powerful associations of melody to childhood experience and family, have provided a most congenial model for my own study.

Yet while pizmonim are composed by individuals and often dedicated to a single person, they record shared memories and are almost always sung by a group. Performance in a variety of social settings is a central mechanism for transmitting songs and reinforcing community memory because

> we all know each other . . . and when we get together in somebody's home when there's an occasion, we sing. We all sing. We all know each other and we all know that these people are singers. (J. Saff, 4 December 1984)

Indeed, a song cannot convey and mediate memory if not performed. Here investigation of the manner in which social memory is conveyed and sustained as bodily practice is most informative (Connerton 1989:1). In particular, Paul Connerton's exploration of the manner in which memory is inscribed as well as transmitted through commemorative ceremonies has sensitized me to the importance of pizmon performance in all its varied contexts. This, in turn, attracts new emphasis to the social situations, both informal and formal, in which pizmonim are sung and committed to memory.

In this manner, then, individual memory joins with and is transformed through the experience of the community. In seeking to understand and interpret the processes through which individual remembering is both a source for and transformed by collective memory, I have been greatly aided by a number of recent studies that have also approached memory within the context of diverse cultural domains. Jöelle Bahloul's ethnographic "excavation" (1996:10) of her grandfather's house in Algeria as a real and metaphorical site for individual and collective memories has helped inform my own approach to song. Studies of memory in vastly different historical times, which demonstrate the ends to which individuals will go to sustain memory (Spence 1983), have shaped my concern with framing memory in relation to both its historical past and other dimensions, such as space.

To maintain a balance between the individual and the group, I have gained greatly from reading studies that approach memory as part of shared, social recollections, including Halbwachs's classic formulation that "the individual remembers by placing himself in the perspective of the group" (1992:40).[11] Several important insights from studies of collective memory proved to be of particular use in this study. Halbwachs's emphasis on the localization of memory (pp. 52–53) as well as the central role of the family (p. 54) and religious life (p. 98) as the collectivities most salient in shaping individual memory has reinforced points clearly present in ethnographic interviews and musical data from this project.

George Lipsitz's *Time Passages* provides a different and extremely useful perspective in exploring what he terms the "peculiar link" of collective memory with popular culture (1990:vii). However, the interactive relationship present in the pizmon case study between what might be characterized on the one hand as a "mass-mediated popular music" and, on the other, as a "traditional genre of religious music" strikes this scholar as not peculiar in the least. Rather, it calls into question both of these traditional analytical categories and the ideologies that have invented and sustained them in musical scholarship.

While I share an interest in collective memory and fully endorse the perspective that individual memory is given meaning only within a social setting, this study purposely seeks to collapse what is often perceived as an opposition between the individual and the collective. Indeed, it is precisely the intersection of individual and group memory, and the manner in which they are inseparable in the past and the present, to which these musical materials speak. It further appears that song, in this case the pizmon, provides a cultural space in which individual and collective memories may both be mediated and juxtaposed.

The manner in which both individual and collective memories can occupy the same expressive space, within and through song, is a subject of great concern here. My thinking about the overlapping and intersecting nature of memories in song has been stimulated by the notion of "heterotopia," a formulation of Michel Foucault's elucidated by Edward Soja (1995:15). Soja explains that "the heterotopia is capable of juxtaposing in a single real place several spaces, 'several sites that are in themselves incompatible'" (ibid. 17, quoting Foucault 1986:25, 27). Soja further suggests that

> Foucault's heterogeneous and relational space of heterotopias is neither a substanceless void to be filled by cognitive intuition nor a repository of physical form to be phenomenologically described in all its resplendent variability. It is another space . . . actually lived and socially created spatiality, concrete and abstract at the same time, the habitus of social practices. It is a space rarely seen for it has been obscured by a bifocal vision that traditionally views space as either a mental construct or a physical form. (Soja 1995:17–18)

In a similar manner, each pizmon may be described as a heterotopology, a site for various constructions of present and past, containing simultaneous commemoration of both individuals and collectivities.

It is germane to note that a study of any modern Jewish community is hard pressed *not* to investigate the role of memory in both constituting and perpetuating expressive culture. The tricky relationship between Jewish memory and history is carefully elucidated by Yosef Yerushalmi in his book

Zakhor ([1982] 1989) and further developed in a later work, *Usages de l'oubli* (1988). Most studies of memory in the Jewish cultural arena, such as Yael Zerubavel's incisive investigation of the construction of memory and myth in Israeli national tradition, necessarily focus on its collective aspects. A notable exception is Langer's *Holocaust Testimonies: The Ruin of Memory,* which presents an archaeology of memory drawn from the "insomniac faculties" (1991:xv) of individual Jews who survived the terrors of the Nazi Final Solution. Langer plumbs oral testimonies to construct a taxonomy of the intensely personal remembering of trauma, articulated as modes of deep, anguished, humiliated, tainted, and unheroic memory. While Langer's attention to the individual provides a welcome counterpoint to the generalizations of other studies, his taxonomy is one of traumatic memory, specifically that of individuals who survived the Holocaust. In contrast, the Syrian pizmonim can be said to sustain memories of meaningful moments, continuities, and a celebration of positive human experiences. This celebratory view of history set forth by the songs is further probed in chapter 6.

In the following pages, then, memory is examined and elucidated on several levels. I mine individual memories shared in the late twentieth century to chart the dimensions of the pizmon heritage and to reconstruct the prior century of its history; these recollections are further used to elucidate the manner in which verbal and musical memories have themselves been encoded within individual songs. Observations of community music-making permit discussion of the manner in which songs are re-experienced as commemoration whenever performed. Memory can thus be charted on two distinct levels (about songs and within songs) and within distinctive modes of representation (through speech and through song). A further duality intrinsic to the songs facilitates exploration of the cultural construction of memory: the song texts provide insight into a world of explicitly Jewish experience, while the melodies relate primarily to extra-Jewish sources and frames of reference. The pizmon is therefore a hybrid,[12] emerging from the bifurcated historical experience of this Judeo-Arab community. On the more specific level of the case study, understanding the different channels through which memories are transmitted helps explain a remarkable "Judeo-Islamic symbiosis" (Lewis 1984) maintained more than seventy years after Syrian Jews left the Middle East. On a broader theoretical level, an analytical approach to the pizmonim in terms of two expressive channels is congruent with the words of the people who remember and perform the songs. Close readings of six pizmonim permit us to explicate these dual channels of meaning and experience, so that the songs can "speak" to us in as cogent a manner as conventional oral testimony.

While this book addresses questions that are primarily social and cultural in character, it is important to note that within the last decade ethnomusicologists have begun to express interest in spanning the divide that has long separated cognitive from cultural studies. It can be said that ethnomusicology is beginning to move away from "the older 'experimental vs. humanistic' controversy towards a more friendly, collaborative arena" (Koskoff 1992:5).[13] However, ethnomusicologists still tend to shy away from earlier research focused on perception of intervallic or rhythmic content, regarding these concerns as reductionist and largely irrelevant to problems of musical meaning (Tolbert 1992:9). Recently, literature addressing larger-scale processes and their relationship to cultural memory has begun to arouse interest.[14] Yet spanning the divide between cultural and cognitive understanding is rendered an even more daunting task because of the need to take into account what has been termed "an explosion" of recent research on memory and the brain:

> Those studying memory include psychologists, neurologists, biologists, mathematicians, and computer scientists. Work is being done at many levels of analysis—from neurons to brain systems and whole behavior. Can the pieces be fit into any coherent, larger picture? (Squire 1987:viii)

While there is little doubt that growing knowledge about the manner in which the brain forms memories will, in the future, expand our understanding of music's role in these processes as well, it is imperative that in the meantime ethnomusicology provide baseline studies of its own. Ethnomusicologists can contribute to understanding the manner in which memory is constituted through processes of musical transmission. In order to begin, they must ask a series of questions: Why is music so frequently implicated in sustaining memory? What is remembered through music? How are memories transformed during musical performance into meaningful acts of commemoration?

If the interpretive focus of the book seeks to convey insider perspectives, I have also endeavored to reflect a deeply embedded musical aesthetic in its literary form. In the Arab musical tradition so deeply loved by many Syrian Jews, it is traditional to precede a vocal or instrumental composition with a more informal, improvisatory introduction (a *layālī* or *taqsīm*) to establish better its "flavor" or mood. Similarly, in Syrian Jewish musical practice, a pizmon is often preceded by a vocal improvisation or *petiḥah,* which literally means "key" or "opening," an "overture" to the coming song (J. Saff, 23 October 1984). I have adapted this aesthetic concept to my text, prefacing each chapter with a more informal yet detailed discussion of a single pizmon and an occasion on which it was performed. The book is therefore structured in a somewhat unconventional manner—each of its six chapters is preceded by a short "prelude" that seeks to introduce the reader to a song and by so doing establish the "flavor" of issues discussed at length in the subsequent chapter. Six songs have been chosen for presentation in the "preludes." They provide cogent examples of characteristics and processes found in the repertory at large. Other songs are discussed more briefly within the text.

Beyond its congruence with the aesthetics of the repertory it discusses, the form and content of the book is intended to strike a balance between the musical source materials and the broader cultural questions motivating their study. While ethnomusicological research and writing until the mid twentieth century tended to emphasize presentation and descriptive analysis of musical data, more recent scholarship has increasingly had cultural interpretation as its primary goal. With ethnomusicologists torn between these musicological and anthropological poles, the result in some cases has been less attention given to the musical materials. A conviction underlying this book is that a broader musical scholarship is both possible and desirable, one that does justice to both the musical and cultural aspects of its subject. This book thus seeks an explicitly cross-disciplinary stance by joining detailed song analysis to ethnographic description in the "preludes" and wedding both to the more synthetic and interpretive chapter essays. This design permits inclusion of the musical materials and further allows them to be more fully mined for the unique cultural and cognitive data they contain. A recording of important songs discussed accompanies the book; a detailed list of its contents is found following the glossary.

The book is structured to explore different domains of memory and remembrance encoded in and conveyed by the pizmonim. Chapter 1 sets the stage for investigating musical transmission and presents background information needed to understand subsequent chapters, including a range of musical, individual, familial, communal, and generational factors. The history and migratory path of the Syrian Jewish community primarily from the late nineteenth through the twentieth century is the subject of chapter 2, identifying centers, peripheries, and way stations as well as movements within international musical networks. Chapter 3 takes a close look at the Judeo-Arab musical tradition sustained by modern Syrian Jews, surveying its musicians, theoretical frameworks, performance practices, and aesthetics. Chapter 4 sketches the pizmon tradition as musical and social practice, correlating notions of genre and repertory with observations of musical occasions and life experience. The role of the individual in commissioning, composing, and performing pizmonim is set forth in chapter 5, framed by a close look at the dynamics of musical reception and transmission. The conclusion, chapter 6, summarizes the role of the pizmon as a carrier of individual and collective memory, as a source for social history, and as a locus for future studies of the relationship between cultural and cognitive processes.

PRELUDE

Ṣur Yah El

An overflow crowd filled the auditorium at the Sephardic Community Center in Brooklyn, the institutional center of the Syrian Jewish community. It was March 14, 1990, and a concert was mounted to honor Meyer (Mickey) Kairey, recognized by the Syrian community as a man "who has dedicated himself to enhancing our community's spiritual way of life" (Sephardic Community Center Program, no page number). For decades, Mickey has trained children in the Syrian Jewish liturgical and musical traditions, including teaching them pizmonim.

The program, the cover of which is reproduced in plate 5, promised two different "sets" of pizmonim to be performed by a choir of young boys and accompanied by an ensemble of Middle Eastern instruments.[1] A third group of solo songs was to be sung by Isaac Cabasso, Mickey's uncle and himself a beloved lay cantor in the community. After a number of speeches and an audio-visual show, the climax of the evening was to be a special presentation to Mickey Kairey.

Around 8:15 P.M., the instrumentalists assembled on stage, which was festively decorated with masks mounted around the proscenium, signaling that the concert also celebrated the holiday Purim. They opened with a musical selection not listed in the program. It was not necessary to identify this piece, for its melody was familiar to virtually everyone as the pizmon "Ṣur Yah El."[2] "Ṣur Yah El," characterized by one longtime Brooklyn resident as "a beauty," is said to have "become so popular in the community that when we open up any gathering we say . . . the song 'Ṣur Yah El' " (G. Shrem, 9 January 1986). (The music, text, and translation of each pizmon is presented following its prelude.)

If the concert on March 14, 1990, was mounted to honor Mickey Kairey's contribution to the spiritual lives of so many within the Brooklyn community and to highlight his role in transmitting pizmonim to subsequent generations, the strains of the pizmon "Ṣur Yah El" evoked for some memories of a similar event to honor another beloved "transmitter of tradition" within the Syrian Jewish community some forty years earlier. Thus performance of "Ṣur Yah El," in establishing the *maqām* (musical mode) *bayāti*[3] and setting the mood for an evening in 1990, implicitly aroused memories of an earlier occasion.

On a September evening in the early 1950s, a party was held at the Magen David Synagogue on 67th Street in the Bensonhurst area of Brooklyn to honor the birthday of Charlie Serouya, who beginning around 1940 had played an important role in the lives of the congregation's children. Born in 1922 in Jerusalem to parents from Aleppo, the same year as Mickey Kairey's birth in New York, Charlie was given the Hebrew name "Shaul" because he was the only boy out of fifteen children born to his parents.[4]

Shortly after Charlie immigrated to New York, he started his work with the kids "by accident." One day when Charlie happened to be at the 67th Street Synagogue, as Congregation Magen David was known, the Rabbi's attempt to instruct students in Torah was disrupted by young children "everywhere, running around, making noise." The Rabbi noted Charlie's presence and asked him to entertain the children. From this inauspicious beginning, Charlie built a youth congregation, known as "Young Magen David," which became so large that the synagogue annex was too small to house it (see plate 6). Charlie's fundraising efforts on behalf of the Young Magen David ("You Must Donate") were legendary, including obtaining supplies of soft drinks and even watermelons for the children. With these resources, Charlie "used to take care of the young boys. He used to take them to baseball games, he used to take them to movies" (G. Shrem, 9 January 1986).

Over the years, Charlie taught the young people pizmonim, also sharing his eclectic repertory of Hebrew, French, and American "cowboy" songs, the latter learned from the films of Gene Autry. Charlie recalls happily that "all the young men in the community were my students" (15 July 1993). In 1965, Charlie moved to the Ocean Parkway neighborhood in Brooklyn and began attending Synagogue Shaare Zion. In 1977, Charlie moved to Deal, New Jersey, where he continues to teach.

One day, Ezekiel Albeg, then cantor at Ahi Ezer Synagogue in Brooklyn, stopped by the 67th Street Synagogue and saw Charlie with the crowd of kids; he decided to compose a pizmon in Charlie's honor. The result was a surprise party for Charlie's birthday, where a group of about twenty men accompanied by Middle Eastern instruments played "Ṣur Yah El" for the first time.

The "Ṣur Yah El" text bears a general religious theme and at the same time refers to the community. The opening words, *Ṣur Yah,* "Rock, God," are a play on Charlie's last name "Serouya." The Hebrew acrostic translates "the youth of the Congregation Magen David."

This pizmon was adapted from an instrumental prelude by the Egyptian composer Muḥammad ʿAbd al-Wahhāb called "Bint al-Balad" ("Daughter of the Country," or more colloquially, "Country Girl"). Widely circulated on radio and TV in Egypt and Israel, "Bint al-Balad" is thought by some Syrian Jews to have been composed in honor of the Egyptian leader, Nasser. However, its relatively early date, 1951, renders such a dedication unlikely.[5]

Since "Bint al-Balad" was an instrumental composition without Arabic text, it might be assumed that composer Albeg was easily able to write a Hebrew text to fit the music. However, Gabriel Shrem remembers that Albeg in fact found it difficult to compose a Hebrew text without the guide of Arabic words and only completed the pizmon after considerable encouragement:

> Ezekiel Albeg was the one that made the words, because this was only a tune, ʿAbd al-Wahhāb never made words. I tell him, "Listen, all the time we try to imitate the words of the Arabic, why don't you try to get this tune right here and put words to it instead of getting words to fit the other kind of way?" He says, "It's a little hard, a little hard." I say, "I know you can make it if you put your mind to it." (G. Shrem, 9 January 1986)

Part of the impetus for using the ʿAbd al-Wahhāb melody was the manner in which it uses "all the ups and downs" of the Arab melodic category bayāti, giving "you a beautiful picture of . . . what bayāt sounds like" (G. Shrem, 9 January 1986).

Indeed, the pizmon closely follows the melody and accompaniment patterns of the Arab model. Comparison with a recording of "Bint al-Balad" made by ʿAbd al-Wahhāb (1976) shows that the differences in the original Arab version include the use of percussion introduction, a larger instrumental ensemble with a number of Western instruments, and emphasis on antiphonal performance. The use of "Ṣur Yah El" by Syrian Jews at the beginning of musical events parallels one function of the Arab *bashraf,* an instrumental composition with a recurring theme, which is intended "to go before" (Faruqi 1981:32). "Ṣur Yah El" has a regular rhythm and is divided into four large sections called *khānah* (ibid.). The first section establishes the maqām (bayātī) and rhythmic mode; the second khānah (beginning at measure 21) introduces modulations in the maqām and variations in the rhythm; the third khānah (beginning at measure 49) takes the maqām into its higher range; and the fourth khānah (at measure 76) returns to the principal theme.

"Ṣur Yah El" is a popular pizmon frequently heard at diverse events in the New York community, ranging from recording sessions to Jewish cultural festivals (Shelemay fieldnotes, 20 November 1985 and 17 September 1989).[6] It is a lively melody recognized by most as a popular instrumental work of ʿAbd al-Wahhāb, but older members of the community know that the song in fact "pays respect . . . to the director of the youth of the Young Magen David" (G. Shrem, 9 January 1986). In this way, "Ṣur Yah El" speaks on multiple levels to Syrian Jews, as a beloved Arab melody, as a familiar pizmon, and as a song associated with a pivotal figure in the education and nurturing of their young people. Its performance at the beginning of the evening to honor Mickey Kairey in 1990 was an auspicious choice testifying to the importance of transmission of tradition and the signal role of the individual within this process. At the end of the evening, Mickey received an oversized framed certificate containing the signatures of some one thousand men whom he had trained as boys between 1955 and 1990. Both certificate and song memorialized Mickey's contribution, the top of the certificate bearing an inscription reading "the mitzvot [commandments] of Hashem [lit. the name, God] are good, enlightening our lives" (Shelemay fieldnotes, 14 March 1990).

Example 1. Ṣur Yah El

Example 1. *(continued)*

Example 1. *(continued)*

צוּר – יָהּ – אֵל – מֶלֶךְ־הָעוֹלָם.

לְךָ־רַעְיוֹנָי.

צִיץ – זַךְ – רָם – בְּנֵה־הָאוּלָם.

חַי – רְצֵה־בִּרְנָנָי:

צוּר – יָהּ – אֵל – מֶלֶךְ־הָעוֹלָם.

לְךָ־רַעְיוֹנָי.

צִיץ – זַךְ – רָם – בְּנֵה־הָאוּלָם.

חַי – רְצֵה־בִּרְנָנָי:

עֶלְיוֹן צוּרָם. – – – בְּנֵה עִירָם.

עָזְרָם, אוֹרָם. – – – חַי – – רָם:

יוֹם־יוֹם – נַקְרִיב. – מִנְחַת־שָׁי.
יָהּ – נְרַנֵּן – שִׁיר. – בֶּן־יִשָׁי:

רְאֵה נָא. – – – יָהּ־צוּר תִּקְוָתִי.
רְצֵה נָא. – – – אֶל־קוֹל זִמְרָתִי.
רְעֵה נָא. – – – אֶת־צֹאן חֶמְדָּתִי:

יָהּ שִׁמְךָ. – – – אַזְכִּיר בִּרְנָנִים.
יָהּ וּלְךָ. – – – כּוֹכְבֵי מְעוֹנִים.
יוֹדוּךָ. – – – כָּל־שְׂרָפִים וְאוֹפַנִּים:

מָגֵן אֵל־עוֹזֵר. – יָהּ אוֹר עֵינָי.
דוֹד נָא הַחֲזֵר. – הוֹד רוֹב בָּנַי:

שִׁיר לְךָ אֶפְצַח. – אֵל חַי זָךְ צַח.
וּשְׁחָקִים תִּפְתָּח. – לְבֵיתִי תְּקוֹמֵם:

צִיר קַל תִּשְׁלַח. – רָם צוּר הַצְלַח.
וְעַמְּךָ אֵל־סַלָּח. – יְהוֹדֶה יְרוֹמֵם.
מָגֵן אֵל־עוֹזֵר. – יָהּ אוֹר עֵינָי.
דוֹד נָא הַחֲזֵר. – הוֹד רוֹב בָּנַי:

שִׁיר לְךָ אֶפְצַח. – אֵל חַי זָךְ צַח.
וּשְׁחָקִים תִּפְתָּח. – לְבֵיתִי תְּקוֹמֵם:

צִיר קַל תִּשְׁלָח. – רָם צוּר הַצְלַח.
וְעַמְּךָ אֵל־סַלָּח. – יְהוֹדֶה יְרוֹמֵם:

וְעַל־הַכֹּל שִׁמְךָ. – יִתְעַל וְיִתְקַדַּשׁ.
נָאֶה־נָעִים לְךָ. – מְנוֹרָה וּמִקְדָּשׁ:

בְּנֵה נָא אֵלִי. – זְבוּלִי – גְּבוּלִי.
גּוֹאֲלִי. –
יַסֵּד הֵיכָלִי. – אֵל־נוֹרָא וְנִקְדָּשׁ:

בְּנֵה נָא אֵלִי. – זְבוּלִי – גְּבוּלִי.
גּוֹאֲלִי. –
יַסֵּד הֵיכָלִי – אֵל־נוֹרָא וְנִקְדָּשׁ:

עַטֵּר כְּאָז. – עִיר־הַקֹּדֶשׁ יְרוּשָׁלָיִם.
עִיר־הַקֹּדֶשׁ יְרוּשָׁלָיִם.
עִיר־הַקֹּדֶשׁ יְרוּשָׁלָיִם.
עַטֵּר כְּאָז. – עִיר־הַקֹּדֶשׁ יְרוּשָׁלָיִם.
עִיר־הַקֹּדֶשׁ יְרוּשָׁלָיִם.
עִיר־הַקֹּדֶשׁ יְרוּשָׁלָיִם:

צוּר – יָהּ – אֵל – מֶלֶךְ־הָעוֹלָם.
לְךָ־רַעְיוֹנָי.
צִיץ – זָךְ – רָם – בְּנֵה־הָאוּלָם.
חַי – רְצֵה־בִרְנָנָי.
צוּר – יָהּ – אֵל – מֶלֶךְ־הָעוֹלָם.
לְךָ־רַעְיוֹנָי.
צִיץ – זָךְ – רָם – בְּנֵה־הָאוּלָם.
חַי – רְצֵה־בִרְנָנָי:

עֶלְיוֹן צוּרָם. – – – בְּנֵה עִירָם.
עֶזְרָם, אוֹרָם. – – – חַי – – רָם.
יוֹצֵר עוֹלָם: תם

Ṣur Yah El

Rock, Lord, God, King of the Universe,
 Unto You are my thoughts.
A crown—pure, exalted; rebuild the sanctuary.
 Living God, accept my cries of exultation.

Rock, Lord, God, King of the Universe,
  Unto You are my thoughts.
A crown—pure, exalted; rebuild the sanctuary.
  Living God, accept my cries of exultation.

Supreme, their Rock; rebuild their city.
Their Help, their Light, Living One, Exalted.

Daily we make offering, a free gift offering,
Lord, we shall shout with joy the song of the son of Jesse.

Behold, Lord, Rock, my hope.
Accept the sound of my song.
Guide the flock of my pleasant portion.

Lord, I will recall Your name with exultation.
Lord, to You belong the heavenly stars.
All the Serafim and Ofanim give thanks to You.

O God, shield and helper; Lord, light of my eyes.
Beloved, restore the glory of the multitude of my children.

I will break forth into song for You, living God, most pure.
Open up the heavens, raise up my house.

Send easy pangs; Exalted, Rock, prosper!
And Your people, God, forgive; let him give praise, let him uplift.
O God, shield and helper; Lord, light of my eyes.
Beloved, restore the glory of the multitude of my children.

I will break forth into song for You, living God, most pure.
Open up the heavens, raise up my house.

Send easy pangs; Exalted, Rock, prosper.
And Your people, God, forgive; let him give praise, let him uplift.

And for everything, may Your name be exalted and made sacred.
Pleasing to you, Menorah and Miqdash.

Rebuild, O My God, my settled place; [reestablish] my [former] border.
O my Redeemer, establish my Temple, awesome and holy God.

Rebuild, O My God, my settled place; [reestablish] my [former] border.
O my Redeemer, establish my Temple, awesome and holy God.

Crown, as before, the holy city, Jerusalem.
  the holy city, Jerusalem.
  the holy city, Jerusalem.

Crown, as before, the holy city, Jerusalem.
  the holy city, Jerusalem.
  the holy city, Jerusalem.

Rock, Lord, God, King of the Universe,
  Unto You are my thoughts.
A crown—pure, exalted; rebuild the sanctuary.
  Living God, accept my cries of exultation.
Rock, Lord, God, King of the Universe,
  Unto You are my thoughts.
A crown—pure, exalted; rebuild the sanctuary.
  Living God, accept my cries of exultation.

Supreme, their Rock; rebuild their city.
Their Help, their Light, Living One, Exalted.
Creator of the World.

ONE

Song and Remembrance

If the relationship of music to remembrance remains a neglected domain in musical scholarship, the pizmonim of the Syrian Jewish community provide an ideal venue for its exploration. We can begin this process by charting the broader dimensions of the Syrian musical heritage, reconstructing memories of its past while beginning to sketch the manner in which this past is remembered and recreated in the present. Memories relating to pizmonim are embedded in two different domains: memories *about* the pizmon repertory, and memories *of* the songs. Additionally, memories about and of pizmonim can be accessed primarily through two modes of representation: most commonly, they can be spoken or they can be sung. Yet memories of the pizmon tradition are also recorded in writing, as well as interconnected to recollections of sight, smell, and taste.

The Syrian Jewish memories posited within the pizmonim are further characterized by an essential duality: the song texts recall a world of explicitly Jewish experience, while the melodies evoke extra-Jewish sources and frames of reference. The pizmonim therefore constitute a hybrid form, with two expressive channels directly reflecting the bifurcated historical experience of this Judeo-Arab community.

Of Tradition and History

The time depth of a tradition within a community is often a source of comment and contestation, and the Ḥalabi community is no exception. Indeed, the loss of historical memory can be invoked to solve any such dilemma pragmatically: "It has been said that . . . if you can't remember where that song came from and when it was sung, that it has become already tradition" (D. Tawil, 4 December 1984). In most cases, however, transmission of the pizmon tradition draws on both documented historical memory and modern experience in a manner calculated to bring the two together. In this instance, the Syrian experience replicates a process widely shared cross-culturally, where collective memories themselves mediate historical events and are then further transformed to articulate new values and ideas (Zerubavel 1995:3). Among Jews, the dialectic between history and memory is of particular importance in ways that are more fully explored below.

Collective memories of the past and realities of the present are further welded together in the transmission process itself. Within musical domains, with transmission vested largely, although not exclusively, within the act of performance, the present tends to predominate. Approaching the pizmonim from the perspective of present-day performance, "transmission of [musical] tradition" can be seen as a tautology since the etymology of the word, from the Latin *traditum,* refers to anything that is transmitted or handed down from the past to the present (Shils 1981:12). In short, tradition is what is practiced as such.

Beyond its practice, musical transmission is surrounded by a complex of concepts and materials that travel alongside actual performance. Therefore, when discussing the "pizmon tradition" in its broadest sense, one must include any communication of or about musical materials from one person to another, whether in oral, aural, or written form, without regard to the time depth of the materials transmitted. The process of transmission is concerned with reconciling the past with the present, a process thoughtfully articulated by a woman who noted that traditions had been conveyed "over the generations" in her family: "My daughter still follows my custom. We had the same custom. They followed the rules." When asked what "the rules" were, she replied with a single word: "Tradition" (S. Cohen, 28 February 1985).

If transmission of tradition by its very nature privileges the present, historical memory is often invoked to justify and explain the perpetuation of tradition. In the case of the pizmonim, biblical models provide a frequently cited source for its legitimacy:

> You will find that song and music are introduced in the Bible in the very earliest chapters of Genesis. There was a man by the name of Jubal [Genesis 4:22]. He was the originator, he created several instruments of music, and the art of singing. Now they sang and they danced when they . . . came out of Egypt you know, after the miracle of the Red Sea. There's a famous song that was composed by Moses. A beautiful song. . . . And those were the men, and they sang and danced separately. Then the women, under the leadership of Miriam, the sister of Moses, she gathered the women around and they sang and they danced. (S. Catton, 30 October 1984)

If the story of Jubal provides an origin myth for music and dance within the broader continuum of Jewish history, it has served the Syrian Jewish pizmon tradition particularly well, providing a tale of its genesis in the distant past, its maintenance through periods of exile, and the celebration of survival in song. That this myth is gendered and provides for separation of men and women while making explicit the role of women in the tradition is worthy of note as well; this feature is explored below.

The connection of this biblical narrative to modern practice is reinforced through an embossed representation of Jubal's lyre on the covers of a recent edition of pizmonim published in Brooklyn (plate 7).[7] Thus the modern pizmon tradition is literally "bound" historically, connected by myth and icon to the oldest forms of musical expression in Jewish religious experience.

The introductions within the modern pizmon edition, penned by famous Syrian rabbis and cantors, cite the words of venerable Jewish religious sources predating them to historicize further the role of melody and song:

> The upshot of what has been said is this: this custom [of singing] is firmly established and well founded in the sources of the Talmud, legal codification, Midrashim, the holy Zohar, as well as in all other holies on high. . . . And so it is, let the righteous ones see it and rejoice; let the just give praise for the printing—for the children of Israel—of this book of supplications of the community of Aleppo. Anyone who rushes off and makes great effort to [possess] this [book] is to be commended—the payback from heaven will be double. (Kassin 1988: 31–32, translated by James Robinson)

On the level of documented music history, the pizmon tradition extant in Brooklyn today shares deep roots with a broader stream of Jewish tradition. The practice of setting sacred Hebrew texts to pre-existing tunes dates from medieval Spain, where it was sanctioned by Jewish mystics.[8]

From the inception of the tradition, the use of melody and song was believed to be vital to the glorification of God and the means by which a man earns life in the next world.[9] However, singing is permitted only in Hebrew, that "holy tongue, that divinely chosen language of ours which is more dear than gold." The singing of "sensual love songs, God forbid, in any language . . . is a criminal offense, since, as we know from our rabbis, forebears, and ancient sages, it stirs up the hearers' inclination to do evil." However, there is an obligation to sing melodies, particularly those of other nations, if they are set to sacred Hebrew texts because "with the tunes that you sing you arouse the Holy One, who is blessed, to take notice of the nation whose tune you sing."

Borrowing melodies and providing them with new, sacred Hebrew texts is done for a

> good reason, a reason of fundamental importance, and it is correct that it is said about it "that it is good." This is so because the melody is a holy spark. Because when one plays sensual love songs, the spark is submerged in the kelippot [husks].[10] It is for this reason that it is necessary to establish a foundation of holy words—drawn from the mouth of scholars and from the mouth of books—for any new tune with a non-Jewish source, in order to lead the spark from the realm of evil to the realm of holiness. This is an obligation in the same way that it is an obligation to draw sinners [to good], to turn many away from iniquity, and to bring out the precious from the vile. [It is an obligation] to make clear the holy sparks. So it is with holy songs. The holy sparks bring light to the just. (Ibid. 32)

Following the expulsion of Jews from Spain in the late fifteenth century, these songs continued to flourish, drawing increasingly on melodies from non-Jewish sources. A central repository for our knowledge about this historical process is the widespread distribution and survival of a *dīwān* (songbook) titled *Zemirot Israel,*[11] published in Safed in 1587 by a Sephardic poet named Israel Najara (c. 1550–1625).[12] Najara noted in his preface that the Hebrew lyrics were intended to be sung to Arabic, Turkish, or other tunes; he preceded most of the poems with the instruction that it was to be sung "to the melody of . . . ," followed by the opening line of the non-Jewish model song (Avenary 1979:186). It is estimated that among the "foreign songs" used by Najara were about 150 of Turkish origin, thirty derived from the oral tradition stemming from Spain, and a couple of Greek melodies (ibid. 186, 188). Recent studies have further investigated the "constant dynamic interaction" between and within various Jewish repertories, implicating a variety of repertories ranging from liturgy to the Judeo-Spanish epic to other genres of Judeo-Spanish folksongs in this process (J. Cohen 1990, I. Katz 1988, Seroussi and Weich-Shahak 1990/91).

In the musicological literature, the use of preexistent melodies as vehicles for new texts is termed "contrafactum." A contrafactum is a vocal work in which a new text has been substituted for the original one (Randel 1986:200). The term itself, while commonly applied to the European secular monophonic repertory of the twelfth and thirteenth centuries (Falck 1980:700), in fact emerged with the above meaning only in the context of twentieth-century scholarship (Falck 1979). Here I use "contrafactum" as a convenient rubric to highlight a musical process that is quite common cross-culturally and that aptly characterizes the pizmon tradition. I return to issues concerning cross-cultural use of the contrafactum and its implications in chapter 6.

The use of contrafacta therefore can be confirmed as an early practice among Sephardic communities in the Levant, their popularity both stemming from the need to provide the masses with an accessible way of incorporating religious ideas in a period of spiritual crisis and based on the mystical interpretation of the secular songs by poets influenced by kabbalistic ideas.[13] There is also no doubt that on some level this practice served to bring Jews into continued interaction with musical traditions they had encountered. In any event, some poems of Najara have "enjoyed uninterrupted continuity of performance down to the present" (Avenary 1979:190) and are still found in the modern collection of pizmonim published in Brooklyn.[14] Pizmonim continued to be composed in this same manner in late nineteenth century Aleppo and twentieth-century Brooklyn, with the outcome in the late twentieth century that those set to "foreign" melodies comprise the majority of the surviving repertory. The definition of "foreign" shifts over time and in relationship to the geographical and national settings in which Syrian Jews find themselves; this issue is addressed in detail in chapter 5.

If individuals are aware of the historical importance of some pizmonim, they are equally sensitive to the reality that the knowledge of many such older songs has declined:

> You know, we don't know all of them [pizmonim]. These are old, hundreds of years old. They are lost, they are gone forever. All we know is the ones we know. (M. Kairey, 6 November 1984)

With the exception of Najara's extraordinary contribution in the sixteenth century, no other single individual is remembered and memorialized by modern Syrian Jews as a leader of pizmon composition until the appearance in late nineteenth century Aleppo of Rabbi Raphael Taboush.[15] In the words of one person, "He's the first one that I remember" (G. Haber, 31 January 1989). During the life of Taboush, pizmon composition and performance evidently were restored and revitalized, initiating a modern school of pizmon transmission that survives most actively in Brooklyn, but also in other Syrian communities in the New World (D. Tawil, 11 December 1984). The close relationships of Taboush with his students and their subsequent role in sustaining the pizmon tradition throughout the twentieth century in the Syrian diaspora are a central focus of this book.

Teachers of Memory

The pizmonim transmitted today in Brooklyn are viewed as the legacy of Aleppo and the creativity of Rabbi Raphael Taboush. Born in Aleppo around the year 1873, Taboush died in Cairo in 1919 (Laniado 1952:148)[16] (see plate 8). Taboush composed many pizmonim still actively performed in Syrian communities around the world, including such popular songs as Yaḥid Ram Le῾olam (no. 238) and Attah El Kabbir (no. 210). Tales about Taboush are vividly retold in late twentieth century Brooklyn.

While she never met her great-uncle Raphael Taboush, Gracia Haber recalls having heard many details about his life and accomplishments (G. Haber, 31 January 1989). The narrative begins with the story of Raphael Taboush's parents, Isaac and Seti Ades Taboush, who had five boys and two girls. Their third son, Abraham, was Gracia's grandfather. Raphael was the fourth son, followed by a younger brother named Joseph, to whom he remained close throughout his life.

Raphael Taboush married Grace Hamouwy, with whom he had three boys and three girls; the eldest boy and girl were named Isaac and Seti respectively, after their paternal grandparents.[17] While the date of Raphael and his family's migration to Egypt is unclear beyond the fact that he died there in 1919, likely the presence of his beloved young brother Joseph, who had left for Cairo as a teenager and became a successful businessman, was a factor in his migration.

The most frequently told tale about Raphael Taboush concerns his blindness:

> *Ḥakham*[18] Taboush was blind, by the way, a phenomenal singer, phenomenal poet . . . and he had somebody else do the writing for him. (D. Tawil, 11 December 1984)

According to Gracia Haber, Raphael became blind after an incident in the environs of Aleppo:

> Raphael used to go places where there is Syrian songs, Arabic songs; he loved tunes. And he wanted to get the tunes in his head. Always. So every time they hear there is a wedding or a party by the Arab, he used to go there. He has some friends that go with him. He had already finished his

> Hebrew school, but not the higher studies to be a rabbi. One day he was in an Arab village and they caught him, realized he was Jewish, and he ran. So, they sent the police after them and he got so scared he ran, breathing very fast, he washed his face with cold water, he was very hot, and he became blind. That's what my grandmother told me. (Ibid.)

After losing his sight, Taboush continued his musical activities and supported himself through selling socks. He also became very religious:

> So, he became blind and then he used to go with his friend also to listen to the music. One day his friend didn't show up. So it was a Saturday, another friend was going to shul [synagogue], he told him, "Raphael, you want to go with me to shul?" He says, "Yes, I'll go." Since that day, he never left the shul. He loved it. (Ibid.)

Many stories circulate about Taboush's special musical skills, said to be all the more acute after he went blind. Most frequently told is the story that Taboush was regarded as a "thief" because he "stole" melodies that he heard (J. Saff, 23 October 1984; G. Shrem, 9 January 1986; M. Arking and J. Mosseri, 14 January 1986).

> This is a true story. You see this Ḥakham Raphael Taboush? Here's his picture over here you see.[19] He was blind, you know. . . . He used to go to hear all the Egyptian singers that come from Egypt to Syria, like they make a performance usually in the coffeehouses. All the musicians used to come. They used to introduce the new songs that they happened to make. So Ḥakham Raphael Taboush used to go with a man.[20] As soon as he comes in they gave their greatest respect. They used to say, "Here comes a thief, thief of songs." This man, he goes up there, he used to sing in Arabic, he used to put his hands on his lap. He used to get the melody. He says it in Arabic, the next day he composed it in Hebrew. . . . This is a gift, you know. . . . And this man had no musical background or anything. It's a gift. (H. Kaire, 14 March 1985)

Some stories tell of Taboush challenging Arab musicians at the end of their performances to compare the melodies of their songs to his. Taboush would sing a melody from one of the bakkashot,[21] challenging the Arab musician to identify it:

> So the [Arab] artist says, with a click of his tongue: "I never heard that maqām before." You know, he couldn't associate it. Then he [Taboush] tells [sings] him something else. [The Arab musician] says: "I give up." "This is a holy maqām," Taboush says. The [Arab] musician says: "I could never

> compare it. It's outstanding, it doesn't compare, it doesn't resemble any other maqām, there's a maqām to it, but the words, it's meaningful." (Ibid.)

Taboush's prolific skill is said to have single-handedly spurred a revival of the pizmon tradition in his native Aleppo:

> He had tunes in his head and every time there was a wedding, or there was a bar mitzvah or a bris [circumcision ceremony], he used to, in Hebrew, translate the words. The music is in Arabic, but the wording was Hebrew. And that's how we start the pizmonim. And for every occasion, there is another pizmon that he used to make. All those pizmonim, they used to sing them in shul. That's how they made them, those songs and they, the young community that loved the music, they add to it. (G. Haber, 31 January 1989)

Taboush is said to have known many Arab melodies and to have been so adept at composing Hebrew texts that he could produce a new pizmon almost on demand:

> This Taboush, he couldn't see. But he was very, very smart and very fine at singing and he was very religious. . . . One time they wanted to make like a joke out of him. So there was one Rav [Rabbi], he came from some other place in Aleppo . . . so they tell him, "You know Ḥakham Raphael, we have Rav so and so." He [Taboush] says, "Why didn't you tell me before that he is here?" And in this minute, the man makes a pizmon for him. (S. Tawil, 30 March 1989)

Despite universal acclaim for his talent, a few intimate that Taboush's voice was not very pleasing to the ear—information transmitted by Taboush's student, Moses Ashear:

> And the funniest thing that Moses, Rabbi Ashear, he used to tell us: "The guy he doesn't have voice. It's something of God, really, how he used to explain you the tune." (Ibid.)

While Taboush's children were said to have been musical, especially his sons Isaac, Ben Zion, and David (G. Haber, 31 January 1989), they did not become the main conduits of the pizmon tradition within the Syrian community. This task fell to his students, most notably Moses Ashear,[22] but also to Eliyahu Menaged and Hayyim Tawil.[23]

The Students of Raphael Taboush

> This Raphael Taboush was in Aleppo, Syria, and I don't know when he died, but I do know that his student was our cantor from the 1920s until he died in 1940 in Brooklyn. He was his adopted son—his name was Moses Ashear. Moses Ashear was an infant and he lost his parents,[24] he was orphaned, and Raphael Taboush, who was a poet, singer, cantor adopted him and Moses Ashear learned from him the art of, since he lived with him, poetry and music and everything else. (J. Saff, 23 October 1984)

Born in Aleppo in 1877, Ashear had a close relationship with Taboush, who passed on to him his knowledge of Arab music, Hebrew poetry, and pizmonim (Ashear 1988:11). Ashear evidently did not go with Taboush to hear Arab music in clubs but studied with him in the synagogue (A. Ashear, 19 July 1989). In 1903, Ashear was appointed official Cantor and Reader of the Torah in Aleppo (Ashear 1988:11). Following his immigration to New York City in 1912, Ashear lived on the Lower East Side of Manhattan, later moving to Brooklyn, where he became the cantor for the Magen David Community in Bensonhurst (see plate 9). Through composing many new pizmonim, Ashear revitalized in Brooklyn the tradition of the *Sebet* ("Sabbath" in Arabic), the Sabbath afternoon domestic gathering where pizmonim are sung (J. Kassin, 30 March 1989).

According to Moses Ashear's son Albert, his father acquired his pizmon repertory in Aleppo from Raphael Taboush. In New York, Ashear sang at the synagogue and at Sebets but never performed at parties. In order to learn new Arab songs, he would listen at home to recordings.

Albert Ashear recalls that his father's dedication to music was so complete, he in effect died singing. While suffering chest pains, he admitted visitors to his house who were trying to identify the melody of an Arab song that had earlier been borrowed and set in Hebrew. Moses Ashear is said to have died as he was trying to recall the melody of the original Arab song (A. Ashear, 19 July 1989).

Taboush and Ashear had a close, almost familial relationship. As an expression of his affection at the time of Ashear's wedding, Taboush composed the pizmon "Melekh Raḥaman," discussed in the prelude to chapter 6.

That Taboush had close relationships with other students besides Ashear is clearly demonstrated by the fact that he composed the pizmon "Ḥai Hazzan" (no. 117) in honor of the wedding of his student Hayyim Tawil. Tawil left Aleppo for Mexico City in 1912, where he taught pizmonim, transmitting a repertory of songs and lively musical imagination to Cantor Isaac Cain and others before his death in the 1950s.[25]

Another Taboush student, Eliyahu Menaged (1890–1964), while evidently not the recipient of a pizmon composed by his teacher, also became a major figure in perpetuating the pizmon tradition. Menaged immigrated to New York in 1912, the same year as Ashear, where he "performed gratis as a cantor . . . in various synagogues for half a century. His honey-sweet voice, his smooth delivery, and his ability to improvise were indeed unique" (SUHV, p. 15). Menaged in turn transmitted his knowledge to many, including most notably Meyer (Mickey) Kairey, whose own subsequent impact as a teacher was celebrated with the concert of pizmonim described in the prelude to this chapter.[26]

Replicating his own experience with Taboush, Ashear forged a close personal and pedagogical relationship with Naphtali Tawil (1902–1963), who along with his brothers Ezra, Moses, and David had learned many pizmonim as a young child from his father. Born in Jerusalem a decade before his parents' immigration to the United States, Naphtali Tawil began to study with Ashear in New York during 1922, "emerging as Ashear's leading and most beloved student, attaining a high degree of proficiency in the knowledge of Makam (modes), Ḥazzanut [cantorial tradition], Pizmoneem and Bakashot" (SUHV, p. 16). Following Ashear's death in 1940, Naphtali Tawil served as cantor at Magen David Congregation and other Brooklyn synagogues. The sustained activity of Naphtali Tawil and later his three brothers at the center of Ḥalabi musical networks over the course of more than half a century provides an unusual example of a pedagogical network reinforced by strong family bonds.

In most other cases, involvement in pedagogical activity tended not to be concentrated in particular families, but sustained through a more extended network of devoted students. Just as the children of Raphael Taboush were not active in perpetuating the pizmon tradition, Moses Ashear's son Albert recalls that he became interested in learning Arab music and pizmonim only after his father's death (A. Ashear, 19 July 1989). Indeed, formal pedagogical responsibility for the pizmon tradition has been maintained by individuals who had not studied with or even known Taboush or Ashear, but had learned the pizmon tradition from others who had. A notable example is Sadegh Harari of Mexico City, who learned the songs of and tales about Taboush and Ashear through Leniado, a Taboush student who immigrated to New York City and with whom Harari was in frequent contact. From Leniado,

Harari learned of Taboush's blindness and his extraordinary memory for tunes, tales Harari recounts in colorful detail (S. Harari, 7 September 1992).

Strong training in pizmonim and the maqāmāt is still considered a requisite for becoming a cantor in the Brooklyn Syrian community, where it is expected that "you went to these people, you sat by them four, five years, pizmonim, setting down pieces, listening to the old music, that's how you become a *ḥazzan* [cantor]" (Y. Nahari, 6 January 1986). Yet there is also nostalgia for the intensity with which the pizmon tradition was once taught, particularly the detailed textual instruction, in which lessons on pronunciation of Hebrew and explanation of its meaning were in the past divided into two distinct stages (M. Kairey, 6 November 1984).[27]

Teaching and Learning

The modern processes of transmitting pizmonim rely on a complex array of oral, written, and aural media. Before exploring these diverse sources, it is necessary first to trace the social settings that frame and sustain them. Most prominent among the settings in which pizmonim are recalled and performed are the synagogue and home.

Although the pizmonim are technically paraliturgical hymns that praise God, the songs are in practice multi-functional and are performed at a variety of religious and social occasions in the Syrian community. One hears pizmonim sung during synagogue services (where the melodies are themselves often reused with texts of statutory prayers), at life cycle rituals, in domestic settings on Jewish holidays, and at parties. Composed in honor of specific individuals to mark important religious and life cycle occasions, pizmonim are sung to both celebrate and commemorate occasions: the birth of a son and his circumcision; the youth's bar mitzvah ceremony at age thirteen; or the recognition of a groom in the synagogue on the Sabbath preceding his wedding. From one vantage point, pizmonim can be seen as musical markers of occasions large and small, formal and informal, within the Jewish life cycle.

While the pizmonim are on the surface composed by, and almost exclusively for, men, and are most often performed by men to mark occasions in the male life cycle, women play vital roles in insuring transmission of the songs, particularly in that most important venue, the home. Men may sing the songs, but the domestic events at which they come together for these purposes are orchestrated by their mothers and wives, often with expressly musical purposes. One woman notes that

> come Sukkot [Festival of Booths] . . . I make sure that one afternoon [is] for my children and for all of their friends, and they know that my house is open to them. The only thing I insist upon—and the boys love it—is that they sit down and they sing pizmonim. Now whenever my father is here, they're thrilled because they grab ahold of him and don't let him go for hours. And they sing all the pizmonim with him. And that's my way, I guess, of just perpetuating the custom. (S. Schweky, 27 January 1988)

The other major context for pizmon performance and transmission is the synagogue, where liturgical performance and other musical activities are most often led by cantors or knowledgeable congregants. Indeed, the very individuals who established Syrian Jewish institutions such as synagogues and schools are explicitly acknowledged as having shaped the broader framework in which pizmonim are remembered and performed; a few are in fact memorialized in the Brooklyn pizmon edition.[28] Other individuals are memorialized within pizmon texts, such as Charlie Serouya, the man to whom the pizmon "Ṣur Yah El" was dedicated in honor of his efforts to teach and mentor Syrian children.

Oral Transmission

> Anybody [who] continually listens to something, they can get it very, very simple. Of course it's easy when you are young, you know, it just comes naturally. (M. Kairey, 6 November 1984)

Pizmonim are learned through repeated exposure in the multiple situations of everyday life. In describing the learning process during ethnographic interviews, individuals tend to separate their knowledge of the borrowed Arab song from the Hebrew pizmon set to its melody:

> How did I learn the songs? The Arabic or the Hebrew? Well, the Hebrew songs, we hear them in the synagogue constantly. There's a period of time when we have a recess in the synagogue on Saturday evening, which lasts about half an hour, and the singers usually get together to sing songs, and that was the beginning of my hearing them. And we get together Saturdays, and one person would sing one song or another, and we all would repeat it, and we picked it up from each other more or less. From people that had been here previously, before us that is, that were singing these songs, we'd pick them up from them.
>
> Also . . . all this music, songs of music, are used in our prayers. In the words of the prayers, not in the words of the pizmonim, nor, of course, the Arabic words. So that's how I picked up pizmonim.
>
> As far as Arabic music, the first song that I heard, my father brought

> the record. Then as I grew older, I loved Arabic music. Why I don't know. And I used to buy records and listen. (J. Saff, 4 December 1984)

While members of the community report knowing a number of songs in their Arabic versions and singing them for hours at home with family members (J. Mosseri, 14 January 1986), most learned pizmonim through constant exposure to them in the synagogue. Repetition of the songs in the company of older men who knew the repertory served to transmit them. In this way, members of the community committed the songs to memory:

> By continuing every Saturday, now we know it by heart. . . . It's not hard if it's continually said, if it's repeated. . . . Nobody knows that, you know it now, now you teach it to somebody else. You know what I mean? Before you didn't know it. It's just like starting or creating something new. Every time something is handed down from one to another. (M. Kairey, 12 December 1984)

One young man described in detail the manner in which an unfamiliar pizmon would be inscribed in long-term memory through repetition during a Saturday afternoon singing session at a friend's house:

> And he said, "Do you know this one on page 186?" No one at the table knew it. So he sang it, two, three times. It was a nice tune, we liked it. We made him sing it maybe another two, three more times 'til we could all sing it. That's how I know it. . . . And then, maybe three, four months later, I was one morning in synagogue and one of the cantors happened to use it, fit into one of the prayers and I recognized it from that. I have it also on tape, that one. (M. Arking, 14 January 1986)

In recent years, children have also learned pizmonim in religious school (J. Mosseri, 14 January 1986). Men who have taught pizmonim at various synagogues and religious schools in Brooklyn are gratified to find that adults remember the songs they learned as children:

> I used to teach pizmonim in Magen David. Today I see these kids married and everything. They still know and that is the only thing they still remember. . . . When they are married and say, "wow, we sing it in the Sebets now." And they always remind me that that was the best class . . . I used to go there 20 minutes a week, I used to teach them two pizmonim a week. Can you imagine they only know about forty or so and they know it. (M. Kairey, 6 November 1984)

Children continue to learn pizmonim at religious secondary schools, where the songs are sometimes sung at graduation ceremonies (J. Kassin,

30 March 1989). Other venues in which children learn pizmonim are youth services where a "catchy tune" is used "to train" children (M. Arking, 14 January 1986). Local Syrian synagogues also sponsor classes for young boys.

Written Transmission

While the oral transmission of pizmonim remains grounded in human relationships, other technologies have been increasingly involved in conveying the songs. Indeed, the transition from oral to written transmission has not been a quick nor an easy one, and many individuals see the emergence of a written tradition as a symptom of loss of memory:

> Because all . . . the people that knows it, they passed away. That's the only thing that I could associate it with. From my memory. You see, all I never knew from the book. All I knew from my heart. When it came to the book it was very strange to me. . . . I don't feel comfortable saying it the other way. Maybe because that's the way I was taught. And all this here, I never knew in the books. From my head. By listening, that's all. (H. Kaire, 14 March 1985)

Throughout the second half of the twentieth century, printed collections have been widely circulated and have served to reinforce individual transmission of the oral tradition. Most important was the publication of an edition of pizmon texts, *Sheer Ushbahah Hallel Ve-Zimrah* in 1964 (see figure 1.1).

Preparation of *Sheer Ushbahah Hallel Ve-Zimrah* began with informal meetings of "three old-timers" who sat down and decided which songs should be included (S. Catton, 24 June 1993). However, responsibility for preparing the printed collection of pizmonim rested largely with Brooklyn cantor Gabriel Shrem's knowledge of the repertory as well as his familiarity with existing collections.[29] Editor-in-Chief Shrem drew upon two existing collections: *Sefer Shir Ushevahah* (Taboush 1920/1921), a collection of bakkashot and pizmonim compiled by Raphael Taboush, edited by Raphael Hayyim ha-Kohen;[30] and Moses Ashear's collection *Sefer Hallel ve-Zimrah* (Jerusalem, 1928):[31]

> I first put the pizmonim of Ḥakham Raphael Taboush and afterwards Ḥakham Moshe Ashear (Alav Hashalom [May he rest in peace]) and then the additional ones. See I didn't make it like a salad, you know. (G. Shrem, 9 January 1986)

Shrem recalled the long hours he worked and the tedious procedures he used:

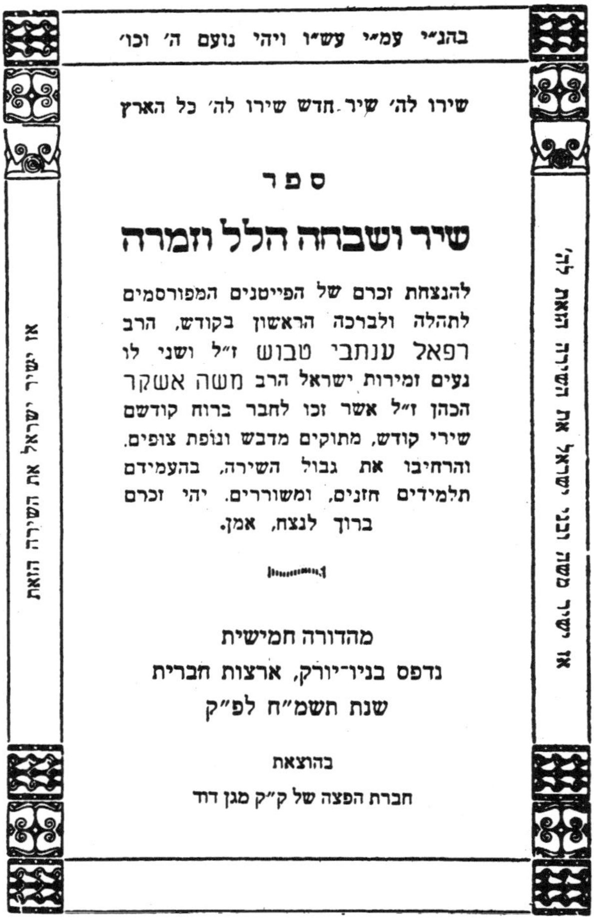

בהנ״י עמ״י עש״ו ויהי נועם ה׳ וכו׳

שירו לה׳ שיר חדש שירו לה׳ כל הארץ

ספר

שיר ושבחה הלל וזמרה

להנצחת זכרם של הפייטנים המפורסמים
לתהלה ולברכה הראשון בקודש, הרב
רפאל ענתבי טבוש ז״ל ושני לו
נעים זמירות ישראל הרב משה אשקר
הכהן ז״ל אשר זכו לחבר ברוח קודשם
שירי קודש, מתוקים מדבש ונופת צופים.
והרחיבו את גבול השירה, בהעמידם
תלמידים חזנים, ומשוררים. יהי זכרם
ברוך לנצח, אמן.

מהדורה חמישית
נדפס בניו־יורק, ארצות חברית
שנת תשמ״ח לפ״ק

בהוצאת
חברת הפצה של ק״ק מגן דוד

אז ישיר ישראל את השירה הזאת

אז ישיר משה ובני ישראל את השירה הזאת לה׳

FIGURE 1.1. Title page, *Sheer Ushbahah Hallel Ve-Zimrah.* Courtesy Sephardic Heritage Foundation.

(top frame) Let the beauty of the Lord [our God be upon us].
(right frame) Then sang Moses and the children of Israel this song to the Lord:
(top of page) O sing to the Lord a new song; sing to the Lord, all the earth.
(left frame) Then Israel sang this song.
(main text) The book

Sheer Ushbahah Hallel Ve-Zimrah [shir u-shevaḥah hallel ve-zimrah]
To perpetuate the memory of the most famous of liturgical poets. Praise and blessing for the most holy of them, R. Raphael Antebi Taboush, and to his second in rank, the sweet singer of Israel, R. Moses Ashear ha-Kohen. They succeeded, with the Holy Spirit, to compose holy songs which are sweeter even than honey and the honeycomb. And they expanded the frontier of song by raising up many students: both cantors and poets. May their memory be revered forever. Amen.

(translated by James Robinson)

> About thirteen, fourteen years of my life [are] in this book. . . . I got four books and I cut off from the book and I pasted the pages on an 8″ × 11″ paper. I also made a copy for myself because you have to send this to the printer and one for me to copy. So I worked on it only at night, because after all I have to take care of my family. I used to work a lot of times 'til one or two o'clock at night. And as it is I used to work with one-sixth of what the average person has sight.[32] I didn't care. . . . I mean, I'm in love with the pizmonim books. You know—I'll tell you—I'm in love with the pizmonim. (G. Shrem, 9 January 1986)

The first edition of SUHV (1964) proclaimed its intent to focus mainly on the "works and creations" of Taboush and Ashear, who are characterized in the original introduction as the "two experts in Hebrew poetry and masters of music of the Middle East" (p. 3). The first edition's introduction also notes that

> All the songs have been arranged systematically according to the "Makam" (a musical scale consisting of intervals of whole, one-half, and one-quarter tones). Vowel points have been supplied. An index has been provided. Israeli songs and other related features of interest have been included. Every effort has been made to make the contents of this book easily accessible to the reader. (p. 4)

The first edition contains several introductions in Hebrew: a lengthy preface (discussed further below) written by the Chief Rabbi of the Brooklyn Syrian community, Jacob S. Kassin (pp. 5–10); a reprint of Moses Ashear's introduction from *Sefer Hallel ve-Zimrah* (pp. 13–14); and a reprint of an introduction by Hayyim Shaul Aboud to *Sefer Shirei Zimrah Hashalem,* the volume of pizmonim widely used in Jerusalem (pp. 16–17). Subsequent editions of SUHV have retained these introductory texts in Hebrew, along with the brief English-language biography of Ashear (originally on pp. 21–23), while updating the editor's introduction and adding short memorial sketches of several other community leaders and singers, including Isaac Shalom (p. 14), Eliyahu Menaged (p. 15), Naphtali Tawil (p. 16), and David E. Franco (p. 17).

A perusal of the contents of SUHV provides an overview of the paraliturgical song repertories and the manner in which they are embedded in Syrian community life. The 1988 edition, which serves as the basis for this discussion, begins with a short section containing prayers for Sabbath Eve (Kiddush Leleyl Shabbat, pp. 1–7). On pages 7a–7L is interpolated the Birkat Hammazon, the grace after meals. On page 8 begin the bakkashot, which extend through page 75. Next follow the songs for Moṣa'ei Shabbat (76–96) [Sabbath evening] and the petiḥot [poetic texts used for musical improvisation before and between bakkashot and pizmonim] (97–106). The pizmonim proper begin on page 107 and extend through page 514, divided among the various maqāmāt; a total of 560 pizmonim are found in the 1988 edition. The final section of the volume includes miscellaneous texts, including a Judeo-Arabic version of the Ten Commandments in Hebrew script (p. 515) and a few Israeli folksongs (pp. 552a and 552b). Two useful indexes located at the end of the volume provide listings of pizmonim both in their order of printed appearance according to maqām (pp. 553–64c) and in (Hebrew) alphabetical order (pp. 578–604). Several additional charts provide correlation between weekly biblical portions and the correct maqām (pp. 565–66), listings of pizmonim appropriate for re-use in various liturgical contexts (pp. 567–69), and charts of pizmonim to be sung for special life cycle occasions (pp. 570–73).

While Shrem compiled the Brooklyn edition primarily from existing collections, evidently some texts required editorial work as well as special permission to be included:

> I started to work on this book right here. . . . It didn't have any punctuation [i.e. vocalization signs] . . . always they chose the cheapest way in the world to print it. . . . I started out, I had two big things to crack. First of all they had like a curse on it. . . . Like you are not allowed to copy it unless with the authority or the willingness of [the] descendants of the author, Raphael Antebi Taboush. Luckily, I spoke to our chief Rabbi. . . . I told him the situation. He says, yes there is that you're not allowed, but we do have his descendant over here. . . . We'll go to speak to him and get his will, let's say, to print the book. (G. Shrem, 10 January 1986)[33]

While the book is a central resource for those interested in perpetuating the pizmon tradition, one occasionally hears criticism of details:

> There's things in this book which have nothing there [e.g., no attributions] and you just wonder where they came from. Or some of them just say "from an old manuscript." They don't know where the tune's from. They just have the words here. Gabriel Shrem knows the tune, so he put it in. (M. Arking, 14 January 1986)

Knowledgeable individuals also note the occasional mistake in classifying a song under the wrong maqām, or an error in attributing a source melody or text.[34] Some individuals more accustomed to oral transmission find the book difficult to use. The placement of punctuation is criticized by one to be hard to read, "like a station—a stop signal" (H. Kaire, 14 March 1985). Yet more problematic is the ordering of songs frozen by the book, "because if you put it together, it has a different meaning" (ibid.). For others who never learned to read Hebrew, written transmission has had little impact, "being I never knew how to read, but I know [the songs] from childhood" (S. Cohen, 28 February 1985).

Most members of the community feel that the publication of SUHV has enhanced transmission of pizmonim:

> I would say up to about twenty years ago, even the interest [in] pizmonim was diminishing quite a bit in the community. But since we printed these books . . . they were printed to make it easier for a person to read because the original books that we used to have, which were very rare, you couldn't come across them, very few people had them, and they were written without the vowels, the *nekuddot*. So it was difficult for the average layman to even read it, so he never even became interested in it. 1964 was the first printing, so that's 20 years ago. Once these books were printed and people started taking it and enjoying it, and it became easier for them, and today there's a rejuvenation in the community to learn as many pizmonim as possible. (I. Cabasso, 13 November 1984)

Frequent reprintings of SUHV have enabled the community to renew the repertory and to add newly composed songs (J. Saff, 23 October 1984; S. Catton, 30 October 1984). The international distribution of the edition also served to increase the Brooklyn community's visibility and prestige among Syrian and Sephardic Jews worldwide. As of 1993, approximately 110,000 books had been sold internationally (S. Catton, 24 June 1993); additionally, thousands of copies have been donated without charge in Israel to needy congregations of Syrian, Iraqi, or "Sephardic Jews of Arab bent who know how to sing" (S. Catton, 30 October 1984). During my fieldwork in Mexico and Jerusalem, I often encountered copies of SUHV. In some cases, individuals were using early editions of the book, indicating that they had received the volume soon after its initial publication.

The pizmon book thus transmits not just songs, but also social history, containing the biographies of important individuals and dedications from a range of families and businesses. The introductory materials also provide a window on the philosophy and rationale behind paraliturgical song traditions among Syrian Jews.

As noted above, the essay by Rabbi Saul Kassin provides a document which frames the pizmon tradition in relation to a world of traditional Jewish thought. Rabbinical prohibitions against singing love songs in languages other than Hebrew are set forth emphatically in this same introduction. The continued importance of song in the present is the manner in which it enhances religious intention:

> It is best that a man accustom himself so that he will be familiar with some melody. This is because a melody is a very great and lofty thing. It has a great power to arouse man's heart and lead it to the Lord. (Kassin 1988:29)

Not incidentally, the introduction composed by Cantor Moses Ashear specifically invokes the importance of memory:

> [Scripture considers] anyone who forgets one thing from his mishnah [to be putting his life in danger, as it is written: 'Only take heed to thyself, and keep thy soul diligently, lest thou forget the things which thy eyes have seen'].[35]

On the title page of SUHV, reproduced along with an English translation in figure 1.1, the power of melody fused to sacred text is invoked to honor and commemorate the cantors and poets who composed the songs and committed their texts to writing.

The Use of Recordings

If the printed editions of SUHV have served to both maintain and symbolize the pizmonim, the use of sound recordings has become particularly important in all aspects of pizmon transmission and composition. From their first days as immigrants in the Americas, Syrian Jews remained part of the Middle Eastern musical tradition through listening to recordings imported from Aleppo and Cairo. In a very real way, recordings of Arab popular music served to link Syrian Jews to the Middle East as well as to conserve and revitalize Ḥalabi liturgical and paraliturgical music in its American diaspora.

Knowledgeable singers continue to learn repertory from cassettes. One man mentioned that he had learned a bakkasha, "Darashti," no. 67, from a cassette recently: "Somebody brought a cassette and I just picked it up" (H. Kaire, 14 March 1985).

Recordings also served to familiarize Syrian Jewish immigrants with music of the new world around them. Elderly members of the community remember learning songs such as "Eli, Eli" from recordings of the famous tenor Yosele Rosenblatt (S. Tawil, 30 March 1989).

A third important function of recordings was to link communities within the Syrian diaspora. In particular, the portability and durability of cassette technology that emerged in the late 1960s made it possible for individuals to share songs among widely separated localities. Virtually everyone interviewed in the Syrian community discussed their personal use of tape recordings. In Mexico, cassettes enabled the immigrants to transmit both old and new songs. A Ḥalabi cantor who immigrated to Mexico in the 1950s mentioned that he subsequently learned old Aleppo pizmonim from private recordings made in New York City, and that he had become familiar with more recent pizmonim through cassettes published in Israel (S. Harari, 7 September 1992).

The cassette is also actively used to teach liturgical music to children within the community:

> I use tapes to teach them their bar mitzvah. . . . I just teach them in about six weeks because they don't have to read much, and I put it on tape and I go to them once a week . . . and circle the things that they're making wrong. (M. Kairey, 12 December 1984)

If the cassette provides a major source for transmitting songs, it has been actively employed by individuals who want to preserve their own performances of pizmonim permanently for the future. Cantor Isaac Cain of Mexico City recorded four cassettes of vocal performances, including Arabic songs, favorite pizmonim, and liturgical selections. Cain reports that he made the recordings because his daughters wanted them for their children's long-term use (I. Cain, 7 September 1992). A number of people in the Brooklyn community have also made cassette recordings, some on their own initiative, others at the request of friends and family; Gabriel Shrem recorded a set of eleven cassettes for use of the Cantorial School at Yeshiva University. The set, which contains pizmonim in different maqāmāt, along with renditions of liturgical prayers using these pizmon melodies, has circulated informally. Moses Tawil noted that his older brothers made tapes near the end of their lives

> because the people just came to them and said, there is not much time on it, so take some of these, they didn't have much. They just taped them to have the melody and the information on record, so to speak. I have some of those. (M. Tawil, 6 November 1984)

Individuals particularly value recordings of songs and repertories that are beginning to recede in community memory and practice, such as the bakkashot; for example, recordings of bakkashot made in Jerusalem are widely circulated (M. Kairey, 6 November 1984; I. Cabasso, 13 November 1984). A complete recording of bakkashot has been made and distributed within the Brooklyn community as well.[36]

Also treasured are recordings of beloved singers now deceased. In this manner, the voice of Eliyahu Menaged singing "Maʿuzzi", preserved on a cassette and presented to the research team by Hyman Kaire, could be included on the compact disc accompanying this book.

Individual and Collective Memories in Song

Pizmonim are among the most deeply valued "customs and traditions" and are "what keeps our community going" (S. Schweky, 27 January 1988). If the goal of written, oral, and aural transmission is to preserve the songs in individual and collective memories, it is crucial to explore what the songs convey.

People in Song Texts

The pizmon tradition carries within it references to people within the Syrian Jewish community: individual names are embedded within the poetic texts, in acrostics, and in dedications preceding the songs. It seems likely that the pervasive manipulation of names derives on the most general level from precedents in Jewish mysticism, where for centuries transformations and permutations of words, names, and numbers served as a link between "gnosis" and "praxis." Indeed, "the use of magical names and seals generated a tradition of 'practical kabbalah' that has lasted until the modern period and still survives in certain sectors of the Jewish community" (Blumenthal 1978:95–96). The incorporation of the poet's first name into an acrostic was a long-standing feature of Jewish liturgical poetry, later adapted into new genres of synagogue poetry that arose among Jews under the Arabic literary influence in medieval Spain (Scheindlin 1991:18, 146–47).

The incorporation of the names of individuals within the songs is also a primary mechanism for linking individual and collective memory. Many members of the Syrian community are aware of the presence of names in songs, and that they were incorporated by the poet/composer:

> He interjects like the name of the person with the song. You know what I mean? Like if there's a song where the father's name is Eliyahu, he'll fit the word "eliyahu" within the song that he's composing. And he makes the bride's name or the groom's name. . . . He mentions his mother's name,

> he mentions his father's name, his uncle's name. (H. Kaire, 17 February 1988)

Songs are subsequently perceived as "belonging" to the individual to whom they are dedicated and secondarily to the families whose names are encoded within; indeed, in many cases the "ownership" has an economic aspect since composers are usually paid to compose a pizmon for an occasion, a subject addressed in chapter 5. The association of individuals and pizmonim is a subject of frequent public comment. At a pizmon concert held at the Sephardic Community Center on October 20, 1985, each song was introduced with explicit references to the person or family to whom the pizmon was dedicated. For example, when introducing pizmon "Romemu Lo Bekol," no. 237d, at a community concert, moderator Joseph Saff noted that it had been composed in honor of the bar mitzvah of a man who was present that evening and singing in the choir (Shelemay fieldnotes, 20 October 1985).[37]

If a song is closely associated with an individual throughout his life, it can become commemorative after death, as indicated by the woman who approached a singer during the intermission of a pizmon concert and asked that he sing the pizmon of her husband who had recently died in order "to remember him" (Shelemay fieldnotes, 27 October 1985). Songs not connected with a particular individual from their inception can also be associated through the act of performance, as was the case when a man dedicated his performance of two favorite pizmonim to the memory of his recently deceased brother (ibid.). Lastly, an individual can "sing himself" into a song, electing to perform as a solo a verse that contains his own name, or the name of a relative. In this manner, the singer joins in bringing a song to life while merging his own identity or the name of a family member with that of someone from the past. For instance, an individual may come

> special to say certain particular part of a bakkashot.[38] Maybe it's named for his father or it's named after him. . . . I mean, it's in the song, something's mentioned, like Abraham or something, so . . . it's a pleasure for him to say it. Say the man's name is Abraham. So he takes it upon himself to say Abraham. You know what I mean? . . . Cause their name is there. They take it upon themselves. It's nowhere, no law. (H. Kaire, 14 March 1985)

So common is the process of an individual performing the verse containing his own name, or his father's as way of commemoration, that specific passages are informally reserved for certain individuals. An example is the case of one man unable to father a child. He often sings a verse referring to procreation in hope that the passage might alter his situation favorably:

> There was one man. He was married and he had no kids. So there was [a text containing the phrase] "zera Abraham," "the seed of Abraham." And his name was Abraham. So nobody's supposed to say it. Only he said it. (H. Kaire, 14 March 1985)

Memorializing individuals in song also served literally to unite early twentieth century immigrants to Brooklyn with their ancestors in Aleppo. Elderly Brooklynites note that this was particularly the case with the pizmonim conceived by Cantor Moses Ashear: Ashear's songs are replete with names, largely because he "knew mostly the people that came from the other side. He knew the families. He knows the mother, grandfather, the father, the whole history of the family" (H. Kaire, 17 February 1988).

The encoding of names further empowers the pizmon through linking it to a central social mechanism in the Syrian Jewish community: one in which personal names are ritually extended to a subsequent generation.[39] In this manner, each living individual through his or her name both remembers and commemorates ancestors.[40] A discussion of the pizmon tradition can thus slide almost imperceptibly into a discussion of genealogies. For this reason, the subject of names as embedded in pizmonim and as related to family lineages frequently arose during ethnographic interviews with members of the Syrian community. In the middle of a discussion of his father's influence upon his own career as a transmitter of pizmonim, Cantor Gabriel Shrem suddenly exclaimed:

> By the way, you know that I am the same name as my grandfather. You know that? I mean, this is a tradition. Naming after the grandparents, whether they are alive or they're not. Just like I have my grandson, who is going to be bar mitzvah in three weeks in Israel . . . he is exactly my name. (G. Shrem, 9 January 1986)

Similar digressions explained the naming traditions of the Syrian Jewish community, which individuals consider to be an important heritage of their "Arab Jewish world" and an important "Sephardic Jewish Syrian custom." The first son is named after the paternal grandfather and the first daughter after the paternal grandmother; the second son and daughter are named after the maternal grandfather and grandmother, respectively. If a child is lost through miscarriage or during delivery, the intended name will not be used for the next pregnancy but may be given to a later offspring. So well known are these naming traditions that they are the subject of good-natured joking within the Syrian community; for instance, Joseph Saff recounted telling his son's father-in-law, who is also named Joseph, that they got along so well that he would let the first grandson be named Joe after him (J. Saff, 23 October 1984).

Individuals can utilize traditions associated with naming to figure out the connection of older songs with living families. One young man was discussing a pizmon (no. 186, "Mi Yesapper") composed early in the century in honor of a groom named Eliyahu Abraham Hadaya. When he was asked if he knew anything about the honoree, he paused and then replied thoughtfully:

> I might know the family, because I know, like his middle name is Abraham and that means his father's name was most probably Abraham and I know an Abe Hadaya. It could be from that family. I don't know the family well enough to know that. (M. Arking, 14 January 1986)

A name may also indicate the locality from which an individual or his family comes. Indeed, Syrian Jewish use of place names preserves traces of a pattern established in classical Islamic practice. Most Arabic names consisted of the *kunya* (name of father or mother), the *ism* (personal name), the *nisba* (one's native place), and the *laqab* (nickname) (Schimmel 1989:1). Taking as an example the name of the beloved Aleppo pizmon composer Raphael Antebi Taboush, "Antebi" is a nisba, derived from Ain-Tab, a town near the Syrian–Turkish border where Taboush's ancestors lived. While the Arabic form would likely have been al-Antebi (the [man] from Antebi), the Anglicization still preserves the long "-i" commonly found at the end of a place name (ibid. 10–11). The name "Taboush" derives from a laqab given to Raphael's father, who crafted gold. Frequently a laqab developed into a family name, and indeed this is the case of the Taboush family, whose surname was actually "Ades."

Time and Place in Song Melodies

If the texts of the songs incorporate people through carrying their names, the pizmon melodies make reference to different times and places. Pizmon melodies are generally taken from songs popular at the period of pizmon composition. In a very real sense, they are associated with the locale and situation at which they were originally heard, whether at a concert, at home, or at school. In many instances, the individual who commissioned a pizmon requested that a favorite melody be used, one that might have circulated in the oral tradition, or in the twentieth century been heard through various forms of sound recordings, radio, or film.

A second level of spatial and/or geographical associations is accessed through melodies. The predominant source for melodies from the late nineteenth century was popular tunes from the Arab musical tradition, and secondarily, melodies of other origins that were heard and sung by Syrian Jews wherever they lived. Thus each pizmon carries with it the local and spatial traces of its genesis outside the Jewish pizmon tradition. In virtually all Syrian diaspora communities, Turkish and Syrian songs of the late nineteenth century gave way in the twentieth century to Egyptian repertories. However, pizmon composers in each diaspora community also contributed songs popular only within that locale. This results in different pizmon repertories:

> He's from Egypt . . . it's very likely that he knows some pizmonim that we don't sing, that we don't know. Because he lived in Egypt for the longest time, and he could be singing songs that we're not acquainted with. (J. Saff, 4 December 1984)

However, enough of the pizmonim are shared that they are able to bridge the differences of time and space between Syrian Jews from various communities. On first meeting her cousins from Mexico, Joyce Kassin remembers her surprise that they had "the same traditions, the same customs." But most marked in her memory is sharing pizmonim: "I'll never forget singing with them," she recalled (J. Kassin, 30 March 1989). The networks that connect Syrian Jews wherever they live and that underpin song transmission are explored in chapter 2.

Furthermore, whatever their immediate national origins, all melodies borrowed for pizmonim are today classified according to the category of melody (maqām) of the modern Arab musical system into which they best fit musically. Many of these maqāmāt are linked by name and historical association with a locality in the Middle East. Those Syrian Jews able to discuss the maqām system in depth are aware that maqāmāt such as ḥijāz, ṣabā, and ʿajam carry names taken from specific places in the greater Middle East:

> As you all realize, each maqām was developed in a certain town, village, borough, country, whatever you want to call it. You still have for instance, in Arabia, two geographical areas called both Ḥijāz and Ṣabā. The Ḥijāz is the northwestern part of it and the Ṣabā is the southwestern part of it.

> That's part of Arabia, southern Arabia. ʿAjam you find it going into the Persian empire. . . . And you'll find all of these are designations of geographical areas in essence. (D. Tawil, 11 December 1984)

However, the choice of which maqāmāt are actually popular in a given community reflects the predilections of a particular area:

> Of course it depends on the locale, who uses what melodies and what songs, and you know, the way you were brought up. Certain areas have a tendency to go toward certain maqāms more than other areas, it depends where, who your composers are, who your singers are, etc. (Ibid.)

Thus people and genealogies are memorialized in pizmon texts, while geography and place are implicitly mapped through melodic usage. Uniting both text and tune, however, is the notion of family: real families named in texts, musical "families" evoked in melody (Y. Nahari, 16 January 1986).

Conclusion: Familial Memories

> I have to tell you first, the background of the Tawil family is very musical and it runs for generations. It happens to run on both my father's side as well as my mother's side. We were six brothers, we are now four. We are all, what do you call, cantors of luxury. In other words, we don't do it professionally, we do it because we love music. And the family is looked up to as probably the leading connoisseur in this type of music, and most of us were born here. But it was just in the family. (M. Tawil, 6 November 1984)

If knowledge of pizmonim is acquired through the course of daily life in the home, school, and synagogue, and ritual passages in the lives of individuals are recorded in the dedications and texts of songs, it follows that memories of the songs are integrally linked to the family unit. According to Halbwachs, each family has its "proper mentality, its memories which it alone commemorates" (Halbwachs 1992:59). These include elements from the past which provide a framework for the "peculiar memory" (ibid. 63) of each family. Like her brother Moses Tawil, Sarah Tawil describes the love of music passed down in the Tawil family. Sarah Tawil particularly recalls sitting with their maternal grandfather, Yosef Haim Shrem, who had "a very, very great voice. So he used to sing pizmonim. I used to sing with him" (S. Tawil, 30 March 1989).

A love of music has been passed on in the Tawil family to Moses Tawil's daughters, who in turn associate family occasions, particularly the Sabbath, with sharing food and pizmonim (J. Kassin, 30 March 1989). So strong is this connection that one of Tawil's daughters, Sheila Schweky, describes music as a "way of life" which her father imparted to his children as he and her uncles got together and sang regularly (S. Schweky, 27 January 1988).

Older women did not learn to read Hebrew, nor did they have formal training in pizmonim; but they did become familiar with songs through hearing them repeatedly. Sophie Cohen remembered attending synagogue with her father when she was a small child and that she used to "hear the services and used to enjoy it." She was active musically as a child and recalled that she continued to lead the cumulative Passover song "Ḥad Gadya" at family seders in "Syrian":[41] "They had to wait for me. I never made a mistake." Sophie remembered that she learned the song when she was seven. Later she taught her Ashkenazic husband to sing Syrian songs (S. Cohen, 28 February 1985).

The performance of pizmonim in domestic settings was the primary context in which women learned the tradition, as Moses Tawil notes: "My daughters, for example, grew up in my home obviously and heard a lot of this music and they sing beautifully" (M. Tawil, 6 November 1984). Joyce Kassin, one of Tawil's daughters, agrees:

> Now, you're asking me how I learned. I'm no different than all of those women. I learned by just being there, enjoying the music, and, yeh, humming along and singing. (J. Kassin, 30 March 1989)

However, Kassin goes on to note that women began participating more actively in pizmon performance during the last fifteen to twenty years, largely as a result of studying music in religious schools and participating in choirs. She sees this exposure as part of the changing role of women in modern Syrian Jewish life:

> . . . Our community's changing. The women are changing. There are a lot of new groups. . . . Our women are being more educated now in religion. They're attending classes now. Years ago when we were going to the yeshiva [lit. "sitting," an academy or school], there weren't many girls from our community that attended yeshiva. They went to the public schools. We went to Flatbush Yeshivah High School and I think that I could count on my two hands all the girls that attended the yeshiva at that time. So, what's happening now is this awareness. The women are being educated in religion, they have classes that are pretty heavy-duty. (J. Kassin, 30 March 1989)[42]

Domestic contexts also served to transmit song repertories such as the bakkashot to women, who did not attend the services at which they were performed early on Sabbath mornings in the synagogue:

> When I was a very young boy, we used to sing on Friday nights after our Friday night meal. We would start singing some of the bakkashot, and my mother and my sisters know many of them. (I. Cabasso, 13 November 1984)

Members of other families also remember singing and dancing to Arab songs as part of their home life (G. Haber, 31 January 1989). Several elderly members of the Kaire(y) family remember the prominent place of pizmonim in their home on the Lower East Side of Manhattan during their childhoods in the late teens and early twenties:

> You know all Friday night, after Shabbat, after we finished eating, we started singing . . . my brother and I. . . . And then in the morning we go to synagogue and listen to songs in the morning. . . . It was a way of life, you know, and it was very nice. (M. Kairey, 6 November 1984)

Sophie Kaire Cohen recalled that her father used to repeat melodies over and over again until her brothers learned them. But she adds that she, too, participated:

> My father would go to the synagogue, he'd come back, make *kiddush* [blessing over wine] and pray on the bread, and we'd have a nice feast. And then we'd sing all these songs after we'd finished our dinners, the Saturday pizmonim. . . . Every Saturday we used to sing the same songs, but on holidays they had extra songs. At Shabbat, at holidays, of course they always sang in my family. And I'd join in sometimes. I used to join in when they used to sing. (S. Cohen, 28 February 1985)

However, transmission of musical memories in some family networks was not unidirectional, moving just from parents to children. Sheila Tawil Schweky remembers that she and her sisters were always asked to sing new Israeli songs that they learned at school, thus introducing a new repertory of songs to the rest of the family:

> My father leads most of it, my uncles take part in it, and then my father always calls me to sing some Hebrew music. So you know, it's like a progression. . . . But the beauty about it was, as we came back with each song, my father learned every one of them. Oh yes. So he knows every single one of the Hebrew songs. (S. Schweky, 27 January 1988)[43]

If biological families have played a major role in transmitting pizmonim and in insuring their place in memory, the movements of these families have physically carried the pizmonim from place to place. The story of the migrations of the Ḥalabi community and the manner in which music traveled with it is set forth in chapter 2.

PRELUDE
Attah El Kabbir

The blended sounds of the ʿūd (lute), violin, qānūn (zither), and darābukkah (hourglass drum) could be heard coming from the open folk arts stage in the South Meadow of the Snug Harbor Cultural Center in Staten Island, New York. After an instrumental prelude composed by Muhammed ʿAbd al-Wahhāb, the ʿūd player and singer Vita Israel introduced the program the ensemble was going to perform:[1] songs with Arab melodies and Hebrew words "praising God" and "describing our longing for Israel." A group of four pizmonim was led off with a long improvisation by each instrumentalist on the melody of the first pizmon, "Attah El Kabbir."[2] The Near Eastern music ensemble competed with amplified echoes of Theodore Bikel performing simultaneously before a much larger crowd in an adjacent tent.

How did the Syrian pizmon "Attah El Kabbir" come to be heard in a Staten Island festival on Sunday, September 17, 1989, alongside the songs of Theodore Bikel, Yemenite music, and klezmer music—not to mention the strains of the New York All-City High School Marching Band? The occasion was "L'Chaim: A Festival of Jewish Arts," a celebration of the sixtieth anniversary of the Jewish Community Center of Staten Island, one of the festival's sponsors, along with the Snug Harbor Cultural Center, Inc. The day-long gathering featured a heterogeneous mix of exhibits, vendors, artisans, and performers which on its broadest level celebrated Jewish survival and creativity. The festival chairperson, Cheryl B. Sherman, wrote in the program that "a Jewish life is on a tenuous tightrope. Only our traditions are able to maintain our equilibrium." In fact, it took a full century of transnational wandering for the pizmon "Attah El Kabbir" to arrive at Staten Island.

The approximate age and provenance of "Attah El Kabbir" are well known. In the words of one Brooklyn native, "that song must be a hundred years old. The music is from Islam" (J. Saff, 23 October 1984). "Attah El Kabbir" was composed by Rabbi Raphael Taboush, as is confirmed by the phrase "I am Raphael" in the acrostic. The title of the song, "You, God, are mighty," conveys a message of religious content and praise of God. The pizmon text calls on God to have mercy on his chosen people, alluding to their exile among strangers; it draws heavily on biblical portions, including Job 36:5, Isaiah 62:6, and Psalm 1:2. The phrase concerning oppression by strangers resembles, but does not draw directly on, passages in the prophetic literature, notably Jeremiah 5:19 and Ezekiel 11:9.

Like most pizmonim, "Attah El Kabbir"'s Hebrew text was composed to match the assonance and rhyme scheme of the original Arabic lyrics, the title of which is recorded in Hebrew script. In this manner, the Arabic text *sudam ya na bir* was transformed to *attah el kabbir.* The original song was a classical Arabic *muwashshāḥ,* a vocal piece with regular rhythm and rhyme, divided into three main sections. The opening section is termed a *dawr;* the middle section is the khānah, which provides a contrast in tune, mode and/or register; the final section brings back the musical refrain of the opening dawr (Faruqi 1981:219).

The pizmon melody, which is set in the Arab maqām nahāwand, is frequently used in Brooklyn to teach nahāwand to students. At the same time, while it is a "model" melody for maqām nahāwand, the tune contains allusions to other related maqāmāt. This reflects an understanding that

> the trained singer never sings in one maqām only. No song is ever written in one maqām. Usually the composer will start with one maqām, he'll reel on to another maqām . . . but he'll always, must and will, come back to the original, opening maqām. "Attah El Kabbir"—you can do whatever you want between it. Maybe if we analyzed the song, I'll show you places where it is not pure nahāwand. Cause no song is ever pure one maqām—always variations. But, however, the close always is the same maqām as the opening. (J. Saff, 23 October 1984)

When it is performed, "Attah El Kabbir" is frequently preceded by an instrumental introduction (taqsīm) or vocal improvisation (layālī) which serves to establish the main maqām, as is heard in the performance on the recording accompanying this book. The performance further incorporates vocal improvisation within the verses of the pizmon. Here Moses Tawil is said to have "sweetened" his performance of "Attah El Kabbir" by exploring the "tetrachords" of maqām nahāwand as well as touching on related maqāmāt (D Tawil, 10 May 1985). In this manner, too, Moses Tawil demonstrates his mastery of an Arab aesthetic where

Example 2.1. Comparison of maqām nahāwand with Western minor scale (Idelsohn 1923:73).

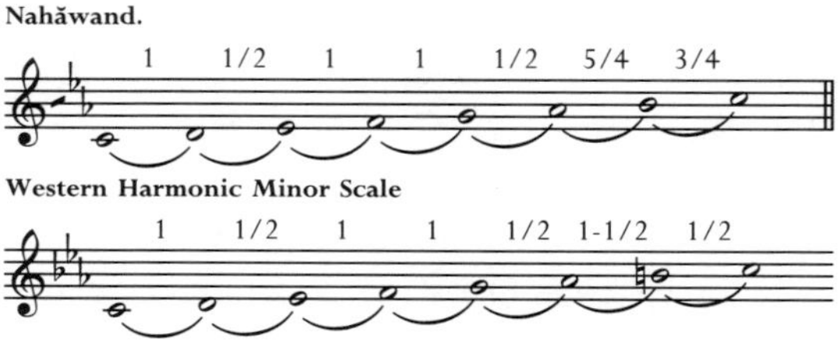

> the singer or the artist has liberty of giving it his own tradition, which is not changing it too radically in any way. But you can see, . . . when he repeats one line the second time, and the notes are a little bit different . . . the more capable a singer is, and the more he can improvise. I mean, it's very easy for a person to learn a song and keep repeating it, but for one that understands music more and has the ability, why he or she . . . has the liberty of changing it and he does it. (J. Saff, 23 October 1984)

The similarity of maqām nahāwand to the Western minor scale has no doubt enhanced its popularity in the United States (musical example 2.1), where the melody of "Attah El Kabbir" is considered to be "very Westernized" (M. Tawil, 6 November 1984). Yet the only musical change in "Attah El Kabbir" acknowledged to have been introduced is said to have occurred in the text. Joseph Saff noted that during his lifetime there has been a small shift in emphasis from the syllable "ra-" in the phrase "ki rab-bim raḥa-mekha," to the last syllable, "-bim." However, Saff also emphasized that he still sings this phrase with the older inflection on "ra," which he recalls as the way the song was sung "when I was a kid" (J. Saff, 23 October 1984).

After its composition, likely around the end of the nineteenth century, the song quickly spread as Syrian Jews migrated to other locales. That the melody of "Attah El Kabbir" was sung abroad no later than the first decade of the twentieth century is confirmed by a transcription found in a 1913 publication by the Jewish music scholar Abraham Zvi Idelsohn (1913:23–24). Idelsohn explains that he gathered and transcribed for this article songs widely known among musicians of that time from Damascus, Aleppo, Jerusalem, and Cairo (ibid. 16). Idelsohn arrived in Jerusalem in 1905, when he was only twenty-three years old, and evidently did not visit other Middle Eastern centers outside Palestine. He almost certainly gathered his examples for the maqām article in Jerusalem after 1905 but before 1913, the year he

EXAMPLE 2.2. Transcription by A. Z. Idelsohn (Idelsohn 1923:74).

went to Vienna in response to an invitation to present the results of his study (Cohon 1984:40).

In Idelsohn's article the song in question is not identified by title but is provided as the first example of maqām nahāwand. Comparison of Idelsohn's transcription (reproduced in musical example 2.2) with the rendition transcribed at the end of this prelude, as well as recent recordings,[3] indicates that the later versions have a slightly expanded form that contains an additional passage in the second system after the second ending of the refrain. While the song may have accrued a new phrase in its middle section during the course of the century, it is also possible either that Idelsohn's informant sang the song differently or that the scholar omitted a phrase in his transcription. Another interpretation also presents itself: the Idelsohn transcription may in fact have been made directly from the Arab tune in circulation, not from the pizmon derived from it. The fact that "Attah El Kabbir" is not included among the "Aleppo-tunes" (pp. 254–474) transcribed and collected in volume 4 of Idelsohn's multi-volume collection, where a revision of the 1913 maqām article also appears,[4] gives this possibility greater weight. The difference in the form of the song represented in Idelsohn's transcription and the versions sung internationally in the late twentieth century could therefore suggest that the melody of the original Arab song may have been intentionally altered when it was set as a pizmon.

Whatever the source of Idelsohn's transcription, it supports the conclusion that the pizmon "Attah El Kabbir" was already circulating in Jerusalem

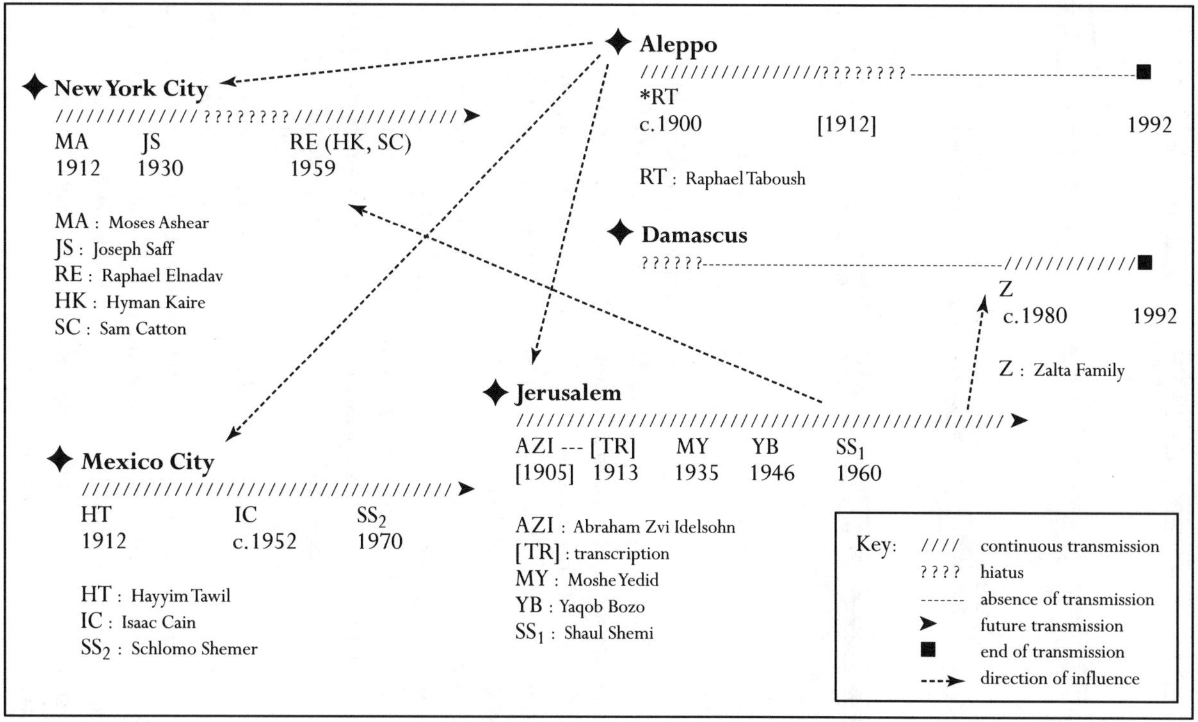

Figure 2.1. The transnational path of pizmon "Attah El Kabbir," c. 1900–1992.

by the first decade of this century (see figure 2.1). In most instances, pizmonim were composed using the melodies of popular (and familiar) Arab songs of their own period; thus if the Arab tune was widely known at that time, likely the pizmon was as well. The "Great Synagogue Ades of Aleppo Jews," founded in 1901, provided an obvious venue for the introduction and performance of popular pizmonim transmitted orally to Jerusalem by members of the Aleppo community who migrated there shortly before or during the time of Idelsohn's sojourn in that city. Certainly we have ample evidence that "Attah El Kabbir" was well established in Jerusalem throughout the rest of the century: this is confirmed by men who migrated from Aleppo to Jerusalem in the 1930s and 1940s.

Menachem Yedid, who was born in Aleppo in 1919 and migrated to Jerusalem in 1935, says that he learned this pizmon in Aleppo (M. Yedid, 23 March 1993). However, Yaqov Bozo, born about the same time (1920) in Aleppo, but who immigrated to Jerusalem a decade later (1946), insists that he learned "Attah El Kabbir" in Jerusalem. To quote Bozo, "In Ḥalab (Aleppo), it was not said at all. It is possible that someone knew it, but I never heard it in Ḥalab. If I heard it, it was in Damascus, not in Ḥalab" (Y. Bozo, 14 March 1993). One can conclude, therefore, that "Attah El Kabbir" must have been on the decline in Aleppo by the 1920s and may have died out entirely by the late 1940s. Indeed, Shaul Shemi, a cantor who was born in Aleppo in 1950, and who immigrated to Tel Aviv in 1960, confirms that he, too, learned "Attah El Kabbir" only after arriving in Israel (S. Shemi, 21 March 1993).

The early introduction of "Attah El Kabbir" to Jerusalem is also rendered likely given evidence of its spread around 1912 to other Syrian communities outside the Middle East. "Attah El Kabbir" has evidently had uninterrupted transmission in Mexico City since that date: it was almost certainly introduced by Hayyim Tawil, a disciple of Raphael Taboush who immigrated to Mexico in 1912 from Aleppo (Ashkenazi 1982:303). Tawil's student, Isaac Cain, learned "Attah El Kabbir" from Tawil in the early 1950s (I. Cain, 7 September 1992). In addition, Shlomo Shemer, a Syrian cantor younger than Cain who was born in Mexico, also performs "Attah El Kabbir" today (S. Harari, 7 September 1992). This pizmon is said to be sung frequently in Mexico City, especially on the holiday Sukkot, within the sukkah (booth) constructed for the occasion.

"Attah El Kabbir" was also transmitted to New York City early on, certainly by Cantor Moses Ashear, who immigrated to New York in 1912. It is also possible that others sang the song in New York prior to Ashear's arrival; almost certainly it was simultaneously introduced by Taboush's student Eliyahu Menaged, who also immigrated to New York in 1912. "Attah El Kabbir"'s continued transmission in New York is confirmed at least until the early 1930s, when Joseph Saff remembers learning the song as a child in Brooklyn (J. Saff, 23 October 1984).

Sometime around mid-century, likely after the death of Moses Ashear in 1940, the trail of "Attah El Kabbir" in New York becomes somewhat fainter. Several longtime Brooklyn residents who immigrated in the teens and who have extensive repertories of pizmonim insist that they did not know "Attah El Kabbir" until it was introduced (or reintroduced) in the 1960s by Israeli cantor Raphael Elnadav, who arrived in Brooklyn in 1959. Hyman Kaire implies that the song was known, but not sung, in New York during the middle part of the twentieth century:

> See, this one we didn't know 'til the new generation came from Israel. I never used to sing this before. But it was known. Because I think it was [by] Raphael Taboush, if I'm not mistaken. So, we didn't know it. . . . The first time I heard it was from Cantor Raphael Elnadav, maybe twenty years ago. I know more or less, but this one I never knew before. It was known, but it wasn't popular. (H. Kaire, 17 February 1988)

Thus, despite its early introduction to New York, "Attah El Kabbir" was apparently neglected by the middle of the century and not widely performed until its revival by an Israeli cantor in the 1960s.

Perhaps most interesting of all, "Attah El Kabbir" is confirmed to have been reintroduced to Syria through cassette tapes from Israel around 1980. According to a recent immigrant from Damascus who arrived in Brooklyn in late 1992, he and his family learned "Attah El Kabbir" in Damascus from an Israeli cassette and he subsequently taught it to his synagogue choir (Anon., 4 February 1993). Thus, the path of transmission can on occasion be reversed, with nearly a century of active performance in the diaspora resulting in the reintroduction of the song to its country of origin.

Today, "Attah El Kabbir" is very much alive in Israel, where "it is used in every synagogue in Jerusalem" (M. Yedid, 23 March 1993). This is also the case in Mexico City, where Cantor Isaac Cain continues the tradition of his teacher, Hayyim Tawil, in borrowing the melody of "Attah El Kabbir" to set the Kaddish prayer in maqām nahāwand for the Sabbath morning synagogue service (I. Cain, 7 September 1992).

Among members of the New York Syrian community, "Attah El Kabbir" is not considered to be "a heavy classic piece of music," but rather a "light" piece appropriate for many occasions (M. Tawil, 6 November 1984). As a result, "Attah El Kabbir" can be heard in a variety of settings, traditional and new. At a gathering of Syrian families at a Catskill Mountains resort, "Attah El Kabbir" was sung within and after several services (Shelemay fieldnotes, 1–4 April 1988). Similarly, in Brooklyn the "Attah El Kabbir" melody was borrowed to set a prayer within the Sabbath morning service, and the entire pizmon was sung at a celebration in honor of a bride and groom later that same day (Shelemay fieldnotes, 20 February 1988). The performance of "Attah El Kabbir" at the Staten Island Festival can therefore be considered a most congenial venue for a pizmon that has traveled worldwide with Syrian Jews over the course of the last century.

Attah El Kabbir

You, God, are mighty, your name is merciful,
Have pity on a chosen people,
For your compassion is abundant,
Without end and without limit.
  For your compassion is abundant,
  Without end and without limit.

My soul shall thank you, every moment and at all times
Accept my faithful praise!
With pity act upon me graciously.
  Accept my faithful praise!
  With pity act upon me graciously.

I shall not hold my peace, not in day or at night
My tongue shall utter your rightness
Desire my prayer as if it were a sacrifice
In place of sacred sacrifice or burnt offering.
  Desire my prayer as if it were a sacrifice
  In place of sacred sacrifice or burnt offering.

See, my rock, how long is the length of my exile
Strangers continue to lord it over me
Hurry now, please, the coming redemption.
  Strangers continue to lord it over me
  Hurry now, please, the coming redemption.

Give beauty and honor and strength
To the son of David, your anointed one
Who, every morning, gives forth hymns
With a voice of song and praise.
    Who, every morning, gives forth hymns
    With a voice of song and praise.

My God, bless and strengthen this righteous people
Bear them on eagles' wings
Yet even higher.
    Bear them on eagles' wings
    Yet even higher.

EXAMPLE 2. Attah El Kabbir

אַתָּה אֵל כַּבִּיר. רַחוּם שִׁמְךָ. רַחֵם עַל עַם סְגֻלָּה. כִּי
רַבִּים רַחֲמֶיךָ. לְאֵין קֵץ וְתִכְלָה:

כי רבים וכו׳

נַפְשִׁי תּוֹדֶךָ. בְּכָל־עֵת וּבְכָל־זְמַן. שְׂעֵה מַהֲלָלִי נֶאֱמָן.
חֹן עָלַי בְּחֶמְלָה:

שעה מהללי וכו׳

יוֹמָם וָלַיְלָה לֹא אֶחֱשֶׁה. לְשׁוֹנִי תֶּהְגֶּה צִדְקֶךָ. רְצֵה
שִׂיחִי כְּמוֹ אִשֶּׁה. בִּמְקוֹם זֶבַח וְעוֹלָה:

רצה שיחי וכו׳

רְאֵה צוּרִי אֹרֶךְ גָּלוּתִי כַּמָּה יָמִים. רָדוּ בִי זָרִים וְקָמִים.
נָא תָּחִישׁ גְּאֻלָּה:

רדו בי וכו׳

פְּאֵר וְכָבוֹד וְעֹז תִּתֵּן. לְבֶן דָּוִד מְשִׁיחֶךָ. כָּל־בֹּקֶר
זְמִירוֹת נוֹתֵן. בְּקוֹל שִׁיר וּתְהִלָּה:

כל בקר וכו׳

אֵלִי בָּרֵךְ וְחַזֵּק לְעַם הַיְשָׁרִים. שָׂאֵם עַל כַּנְפֵי נְשָׁרִים.
בְּיֶתֶר מַעֲלָה: שאם על וכו׳ תם

TWO

Music and Migration in a Transnational Community

Syrian Jews in the late twentieth century present a paradoxical profile to the outsider seeking to characterize their history and identity. With the exception of a few hundred mostly elderly individuals remaining in Aleppo and Damascus, virtually all Jews of Syrian descent today live outside of Syria; and many, outside the Middle East altogether.[5] Their dispersion to major urban centers around the world can be seen within several historical contexts: as a Jewish diaspora community with a complex past that includes multiple migrations; as a Middle Eastern diaspora community, part of a significant movement of peoples from the broader Middle East to the New World (Naff 1985); and as a well-bounded, yet adaptive American ethnic community with internal movements within the United States (Zenner 1988:386). Their strong identity as Syrian, or more specifically in this case Ḥalabi, Jews is sustained in the face of decades of separation from Aleppo.[6] Yet while they maintain a strong emphasis on locality and boundedness in the United States and other countries of relocation, the twentieth-century Syrian community is an emphatically transnational one, distributed among urban centers widely separated on the map. In many ways, the very circumscribed nature of Syrian social and religious life in each local community can be said to feed and reinforce the connections between these widely dispersed urban centers, constructing a transnational network of extraordinary range and vitality.

"Hillel said, Separate not thyself from the congregation."[7] Read aloud and interpreted by a member of the Syrian Jewish community at an informal study session for a small group of Syrian men gathered together for Passover, this short passage encapsulates constraints "not to leave your community and how important it is to stay with your own" (Shelemay fieldnotes, 2 April 1988). This maxim in fact expresses a central value of Syrian Jewish life in the late twentieth century, a life lived at once with deep local roots and strong international ties.

While ethnomusicologists have long theorized about the manner in which the local and international interact in urban musical traditions,[8] this multilayered reality has only recently been examined through grounded ethnography in the field.[9] Similarly, the pizmon case study provides an open window on music as part of both an intensely local phenomenon and simultaneously a global pursuit. Syrian Jews in Brooklyn talk about the local and the transnational as part of a larger whole. For example, one Syrian Jewish community leader began a group interview with the following statement:

> I come from a community of Syrian Jews that live in Brooklyn. There are Syrian Jews all over the world, about 125,000.[10] They are in New York City and a small group in California. There are two large congregations in Mexico City, they number about 30,000. They have a large group in Panama, about 10,000 in Brazil, in São Paulo, and then in Argentina, they have a community as large as that in New York, about 25,000–30,000. They are very clannish. They live with each other, they know each other. . . . It's a very, very interesting life when you see it in action. (S. Catton, 30 October 1984)[11]

Thus the widely flung pathways of immigration have over the years coalesced into a transnational network that is an integral part of the modern Syrian Jewish world view. Here we examine this network primarily from the perspective of Syrian Jews in New York City. The Syrian community in Brooklyn—termed "Aleppo-in-Flatbush" in one publication (Sutton 1979)—is organized in close proximity to the myriad religious and communal institutions at its core (see figure 2.2).[12] Many in the Brooklyn community speak spontaneously and warmly of longtime residency alongside family members, such as the elderly cantor who boasted proudly that all his daughters except one lived "on the same block" (G. Shrem, 9 January 1986). Others lament factors that have caused family to move away from the neighborhood since "before we were in the radius of three blocks, easy, so we saw each other every single day" (S. Cohen, 28 February 1985). The Syrian neighborhood in Brooklyn is said to become a "ghost town" (H. Kaire, 17 February 1988) in the summer when many families shift to their vacation homes in Deal and Bradley Beach on the New Jersey shore, where new permanent Syrian neighborhoods have also been established. The cold winter months see many retired members of the community migrating together to Florida, where in one Miami suburb forty Syrian families live in the same apartment building (Shelemay fieldnotes, 1–4 April 1988).[13]

Business ties also bind, with a good portion of the Brooklyn community

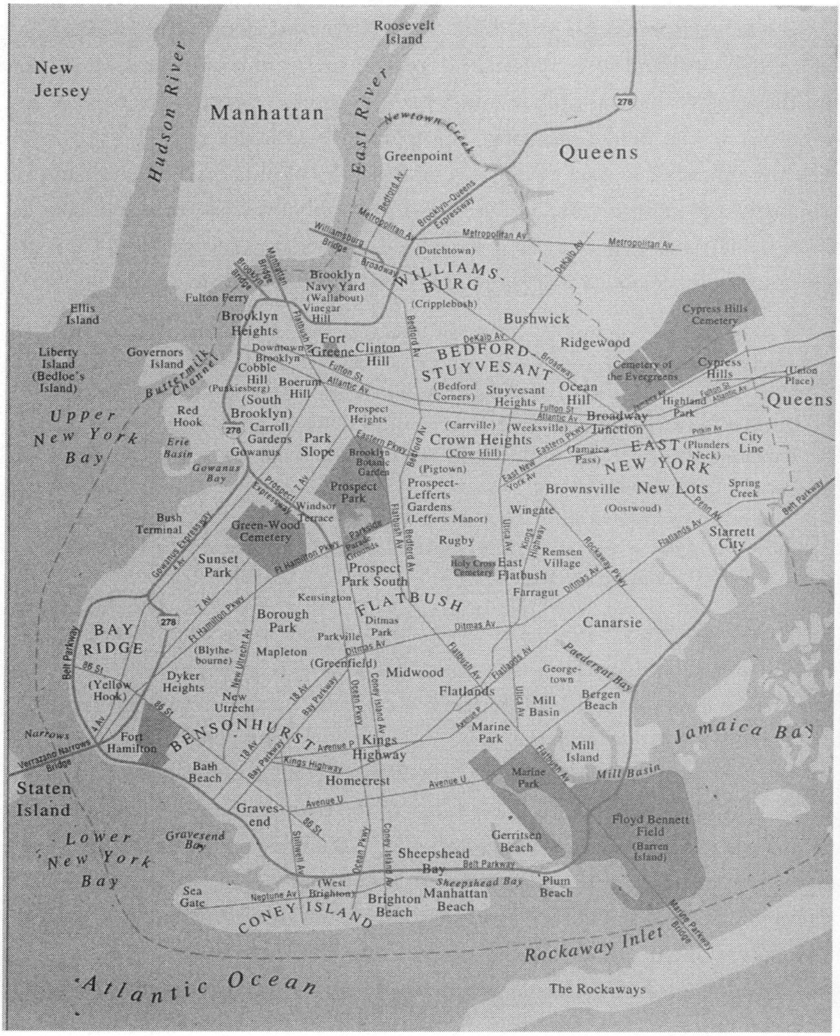

FIGURE 2.2. Map of Brooklyn. Courtesy Yale University Press (Kenneth T. Jackson, ed., *The Encyclopedia of New York City,* 1995:150)

engaged in family firms supported by a kin and ethnic network; the little research done in this area in the late 1950s indicated that at that time Syrians only hired members of their own group, often "importing" relatives from other Syrian communities internationally (Zenner 1983:176–77). Many of these business connections, including clothing companies and discount stores, are still active (Bnai Brith 1991:24). Economic ties often overlap with marital bonds, which emphasize marriage within the group, often between cousins from different centers (Zenner 1988:384–85). Testimony by many members of the community indicates that cousin-marriages are still quite common. Although, as noted above, there is substantial intermarriage with Jews of non-Syrian, primarily Ashkenazic descent, a 1935 community proclamation forbidding marriage to converts was reaffirmed on June 3, 1984 (Kassin 1984).

Within the Syrian community, familial connections are maintained and reinforced through myriad life cycle events ranging from circumcisions to bar mitzvahs and weddings that dot the calendar; members of the community report typically attending several circumcision ceremonies a week (J. Saff, 16 February 1985; G. Haber, 31 January 1989). The high level of ritual activity is acknowledged to provide a continuing challenge to professionals in the community, especially for men who, in order "to honor the family," need to miss work (Anon).[14]

Alongside strong inter-community familial and economic ties, many Syrian Jews in Brooklyn also participated in the world around them. During their early years on the Lower East Side of Manhattan, many Syrian Jewish men frequented local coffeehouses (Sanua 1977:282). As they acclimated to American life and gained financial resources, members of the community began to attend cultural events in New York City, patronizing New York theatres and other institutions. Many Syrian men served in the U.S. Armed Forces during World War II, a period closely documented by those remaining at home in Brooklyn through publication of newspapers called "Victory Bulletins" which described the patriotic work of the broader community while memorializing the service of individuals (Sephardic Archives c. 1985). Yet interaction in the spheres of domestic and religious life was and remains largely restricted to other Syrian Jews.

Community boundaries, while tightly circumscribed in Brooklyn, are at the same time highly permeable in terms of Syrian Jews' relationships to other Aleppo immigrants in their pan-American locales. Just as urban research has had to proceed on several levels of analysis (Reyes Schramm 1975), so any approach to Syrian Jewish history and culture must simultaneously operate on the levels of the local and the transnational. To approach the subject of music in a transnational context, one must acknowledge that the community that transmits the tradition is no longer "tightly territorialized, spatially bounded . . . or culturally homogeneous" (Appadurai 1991:191). In the case of Syrian Jews, one must consider several levels of time and space: their conceptualizations of their distant past; the manner in which aspects of their various identities as a Syrian/Arab/Jewish diaspora/Sephardic community still shape their outlook; the various routes they traveled to arrive at their late twentieth century locations; and the manner in which their community remains one in continual motion, linked through kinship, marriage, travel, and communications within a transnational grid.

Discussing the relationship of Syrian Jews to the realities and mythologies of a Jewish diaspora is complicated by the scholarly application of the term "diaspora" to a range of peoples living outside their historic homelands. In the growing literature on diaspora peoples and cultures, one finds a diaspora generally regarded as "an expatriate minority community (1) that is dispersed from an original center to at least two peripheral places, and (2) that maintains memory of the original homeland" (Safran 1991:83). It has further been proposed that diaspora communities necessarily feel unaccepted by their host countries and that there is a commitment to return to and/or to maintain the homeland (ibid. 83–84).

While the Syrian Jews share dispersal and memory, it is less clear that they feel unaccepted by their host countries. Some individuals report having experienced and heard of anti-Semitic incidents in Mexico that caused them discomfort as children and contributed to their later moves from Mexico City to other locales (E. Goldfein, 7 September 1992; S. Schweky, 27 January 1988). The destruction of the Jewish Community Center and casualties caused by a car bomb in Buenos Aires, Argentina, on July 18, 1994 (*The New York Times,* 19 July 1994) have caused concern and necessitated additional security precautions at Jewish institutions in Central and South America, including Mexico City.

Certainly there is absent any commitment to return to or to maintain contact with their native Syria. Rather, Syrian Jews in the late twentieth century occupy a "transnational diaspora" that does not necessarily involve a single "center." In sketching a decentered view of a modern diaspora, I follow the anthropologist James Clifford's suggestion that we need to give more attention to a diaspora's "lateral axes" (1994:321–22).

The Syrian Jews further illustrate what has been termed "multiple experiences of re-diasporization" (Clifford 1994:305, quoting a personal communication from Jonathan Boyarin; Boyarin and Boyarin 1993); the term "Second Diaspora" is also applied to the Sephardic experience (Días-Mas 1992:179). The multiple diasporas of Syrian Jews from their distant past until the present is our subject below (see figure 2.3).

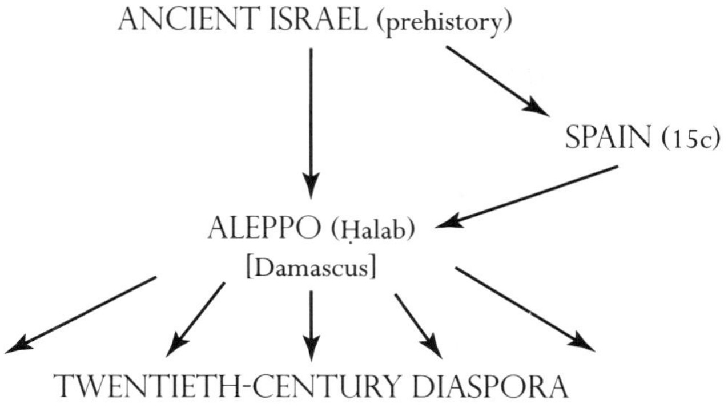

FIGURE 2.3. Multiple diasporas of Syrian Jews.

Defining a Diaspora Community
Jews in and of Aleppo

The Syrian Jews present a complex history, one in which multiple sources and influences overlap and intersect over time. Most relevant for our study here, which seeks to understand the Syrian Jewish self as expressed through music, are two perceptions of history: first, the historical continuum as remembered and commemorated through the eyes of late twentieth century Syrians; and second, documented events that may not be important from an insider's perspective, but that are salient to cultural transmission and identity.

The beginning, at least from the perspective of Syrian Jews, would start somewhere around the year 1,000 B.C.E., when the founding of the first Syrian synagogue is traditionally dated to the activity of King David's troops in Aram Zobah (1 Chronicles 18:1, 19:1; also 2 Samuel 8). Although many Jews call Aleppo itself "Aram Zobah," there is in fact considerable question as to its exact location (Young 1978:951). Recent discussions of Syrian Jewish history by members of the community incorporate this story as ancient history (Sutton 1979:155), and a published chronology of historical events concerning the Jews of Syria begins with an entry from 1004–965 B.C.E. noting that "King David conquers Syria from the Arameans" (Bnai Brith 1991:25). An oral tradition surrounding David's commander, Yoab Ben Suria, is circulated among Syrian Jews internationally (Sutton 1979: 155; M. Tawil, 2 April 1988; M. Antebi, 3 September 1992; R. Betech, 2 September 1992).

While it is thought that Jewish settlement in Aleppo was uninterrupted from its inception in Roman times (64 B.C.E.–323 C.E.; Hitti 1951:280–84), archaeological evidence for a Jewish presence in Aleppo itself provides a later dating.[15] Thus, the tradition surrounding Yoab Ben Suria at once establishes a direct, if mythologized, link to ancient Israel while pushing back the arrival of Jews in Aleppo centuries before the generally agreed inception of the Jewish diaspora during the period of the Roman empire. The relationship of modern Syrian Jews to exile from the historic homeland Israel is clearly of metaphoric significance; the establishment of the Jewish state in the mid twentieth century has served to underscore this connection. Indeed, it has been suggested that "in some ways, Israel has become the impoverished homeland, especially since Syria now has lost most of its Jews, and contact with those remaining is restricted" (Zenner 1988:386). The complexity of this relationship is also reflected in the story of a man who carried a bag of soil from holy Jerusalem back with him to Aleppo, so that when his father died, he could be buried, symbolically, in sacred soil (Sutton 1988:299).

Within the context of Islamic societies, Jews were tolerated and protected by a pact called *dhimma,* and those benefiting from this pact were known as *dhimmi*s (Lewis 1984:21–25); other minorities, including Greeks, Armenians, and Arab Christians, were also dhimmis who competed with each other and Jews "for a position in society complementary to that of the dominant Muslims" (ibid. 55). The various pacts of the seventh and eighth centuries acknowledged the primacy of Islam and specified that dhimmis were to pay taxes and adhere to certain restrictions in dress and behavior specified by Islamic law (ibid. 21; Stillman 1979:157–62). Dhimmis tended to concentrate in professions scorned by Muslims, especially trade and finance (Lewis 1984:28), which led to a high proportion of Jews engaged in mercantile activities in their native Aleppo.

From an early date, the Jewish community participated actively in Aleppo's commercial life. Evidently a pre-Islamic market center, Aleppo continued to produce and sell wheat, cotton, and pistachio nuts from its local region as well as serving as a way station for passing caravan trains (Sauvaget 1971:85–86). Throughout the centuries, as various political powers ascended and declined, including a Mongol conquest of the city in 1260 that resulted in the deaths of many Jewish residents, Aleppo continued to be a focal point for trade (Ashtor 1972:563). By the fifteenth century, Aleppo became a starting point for caravans that brought silk from the East to resell to Venetians in exchange for cloth; by the sixteenth century, Aleppo had become the principal market for the whole of the Levant (Sauvaget 1971:88).

Throughout this period Jews were prominent in trade and scholarship (Ashtor 1972:563). While religious differences were of paramount importance, the historical record indicates that the several religious communities were not segregated into social worlds of their own. Notably, Muslims, Christians, and Jews shared "much of the same repertoire of attitude, tastes, superstitions, and prejudices" (A. Marcus 1989:43).[16] While truly intimate circles exclusively involved family units and co-religionists, members of different communities often worked together. Since Muslims often employed dhimmis, and residential areas were mixed, a combination of business relationships and residential proximity narrowed the social distance between individuals of different faiths (ibid. 44).

Jews were also active participants in an increasingly international milieu. The mid sixteenth century saw the establishment of a variety of European consulates and commercial headquarters, including the French (1562), English (1583), and somewhat later (1613) the Dutch (ibid. 88). By 1700, European Jews joined this influx and many arrived from Italy and France in Aleppo, where they came to be known as "Francos" (Ashtor 1972:564). Local Jews found "a particularly useful source of privileges in their Italian co-religionists," who held the status of protected foreign nationals, not dhimmis. Many local Jews were employed in the commercial businesses of these newly arrived merchant families (A. Marcus 1989:46).

The early sixteenth century also saw a migration to Aleppo that had a lasting impact on Syrian Jews: the arrival of Spanish (Sephardic) Jews in the aftermath of their expulsion from Spain. Indeed, for some members of the Syrian community, the influx of Sephardic Jews to the long-standing Aleppo Jewish community is the pivotal event to which they trace their own ancestry.[17]

The Sephardic migration to Aleppo resulted in the establishment of a Sephardic community separate from that of the long-time Jewish residents of Aleppo, who were termed *mustaʿarbim* ("Orientals") by the newcomers (Ashtor 1972:563).[18] The word *mustaʿriba* evidently originated in the Ottoman empire after its conquest of the Fertile Crescent and Egypt (1516–1517) to distinguish between Arabic-speaking Jews of Syria, Iraq, and Egypt, and the Greek, Turkish, or Spanish-speaking Jews who were more familiar (Lewis 1984:120–21). Eventually the two communities merged, and as a result Syrian Jewish views of their history in Aleppo are subsequently mediated by the historical connections with Jewish exiles from Spain and the changing sensibilities and traditions of the Sephardic diaspora.

By the late eighteenth century, Aleppo began to decline economically under pressure from a variety of forces including the diminishing industrial and maritime activity from France, corrupt administration at home, and expansion of trade to other centers in Asia and the Americas. An 1822 earthquake and increased taxes during an Egyptian occupation in the 1830s exerted further economic pressures (Sauvaget 1971:88–89). The opening of the Suez canal, on November 17, 1869, decreased use of overland trade routes (Longwood 1957:52).

Thus by the period of twentieth-century migration, the longstanding immersion of Syrian Jews in Arab culture and subsequent adoption of a Sephardic heritage led to a complex Ḥalabi self-identification as "Arab Jews" that continues into the present (D. Tawil, 11 December 1984; S. Catton, 30 October 1984; J. Saff, 23 October 1984). Both aspects of this identity are important to understanding Syrian Jewish identity in the Americas.

Syrian Jews as Sephardic Jews

The term "Sephardic" has accrued widely divergent modern meanings depending on the background, training, and intention of the writer/speaker. The name "Sepharad," which originally appears in Obadiah 20, refers to one of the (unidentified) places to which Jews were exiled. During the Middle Ages, Spanish Jews called themselves "Sephardim," singular Sephardi (Días-Mas 1992:7). In general, modern definitions of "Sephardic" fall into two main categories: the first confines the use of the term "to the actual descendants of Jews from the Iberian Peninsula who have preserved Judeo-Spanish or Ladino as their language of communication and whose customs, rituals and folklore reflect the intonations and flair of their Iberian past"; and the second applies it to a wider category that "includes Jews who have no ancestral ties with Spain, and whose languages reflect their centuries-long abode in various countries, but whose rituals and observances bear kinship to the Iberian ones, albeit adapted to the mores of their respective native lands" (Papo 1987:3). Given their mixture of Sephardic and Arab background and culture, in particular their maintenance of an Arabic vernacular rather than Judeo-Spanish,[19] Syrian Jews occupy a Sephardic borderland that can be included or excluded from definitions of the Sephardic community, depending on the perspective of the individual using the term. Modern authors who are members of the Sephardic communities about which they write have tended to offer more inclusive definitions, arising largely from twentieth-century political contexts, that subsume as Sephardic all Jews not of Ashkenazic (largely Germanic and Slavic) heritage (Elazar 1989:14–17). Others (including Papo 1987), after acknowledging divergent uses of the word "Sephardic," adopt a working definition for Sephardic within the Americas based on both place of origin and ascription, thus incorporating all Jews who emigrated from the Ottoman Empire to the New World and who consider themselves to be Sephardic.

Of particular import to this study is the extent to which the Sephardic influx, both in Syria and in other Middle Eastern locales, is presented in many sources as an influence that "restored the religious and cultural life of the local Jews" (Haddad 1984:57; see also Elazar 1989:118); frequently one finds the "Arabized language, clothes, names, and manners" of Jews long resident in Syria presented as inferior to the "wealthier, more educated, and more religious" descendants of Jews from Spain (Haddad 1984: 59; Elazar 1989: 29). This perspective has been reinforced during the twentieth century on the occasions during which Jews of Ashkenazic descent have been actively antagonistic to the Arab cultural traditions of Syrian Jews (Shelemay 1996a:45).

While Syrian Jews in Israel have been absorbed into a larger Sephardic world that comprises nearly half the Jewish state's population,[20] the minority status of Sephardic Jews abroad has tended to reinforce their special identities and different countries of origin; in the words of one researcher, "each group goes its own way" (Zenner 1965:332). In the case of Syrian Jews, their minority status in New York and other centers such as Mexico City has encouraged them to maintain separate communal and religious institutions (ibid. 333). Thus one member of the Brooklyn community notes that "although I occasionally use 'Sephardic' to describe Syrian Jews, the term is not altogether accurate. It is usually used by Syrian Jews when they describe themselves to outsiders, but to describe themselves to each other they use the term Syrian" (Esses 1992:13 n. 1).

An additional factor is that the twentieth-century Arab–Israeli conflict has tended to mask centuries of creative interaction in literature, philosophy, and musical expression between peoples of Islamic and Jewish heritage in the Levant (A. Alcalay 1993:27). This is complicated further by the twentieth-century ambivalence of many Sephardic Jews long resident in Arab countries who were forced to relocate in the early years of the Arab–

Israeli conflict and at times manifests itself in a self-consciousness about their own Arab culture (Haddad 1984: 143–44).[21]

The dual Sephardic–Levantine identity of the Syrian Jews emerges as a particularly important factor in the United States, where the Sephardic community is "a small minority within a small minority" (Elazar 1989:167). While exact numbers are notoriously hard to come by, estimates of the number of Sephardim in the United States today range from 60,000 to 180,000, approximately 2.8 percent of the general Jewish population, which has been estimated at 2.7 percent of the overall population of the United States (Elazar 1989:166–67). A majority of Syrian community members interviewed for this study voluntarily identified themselves as Sephardic Jews in formal interviews, often elaborating the term Sephardic within a qualifying phrase such as "Sephardic Jewish Syrian" (J. Saff, 23 October 1984). Equally complex is the relationship of Syrian Jews in the Americas to their Arab heritage: individuals comment on closely linked identities "being that we are Sephardic, and being that we are Arabic" (S. Catton, 30 October 1984). In general, and in contrast to models that assume second-generation rejection of immigrant parents' old world customs,[22] descendants of Syrian Jews in the Americas take pride in their dual heritage.

Just as Aleppo provided the context in which this multiplex identity was formed, so their Syrian origins remain a primary factor in self-identification and bonding—indeed, the overwhelming identification of the community is as "Ḥalabi Jews." The concept of place so deeply felt among Middle Eastern peoples, particularly in relationship to travel and movement (see Eickelman and Piscatori 1990b), is clearly maintained among Syrian Jews in a metaphoric sense. Of particular interest is the close connection in Middle Eastern urban centers between a contiguous physical space and social life, where the "quality of life is defined by the extension in contiguous physical space of the notion of closeness (*qaraba*)"; this closeness can be "symbolized in a number of ways: the exchange of visits on feast days, assistance and participation in the activities connected with births, circumcisions, weddings and funerals of component households, and the like" (Eickelman 1981:272). This strength of attachment to the city as a focus of territorial loyalties derives from the premodern period, where the concept of home *(waṭan)* "lacked the connotation of national homeland which was to be attached to it in the nineteenth century in the wake of contact with European ideas. People spoke of territorial home in the narrow terms of specific localities" (A. Marcus 1989:34).

The territorial sense that existed among Jews in historic Aleppo has been largely maintained in twentieth-century Brooklyn and is now applied conceptually to link diaspora centers. Indeed, "the *imageability* of residential space in the Middle East is not principally in terms of physical landmarks, but in shared conceptions of the social order."[23] A notion of Syrian place continues to inflect various cultural domains in late twentieth century Brooklyn: while one Ḥalabi Jew refers to his parents having spoken "Arabic" at home (M. Kairey, 12 December 1984), his sister referred to this practice as "speaking Syrian" (S. Cohen, 28 February 1985). Likewise, all Arab music can be subsumed under the rubric "Syrian" music, with tunes of non-Arab provenance sometimes referred to by their place of origin.[24] Yet Aleppo itself, ever present, is no more than a faint reflection. This is true, paradoxically, even for first generation American immigrants. In the words of one Syrian woman who arrived in New York during the 1920s, "I never knew Aleppo. I knew all other places, but not Aleppo" (G. Haber, 31 January 1989).

Migratory Paths

In responding through migration to the economic downturn in late nineteenth century Aleppo, Syrian Jews were only one small part of the broad movement during this period of Middle Eastern peoples of various ethnic and religious backgrounds to the New World. Between 1881 and 1914, when migration was curtailed by World War I, approximately 110,000 Arabic-speaking immigrants entered the United States. It is difficult on the basis of immigration data alone to separate out the homelands of Middle Easterners entering the United States during this period, let alone to distinguish Syrian Jews amid this great population flow. Before 1899 immigration officials in the United States identified Middle Eastern immigrants by place of origin, distinguishing as categories Syrians, Turks, Ottomans, Greeks, and Others (Hooglund 1987:3–6). Yet at this time, Ottoman Syria alone had three main districts—Mount Lebanon, Syria, and Palestine—leaving room for considerable ambiguity in the Syrian category. To complicate the situation further, United States immigration from 1899 to 1920 listed all Arabic-speaking Middle Eastern immigrants as Syrian (ibid. 3). The dissolution of the Ottoman empire in 1918 gave way to separate mandates in the Levant (ibid. 3–6), followed by the establishment of the modern political entity of independent Syria, which occurred only in 1936 (Hourani 1991: 330–31). An understanding of the migratory paths of Syrian Jewish, and specifically

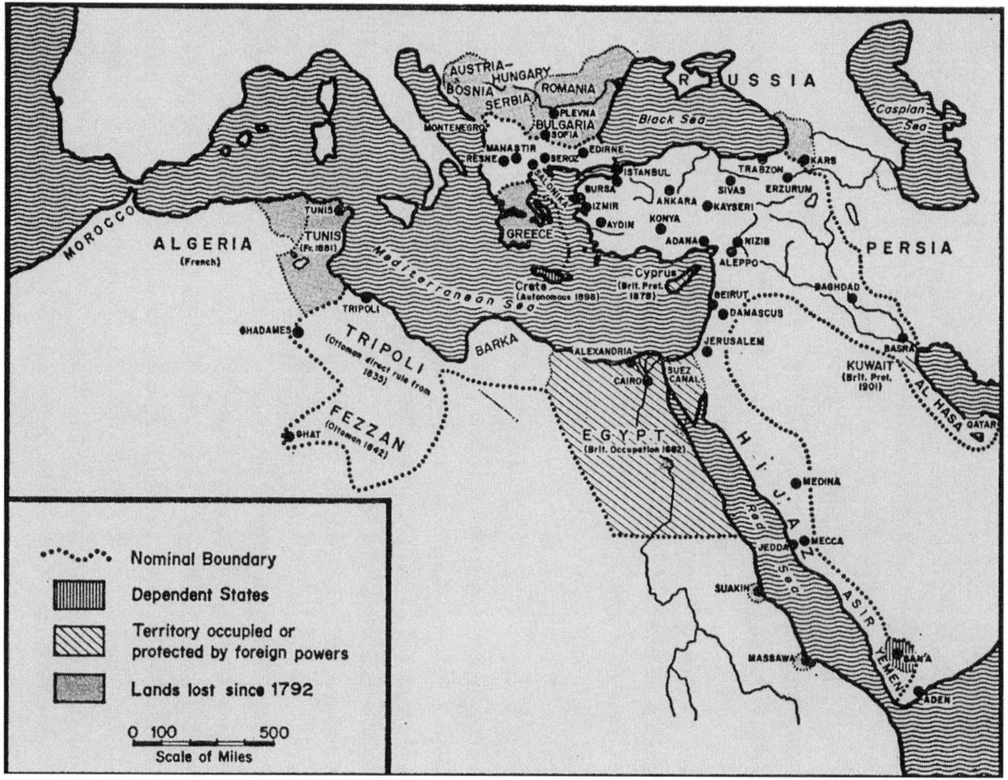

FIGURE 2.4. Map of the Ottoman empire in 1908. Courtesy Peter Mansfield, *The Ottoman Empire and Its Successors* (New York: St. Martin's Press, 1973), Map I, p. viii.

Ḥalabi, immigrants therefore requires focused ethnographic inquiry. Data from interviews, combined with insights gleaned from the few written accounts by members of the Syrian Jewish community, in fact construct a distinctive picture. Some Syrian Jews left Aleppo for nearby Middle Eastern destinations such as Jerusalem and Cairo (see figure 2.4); often this was an initial move within the Levant before proceeding to the New World. An inability to enter the United States was one underlying cause of the circuitous routes that many Syrian Jews followed. The Immigration Quota Act of 1921 reduced the number of immigrants from about one-half million to three hundred thousand per year, each region being limited to a percentage of the number of its immigrants in 1910 (Hooglund 1987:1–2). In 1924, another law limiting immigration to two percent of the 1890 figure was instituted, a quota system weighted in favor of England and Germany and against the Levant, Russia, and Poland (Angel 1982:17–18).

There were also strong "pull" factors leading many Ḥalabi Jews to join families in disparate New World urban areas, ranging from Mexico City to Buenos Aires. In general, Syrian Jewish migration fits a pattern known to sociologists as "chain migration," in which the movement is largely determined by personal contacts, communications, and rendering of services among family and friends in both the sending and receiving societies (Baily 1982:74). "Prospective migrants learn of opportunities, are provided with transportation, and have initial accommodation and employment arranged *by means of primary social relationships with previous migrants*" (MacDonald and MacDonald 1964:82).

The concept of chain migration, which has been widely applied in studies of Italian New World immigrants (see Barton 1975 and Briggs 1978), seems to characterize aptly the Syrian migration as well: in general, one Syrian immigrant would urge others to join him, resulting in the movement of breadwinners, either accompanied or followed closely by the migration of their families. One methodological observation emerging from these studies is that chain migration processes are "best studied at the micro level, at the level of specific individuals, families, kinship networks, and villages or clusters of villages" (Baily 1982:75). The course of Syrian Jewish migrations and the complex links between resulting diaspora centers are in fact best understood by mapping the movement of individual Syrian Jewish families from the beginning of the twentieth century as they moved from Aleppo, and other cities of the Levant, to form new Ḥalabi communities in New York by 1903 (Sutton 1979:7–8), Mexico City in 1912 (Askenazi 1982:17), and other new world urban centers (see Sutton 1979, Chira 1994, and Zenner 1988). Sutton suggests that most Syrian Jews chose to go to Egypt; Manchester, England; or New York. Only those "unfortunates" who were rejected for reasons of health by United States immigration went to South America (1979:119), or secondarily to Mexico City and other locales in Central America (ibid. 9).

Such was the route traveled by the family of Gracia Taboush Haber, who was born in Jerusalem in 1910 to parents from Aleppo. After her father's death in the early 1920s, Gracia, her mother, and her siblings left Jerusalem for Egypt, where they lived with extended family for a year. There the family received Egyptian passports but failed to get visas to join other family members in the United States. After living with relatives in Mexico for more than three years, the family finally reached New York City, where Gracia married a cousin. While it may appear that 1928 marked a period of final settlement, in fact Gracia Taboush Haber was on the move throughout her life, visiting widely scattered Syrian relatives, including a daughter who lived for 24 years in Manila. At the time I interviewed her in 1989, Gracia still talked of her life as a transnational experience, mentioning her continuing desire to travel to Israel to visit cousins, one of whose sons she had "married off" in Brooklyn,[25] and to spend time with a brother who had lived in Puerto Rico for 40 years (G. Haber, 31 January 1989).

Many of the Syrian Jewish migration histories are similar to Gracia Taboush Haber's, tracing circuitous routes from Syria to urban centers abroad. Albert Sitt's father left Aleppo in 1906 for the United States. Rejected because of eye infection and returned to Syria, he next went to France for a brief period. Disembarking from Marseilles, he is said to have gotten on the wrong boat and ended up in Argentina (1907). Sitt finally arrived in Manchester, where he married a member of the Syrian community resident there, and where his son Albert was born in 1931. Shortly thereafter, financial reversals forced the family back to Aleppo, where the elder Sitt died in 1949. At that time, Sitt's widow and her children were brought to Mexico by relatives, where Albert Sitt remains, although others in the family have moved within the Syrian American diaspora, his sister residing in Houston, his daughter in New York City (A. Sitt, 10 September 1992). Other than short trips to Aleppo to find a bride, longterm returns to Syria, such as that of the Sitt family, appear to have been relatively rare.

Other Syrian-Jewish immigrants came directly from Aleppo to New York City (D. Dweck, 28 February 1985; S. Cohen, 20 February 1985; Shelemay fieldnotes, 1 April 1988). Some confirm that the men arrived first and then sent for their families. Albert Ashear (19 July 1989) remembered that his father borrowed money to pay the $16 fares, came to the United States with his eldest son Joseph, and then quickly sent for the rest of the family.

Others married in New York, as did the father of Louis and Moses Massry, who after his 1910 arrival met and married a recent immigrant from Lebanon (Shelemay fieldnotes, 1 April 1988). Later in the century, as immigration from Syria became increasingly difficult, the small number of people who managed to leave Aleppo and Damascus tended to travel directly to New York with the support of those already residing in Brooklyn (M. Arking, 28 April 1988; B. Zalta, 16 March 1990).

From the early nineteenth century, Egypt attracted Jewish immigrants from throughout the Ottoman empire, North Africa, Italy, and Eastern Europe (Laskier 1992:4–6), and many Syrian Jews spent considerable time in Egypt before leaving for the New World. For example, Gabriel Shrem was born in Egypt around 1917 to parents who came from Kilis, a town in historical Syria earlier ceded to Turkey.[26] Although his father left for New York in 1920, three-year-old Gabriel remained in Egypt with his mother and brother but was prevented from immigrating with them in 1928 because of his eye infection. In 1930, his father returned to Egypt to retrieve Gabriel and brought him to New York, where he was forced to remain on Ellis Island for a week (G. Shrem, 9 January 1986).

The 1956 Sinai/Suez war prompted a final mass migration of Jews from Egypt. At that time, most Ḥalabi families residing in Egypt went to Israel; a minority proceeded, then or afterward, to the United States (J. Harari, 23 July 1992). Between 1956 and 1960, some 36,000 Jews left Egypt (Laskier 1992:264). Records of 27,883 Egyptian Jewish refugees assisted by Jewish organizations between 1956 and 1963 (summarized ibid. 276) indicate that 15,723 of these immigrated to Israel, while the remainder went to various destinations in the United States (3,638), Latin America (4,220), Australia, Canada, and miscellaneous other places.

One example is provided by Albert Cohen-Saban, who was born in Egypt to Ḥalabi parents, immigrated at age 15 to Israel, and in 1965 came to New York. Cohen-Saban's childhood migration and later travels directly shaped his musical knowledge, which he employs as a lay cantor in Brooklyn: he was a soloist for the choir at the largest synagogue in Cairo from ages seven to fifteen and later taught cantorial skills to boys in Israel. He studied "Ḥalabi-style" in the United States and still travels frequently to serve as a cantor at Ḥalabi congregations in Panama, Mexico, and Israel (A. Cohen-Saban, 10 January 1985). Likewise, the parents of Joseph Mosseri were born in Egypt. His mother's family left Egypt in 1958, his father's three years later in 1961. Both families went to France for short periods and then on to New York City (J. Mosseri, 14 January 1986).

Some families followed paths that took them for a time to Mexico or South America. Sophie Shafia Ashkenazi's oral history recounts that her father went from Aleppo to Mexico in 1908, seeking to avoid conscription into the Turkish Army: "Since his friend was in Mexico, he decided to go there. . . . But he left alone. It was a year later when he sent for us" (Sutton 1988:240). Other families went to different locales for economic reasons; one Syrian woman tells of her father, who left Aleppo in 1906 for Cairo; his brothers followed "better commercial opportunities" and moved to Buenos Aires and New York (ibid. 266). Another story is that of the Tawil family, born in Palestine to Ḥalabi parents. The family emigrated to America in 1913, at first living on the Lower East Side. In 1921 the Tawils moved to Brooklyn, only to shift to Mexico City between 1923 and 1929, returning to New York shortly before Abraham's untimely death (S. Schweky, 30 March 1989; J. Kassin, 30 March 1989).

Some more recent immigrants ended up in a given locale by chance. Rabbi S. Harari, who left Aleppo in 1949 and remained for some years in Lebanon, wanted to immigrate to Argentina to join a friend there, but he delayed and the friend died. In the end, the Mexico City Syrian community invited Harari to officiate at a historic Ḥalabi synagogue, an invitation Harari accepted in 1957 (S. Harari, 7 September 1992).

A small number of Syrian Jewish families arrived at ports other than New York City or lived for different periods of time in a variety of North American locales, including Seattle (J. Mosseri, 14 January 1986) and Sarasota, Florida (I. Abadi, 21 November 1984). Sam Catton was born in Atlantic City, New Jersey, "about half a block away from the Golden Nugget" to Ḥalabi parents who had arrived there around 1912; Catton remembers that the ten Jewish families joined to bring a Hebrew teacher from New York City to instruct their sons (S. Catton, 30 October 1984). Gabriel Shrem's family left New York after their arrival for Macon, Georgia, and later Florida; the family traveled by the seasons selling giftware in the southeastern United States. While Gabriel Shrem was fortunate to marry his Egyptian-born wife in Winston-Salem, North Carolina, they later moved to Brooklyn where "a lot of our people are" (G. Shrem, 9 January 1986). Indeed, many Syrian families in smaller communities tended to gravitate to New York once their children approached adolescence. Sophie Shafia Ashkenazi, whose own migratory path took her from Aleppo to Mexico to North Carolina (with multiple intermediate stops),[27] explained her final return to New York City as follows: "Why? My concern is with my children. Here my children could marry, and did marry Syrian Jewish mates. . . . I wanted to bring them where they could take [marry] people of our own faith, our own kind. We closed up and came to New York!" (Sutton 1988:246).

At Home in New York

During the first three decades of the century, Syrian Jewish immigrants tended to settle on the Lower East Side of Manhattan.[28] In 1911 or 1912, a synagogue was established on the top floor of a tenement at 48 Orchard Street, where Moses Ashear chanted the prayers following his 1912 arrival from Aleppo (Sutton 1979:24). Many elderly members of the Ḥalabi community remember the years in Lower Manhattan as a time of economic struggle. A now-elderly man recalls his family's financial misfortune and eventual eviction from a Lower East Side tenement as "the shame of the century"; only through the intercession of the Bikur Holim was the family relocated (Anon.).[29] Albert Ashear recalled that his family's first apartment at 54 Orchard Street was "poor, but they were happy to be here. They wanted a better life. Everybody heard that there's gold, that you sweep gold in America" (A. Ashear, 19 July 1989). In reality, difficult economic times meant that Albert's father, Cantor Moses Ashear, had to work as a bookkeeper during the weekdays to support his family.

Beginning around 1919 or 1920, the first Syrian families moved to Bensonhurst in Brooklyn (Sutton 1979:360) and in 1921–22 founded the Magen David Congregation on 67th Street (ibid. 39). By the late 1930s, some members of the community moved to Flatbush, near Ocean Parkway (ibid. 41). The Ocean Parkway neighborhood quickly became a Syrian center, with Middle Eastern grocery stores established later on Kings Highway and many religious and communal institutions built throughout the neighborhood. In contrast to Syrian communities in Jerusalem, where Syrian Jews tend to mix with others of Sephardic origin (E. Barnea, 10 March 1993), Syrian Jews in Brooklyn established their own synagogues.[30] Some members of the Brooklyn community are aware of these differences, noting that in Jerusalem, Jews from all over the Middle East "sing together" (I. Cabasso, 13 November 1984). The Brooklyn Syrian community also maintains clear boundaries between individuals born in Aleppo and Damascus—a distinction less clearly drawn in Jerusalem, where it is noted that "we bring the Shāmī's and everyone else who wants to come" (S. Shemi, 21 March 1993).[31] Members of the Brooklyn community point out the manner in which these differences reshape longtime musical practices:

> Of course today in Jerusalem [bakkashot] is sung not only by the Jews from Aleppo but from all Sephardic Jewry, [who] have accepted it as not only an Aleppoan bakkashot but a Sephardic bakkashot. So you go to Israel today and you find people from Iran, Iraq, Morocco, Jews from all over who are singing these bakkashot. (I. Cabasso, 13 November 1984)

Interaction between Syrian Communities

Despite differences in the structure and degree of boundedness of the various Syrian communities, all remain in close contact with each other. These connections range from travel by individuals between communities to circulation of recordings.

In addition to private family visits between members of different Syrian communities, young boys were sent to study in Brooklyn, sometimes at the behest of emissaries traveling on behalf of the schools (Sutton 1979:313). One Ḥalabi man born in Mexico City in 1937 noted that many boys of his generation studied in Brooklyn, including several who are now active leaders in the Mexican Syrian community; he also recalled that his father, who immigrated to Mexico from Kilis, Turkey, in 1926 or 1927, worked "all his life" to help establish a Yeshiva in Israel (R. Betech, 8 September 1992).[32]

A second major aspect of transnational interaction was marriage between members of different communities over the years. Ruth Cain is only one of many Syrian women who migrated in order to marry, in her case leaving New York to wed Isaac Cain in Mexico City (R. Cain, 7 September 1992). A most notable instance of intercommunity marriage occurred in August 1977, when a dozen Syrian Jewish women from Damascus were flown to New York City to meet Syrian American husbands to whom they had been wed by proxy (Bnai Brith 1991:4).

An additional network within and between Syrian diaspora communities is a rapidly circulating group of rabbis and cantors. One young cantor from Damascus, now resident in New York City, views this as a modern phenomenon deriving from a pattern established during the earliest years of Syrian immigration to both Palestine and the Americas:

> All these, they used to be rabbis and ḥazzanim as well. Some of them came to America. I don't know the exact number, but a few of them came to America, and many of them went to Israel. Before, I mean early 1900s, 1920s, and they also established in Jerusalem bakkashot, and they taught. And if you ask all ḥazzanim now in Israel, now, the popular ones, who did you learn from and he tells you, I learned it from somebody who learned it from some Syrian rabbi. (B. Zalta, 16 March 1990)

If the transmission of pizmonim such as "Attah El Kabbir" can be traced to the movement of students of Rabbi Raphael Taboush early in the century, one can follow the continued circulation of repertory and musical styles by a small group of professional cantors within and between Syrian communities throughout the world. Several talented Israeli-born cantors have within the past twenty or thirty years settled permanently in New York City.[33] This serves to promulgate disparate cantorial styles, each ḥazzan coming "with a new style, a new taste of music, from where he came from" (B. Zalta, 16 March 1990). However, the Brooklyn community is particularly sensitive to the influx of new pan-Sephardic cantorial traditions and is concerned that they not overwhelm the traditional Ḥalabi practice considered to be perpetuated in Brooklyn (I. Cabasso, 13 November 1984; M. Kairey, 6 November 1984). New cantors, upon arrival in Brooklyn, are usually given special instruction in Ḥalabi musical and liturgical practice. Indeed, most cantors view Brooklyn as a locale in which they can learn aspects of the "original" Ḥalabi musical tradition no longer perpetuated in Jerusalem or other Syrian centers:

> In Israel, the people who study the pizmonim, they already lived in Israel for seven generations. So in Israel, they already accomplished [a] different style. Same song, but they made changes. Over here, the great cantors . . . [such as] Moses Tawil was born here, but his father was born in Syria. His house in the States was the same thing as his house in Syria. That's the original Syrian community today in the world. Many Syrian people in Israel, but they aren't original. (Y. Nahari, 6 January 1986)

Some cantors maintain primary residence in Israel and travel abroad to officiate in various Syrian communities on holidays; a particularly notable example was a group of sixteen cantors who in 1982 traveled to Israel and South America to officiate for the High Holy Days (S. Shemi, 21 March 1993). Others have moved from one diaspora location to another, as is the case with Cantor Edward Farhi. Born in Aleppo in 1938, Farhi left at age 17 for Beirut. Soon he joined an uncle in Rio de Janeiro, Brazil, where he studied and became a professional cantor. Seeking a change, he visited several other Latin American and Central American countries as well as New York, finally marrying and settling in Mexico City in 1966. Some years later he received an invitation to become chief cantor at Shaare Zion congregation in Brooklyn. In 1983, he settled in New York, where he remains, having declined in the interim an offer of a cantorial post in Brazil (Sutton 1988:208–15).

Many lay cantors exchange materials during family visits abroad. Isaac Cain spends time each winter in Miami Beach, where he had an apartment near that of Albert Ashear. Since 1953, Cain has also visited Brooklyn several times a year, where he is frequently asked to help chant the liturgy at Syrian synagogues (I. Cain, 7 September 1992). In the words of Cain's wife Ruth, "Every time we go, they like to get together with my husband and sing along and learn a few things" (R. Cain, 7 September 1992). In general, members of the Syrian community are aware of the active transnational cantorial connections and that the "people who were cantors in Argentina . . . were the same group who were in Mexico and in Israel" (S. Shemi, 21 March 1993). Most cantors are respected because, despite some differences in style, they are seen as "guarding the gate of the songs, of the pizmonim" (ibid.).

A number of rabbis also connect the different Syrian communities. Shimon Alouf, a rabbi of Iraqi descent who lived in Israel for many years, settled in Brooklyn in 1984. Widely respected for his musical expertise and his ability to sing Arab music, Alouf originally learned from his father's recordings of Egyptian musicians ʿAbd al-Wahhāb and Umm Kulthūm (S. Alouf, 21 February 1985). Israeli-born Ḥalabi Rabbi Meir Entebi, currently the leader of Congregation Maguen David in Mexico City, served in Argentina before taking the post in Mexico (M. Antebi, 3 September 1992).[34]

As noted in chapter 1, Syrian communities also communicate through ritual materials circulated internationally, including the various editions of *Sheer Ushbahah Hallel Ve-Zimrah*. Cassette tapes also travel widely, providing liturgical and musical interaction with broader Sephardic networks. Recordings of Israeli cantors circulate widely. Prominent examples include *Nishmat Kol Hay* ("Saturday Sephardic Prayers," n.d.), a collection of eight cassettes performed by Yehezkel Zion and Ephraim Avidani, and *Halleluyah Betzalzali Samaʿa* ("Sabbath Prayers According to the Jerusalem Tradition," n.d.), a set of six cassettes with examples in the various maqāmāt performed by Cantor Yigal Ben Hayyim (D. Tawil, 11 December 1984). Brooklyn cantors have issued recordings as well, most prominently Raphael Elnadav's *Sephardic Prayer Songs for the High Holy Days* (1980).[35]

Members of the Mexican Jewish community proudly discuss their collections of cassette tapes, which include numerous Israeli recordings (S. Harari, 7 September 1992). In 1993, Middle Eastern music cassettes were available at two shops in Mexico City: "Adonis" carried Arab music, while "Gindi" had only Israeli-issued cassettes. When I presented him with a copy of the tape made during our team project in New York City (Shelemay and Weiss 1985), Cantor Isaac Cain of Mexico City showed me a copy he had already obtained himself in New York.

Cassettes are also widely used and distributed among Syrian cantors in Israel, who refer to them throughout their discussions of Syrian liturgical music and pizmonim (S. Shemi, 21 March 1993). And as noted earlier, even Syrian cantors in late twentieth century Damascus have acquired pizmonim through listening to cassettes from Israel (B. Zalta, 16 March 1990). It is clear that Syrian cantors throughout the world refresh and expand their pizmon repertories through the circulation of cassette tapes from other centers. Collecting recordings has furthermore become an avocation for many: "I've got so many cassettes I want you to hear exactly what I'm talking about," reports one cantor who collects cassettes of Arab music from all over the world (Y. Nahari, 6 January 1986). Two younger members of the Brooklyn Syrian community, avid collectors of pizmon recordings, enthusiastically compare recordings they have of various pizmonim (M. Arking and J. Mosseri, 14 January 1986).

Individuals recount the extensive exchange of cassettes. One member of the community brought back records and tapes from a trip to Egypt, which he sold to interested friends. After buying a recording of a favorite song from this individual, another man then loaned the tape to a Brooklyn acquaintance from Israel who wanted to learn the song (J. Saff, 19 December 1985). In the case of women, male friends and relatives are often the most convenient source of tapes of Arab music (G. Haber, 31 January 1989; J. Kassin, 30 March 1989; S. Harari, 7 September 1992).

Within and between Syrian Jewish Diaspora Communities: Insiders' Comparisons

Perhaps because most Syrian Jews experience multiple centers of the Syrian diaspora as part of their everyday lives, many, whether religious leaders or laypersons, are quite articulate about both the strong ties among diaspora

Syrian communities as well as differences between them. When comparing the Syrian Jews of New York and Mexico City, one individual commented: "A seed from the same apple tree, planted in different places, produces similar fruit. The trunk is the same, branches different. Different soil, different climate" (M. Antebi, 3 September 1992).

The practice of comparing communities is a lively one among Syrian Jews and likely has its roots in the longtime divisions within Syrian Jewish life. Apart from the religious differences between Muslim and Jewish spheres so ingrained during centuries in Syria, for centuries distinctions were also made between Jews resident in either Aleppo or Damascus; no doubt these differences were exacerbated in the nineteenth century when the economic and religious life of the Damascus community came under particular pressure. Damascus was severely affected by reversals in trade, particularly upon the opening of the Suez Canal. In addition, the 1840 Damascus Affair, with blood libels against Damascus Jews, resulted in persecution (Sutton 1979:140–41).[36] Thus the considerable energy devoted to characterizing and contrasting communities appears to be a deeply embedded process stemming from the pre-migratory period. The Aleppo/Damascus split has been maintained to a greater extent in Syrian communities outside Israel. While in the twentieth century Aleppo and Damascus are only "four hours apart by car" (B. Zalta, 16 March 1990), this was a lengthy journey in early years that allowed the communities to establish separate identities. Liturgical and musical differences between the Aleppo and Damascus traditions in Syria, although evidently subtle, continue to be a subject of discussion. In the words of one recent Syrian Jewish immigrant: "We say [sing] the same thing, the same song, but [with] a few adjustments here and there" (ibid.).[37] The Aleppo/Damascus split has been continued and institutionalized in many New World communities, including separate residential areas and independent mutual aid societies for each group in Buenos Aires (Mirelman 1987:29 and 1990:194).

Each of the widely separated Syrian communities has established organizations that support and perpetuate Syrian Jewish culture. The Sephardic Community Center in Brooklyn (see plate 10) and the activities of its Sephardic Archives have a direct parallel in the World Center for Traditional Aleppo Culture in Tel Aviv.

Individual Syrian Jews provide interesting insights into differences between the various transnational centers. In part because the fieldwork for this study was carried out in Brooklyn, Mexico City, and Jerusalem, these three centers were the subjects of most comment. However, the complex pathways of migration and travel sketched above insured that other Syrian communities were the subjects of commentary; in particular, two of the largest, those in Buenos Aires[38] and Manchester,[39] were included.

It is widely acknowledged that there are significant differences between Syrian Jewish communities in the New World and Israel:

> Now, the community in New York lives mostly in East Flatbush. . . . And all of them have to live within walking distance of the synagogue because riding on the Sabbath is not permitted according to Orthodox Jewish law. . . . But you'll find this in almost every country except Israel. In Israel, they have synagogues all over; wherever you live, you can find a synagogue within walking distance. . . . But there again, even in Israel where it's all Jewish, they are not so closely knit, like they are in the diaspora. (S. Catton, 30 October 1984; see also Zenner 1965)

The Syrian community in Jerusalem is quite integrated into the general Sephardic community, and specialists in particular traditions remain only among the older generation. Thus in Israel, Syrian musical traditions are handed down to and transmitted by descendants of other backgrounds (Y. Bozo and E. Barnea, 10 March 1993).[40] The strong Sephardic mainstream in Israel necessarily serves to homogenize the musical practices of Israeli cantors, who are perceived by some Brooklynites as "all following the same artist" (H. Kaire, 14 March 1985).

Pizmon repertories are also acknowledged to be different in Israel. Brooklyn Ḥalabis who are well versed in Arab music point out that some pizmonim sung by Israeli cantors are not known in New York while the Arab source melodies are known: they sing "a lot of songs that we don't have words for; we know the music, but we don't have words for them" (J. Saff, 4 December 1984). One Syrian woman characterized the differences in much stronger and more general terms: upon first visiting Israel, she remarked that she was "more comfortable with Arabs than the Israelis—the Israelis have a different culture" (Anon.).

A striking difference between the Israeli and New York communities is in their relative emphasis on the bakkashot or pizmonim. The bakkashot are actively performed by a diverse group of Sephardic Jews in Jerusalem and Tel Aviv, while only a small group of elderly men maintain bakkashot performance in New York (I. Cabasso, 13 November 1984; B. Zalta, 16 March 1990). Conversely, pizmon composition and performance in New York during the twentieth century has taken a distinctive path, to be explored in subsequent chapters. Members of the New York community are keenly aware of these differences and comment at length on bakkashot performance in Israel.

In general, New York Ḥalabis consider that they sing pizmonim and bakkashot the "way we were taught from Ḥalab," while in Jerusalem they make it "a little fancy," only "about 80% pure." "They have nice voices and they change it around a little, but it's marvelous" (M. Kairey, 6 November 1984). There is also ambivalence about the changes underway in Israel:

> The words are all the same but unfortunately . . . they are changing some of the melodies. I say unfortunately because it's going away from tradition. And they're implementing some of the melodies that they brought in from, say, Iran or Morocco and we feel sad about it because, you know, we would like to have our own music and our own tradition be kept up. But if you do go to Jerusalem, they have some groups over there that are singing the bakkashot magnificently. . . . You go to the synagogue at 3 o'clock, 4 o'clock in the morning and you would see Jews from all over the world getting together. (I. Cabasso, 13 November 1984)

The circulation of recordings of bakkashot from Israel in Brooklyn concerns members of the community who wish to maintain the Brooklyn style.

> Every once in a while somebody stops and says we did a good job. People that don't even know from A to Z in as far as music's concerned. This one fellow says: "My son, every night he puts on the tape before he goes to sleep and memorizes a couple of bakkashot songs." I say: "Very good. Let him come in the morning." (H. Kaire, 17 February 1988)

While some longtime residents of both communities think that the prayers are more generally "the same" in Mexico City and Brooklyn (R. Cain, 7 September 1992), the population of the Mexican Jewish community since the early 1980s has grown, moved to new outlying suburbs of Mexico City, and been split by religious controversies that have engendered changes in religious practices (S. Schweky, 27 January 1988; R. Betech, 8 September 1992). For example, the bakkashot are no longer performed in Mexico City (R. Betech, 8 September 1992). However, decline in musical practice in Mexico should not be interpreted as indexing a lack of ritual involvement; indeed, it appears that the opposite may be the case. An increase in the size of the community was given as the primary reason a cantor was not able to perform a pizmon in honor of a baby girl's naming ceremony during Sabbath morning services. Indeed, in the past

> . . . they sang all the songs for the girl. . . . But the community was small, now the community is too big, and if they are going to sing to each, do you know how many we have each Shabbat? Sometimes, for example, we have twenty, so they cannot sing to everybody. Because the service is going to be late, and people start to go. They came very early . . . too many hours in the shul. So they don't sing anymore. (R. Betech, 8 September 1992)[41]

It is also clear that each community develops its own patterns over time, depending on its own constitution and local conditions. A good example is presented by Y. Bozo, who was born in Aleppo in 1920 and immigrated to Israel in 1946, becoming a widely acknowledged expert on the pizmonim; his extensive repertory is said to include some three hundred songs. However, Bozo sings from his own private, handwritten compilation of pizmonim, not all of which are included in the Aboud collection widely used in Jerusalem. While he does not transmit stories about Raphael Taboush, he acknowledges the influence of Hayyim Shaul Aboud: "Aboud is our yardstick" (Y. Bozo, 14 March 1993).[42]

The vagaries of migration and the integration of pivotal individuals into their respective communities have shaped musical life in the various Syrian urban centers. The immigration of Moses Ashear, Eliyahu Menaged, and other students of Raphael Taboush to New York, and their active careers as cantors and teachers, insured the lively continuation of pizmonim as well as the commemoration of Taboush in New York City. Today, in part due to the contribution of the late Ashear student Naphtali Tawil (1902–1963) and the on-going role of men such as Moses Tawil and Meyer (Mickey) Kairey, the Ḥalabi community in New York is regarded internationally as "stronger in respect to pizmonim" (B. Zalta, 16 March 1990). In contrast, and despite the fact that two Taboush students immigrated at early dates to Mexico City,[43] and both were active as teachers, their impact has faded under the pressure of individual innovation[44] and the entry of pan-Sephardic traditions.

If there are differences between the various international centers of modern Syrian Jewish life, there are also subtle distinctions acknowledged within communities. For example, there are some differences in musical practices within Syrian synagogues in Brooklyn, Deal, and Manhattan (B. Zalta, 16 March 1990). This is particularly true in the Manhattan congregation, which was established by people who have lived in Manhattan for many years and who rarely attend the Brooklyn or New Jersey shore Syrian synagogues (ibid.).

Conclusion

The relative stability of pizmon form and content provides an interesting counterpoint to the rapid changes in Syrian Jewish life. Indeed, the pizmon at the end of the twentieth century appears to be an important agent of continuity in a community that has undergone extraordinary dislocation. As other aspects of expressive culture are slowly transformed—or discarded altogether—the role of the pizmon, as well as the broader Arab music culture of which it is a part, assumes a larger significance. Studies of other transnational musics have tended to emphasize the manner in which musical expression is a form of political agency, with music serving as a locus for political commentary and action against repressive agents within a particular historical arena (see Erlmann 1993). The Syrian case study offered here, in contrast, provides an example in which a transnational music serves as a locus for sustaining positive historical memories in face of diasporization and the challenge of modern political conflicts. A study of the pizmon additionally highlights ways in which music can shape and otherwise be instrumental within the internal social life of the community in question. In this case, the pizmon is an important agent for continuity in ritual and life cycle events, in terms of both their formal structure and continued performance; the ongoing composition and performance of these songs further reinforce traditional values related to community and patriarchy.

The transmission of pizmon "Attah El Kabbir," mapped in the prelude to this chapter, elucidates the complicated path of a single song as well as the geographical and human contexts of its transmission. In the same way, we have been able to map the course of Syrian history and migration, tracing the emergence of a "multiply-centered diaspora network" (Clifford 1994:305), in which emphasis has shifted from a historic homeland to interacting "lateral connections" on a larger map (ibid. 306).

If we are to try to summarize the transnational Syrian Jewish experience, it may be desirable to look at insiders' maps. Of great interest is an image used as the logo by the Sephardic Archives, the central cultural organization of the Brooklyn Syrian Jewish community (see figure 2.5). This image contains a stylized skyline of a modern Western city (Manhattan), a bridge (the Brooklyn Bridge), and a landscape of Middle Eastern–style domed houses (orientalized Brooklyn). Reading left to right, the eye moves from the skyscrapers (of Manhattan), over the Brooklyn Bridge, to the Syrian enclave in Brooklyn. Reading the logo in the opposite direction, more likely for those

Figure 2.5. Logo of the Sephardic Community Center, created by Mazal Husni in 1982. Courtesy Sephardic Community Center.

who read Hebrew from right to left, the movement goes from an (unidentified) Middle East cityscape to the Western urban center, and then to the bridge, which seems to lead back to the beginning of the cycle. Read this way, the logo speaks to the past with a cityscape that could represent any Middle Eastern locality, from the old city of Aleppo to the old city in Jerusalem. Finally, particularly when read from right to left by a practiced eye, the logo further gives an effect of Arabic calligraphy.

To a great extent, it is the pizmonim and other Syrian song genres that help weld the disparate world of Syrian Jews into a whole, bringing widely dispersed centers together, evoking memories, however idealized, of a shared past. Yet to understand the world of Syrian Jewish music and the transnational heritage of the pizmon, we must more fully explore the pervasive presence of Arab music among Syrian Jews in the Americas.

PRELUDE

Ani Ashir Lakh

A large and lively crowd enters the restaurant at a country club on the Jersey shore, everyone greeting their hosts with exclamations of "*mabrūk*," "congratulations" in Arabic. It is June 30, 1988, and Moses and Alice Tawil are celebrating their golden wedding anniversary at a party given by their four adult children. Rented in its entirety for the evening, the sprawling, peach-colored restaurant is decorated with an Oriental motif of flowers and Japanese fans.

One enters through a spacious bar area partially filled with small, round tables grouped around a larger table holding a light cocktail buffet of fruits and vegetables. From there, guests walk through a wide hallway into one of two halls. In the center of the large, rectangular dining room directly ahead, an elaborate buffet is displayed. Although much of the offering is continental cuisine—lamb chops, roast beef, veal, vegetables, salads—there are many Middle Eastern dishes as well. Appetizers of kibbe and tahini are in good supply, along with tabouli salad. Later in the evening, baklava and halva appear on trays adjacent to French pastries for the dessert buffet.

Between the bar at the far end of that room and the buffet island are numerous dinner tables with chairs; at the other end a large table holds a multi-layered anniversary cake. Around nine in the evening, a lone male musician assumes a position behind the cake and begins singing with guitar accompaniment, alternating Latin songs like "La Bamba" with popular American and European standards. Well known to many of the partygoers from other community parties, the musician is described as a "local Julio Iglesias."

The second large hall is dominated by a dance floor at its center, surrounded on three sides by chairs and ringed more widely by tables. Also around nine, seven male musicians take their seats along the wall behind the dance floor. That these are professional musicians hired for the evening and not guests was made clear by the club doorman, who directed the musicians to enter through the rear service door.[1] These men, all of Middle Eastern descent and residents of the New York metropolitan area, make up an orchestra consisting of a synthesizer, violin, zither, ʿūd, flute, frame drum, and hourglass drum. In front of the male musicians sits a female singer, a young Palestinian woman born in Israel who lives in New York. I am advised by my hosts that the orchestra will begin its performance playing "light songs," moving on to "the heavy numbers" sometime after midnight, according to Arab tradition.

Conversations are heard all around, many in English, others in Arabic or Hebrew; some people converse in a mixture of all three languages. Topics of discussion include politics—primarily the upcoming American elections and prospects of support for Israel by the major presidential candidates—and speculation about the future of Brooklyn real estate prices, which have increased in recent years and now threaten to drop.

As we sit, talk, eat, and listen to the orchestra, conversation frequently turns to the music. At different points, two of the men at the table quiz me to see if I can identify the melodic category, or *maqām,* being played at the moment. The orchestra performs continuously, drawing on a variety of modern Arab composers and repertories. Occasionally, guests move to the dance floor and perform Oriental-style dancing, their arms swaying gracefully above their heads. The singer particularly pleases the crowd, which quiets somewhat during her renditions of songs made famous by the great Egyptian singer, Umm Kulthūm.

The evening's performances are not limited to the polished offerings of the professional Arab musicians. A song by Muḥammad ʿAbd al-Wahhāb is performed in Arabic to the accompaniment of the orchestra by a guest, a young cantor from Israel who has recently arrived to serve the Brooklyn community and who has begun studying Syrian liturgical music with Moses Tawil to acquire a true "Ḥalabi" style.

Shortly before midnight, after a general toast, the three Tawil daughters move to the front of the room and sing the "Anniversary Waltz," accompanied by the Arab orchestra. The Anniversary Waltz melody, said to have been popularized in the community through a recording by Al Jolson, was evidently once used for a pizmon the text of which "was not printed." The song melody is also said to be borrowed in the synagogue for prayers (J. Saff, 23 October 1984).

Next, the family leads the way into the buffet room, where, with great flourish, the senior Tawils cut their anniversary cake. Once again the Tawil daughters sing, this time joined by their brother, performing a rendition of "A Yiddishe Mameh,"[2] for which Sheila had written special words for the Tawils' Silver Anniversary and updated for revival on their fiftieth (see plate 11). Still sitting at his station behind the cake, the Latino musician next leads the crowd in a raucous rendition of a humorous song about a bride and groom set to the tune of "The Farmer in the Dell"; at the end of the song, many of the Syrian women ululate, giving out the high, piercing cries of joy traditional among Middle Eastern women. Not to be outdone, Moses Tawil himself launches into a rendition of the Hebrew folksong "Havah Nagilah," everyone enthusiastically joining in, after which most return to their tables in the other room and to the music of the Arab orchestra.

At one point during this long evening of revelry and music-making, I enter the ladies' room and encounter two of the Tawils' teenage granddaughters, both looking rather subdued, perched on a wide marble counter. "Aren't you having fun?" I ask. One answers, with a sigh, "No, we're bored. It's not our music."

But it is certainly their grandfather's music, and shortly after midnight, Moses Tawil takes the stage and sings his favorite Arab song, which is also his favorite pizmon, "Ani Ashir Lakh." Although this pizmon is based on the melody of "Aḥibb Ashūfak," a song likely composed in the late 1920s by Muḥammad ʿAbd al-Wahhāb, with an Arabic text by Ḥasan Anwar, the pizmon entered into the repertory of Syrian Jews in New York considerably later.[3]

While no documentation exists concerning the identity of the composer of pizmon "Ani Ashir Lakh," nor the occasion for which it was composed, its relatively recent appearance in Brooklyn in the third edition of SUHV (1983) suggests that it originated in Israel and was later transmitted to Syrian communities in the Americas. While few amateurs can sing "Ani Ashir Lakh" because of its technical difficulty and considerable vocal demands, the song is in fact best known and most frequently performed by cantors trained in Israel who now live and work among Syrian Jews in the Americas. Apart from Moses Tawil, the only singer to perform "Ani Ashir Lakh" during research sessions in 1984–85 was Shimon Alouf, the Israeli rabbi and accomplished singer who had recently moved to Brooklyn from Jerusalem. A similar situation exists among Syrian Jews in Mexico, where Mexican-born or longtime resident cantors are familiar with this pizmon as an ʿAbd al-

Wahhāb song, but note that it is only performed by a young Israeli-born cantor working in their community. Slight differences between the Hebrew words sung to "Ani Ashir Lakh" by Moses Tawil and a recorded rendition by a well-known Israeli singer, Yehezkel Zion, indicate that the pizmon is transmitted in more than one version (J. Saff, 4 December 1984).

The relationship between the Arabic song "Aḥibb Ashūfak" and the pizmon "Ani Ashir Lakh" is complex and interactive: while Moses Tawil recorded the Hebrew pizmon several times during research sessions in the mid 1980s, at his anniversary party he sang the Arabic version. When once asked if there were some pizmonim performed only at the synagogue and others sung for secular occasions like parties, Tawil explained that any pizmon could be sung either place:

> There is no particular song that we don't sing, if that's what you mean. If it's known, if it's popular, we sing it. (M. Tawil, 6 November 1984)

Rather, the occasion determines the language in which the song is to be sung and thus arbitrates whether the pizmon or its Arabic model is performed:

> Basically the Hebrew pizmonim belong at the Sebets (Saturday afternoon domestic gatherings). And our Arabic songs belong at our parties, our *ḥaflahs*, our *nawbahs*, so we say, that's what we call them. We don't sing Hebrew songs at the nawbahs. That's a definite distinction. (J. Kassin, 30 March 1989)

When asked to give an example of one song that he knew in both its Arabic and Hebrew versions, Tawil hummed the melody of "Ani Ashir Lakh." Next he sang its opening line in Arabic ("Aḥibb Ashūfak"), and finally the beginning of the Hebrew version. Only then did he identify the song as the pizmon "Ani Ashir Lakh" (M. Tawil, 6 November 1984).

Tawil went on to explain that the melody of the two songs was the same and that the Hebrew words had been written to match the rhyme and meter of the Arabic original. Comparison of the opening verses of the two texts shows the close degree of correspondence:

Arabic: A-ḥibb a- shū- fak ku- l yawm yir- tāḥ fu- ʿā- dī
Hebrew: A-ni a- shir lakh be- khol yom be- tokh ke- ha- li

Arabic: Wa- al- qalb dāb min al- bi- ʿād yā kul ʿa- dhā bī
Hebrew: Lib- bi yit- av le- vet va- ad be- khol ze- man- ni

However, paralleling the Hebrew and Arabic texts reveals their different meanings.

"Aḥibb Ashūfak"[4]

I love to see you every day
[so that] my heart feels at ease.
My heart wore out from the distance [between us]
How long is my suffering!
Oh sir, look at my submission and my compliance: Shame on you!
Have mercy on my love.
I saw his shadow in my dreams, What is sweeter? How beautiful it is,
how lucky I am to have this fate.
And my thoughts got lost in the beautiful one.
You increased my passion.
Oh my soul, my mind is gone thinking of you and I say again:
For the sake of your eyes, keep your promise to me.

"Ani Ashir Lakh"

I shall sing to you every day in the midst of my congregation; my heart desires Your meeting place at all times.
Lord, God, return, be gracious to me; rise for me, Lord, God, like the light of the day; and be merciful, Lord, God, O God who lives and endures.
Send my redeemer, O Faithful One; rebuild my sanctuary, O Merciful Father; ah ah send my redeemer. . . .

My heart desires Your meeting place at all times, God of my life.
Raise up light for me, Lord, God, like the light of the day; and be merciful, Lord, God, who lives and endures.
My heart desires Your meeting place; ah Lord of my life, raise up light for me.
Return, be gracious to me; rise for me, Lord, God, like the light of the day; and be merciful, Lord, God, on the assembly of my congregation.

"While the Arabic version is obviously one lover talking to the other ['I love to see you every day'], the Hebrew words 'I will sing to you, every day,' refer to the Lord" (M. Tawil, 6 November 1984). Thus a love song is transformed into a straightforward hymn of praise seeking closeness to "the Holy One, the Merciful One, and the Redeemer."

In terms of its musical structure, "Aḥibb Ashūfak" is a dawr ("turn," Faruqi 1981:58; El-Shawan 1981:303), a classical Egyptian vocal form divided into two main sections (Danielson 1997:70). The first section, the *madhhab,* presents the main theme punctuated by instrumental repetitions.[5] The second section, also named dawr like the entire composition, begins at the second appearance of the text *shelaḥ goali* and includes solo improvisations on the original theme, choral renditions, and virtuoso passages moving to the upper registers of the mode. During the dawr, passages are sung to the syllable "ah," a section known as the *āhang* or *hank*. The song concludes with a brief return to the main theme of the madhhab set with different words, descending to the tonic at the end.

As in the performance of all pizmonim, Tawil's rendition of "Ani Ashir Lakh" follows its Arabic model with great precision, although Tawil's recording on the enclosed compact disc[6] contains more internal repeats than does the vintage 78 RPM Arabic original by ʿAbd al-Wahhāb, likely because of time constraints of early recording technology. The instrumental accompaniment for the pizmon follows precisely the instrumental introduction and interludes of ʿAbd al-Wahhāb's rendition, with Tawil occasionally bending the rhythm to vary a well-established meter. Indeed, a comparison of recordings of several pizmonim by Tawil and their Arabic models by ʿAbd al-Wahhāb showed that Tawil tends to vary rhythm more than melody (Groesbeck 1984).

While many songs modulate between different maqāmāt, "Ani Ashir Lakh" maintains maqām nahāwand with some brief and subtle moves toward maqām bayāti beginning in the dawr section of the song. Modal ambiguity is achieved through using one of the four varied inflections said to exist within maqām nahāwand. Three inflections closely parallel the three varieties of Western minor scales (natural, harmonic, and melodic). The fourth, called "nahāwand morasa," is said to be used very often instead of the third variety and to resemble maqām bayāti. Indeed, both the natural and harmonic forms of maqām nahāwand are used, along with gestures toward nahāwand morasa with its lowered second scale degree (in this case, E♭) which implies the lower tetrachord of maqām bayāti (D. Tawil, 10 May 1985).

After Moses Tawil completed singing "Aḥibb Ashūfak," friends and family applauded appreciatively. Tawil thanked the musicians and rewarded each with a gratuity. The music started up again, featuring classical Arab repertory. When we left the party just before two in the morning, the ensemble was still playing. About thirty people remained, devotees of the Arab musical tradition.

Example 3. Ani Ashir Lakh

Example 3. *(continued)*

Example 3. *(continued)*

Example 3. *(continued)*

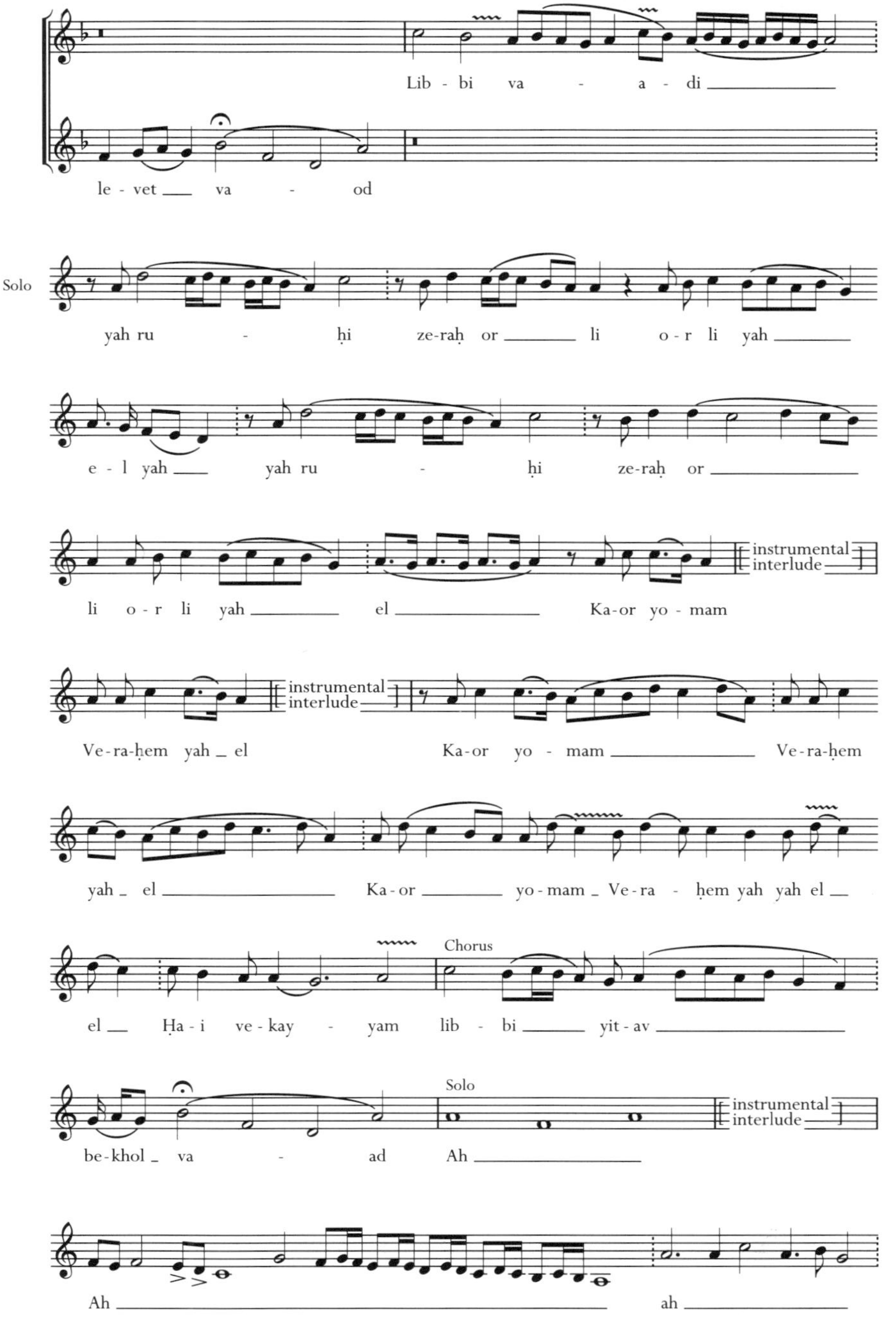

Example 3. *(continued)*

אֲנִי אָשִׁיר לָךְ, בְּכָל־יוֹם בְּתוֹךְ קְהָלִי לִבִּי יִתְאַב לְבֵית וַעַד בְּכָל זְמַנִּי:

יָהּ אֵל שׁוּב חוֹן לִי (3) זְרַח לִי יָהּ אֵל כָּאוֹר יוֹמָם וְרַחֵם יָהּ אֵל אֵל חַי וְקַיָּם:

שְׁלַח גּוֹאֲלִי (3) נֶאֱמָן. יִבְנֶה וַעֲדִי. אָב רַחְמָן. אָה אָה שְׁלַח גּוֹאֲלִי וכו׳:

לִבִּי יִתְאַב. לְבֵית וַעַד. בְּכָל זְמַנִּי יָהּ רוּחִי, זְרַח אוֹר לִי יָהּ אֵל. כָּאוֹר יוֹמָם. וְרַחֵם יָהּ אֵל. חַי וְקַיָּם, לִבִּי יִתְאַב. לְבָית וַעַד. אָה יַהּ רוּחִי זְרַח אוֹר לִי. שׁוּב חוֹן לִי (5) זְרַח לִי יָהּ אֵל. כָּאוֹר יוֹמָם וְרַחֵם יָהּ אֵל, עֲדַת קְהָלִי:

תַּם

Ani Ashir Lakh

I shall sing to you every day in the midst of my congregation; my heart desires Your meeting place at all times.

Lord, God, return, be gracious to me; rise for me, Lord, God, like the light of the day; and be merciful, Lord, God, Oh God who lives and endures.

Send my redeemer, Oh Faithful One; rebuild my sanctuary, Oh Merciful Father; ah, ah, send my redeemer . . .

My heart desires Your meeting place at all times, God of my life.

Raise up light for me, Lord, God, like the light of the day; and be merciful, Lord, God, who lives and endures.

My heart desires Your meeting place; ah, Lord of my life, raise up light for me.

Return, be gracious to me; rise for me, Lord, God, like the light of the day; and be merciful, Lord, God, on the assembly of my congregation.

THREE
A Judeo-Arab Musical Tradition

We took from them their music and put it in our Hebrew words. So in other words, the culture was the same. . . . We got along with them, we ate the same food, we listened to the same music, only we changed the Arabic words to Hebrew words. (M. Kairey, 6 November 1984)

Despite its longtime residency outside the Middle East, Syrian Jewish music at the end of the twentieth century continues to be closely tied to the Arab musical tradition. Its relationship to the Arab orbit transcends the historical connections that necessarily link an immigrant community, if only through distant memory, to its pre-migratory home. In the case of the Syrian Jews, the Arab musical world has remained a continued source of musical concepts and practices more than seventy years after much of the community left the Middle East for various destinations in the New World. This, too, despite the otherwise strained relations between the Jews and Arabs for much of that period.

Syrian Jews discuss their Arab heritage with great pride:

> Now in the Syrian Jewish community, in our community, we have something that's a little different. Being that we are Sephardic, and being we are Arabic, of Arabic origin, or we mixed with the Arabic. . . . our ancestors picked up the Arabic music. (S. Catton, 30 October 1984)

Many traditions from Aleppo, ranging from use of Arabic language to food, were preserved in the New World after the period of immigration. As one Syrian woman recalled, "When my father came from Syria, we had the same customs they had in their homeland . . . and they kept it up" (S. Cohen, 28 February 1985). Even after marrying an Ashkenazic husband, she said that her family spoke "Syrian" and that she "used to cook half Syrian and half Jewish." Her family "liked the Syrian food more" (ibid.).

Among those customs that were maintained were the musical traditions of the Arab world. But the Arab musical world is vast in historical and geographical range. If we are to understand the manner in which this Jewish music is conceptualized first and foremost as Arab music, we must locate it in relation to the Arab musical traditions by which it has been shaped both in the past and in the present.

From a geographical perspective, Syrian Jewish music was for centuries nurtured in Aleppo, at the center of what has been termed the Mashriq, a region stretching eastward from Egypt to Iraq, united by Islamic religion, Arabic language, and a series of rulers.[7] While aspects of classical Arab music theory were transmitted and shared throughout this area of the Islamic world from the Middle Ages forward, centers such as Aleppo over the years developed and were celebrated for their own distinctive regional musical styles.

The Syrian Jews were first and foremost, then, heirs to the grand sweep of Arab musical tradition filtered through the locality of Aleppo. There is evidence that they were active in Aleppine musical life from early dates. A Damascene chronicler in 1744 mentioned a visit to his city of "three Jews from Aleppo, expert musicians in command of the finest repertoire. . . . They performed in the coffeehouses of Damascus and entertained both the high and the low" (A. Marcus 1989:43–44).

Jews took great pride in the music of their Syrian city, which was widely renowned for its excellence. Syrian Jews in the 1990s still regard Ḥalabi music as a distinctive style as well as "the finest type of music in the Arab world" (M. Tawil, 6 November 1984). One Aleppo-born Jew has written that

> Aleppo's people are known to have very developed taste in music, in their clothes, their architecture; all of them, Muslims, Jews, and Christians. Especially in music, they are world-known. It is said that every Arabic musician, if he has won the approval of the people of Ḥalab [Aleppo], he has *carte blanche* to audiences everywhere. (Sutton 1988:228)

For Syrian Jews, the high general standards of Ḥalabi music also extend to their own liturgical styles and have been maintained since they left Aleppo for the New World.

> In Ḥalab, they were very discerning and very exigent. You might say that they insisted on the finer type of music, and the artists delivered it that way. In this country, we have singers and artists that sing this type of music. And they would tell you, "Oh well, last week I went to a party, an affair where there were Ḥalabi." That means we have a different, a finer type of music. So I say this because in my opinion, when it comes to religious type of music, I feel that the Ḥalabi is the finest, the one with the

> Ḥalabi background is the finest, which is the one that we adhere to. (M. Tawil, 6 November 1984)

Musical life in Aleppo is still remembered by those who spent their childhood years there before emigrating. At the center during this period were the neighborhood coffeehouses, which rose to popularity in the sixteenth century and were subsequently targets of criticism and attempted closures. There men socialized, played backgammon, sipped hot coffee, and smoked water pipes (A. Marcus 1989:227, 231–32). Bands of musicians often entertained as well. The coffeehouse was a "meeting place for men of all religions in Aleppo, a central setting for the transmission of oral culture" (ibid. 227).

In addition to the musical performances in the coffeehouses,

> Once or twice each year there was a gala concert of Arabic music, which featured a visiting performer such as Muḥammad ʿAbd il-Waháb [*sic*]. . . . A little music was available publicly in some cafés, mostly by means of phonograph records. The "Shahh-bandar," a large café on what was then the outskirts of the city . . . featured vocalists and a live musical ensemble. . . . On a pleasant evening, one of the hohsh[8] residents, usually among those in humble circumstances, would procure a ʿ*ood,* a lute, to be joined by neighbors in his courtyard, and often by those of a adjoining hohsh, who would enjoy and contribute to the quiet entertainment. (Sutton 1988:43–44)

In part because of its reputation for excellence, musical life in Aleppo was cosmopolitan. A range of Arab musics had an impact upon the musical world of Syrian Jews (the influence of European musical traditions is discussed further in chapter 5). Elderly Syrians in Brooklyn remember hearing tales about visits of famous musicians from Damascus, Beirut, and Cairo to late nineteenth century Aleppo (Sutton 1979:191). These include the Egyptian musician Salāmah Ḥijāzī (Sutton 1988:44), who was "the father of Egyptian musical theatre" around the turn of the century (Danielson 1991: 98 n. 12).

Aleppo's proximity to Turkey and its incorporation into the Ottoman state during the early sixteenth century (Hourani 1991:215) rendered Turkish music particularly well known to Aleppo musicians. The brother of Cantor Moses Ashear, a qānūn (zither) player named Charles Ashear, is said to have performed in Istanbul before "the dictator of Turkey" around 1908 (A. Ashear, 19 July 1989). But even before the Ottoman Empire formally disbanded in 1923 (Hourani 1991:316), the popularity of Turkish culture and music had evidently already waned throughout much of the Arab world (Danielson 1991:133).[9]

By far the most important change in the broader arena of Middle Eastern music grew out of stunning technological innovations of the late 1880s: the development and rapid proliferation of recording technology. This new form of musical reproduction had a dramatic effect on the transmission processes and content of Middle Eastern music in general. It further served eventually to establish Cairo as the new Middle Eastern musical center.

Shortly after the turn of the century, well over a decade before large-scale Syrian Jewish immigration commenced, commercial recording on both cylinders and disks spread throughout the Middle East. The Gramophone Company, an offshoot of the American Victor Talking Machine Company, was established in Cairo, Egypt, in 1903. By 1910, it had issued 1,192 discs from Egypt,[10] as well as nearly 2,000 from Turkey, 158 from Syria, and hundreds of others from Algeria, Iran, and Tunisia (Gronow 1981:255). By 1908, special Syrian music catalogues were issued regularly as well (ibid. 257). Other national and independent companies also entered the Middle Eastern market.

In 1904, advertisements for records and recording machines proliferated in Cairo newspapers (Racy 1976:24), a dramatic increase in the visibility of recording technology that has led one scholar to suggest that there was already underway

> the gradual transformation of the phonograph from a curious toy into a serious musical mass medium that involved the performer, the audience, and the businessman. It evidenced a significant change in musical life represented by the emergence of the recording artist and by a musical market sustained by a record-consuming audience. (Racy 1976:25–26)

By 1900, too, Ottoman Egypt had already been under British political and economic influence for several decades, and Cairo had become a center of cosmopolitan cultural activity (Hourani 1991:282–83). The city provided a receptive environment for musicians from all over the Arab world, and outstanding musicians either visited Cairo occasionally or moved to Egypt permanently (Racy 1976:28). Given the strong spirit of artistic innovation in the air and the presence of a growing record industry to disseminate music, a new repertory (called *fann* ["art"] or *ṭarab* ["enchantment" or "entertainment"] music) emerged to dominate Arab music, spreading from

Cairo throughout the Middle East and, eventually, worldwide in the years following World War I (Racy 1982:391). Propelled by the ascendancy in the 1920s of international stars such as Muḥammad ʿAbd al-Wahhāb and Umm Kulthūm, and featuring solo singers accompanied by instrumental ensembles of increasing size, ṭarab extended and built on the older genres of Arab music once performed informally by soloists with small groups of instruments for connoisseurs. Generally termed *turāth* "heritage," this older repertory included both improvised and precomposed pieces such as the *qaṣīdah* and muwashshāḥ,[11] quite fashionable through the beginning of the twentieth century in Cairo, Aleppo, and Istanbul.

Thus, the Syrian Jews left Aleppo sustaining a strong local tradition of turāth in which they had been immersed for centuries, while also aware of the new musical world of ṭarab emerging from Cairo. Both styles were to play an important role in their musical tradition as expatriates. Furthermore, the proliferating record industry, to which they had been exposed for some time in the Middle East, permitted them literally to carry Arab music along to the New World and to continue to supplement their musical repertories from recordings readily available in their new locales (see plate 12).[12]

Without exception, individuals consulted for this study consider "Arabic music," or more colloquially "Syrian music," to be a living tradition at the center of their religious and social lives. They keep abreast of the latest songs from the Middle East through recordings and as a result view Egyptian ṭarab as the dominant stream of Arab musical tradition today. An explanation by one leading member of the Brooklyn community reaffirms his status as an American while expressing his deep admiration for and knowledge of Arab music:

> Well, first I should tell you I am American-born. Pizmonim basically are Arabic music. I could call it Oriental, but really, that would not describe it. It's more Arabic. Now, that encompasses a very large area and there are different types of Arabic music, just like you have different types of music in the United States. And you have the Western music, you have the go-go music, you have the more classic music, you have the operatic music, and so on. The finest and most delicate music in the Arabic area is the Egyptian music. Well, we could probably trace the Egyptian music back to, I would say, maybe 4,000 years ago or even more. Let's talk about the Egyptian part of it, which is my favorite, because professionally, I can tell you that, it's a certainty, that it is the finest Arabic music. They have the most delicate, the most pleasant type of melodies and sound. (M. Tawil, 6 November 1984)

The overwhelming impact of modern Egyptian music among Syrian Jews can be attributed both to the domination of the Cairo recording industry detailed above (see also El-Shawan 1987) and to idiosyncrasies of Syrian Jewish immigration patterns discussed in chapter 2, which led many in the Syrian Jewish community to live for interim periods in Egypt (S. Catton, 30 October 1984).

Memories of Arab Musicians

Discussions of music by Syrian Jews are filled with references to famous Arab musicians. Indeed, the many stories about these individuals and familiarity with their music testifies to the continued resonance of turāth in late twentieth century Brooklyn. There are repeated references to the oeuvre and impact of the composer/singer Sayyid Darwīsh (1892–1923), an Egyptian who worked in traditional musical forms such as the muwashshāḥ and *mawwāl* (Danielson 1991:54; D. Tawil, 11 December 1984; J. Saff, 19 December 1985; G. Shrem, 9 January 1986; and S. Tawil, 30 March 1989).[13] Described as "a star [who] came into the horizon in the Arab music world," Darwīsh is remembered as the foremost Arab musician of the 1920s. He is also acknowledged as a teacher of many Egyptian musicians, including Muḥammad ʿAbd al-Wahhāb (Y. Nahari, 6 January 1986).

Other musicians still remembered by members of the Syrian-Jewish community in the Americas include composer Dawud Ḥusni (1870–1937; Y. Nahari, 6 January 1986), an Egyptian closely associated with innovative vocal forms such as the *ṭaqṭūqah,*[14] first performed by professional female singers around the turn of the century (Danielson 1991:355). Also mentioned is Zakariya Aḥmad (1896–1961; Y. Nahari, 6 and 16 January 1986), best known for the populist songs that he composed for Umm Kulthūm during and after World War II (Danielson 1991:164). Most of Aḥmad's songs were *ughniyāt* (lit., "song or tune," Faruqi 1981:380), which drew on the mawwāl and other distinctively Egyptian styles (Danielson 1991: 168–70).

Farīd al-Aṭrash and his sister Asmahān, important singers of Druze descent who lived in Cairo and starred in Egyptian films of the 1930s, are also remembered by Syrian Jews (J. Saff, 23 October 1984; Y Nahari, 6 and 16 January 1986; B. Zalta, 16 March 1990). A "very pretty" song of al-Aṭrash is reportedly still used by an Israeli cantor for the Kaddish prayer in Syrian synagogues in Mexico City (S. Harari, 7 September 1992). Yet while one Ḥalabi man mentioned that he preferred al-Aṭrash's songs because they fit his own voice better than did those of ʿAbd al-Wahhāb (G. Shrem, 9 January 1986), not everyone liked al-Aṭrash's style: "Farīd al-Aṭrash composed hundreds of songs—he's got five versions of music, and dammit, every song you hear repeats itself, the same five versions! . . . I get tired of listening to his music" (Anon.). Asmahān before her death was a competitor of Umm Kulthūm, who some members of the Ḥalabi community believe was "murdered by Umm Kulthūm's people" because they feared her talent (Y. Nahari, 6 January 1986), one of many stories in circulation about Asmahān's private life (Danielson 1991:148–50).

Considerable comment is still heard about the singer/composer Zakī Murād, whose recordings were well known among Syrian Jews in Brooklyn by the mid-1920s (J. Saff, 23 October and 4 December 1984).[15] A brother of Zakī Murād is said to have lived in New York for "thirty to forty years," where because of the Depression "no one had time to do music" (D. Dweck, 28 February 1985). Zakī Murād's singer/actress daughter Layla made her own Cairo debut in 1927 and later became a film star (Danielson 1991:144). Her recordings of "perhaps fifty years ago" still circulate by tape among Syrian Jews in Brooklyn (G. Haber, 31 January 1989).

The Egyptian violinist Sāmī al-Shawwā made a strong impression on Syrian Jews abroad, both through recordings and during a 1927 concert tour to the United States (Danielson 1991:124–25). One member of the Brooklyn Ḥalabi community volunteered a tale about Shawwā's extraordinary instrumental technique:

> I was told this story. I'm sure it's true. There was a violinist whose name was Sāmī al-Shawwā. Shawwā was an excellent, excellent violinist who knew nothing about sheet music. I saw him in the '40s or early '50s—and I'm sure the guy—if he's alive now, he's over 100—let's say he's not alive. He interpreted music on the violin just fabulously, just unbelievably. He can practically repeat on the violin words that I would be speaking—just amazing, that's how professional he was at playing the violin. Jascha Heifetz was in Egypt and he heard Sāmī al-Shawwā play. Now to Jascha Heifetz, he doesn't know anything about quarter or eighth notes,[16] as great a violinist as he was. He went over to him and said, "I'm hearing notes from you that I never knew existed on the violin. Show me how you get these *dawzet*." Dawzet means position. (J. Saff, 23 October 1984)[17]

But the bulk of Ḥalabi concern centers around the two musicians who dominated the world of Arab music throughout much of the twentieth century, Umm Kulthūm (1904?–1975) and Muḥammad ʿAbd al-Wahhāb

(1910?–1991; see plate 13). They were discussed, often at great length, by virtually everyone interviewed for this study. These two musicians in a sense unite the dichotomous worlds of twentieth-century Arab music, incorporating its conservative past within an innovative present. In the words of one research associate:

> Now, Umm Kulthūm sang pure, old-fashioned Oriental music, always did. Just the old, basic, beautiful Oriental music. Whereas ʿAbd al-Wahhāb came out with this new version of Arabic music. (J. Saff, 23 October 1984)

Umm Kulthūm, renowned for having a voice "prettier than a nightingale," is especially appreciated for her ability to repeat the same phrase with endless variations and to modulate between maqāmāt (ibid.; Y. Nahari, 16 January 1986). To hear her sing "is to get drunk without beer," recalls a young man who discovered her music when he was six years old by listening repeatedly to her recording of ʿAbd al-Wahhāb's song "Inta ʿUmrī" (Y. Nahari, 6 January 1986).

Ḥalabi women report enjoying Umm Kulthūm's singing (S. Schweky, 27 January 1988; G. Haber, 31 January 1989). One recalls learning the music of Umm Kulthūm from tapes that she copied from male relatives and friends during her college years:

> I would say that I was into her music for about five, eight years, or so. I would just play it in my car. I would walk around with the cassettes. Nobody did those things and especially with Syrian music on it. . . . I would take it to the beach in Bradley, you know. (J. Kassin, 30 March 1989)

Kassin particularly enjoyed the "tremendous orchestration" behind the Umm Kulthūm songs, which reflects a transition from the traditional small ensemble called the *takht* to a larger orchestra called the *firqah* that occurred in the 1930s. She also noted that one of her favorite Umm Kulthūm songs had been made into a pizmon. Umm Kulthūm was equally familiar to Syrian Jews who were born in Mexico City (I. Cain, 7 September 1992) and to those who remained in Syria. Indeed, one immigrant to New York from Syria in the mid 1980s mentioned listening to Umm Kulthūm frequently and using one of her songs to set the Kaddish prayer for the Sabbath morning service (B. Zalta, 16 March 1990). While Lebanese-born singers such as Fairuz and Warda have gained some popularity among Syrian Jews since the death of Umm Kulthūm in 1975, they have not replaced her in their affection

(J. Saff, 23 October 1984 and 19 December 1985; Y. Nahari, 6 January 1986; S. Schweky, 27 January 1988; S. Tawil, 30 March 1989). Individuals continue to recount stories about Umm Kulthūm's career, her competition with other female singers, and the elaborate measures used to entice her to perform ʿAbd al-Wahhāb's compositions after many years of estrangement between these two famous musicians (J. Saff, 23 October 1984).

To an even greater extent, the music of Muḥammad ʿAbd al-Wahhāb has been beloved by many in the Ḥalabi community virtually all their lives:

> Of course, I'm very partial to ʿAbd al-Wahhāb. . . . There was a period in my life where I listened to ʿAbd al-Wahhāb for one year only. I never listened to any other singer, male or female. Only ʿAbd al-Wahhāb. (J. Saff, 4 December 1984)

ʿAbd al-Wahhāb's music spanned the worlds of turāth and ṭarab. His earliest songs, such as the "Aḥibb Ashūfak" (discussed in the prelude to this chapter), exemplify the dawr and qaṣīdah genres, which were common from the mid nineteenth century until around 1930 (Danielson 1991:355), while many of his later songs incorporated a range of innovations. Of all the Arab musicians of the twentieth century, it is to ʿAbd al-Wahhāb that the Syrian Jews interviewed in this study expressed the greatest attachment:

> I love ʿAbd al-Wahhāb music. I'm very much in love with listening to him, and he intrigues me tremendously, with the change that he made in the Oriental music, from the time he started composing, until the present day. It's so up to date, and he sings in such a heartfelt way. . . . And his music is unlike the old-fashioned Oriental music that we knew up until the time he started. (J. Saff, 19 December 1985)

Many tales are told about these famous Egyptian musicians of the past. Composers thought to be of Jewish descent, such as Zakī Murād, were most frequently discussed (J. Saff, 23 October 1984; G. Haber, 31 January 1989; S. Tawil, 30 March 1989). However, a particularly distinctive genre of stories circulates concerning ʿAbd al-Wahhāb. It appears that the strong attachment of many Syrian Jews to his music, combined with the lack of direct contact with the modern Arab musical tradition, has given rise to stories linking ʿAbd al-Wahhāb in some manner to the Syrian Jewish community and/or to the broader world of Jewish experience. One such tale constructs ʿAbd al-Wahhāb's role as part of Anwar Sadat's entourage during the Egyptian President's historic visit to Jerusalem for peace talks:

> During that time, ʿAbd al-Wahhāb was commissioned to write a new Egyptian national anthem, which is a victory song, or a peace-victory song. . . . But when Sadat came off the plane—I saw it on TV—and was coming down the ramp, the band was playing this new victory song, and they weren't playing it right. The leader was not leading them. So finally, they stopped playing, the leader came down from the dais, Mr. ʿAbd al-Wahhāb with his army uniform and cap came up, took the baton, and led, and they played it perfectly. . . . But it was really something, ʿAbd al-Wahhāb came there and he led, and they played it perfectly. (J. Saff, 4 December 1984)

Several individuals tell of a Syrian Jew who is said to have visited ʿAbd al-Wahhāb in Egypt and described for him the way in which his songs are borrowed for the pizmonim. The composer is said to have been very excited and pleased by this information (Anon.). However, another researcher heard a version of this tale with the composer inquiring (perhaps facetiously) if he would receive royalties (M. Kligman, personal communication). One story concerning the past relates that ʿAbd al-Wahhāb credits the Jews of Aleppo with giving him his first recognition (M. Antebi, cited in Sutton 1988:228). Other tales involve cantors who have expressed a desire to meet ʿAbd al-Wahhāb (A. Alcalay 1993:254). One cantor seeks to understand the compositional process in Arab music through knowing "when they compose a song, in which room they sit, what kind of environment they had, what kind of food" (Y. Nahari, 6 January 1986). These oral traditions, whether invented or not, instill a measure of human experience into a musical tradition today openly acknowledged to be sustained solely through recording technology:

> Unfortunately, all the people . . . the sources already died. . . . Unfortunately, you can't live for two hundred, three hundred years except in the Bible. . . . But it's such a big shame. Because once you pass away, even your son, even the one who heard you all the time, he cannot be like you. So that's why we have the cassette. . . . I can always learn the music. (Ibid.)

No doubt the dependency on recording technology by Syrian Jews since the period of immigration has been intensified by the fact that they have had little face-to-face contact with live Arab musicians during that time. Beyond the hiring of professional Arab musicians for private parties and community concerts, there is little contact between Jewish, Christian, and Muslim immigrants of Middle Eastern descent. While their absence at live performances mounted by Arab Americans stems in part from the reluctance of Syrian Jews to socialize outside their own community, this predilection has clearly been reinforced by the on-going political tensions between expatriate Middle Eastern peoples of different religious and national backgrounds. As one Syrian Jew remarked with unusual bluntness, "I can't enjoy Arabic music in the company of Palestinians." Another explained that he would only attend Arab nightclubs or concerts when he was away from home in a distant city and would therefore not be recognized; he went on to describe an evening he had enjoyed greatly at an Arab nightclub in Los Angeles. One man further reported having made a special trip to Cairo only "because I wanted to hear Arabic music." He reports that he went to a club in his hotel and listened to the music until 3 A.M. (Anon.).

Opportunities for Syrian Jews to attend public concerts of Arab music held in New York City are in fact rare, since the few such events are generally held outside of Brooklyn and often are scheduled on the Jewish Sabbath. For example, a concert by Sabah Fakhri, a singer from Aleppo well known to individuals in the Syrian Jewish community (J. Saff, 19 December 1985), was held on a Friday evening in a concert hall in midtown Manhattan (Sabah Fakhri, "Classical Music and Songs of the Arab World," 29 May 1992). One individual mentioned having attended a concert of Warda at the Forum in New York City during summer 1984, adding that this was the only time in years he had heard an Arab singer performing publicly in New York; he was glad he had gone since he did not know when he would ever be able to go again (Anon.). A similar situation exists among Syrian Jews in Mexico City, who explain that they do not go to hear Arab music at a local nightclub for several reasons: they would not be "comfortable" socially; they do not like the "popular" music played; and they are offended by the presence of belly dancers (Anon.).

Thus, throughout the twentieth century, sound recordings provided the primary model from which Syrian Jews with musical inclinations could shape their own performances.

> As I grew older, I loved Arabic music, why I don't know, and I used to buy records and listen. And I picked them up from records. In those days we didn't have tapes. I picked them up all from . . . records. (J. Saff, 4 December 1984)[18]

Syrian Jewish music has in these ways continued to draw regularly on the central Arab tradition and to incorporate it within a musical life on its furthest periphery, enabling a Jewish people to perpetuate a tradition shaped by Arab values as they integrated into modern American life.

The Acquisition of Arab Musical Traditions

During their centuries of residence in the Middle East, Syrian Jews were able to acquire and extend their knowledge of Arab music as a part of their everyday lives and social interaction. Within Aleppo,

> Most of the Jewish community lived, not in a ghetto like it was in Europe which was completely closed off by gates during the night, but they lived close to the Moslem communities and they came in contact with the Moslems pretty often. (I. Cabasso, 13 November 1984)

Indeed, wherever Syrian Jews lived throughout the Middle East, they evidently had considerable contact with their neighbors. A descendant of Rabbi Raphael Taboush, herself born in Jerusalem, remembers seeing a picture of Raphael's brother Joseph taken in his house in Egypt, where he had lived from his teenage years, socializing with a large group of Arab men (G. Haber, 31 January 1989). Interaction extended to attending cafes and local coffeehouses as well, which brought Syrian Jews into contact with local musical styles on a regular basis:

> Any time you heard any form of music, which would have been at the local coffeehouse, would have been that Arabic type of music. And if you went home and you wanted to sing to yourself . . . it would have been that music that you heard in the coffee shops. (D. Tawil, 11 December 1984)

While contact with the environment around them was a constant source of music for Syrian Jewish men, the process of transmitting music within the community itself and inculcating children, male and female, with a love of the Arab tradition actually began in the home. After the period of immigration, musical activity at home became even more central to the survival of the Ḥalabi tradition.

Many individuals relate memories of Arab music in their daily lives. One of the most detailed statements came from David Tawil, who reminisced about the integration of Arab music, and especially the songs of ʿAbd al-Wahhāb, into his family's Sabbath observance during the 1920s:

> This is like an inside kind of thing. Saturdays were usually spent around the lunch table after having come from synagogue and we would sit for approximately an hour, an hour and a half, munching on some hors d'oeuvres, after which the . . . main meal was brought. . . . The point is

> that at that period of the day, of the Sabbath, many people would come to the house and listen to some Arabic music being sung by either my father or an uncle or I have an older sister that is presently blind who had an incredible voice . . . absolutely beautiful. Well, my father was quite a lover of Arabic music, he used it a great deal in the prayers of course, he too was a cantor, and he encouraged my brother Moe to learn these Arabic songs that ʿAbd al-Wahhāb had brought to the forefront. And Moe had such a tender voice that he was really able to emulate every note that ʿAbd al-Wahhāb was ever able to sing. . . . Saturday night sessions were in order, whose house shall we go to, and there they would pile in about 70 or 80, 90 or 100 people and they would sit and sing all night Arabic songs. And in this manner, a great deal of the community took flavor from the Arabic music itself. (Ibid.)

David Tawil's sister Sarah vividly remembers long hours of hearing Arab songs at her house on the Sabbath, as well as her own highly unusual participation as a female singer. Her father encouraged her to sing Arab music and bought her recordings from which she learned. Although she used to hear her father and grandfathers sing pizmonim, most of her singing was "Syrian Arabic. . . . I don't really sing the pizmonim" (S. Tawil, 30 March 1989). One of Sarah's nieces remembers hearing her aunt humming along at Sabbath afternoon gatherings, where she would sing "the words in Syrian" along with the pizmonim (J. Kassin, 30 March 1989; see plate 14).

Gracia Haber recalls her uncles and grandfather singing and dancing to Arab music at her home in Mexico City between 1925 and 1928, and subsequently in New York. She emphasizes that they were "modern, not old-fashioned," and that they'd play records of musicians "whether they were Jewish or not Jewish." A young man of Ḥalabi descent also recalls singing Arab songs with his father and other relatives "day and night," but in a rare reversal of the usual process that may be attributed to generational differences in the transmission process, he first learned the Arab songs as pizmonim by singing in a children's choir directed by the cantor at his Brooklyn synagogue (J. Mosseri, 14 January 1986).

But while hearing both live and recorded music at home was an important factor in the continued transmission of Arab music among Syrian Jews in the Americas, many Syrian men mentioned childhood participation in the bakkashot[19] at the synagogue as the seminal experience through which they first developed their love of Arab music (I. Abadi, 21 November 1984; H. Kaire, 14 March 1985; G. Shrem, 9 January 1986). Bakkashot provided "the best school" for Arab music

> because every chapter, it's [a] different maqām. So you go from maqām, to maqām, from maqām to maqām. Can you imagine after ten, fifteen, twenty years, that you wake up to bakkashot, and you sing the bakkashot every single week . . . they knew it. (Y. Nahari, 6 January 1986)

Although few oral traditions survive concerning the singing of the bakkashot in Aleppo before the period of immigration, a number of men of different generations who grew up in Syrian communities in various locales described their own early memories of the bakkashot. Most began attending the bakkashot at very early ages. One started at eight years of age in Cairo (G. Shrem, 9 January 1986) and another at age five in Jerusalem (Y. Nahari, 6 January 1986). Isaac Abadi describes being awakened at 1 A.M. to sing the bakkashot in the Old City of Jerusalem, joking that the sleeping Arabs must have thought what "donkeys" the Jews were to go out in the middle of a cold winter's night (I. Abadi, 21 November 1984). Since the individual bakkashot are set in different maqāmāt, and many of the hymns have internal modulations as well, their performance provides a powerful training ground for young boys, serving simultaneously to introduce them to the pizmonim and to Arab music. In the words of one, "I had the foundation of pizmonim from bakkashot already in my blood" (G. Shrem, 9 January 1986).

The Syrian bakkashot are still performed today in a traditional manner at the Ades Synagogue in Jerusalem, where men, many with young sons, begin to congregate around 2:30 A.M. They sing in unison until about fifty individuals have arrived and at that point divide into two groups who alternate singing. This lively congregation of some eighty to ninety men and boys sings in increasingly spirited manner until around 7 A.M., buoyed by steaming cups of coffee and tea passed around at regular intervals. The one week I witnessed the singing of the bakkashot at the Ades Synagogue, three other women were present, two of whom clearly knew the songs by memory and who sang along quietly from their seats upstairs in the women's section (Shelemay fieldnotes, 14 March 1993). The bakkashot are still performed at a number of other Syrian and Sephardic synagogues in Jerusalem as well, but in a condensed format beginning only an hour or so before the Sabbath morning prayers.

The bakkashot have been sung by Syrian Jews in New York since their arrival. Hyman Kaire remembers that his father would wake him about 6 A.M. to sing bakkashot during his immigrant youth in the early 1920s on the Lower East Side of Manhattan. Walking hand in hand, they would sing quietly on their way to the synagogue in order to warm up their voices. At the synagogue, after bringing out the books and rock candy and licorice to soothe their throats, they would divide into two groups, one starting, the other finishing a paragraph in alternation (H. Kaire, 14 March 1985).

In Brooklyn, the bakkashot are presently performed at Congregation Shaare Zion in a condensed version beginning around 7 A.M. (Shelemay fieldnotes, 16 February 1985). Women do not usually attend the singing of the bakkashot in New York, although one research associate mentioned that his mother and sister had in fact learned many of the hymns through singing them with the family after the Sabbath evening meal (I. Cabasso, 13 November 1984).

While research associates report that pizmonim (of the same maqām) would be interpolated between bakkashot (H. Kaire, 14 March 1985), as is still the practice in Brooklyn, no pizmonim were performed when I observed the bakkashot in Jerusalem. The once lively bakkashot tradition among Syrian Jews in Mexico City has been discontinued in recent years (R. Betech, 8 September 1992).

The Arab Musical System and the Notion of Maqām

If the bakkashot provided an introduction to the world of Arab music, they also served as the primary context in which the Syrian Jew becomes steeped in specifics of the Arab musical system. At the center of the world of Arab music is the concept of maqām, considered by Syrian Jews to be the "science behind Arabic music" (M. Tawil, 6 November 1984), and the "bottom line of the entire culture that we have absorbed and used" (D. Tawil, 11 December 1984). In general, the maqām concept and its realization among Syrian Jews parallels that governing melodic practice in contemporary Arab music, most particularly that of late twentieth century Cairo. The term maqām (pl. maqāmāt) has been used in Arab music since at least the fourteenth century, referring to categories of melody sharing pitch content, motion, ambitus, and a hierarchy of tonal relationships (Faruqi 1981:169–70).

A parallel conceptual field concerning rhythm exists in Arab musical practice, subsumed under the term *īqāʿ* (pl. *īqāʿāt*), incorporating rhythmic cycles of various lengths that are repeated for the duration of a vocal or instrumental performance. While the maqāmāt are widely discussed among Syrian Jews in great detail, the īqāʿāt are not generally mentioned; even the term appears to be unknown (M. Kairey, 6 November 1984). The contrast between a sophisticated theoretical grasp of pitch content and a dearth of knowledge about rhythm is evidently common among musicians in the Middle East as well (Danielson 1991:341–42).

Theoretical knowledge of maqām among Ḥalabi Jews is anchored in an abiding interest in the "*laḥan*" ("tune") to which a song is sung, the characteristics of which determine its maqām (J. Saff, 4 December 1984). A few individuals also have impressive knowledge of the history of Arab music acquired from independent study, which was recounted in great detail during the early stages of this project. The most nuanced overview is that of David Tawil, who traces Arab music history from its roots in the pre-Islamic Middle East, through the flowering of musical life in Spain under Muslim rule during the Middle Ages, to the consolidation and systematization carried out by scholars in the mid twentieth century (D. Tawil, 11 December 1984). Of particular interest is the acknowledged impact on Tawil and others in Brooklyn of the Congress of Arab Music, held in Cairo during 1932. The goal of the Congress was to revive and systematize Arab music through establishing a "fixed musical scale," organizing a notational system, recording music from different locales, and discussing relevant scholarly studies (Racy 1991:70).[20]

In part because the words of any given pizmon are in fact composed after the melody is selected, it is on the melody of the songs that attention seems mainly to focus. Women, who do not customarily learn or sing the Hebrew pizmon texts, are perhaps most explicit in their separation of tune and text. In the words of one, "I do not know the pizmonim by name, I know [them] by sound" (S. Schweky, 27 January 1988). Similarly, another woman points out that the first thing she hears is the music, and only afterward does she listen to the words (J. Kassin, 30 March 1989).

Among Syrian Jews, secular songs often provide melodies for chanting sacred texts, the texts "elevating" the status of the borrowed melody. This contrasts with Islamic practice, in which pitched recitation of the Qur'ān is conceptualized as "reading" *(qirā'ah)* rather than musical expression (Faruqi 1985:9) and is at the apex of a strict Muslim hierarchy of various types of *handasah al-ṣawt* ("sound art expressions"). Secular vocal and instrumental styles *(mūsīqā)* are of diminished status, their precise reputation depending on their relationship to entertainment and sensuality (ibid. 8). However, what may be a residue of Islamic practice seems to be reflected in the occasional use among Syrian Jews of the phrase "to say" a song, as in the following description of singing bakkashot in the synagogue:

> This guy wants to say the high part, this guy wants to say the [low part], all right. . . . it's a pleasure to him to say it. (H. Kaire, 14 March 1985)

This terminology seems to be used mainly by older members of the community in relation to the performance of bakkashot and liturgical prayers: for instance, a cantor used to "say" the kedusha prayer with a lot of vibrato (G. Shrem, 9 January 1986). But one can also "say" the maqāmāt, for example "say rāst" or "say ḥijāz" (ibid.).

Since most of the song repertory of the Syrian Jews is today acquired from Middle Eastern recordings (and in prior years derived from the Aleppo oral tradition), it follows that it also shares musical organization, and categories of melody (maqāmāt), with Middle Eastern sources. The number and names of maqāmāt vary depending on historical period and geographical area within the Arab world. Even within the same modern locale, the total number named by musicians will vary according to the way in which closely related maqāmāt are considered to be independent or part of the same "family" (see Faruqi 1981:169–70; Powers 1981:502; and S. Marcus 1989: 330–53).

Maqāmāt included in the Brooklyn pizmon collection *Sheer Ushbahah Hallel Ve-Zimrah* (1988) are *rāst, māhūr, sasgar,*[21] *ʿajam, lami,*[22] *nahāwand, bayāt, muḥayyir bayāt,*[23] *ḥusaynī, ʿushayrān,*[24] *rahawy nawā,*[25] *ṣabā, awj,*[26] *sīkāh,* and *ḥijāz.* Other maqāmāt mentioned by members of the community during interviews that are not found in the pizmon book include *ʿirāq,*[27] *kurd,*[28] and *jihārkah.*[29]

Although eighteen maqāmāt either are included in *Sheer Ushbahah Hallel Ve-Zimrah* or were mentioned in interviews, only half of these are considered to be important and to head their own family of subsidiary maqāmāt. When asked the number of major maqāmāt in use in their community, the smallest number offered was seven (M. Tawil, 6 November 1984), while the highest estimate was an even dozen (A. Ashear, 19 July 1989). The majority of respondents identified between seven and nine major maqāmāt. In several cases, the precise number was determined by how many maqāmāt that particular individual could distinguish; there was general consensus that the principal maqāmāt include ʿajam, bayāt, ḥijāz, nahāwand, rāst, ṣabā, and sīkāh.[30]

Technical knowledge of the maqāmāt is largely the domain of professional cantors in the community, many of whom are from Israel and are not of Syrian descent. An exception is the extraordinarily detailed knowledge

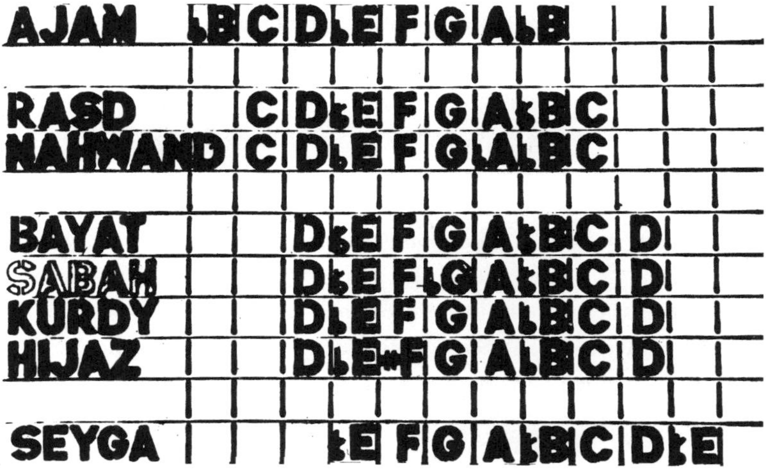

FIGURE 3.1. A summary of eight major maqāmāt prepared by David Tawil. Courtesy David Tawil.

of lay cantor David Tawil, whose involvement with the pedagogical process has led him to prepare materials such as the summary of maqāmāt found in figure 3.1.

Tawil uses the standard terminology of twentieth-century Arab music theory, conceptualizing an individual maqām as a "basic scale" divided into two tetrachords (D. Tawil, 10 May 1985). The concept of scale is apparently an artifact of modern Middle Eastern thought which was only applied to the definition of maqāmāt in the late nineteenth century (see S. Marcus 1989:448–57). The concept of scale is almost certainly an even more recent one among Syrian Jewish musical amateurs: indeed, David Tawil remembers that his father could not reduce a maqām to its scalar content, but rather sang the song to demonstrate a maqām. But the scalar concept is now quite widespread, leading one member of the community to offer to bring an ʿūd player to demonstrate "the scales of the major maqāmāt" for the NYU Urban Ethnomusicology Seminar (J. Saff, 4 December 1984). Modern tetrachordal theory evidently dates from the 1932 Cairo Congress publications (*Kitāb Muʾtamar* 1933:182ff. and *Recueil* 1934:188ff., cited in S. Marcus 1989: 281), although it does seem also to have precedents in early sources (S. Marcus 1989:282).

Syrian Jewish maqām theory emphasizes that the "nucleus of a maqām" is found by identifying its last pitch and the two preceding; only maqām ṣabā is said not to be easily defined in this manner (D. Tawil, 11 December 1984; Y. Nahari, 16 January 1986). Such knowledge can emerge from practical experience as well: one man reported being taught to listen "to the end of the tune" and to match it to a song he already knew (A. Ashear, 17 July 1989). This process works on maqāmāt with distinctive lower tetrachords that clearly signal maqām identity, for example, maqām ḥijāz.

Detailed exegesis on modulation between maqāmāt employs the concept of a pivot tone (a "golden note"; D. Tawil, 16 March 1990; Y. Nahari, 16 January 1986) as the point of transition; one termed the pivot tone a "door" (B. Zalta, 16 March 1990). Some individuals, while they may not be as conversant with the fine points of maqām theory, can demonstrate the structure of the various maqāmāt through improvisation and most certainly are aware "when they or someone else makes a mistake" (H. Kaire, 14 March 1985). As a rule, Syrian Jewish women are not conversant with Arab music theory, although several acknowledge knowing or are said to know "a few" maqāmāt (G. Haber, 31 January 1989; S. Schweky, 27 January 1988; S. Tawil, 30 March 1989).

Acquisition of the maqāmāt is linked to learning individual songs; thus extensive theoretical knowledge correlates directly to mastery of the repertory. As one member of the community explained, he had acquired an impressive grasp of maqāmāt

> by my close association to music. I mean, well, in the beginning you hear the word maqām, so you go to a guy that knows, "What does maqām mean?" If you're interested, then he'll tell you. "Well, . . . maqām bayāt." "How could I recognize maqām bayāt?" So he'll say, "Do you know this song?" and I'll say, "What song?" "Well, this song, if you listen to it, and you get the closing of it, you hear the music, you'll hear that the song is bayāt. So now you'll have to remember that this is bayāt." So if ever anybody sings a song in bayāt, and I can coordinate the music into what I know of bayāt, then I see, they fit. Now I know this is bayāt. That was the beginning. (J. Saff, 4 December 1984)

Although bayāt is said to be the first maqām that beginners learn because of its popularity (J. Saff, 4 December 1984), individuals report that the same process was used to teach them other maqāmāt as well (D. Tawil, 11 December 1984; A. Ashear, 19 July 1989). "If they ask you to recognize how maqām ḥusaynī goes, so you relate it to one song" (Y. Nahari, 6 January 1986).

But an understanding of maqām does not exist merely on the level of theoretical concept or as a system for classifying song melodies. Rather, it has a meaning and significance nurtured at the very heart of Syrian Jewish ritual life, in large part because of its multi-faceted association with the weekly reading of the Five Books of Moses:

> Many parts of the services were sung to the tunes of Arabic music. And since we have what is called as the maqām, or modes, we have different types of music every single week. Depending on the portion of the Torah that is read every week. The services never get monotonous. (S. Catton, 30 October 1984)

The use of maqām in the Sabbath service has two main aspects. First, the cantillation of the Sabbath biblical portion *(parashah)* is always performed in maqām sīkāh (H. Kaire, 17 December 1988; M. Tawil, 21 August 1991; I. Cain, 7 September 1992; Nulman 1977–78). The fixed association of the Torah reading with maqām sīkāh is so strong and pervasive that

> if you hear some song in maqām sīkāh, and you know how to read the Sefer Torah, although you don't know which maqām is the song, you say to yourself, "Ah, it's very similar to how we read the Sefer Torah. So, is that maqām sīkāh?" (Y. Nahari, 6 January 1986)

The reason for the exclusive use of maqām sīkāh for the Torah cantillation is obscure. One member of the community suggested that it stems from hearing the call to prayer in the Arab world sung in that maqām (J. Saff, 4 December 1984). Recent research on Qur'ānic chant in Egypt indicates that it is conventional to begin and end a Qur'ānic recitation in maqām bayātī, but there is no indication whether this also applies to the call to prayer (Nelson 1985:126–27). It further should be noted that maqām bayātī and maqām sīkāh share pitch content, although they start on different pitches (see figure 3.1). Whether the practice of issuing the call to prayer in sīkāh was prevalent in Aleppo is unknown.

A second aspect of maqām usage within Syrian Jewish liturgical practice is that on every Sabbath morning, melodies within a single maqām are used to chant certain portions of the statutory prayers; additionally, pizmonim within the "maqām of the day" will be interpolated at points in the ritual, such as when individuals are called forward to read the Torah. The choice of maqām for a given Sabbath is determined by the subject matter of the biblical portion and is set forth in an index to SUHV (pp. 565–66). The first portion of four of the Five Books of Moses is set in maqām rāst (the exception being Numbers, which begins in ḥijāz), which is considered to be "the father of the maqāmāt" (J. Saff, 20 November 1984). Here a possible correspondence exists with Arab practice, since rāst is traditionally the first maqām used in a collection *(dīwān)* of Arab songs (S. Marcus 1989:422; Idelsohn 1913:14–16).

The correlation of maqām to a given portion of biblical text is highly charged with meaning: for example, maqām ʿajam is used on Sabbaths when the biblical portion concerns happy events, while maqām ḥijāz is sung on those Sabbaths when the parashah pertains to death or misfortune (A. Ashear, 19 July 1989; H. Kaire, 17 February 1988; B. Zalta, 16 March 1990; I. Cabasso, 13 November 1984). A detailed exposition of these affective associations (Kligman 1997:261–68) indicates that while the association of ʿajam with joy is consistent with pan-Arab musical practices, ṣabā rather than ḥijāz signifies sadness to Arab musicians (ibid. 302).

On some major Jewish holidays, the associations to the maqām of the day used to set prayers are further reinforced by references within the pizmon texts to the holiday at hand. For example, on Passover, songs will be sung that mention crossing the Red Sea and "they sing it and think of the holiday" (H. Kaire, 17 February 1988).

Because of the centrality of the maqāmāt to Syrian Jewish worship, a cantor's mastery of this musical system largely determines his reputation and prestige. Cantors within the Syrian community emphasize that "after you know the maqām[āt], that's when you establish your personality as a cantor" (Y. Nahari, 6 January 1986). Because of the use of a different maqām every Sabbath, and the further expectation that a cantor will vary melodies within the particular maqām of the day, the cantor is judged by very specific criteria in addition to the quality of his voice. These considerations include the manner in which he returns at the end of a prayer to the maqām in which he began (G. Shrem, 9 January 1986; Y. Nahari, 16 January 1986), as well as his ability to modulate smoothly between maqāmāt:

> In ḥazzanut, in [a] cantorial career, if you sing the maqāmāt you have to be very, very careful. How you connect the two different maqāmāt together, like two [pieces of] wallpaper. . . . When you see wallpaper, the smart thing is that you won't see the cut in the middle. Like the wallpaper is well done all over the house. (Y. Nahari, 6 January 1986)

It is equally important not to modulate too often. A cantor should just "give the flavor" of a different maqām and then go back to where he started. If a singer jumps from one maqām to the other, he risks repeating himself and "mak[ing] it boring" for listeners (ibid.). Cantors also discuss "legal" and "illegal" ways to move between maqāmāt (Y. Nahari, 16 January 1986).

The flexible use of maqām within the Syrian Sabbath liturgy places a pressure on the cantor to improvise that is felt by some to exceed the skill demanded of most other singers within the Arab tradition:

> To be a singer, and to be a cantor, it [is] something totally different. If I decided to be [a] pure singer, I'd take a song of Umm Kulthūm, I'd take a song of many, many singers, and I'd copy from them. . . . But when it comes to be a cantor, not only did you have to listen to the original song, you have to be the one to create a music. (Ibid.)

If cantors acquire prestige from their virtuosity with the maqāmāt, the maqāmāt acquire additional temporal and situational associations by virtue of their use in Syrian Jewish Sabbath liturgy. Just as certain maqāmāt, and the pizmonim set to their melodies, are associated with specific days of the liturgical year, maqāmāt are used for life cycle occasions that both derive from and reinforce liturgical associations. For example, maqām ṣabā, used to set prayers on the Sabbath when chapters are read concerning the life of Abraham, is the maqām used for pizmonim sung at the circumcision ceremony (H. Kaire, 17 February 1988).

The affective associations of the major maqāmāt also extend beyond the liturgy and inform response to melodies in whatever context they are sung. "It's a question of moods. Got a lot to do with moods" (Y. Nahari, 16 January 1986). Thus maqām ḥijāz, considered to be a "sad melody," is rarely played at parties. The "atmosphere" or "mood" of a musical performance can be further transformed through change of register and volume at which a maqām is sung or played. An "aggressive mood" can be conveyed through using a high register, while sadness is implied by "singing low and to himself" (Y. Nahari, 16 January 1986).

Many metaphors are employed to convey the finer points of maqām identity and meaning. Each maqām is considered to have its own "color," a notion drawn from the wider world of Arab aesthetics (Y. Nahari, 6 January 1986). Some Arab musicians and their audiences invoke the concept of *lawn,* literally "color," to describe musical character and style. While Arab musicians tend to associate the notion of "color" with different genres (for example, *lawn jāz* "jazz color" or *lawn gharbī* "Western color" [Racy 1982:396–97]), musicians in the Brooklyn Ḥalabi community tend to apply the notion more literally.

> But I cannot sing maqām nahāwand and two minutes later sing maqām ṣabā. . . . In other words, you take . . . this length of the wall, you paint it black and then gray, and brown. From the brown you go into the gray and from the gray you go into white, so it's continuation, nice continuation. You don't break the colors drastically. But if I paint it black and then yellow and then red, it looks like a flag. (Y. Nahari, 16 January 1986)

Each maqām is also said to have its own "flavor" (I. Cain, 7 September 1992), which can be "sweetened" by the process of ornamentation and improvisation (D. Tawil, 10 May 1985). The emphasis on improvisation, and the importance of purely improvised forms such as the layālī and the taqsīm,[31] appear to derive in large part from their role in establishing both the color and flavor of the maqām:

> A taqsīm has no rhythm, no body to it, no nothing, but it has a magnificent rendition of the flavor and according to the capacities of the individual, how to handle that particular maqām, how he intertwines it, goes out, comes in, but that's taqsīm. . . . We've warmed up the audience for you, we've put you in the mood, we've told you what the maqām is, now you go ahead. (D. Tawil, 11 December 1984)

Some of the metaphors evoke synesthesia, as exemplified in remarks about the similarity between two songs in a single maqām:

> You see it's the same source, it's the same tree. It's the olive tree. And not the rose tree. You understand? You smell, you have the ear for that. You smell through the ear, you understand, that's how I call it. (Y. Nahari, 16 January 1986)

So totalizing is the concept of maqām among Syrian Jews that it extends beyond the domain of Arab music to incorporate other musical traditions as well. Many of the maqāmāt are described in comparative, cross-cultural terms: Maqām ḥijāz is characterized as "a very European maqām" (Y. Nahari, 6 January 1986), and maqām ṣabā is said to sound like Scottish music (S. Catton, 30 October 1984).

Conversely, foreign songs and even entire musical traditions are easily accommodated within the ever-flexible maqām framework. In this manner, the song "America," rhumba, and most Spanish American music are said to be set in maqām nahāwand. Syrian Jews perceive the maqāmāt as a nearly universal musical system able to interact with and even subsume other musical systems. This perspective has almost certainly been shaped by the extensive quotations of foreign musical styles in modern Arab music, which often draws on multiple sources within the same song. This "additive approach" is found most prominently in the music of ʿAbd al-Wahhāb, who both incorporates a range of non-Arab musical styles and even quotes well-known melodies by foreign composers (Racy 1982:396–97; El-Shawan 1985). It is not surprising that a Ḥalabi musical connoisseur, when asked if non-Arab tunes could be classified according to the maqāmāt, responded: "Any sound in the world fits into maqām. . . . Give me a Western song! "Happy Birthday"? That will be rāst" (Anon.). The intense appeal of ʿAbd al-Wahhāb's music for so many in the Ḥalabi community may in part stem from the fact that his liberal borrowing from a panoply of musics provided both a model for and a reflection of Ḥalabi musical practice in the Americas.

Beyond the interactive relationship of Arab music with the materials of other musical traditions, individual singers are considered to have their own distinctive vocal "color," stemming from the timbre of their voice or their idiosyncratic use of ornaments (Racy 1982:400). Similarly, a Ḥalabi singer can impart an "Arabic flavor" to songs outside the Syrian Jewish or broader Arab repertories:

> You know Spanish music, of course it's so related to the Syrian music. . . . My father could take a Spanish song and put a little twist on it. And you'd say, "Gosh, I think I know that song from some Syrian song or another." (J. Kassin, 30 March 1989)

The maqām principle and its realization in musical performance thus provides a connective tissue linking all forms of musical expression within Syrian Jewish religious and social life. It extends also to shape the materials of music and the concept of the musician.

The Materials of Music

For many in the Ḥalabi community, a love of Arab music stimulated by exposure at synagogue and home and nourished through recordings eventually became a more active pursuit. While many individuals in the community were familiar with and sang along with Arabic songs, a relatively small group possessed a level of specialist knowledge. Most of these individuals would not be identified as "professional musicians." The strong distinction between the status of amateur and professional musicians within the community likely grows out of the ambivalent or negative status of musicians in the Arab world. While the art of reading the Qur'ān has always been highly respected within Islamic societies, musicians who performed other genres of mūsīqā were more constrained (Faruqi 1985:22–23).

Among Syrian Jews, one finds a great deal of ambivalence toward musicians and professionalism superimposed on music-making in modern life. While professional musicians are respected for their knowledge, particularly of details of the Arab musical system, individuals within the Syrian community are very emphatic about their amateur status and the distinction between their knowledge and that possessed by the professionals only:

> One has to be a real high professional to be able to really get to that [knowledge of maqāmāt]. And I'm far away from that. I'm a lay person. I'm not a singer, I don't play an instrument, I don't read music. I'm just interested in Arabic music, and because of my interest in it for the last fifty years, fifty some-odd years, I've developed knowledge of music, of maqāmāt . . . that has been with me, so I am able to speak of it. I'm not, it's not saying that other people don't know what I know. (J. Saff, 19 December 1985)

Thus there is a clear dichotomy between professional and nonprofessional musicians in the Syrian Jewish community. A major distinction is first made on the level of knowledge and musical skill. Professional musicians are generally acknowledged to have studied and to possess considerable technical musical expertise, to be accomplished instrumentalists, or to have beautiful voices (S. Catton, 30 October 1984). An increasingly important aspect of professionalism in the late twentieth century is musical literacy, the ability to "read notes" (M. Kairey, 6 November 1984; H. Kaire, 14 March 1985). Indeed, the most important historical figure in the pizmon tradition, Rabbi Raphael Taboush, was considered a musical amateur because he did not have musical training; the great respect he commanded among both Jews and Arabs was due to his extraordinary ear and musical memory (H. Kaire, 14 March 1985). Of final, and paramount, importance to the distinction between professional and amateur is the amount of time devoted to musical pursuits and whether it is done for economic gain (M. Tawil, 6 November 1984; Y Nahari, 6 January 1986; B. Zalta, 16 March 1990).

In addition to the simple amateur/professional dichotomy, a further distinction is made between professional singers and those who chant the Jewish liturgy, the cantors *(ḥazzanim)* (S. Catton, 30 October 1984). However, even within the cantorial category itself an amateur/professional opposition exists, separating professional cantors from "cantors of luxury" according to the same criteria set forth above. Lay cantors perform the liturgy "because we love the music" (M. Tawil, 6 November 1984); they are never full-time, are not paid, and are usually well known within their own community (Y. Nahari, 6 January 1986). In contrast, the professional cantors are full-time and derive their living from their roles as singers; many have served synagogues in different communities both in Israel and abroad.

While famous female professional singers such as Umm Kulthūm exist in the Middle East and are greatly admired by Syrian Jews, there are few female counterparts among women in Brooklyn, where discussions of the status of musicians applies entirely to males. Evidently no Ḥalabi women in memory played musical instruments; and only one, Sarah Tawil, has been praised as a singer of extraordinary talent, although today her vocal skills are remembered primarily by her family members, who recall that she sang "like a lark" (M. Tawil, 20 October 1984). Blind since she contracted an eye disease as an infant in Egypt, Sarah Tawil evidently began to sing publicly after her family immigrated to Mexico in the mid 1920s and continued to perform during her early years in New York City. She remembers her experiences wistfully:

> I was very famous there, not only me, but my brothers, my dad, when . . . they used to pray in shul, it was out of this world. . . . And then, I tell you, they used to make me sing. Because if they have any parties, I have to be there. . . . They brought . . . music [instrumentalists]. And they brought singers and everything, but they wanted me. . . . I used to sing the most, . . . very high Syrian singing, because my Dad . . . used to buy me the better records. He used to love to hear me singing. (S. Tawil, 30 March 1989)

In addition to singing, a surprising number of individuals in the community learned to play Middle Eastern musical instruments. The instrumental resources most commonly encountered among Syrian Jews in Brooklyn are those of the takht:

> In Arabic music, basically there were only four or five instruments used up until the time where Arab music was modernized. . . . So the instrumentations would have been in the past, I'm talking about fifty, sixty, seventy years ago. A singer might have an ʿūd (the lute), the violin, the darābukkah, and the qānūn, which is the zither, and that was it. Sometimes he'd have only a drum; I call it a drum—it's darābukkah—and a ʿūd. . . .
>
> But today's music, the new Arabic music, you got all instruments.

> There are pianos today that play quarter notes. They use guitar, all types of guitar. They use the accordion and they use the flute, the lute—all wind instruments are used, it's amazing. (J. Saff, 23 October 1984)

Syrian Jewish practice thus corresponds to the classic Middle Eastern takht, which included an ʿūd (lute), qānūn (zither), violin,[32] *nāy* (flute), and *riqq* (frame drum); when needed, a solo male or female vocalist was supplemented by a chorus of four or five male singers (El-Shawan 1981:143–44; 1984). The precise instruments of the takht often varied in the Middle East itself, and sometimes only two of the five instruments would be used, depending on availability. In the Middle East, the qānūn was the only indispensable member of the group (ibid. 150–53); in Brooklyn the ʿūd or violin are more commonly present.

Yet despite the widespread use of instruments, Ḥalabi Jews share with other aficionados of Arab music a greater appreciation for the singing voice than for instrumental music:

> In Arabic music you'll find that the master of the music is the singer alone. As a matter of fact, a singer alone can do it without the need of any instruments. (D. Tawil, 11 December 1984)

The clear priority given to the singer may stem from a deep-seated regard in Islamic culture for unaccompanied Qur'ānic chant as the prototypical sound art (Faruqi 1985:24). Moreover, this sentiment is reinforced among Jews by prohibitions against using instruments in the synagogue or playing any instrument on the Sabbath or holidays. Indeed, it is explicitly noted that the chorus is used to "support and carry" the solo voices, especially on Sabbath when instruments are not permitted (M. Tawil, 6 November 1984).

Yet, even given the preference for vocal music and corresponding limitations on instrumental usage, many Ḥalabi individuals indicate both extensive knowledge of and great love for Middle Eastern musical instruments. Even a cantor who performs with instruments only "every three months" acknowledges that it aids him in singing and that he in fact prefers having instrumental accompaniment (Y. Nahari, 6 January 1986). The increasing size of ensembles in the Arab world, while not replicated in Brooklyn nor among Arab-Americans (Rasmussen 1991:311), have no doubt engendered interest in musical instruments.

Several members of the Brooklyn Ḥalabi community play Middle Eastern musical instruments. The ʿūd, played by Louis Massry and Joe Catton, is described as the "most beautiful instrument" (S. Catton, 30 October 1984) and like "half an egg" (M. Tawil, 6 November 1984). It is particularly popular in Brooklyn because of its flexibility and lovely sound. While famous Arab singers (including ʿAbd al-Wahhāb) who accompanied themselves on the ʿūd provided models for performance practice in Brooklyn (G. Haber, 31 January 1989), the ʿūd was a practical choice in Brooklyn because it is "easier to tune up than the qānūn" (J. Saff, 23 October and 4 December 1984). ʿŪds are imported from the Middle East, richly decorated with ivory and mother-of-pearl inlays, and tuned according to the modern Arab tradition (see plate 15).[33] Players use plastic plectra, although one carries along with him the traditional eagle feather *(rīshah)* both as a backup and to "keep tradition" (L. Massry, cited in Garcia 1984).

In contrast, the qānūn is more rarely used because of the time needed to tune the twenty-six courses of three strings stretched over its trapezoidal body; individuals noted that it takes "one-half hour to tune up" (J. Saff, 4 December 1984) and needs frequent re-tuning because the "pegs keep turning" (M. Tawil, 6 November 1984). While oral traditions record that at least one Syrian Jew, Charles Ashear, played the qānūn professionally in Syria (A. Ashear, 19 July 1989; H. Kaire, 17 December 1988), Syrians in Brooklyn have learned to play qānūn informally, both from recordings and from each other (A. Ashear, 19 July 1989).

For concerts and parties in the Ḥalabi community, individuals hire a local, professional Arab qānūnist, often Mohamed Elakkad, an Egyptian living in New York whose grandfather of the same name (1850–1931; El-Shawan 1981:167) was a famous qānūnist in Cairo. Elakkad participated in one music session (Shelemay fieldnotes, 10 January 1985) and played at a community concert (Shelemay fieldnotes, 27 October 1985).

The violin is frequently used in Brooklyn both to accompany singers and to play solo improvisational pieces, taqāsīm. For informal community events, the violin is usually played by community member Moses Massry. At more formal concerts and parties, the professional violinist Hakki Obadia is hired.[34]

In addition to the three chordophones, one finds percussion accompaniment used on a regular basis. The darābukkah is the instrument of choice and is played in the Brooklyn community by Ezra Ashkenazi, a Syrian Jew born in the United States. Ashkenazi, who recalls that "my father used to play the drum and I listened," was given a darābukkah when he was eight years old. He also learned from records, playing along with the drummer (E. Ashkenazi, 28 February 1985).[35] Ashkenazi used both a metal and a clay darābukkah to accompany "music sessions" (see plate 16; Garcia 1984). Frame drums, generally known as *daʿire,* are mentioned by members of the community (M. Tawil, 6 November 1984) but were not played at any music sessions. The frame drum played as part of the professional takht hired for the Tawil anniversary party (discussed in the prelude to this chapter) was termed a riqq (Faruqi 1981:282).

Of the other instruments commonly used in the Middle Eastern takht, the nāy (flute) is not often heard at Syrian Jewish musical events in Brooklyn. No one within the Ḥalabi community evidently plays the instrument, although a professional nāy player is occasionally hired for an important concert or party.

A synthesizer, calibrated to accommodate the Middle Eastern tuning system, is used in Brooklyn when a professional music ensemble is hired, particularly at parties. It is also used in the Mexican Syrian community, where it can be heard accompanying a selection of pizmonim and Arabic songs privately recorded in 1992 by Cantor Isaac Cain.

Conclusion: Performing Pizmonim

The close relationship of the pizmon to its Arab models extends to the broader context of musical performance. At the evening music sessions held during the first year of the team project (1984), pizmonim were selected and arranged according to a suite concept. Known as the *waṣlah* (lit. "a connection," Faruqi 1981:387–88; see also Racy 1983), this vocal-instrumental suite was widely used in Egypt and other areas of the Mashriq. Among Ḥalabi Jews in New York, the term *nūbah* ("turn or rotation," ibid. 234–35, 242) is more often heard than *waṣlah.*

In Arab practice, the waṣlah centers on a single maqām, with modulations to other maqāmāt inevitably followed by a return to the principal mode. Slower songs are generally performed at the beginning of the suite, with a progression to faster rhythms near the end (Faruqi 1991:387–88). Before the singer begins, it is customary to have an instrumental introduction, played first by an improvising solo instrument which is later joined by the ensemble in unison. As a preface to the first song, the soloist would improvise a layālī.

This format is generally present in Brooklyn, where Syrian Jews acknowledge following the pattern of "the great Egyptian singers" (M. Tawil, 19 November 1984). After a brief instrumental introduction (truncated in

Brooklyn because only a few amateur musicians were available), a music session generally continued with a lively group song to set the mood and establish the maqām. The soloist would perform an improvisation, either a layālī or a poetic Hebrew text with an improvised melody called a petiḥah (M. Tawil, 11 November 1984). This would be followed by a rendition of a "heavy classic" song of considerable length. The suite would end with a fast number emphasizing the central maqām (M. Tawil, 19 November 1984).

Just as the form of the music performed for recording sessions or at private Ḥalabi parties adheres to classical Arab norms, so does the broader aesthetic which dictates how musicians relate to their listeners. The process of singing a pizmon in a public forum draws on a similar set of responses to those evoked by Arab music. Most important is the communication established in the course of a performance between the solo singer or instrumentalist and the knowledgeable listener. A skilled musician is expected to create ṭarab in his or her music and to create a mood of musical involvement which is then acknowledged by the listeners, who exclaim aloud in Arabic at particularly moving moments during the performance. The soloist is then further inspired and performs at an even higher level of accomplishment (Racy 1982:392). This central aesthetic of Arab music continues to shape musical performance in Brooklyn:

> When you're singing in front of an audience, at a concert, then you have liberties to do whatever you want. And if the audience responds, and you get that inspiration, you do things which normally you won't be doing. (J. Saff, 4 December 1984)

Members of the Syrian community describe moments of intense inspiration and communication with their audience when improvising within the maqām system during religious rituals as well. One Ḥalabi man talked at length about an occasion when he served as a lay cantor at High Holy Day services at his synagogue. While singing a lengthy, solo portion of the ritual for the Day of Atonement, he said that he felt like "two insulated wires" went down his back "to his heels" and that he was "in a communion with the Almighty." Afterward, one congregant came up to him and told him that there had been a period of several minutes when he had been "amazing." Thus it appears that the communication of cantor and congregation, while certainly shaped by the conventions and ethos of the Jewish liturgical setting, also derive at least in part from the broader aesthetic framework associated with performing the maqāmāt. Ḥalabi cantors are aware of their congregations and are sensitive to their response: "You hear them, sure, and you feel it too" (G. Shrem, 9 January 1986; Kligman 1997:375–78).

But to understand more fully the dynamics of the Judeo-Islamic musical tradition within the Ḥalabi community and its flexible relationship to the new exigencies of time and place, we must turn to the manner in which pizmonim are performed within everyday Syrian Jewish life.

Plate 1 Brooklyn participants in team research project: (*left to right*) Isaac Cabasso, Joseph Sutton, Joseph Saff, Moses Tawil. Courtesy Kay K. Shelemay.

Plate 2 Brooklyn participants in team research project: (*left to right*) Hyman Kaire, Harry Tawil, David Tawil. Courtesy Kay K. Shelemay

Plate 3 Brooklyn participants in team research project: (*left to right*) Louis Massry, Meyer (Mickey) Kairey, Moses Massry. Courtesy Kay K. Shelemay

Plate 4 Research team student members: (*left to right*) Amy Horowitz, Geoffrey Goldberg, Rolf Groesbeck. Courtesy Kay K. Shelemay

Plate 5 Program cover, Purim Pizmon Concert in honor of Meyer 'Mickey' Kairey. Courtesy Sephardic Community Center.

Plate 6 Young Magen David. Courtesy Charles Serouya.

Plate 7 Cover, *Sheer Ushbahah Hallel Ve-Zimrah*, third edition (1983). Courtesy Sephardic Heritage Foundation.

Plate 8 Rabbi Raphael Taboush. Courtesy Sephardic Community Center.

Plate 9 Cantor Moses Ashear. Courtesy Sephardic Community Center.

Plate 10 The Sephardic Community Center, 1901 Ocean Parkway, Brooklyn, New York. Courtesy Kay K. Shelemay.

Plate 11 The Moses Tawil family, Golden Anniversary celebration: (*left to right*) Joyce Kassin, Judy Nasar, Sheila Schweky, Abraham Tawil, Moses and Alice Tawil. Courtesy Tawil family.

Plate 12 "Jewish Family in Aleppo," painting by Avi Shemi, from a photograph taken in the 1940s of the Sakka family at home in Aleppo with their phonograph. Courtesy Aleppo Heritage Center, Israel.

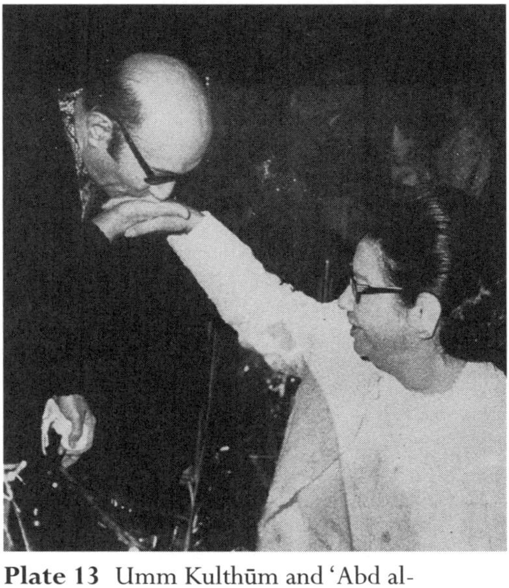

Plate 13 Umm Kulthūm and ʻAbd al-Wahhāb. Courtesy Fārūq Ibrahīm.

Plate 14 Moses Tawil and musicians at housewarming, Deal, New Jersey, 1973. Courtesy Tawil family.

Plate 15 Louis Massry and his ʻūd. Courtesy Maria Garcia.

Plate 16 Metal and clay darābukkahs. Courtesy Maria Garcia.

Plate 17 Moses Tawil and grandson Alan Nasar at bar mitzvah. Courtesy Tawil family

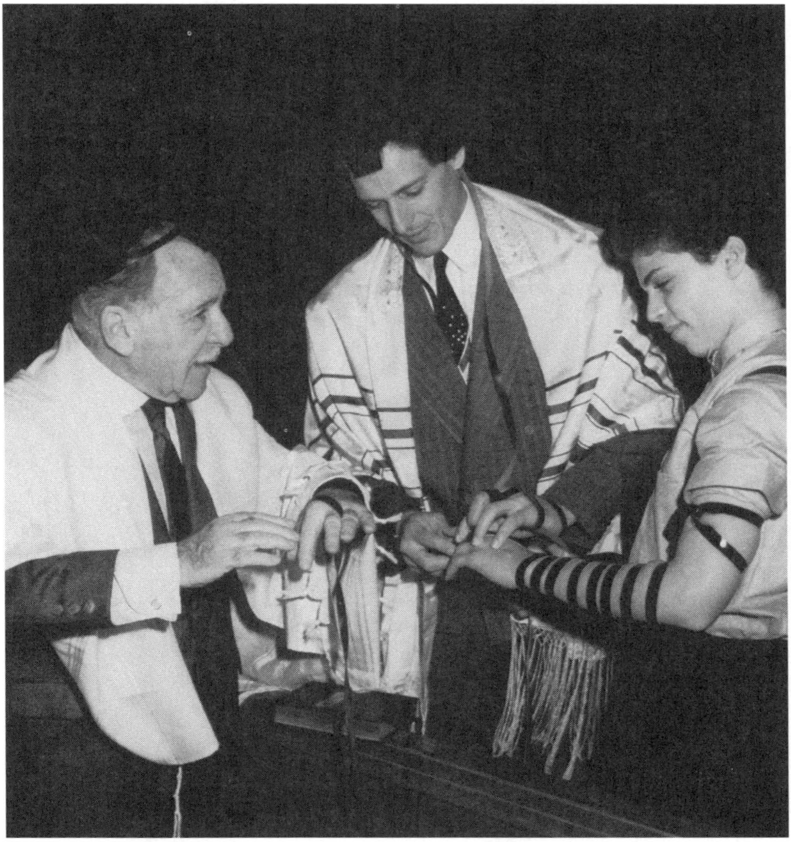

Plate 18 Alan Nasar puts on the tefillin. Courtesy Tawil family.

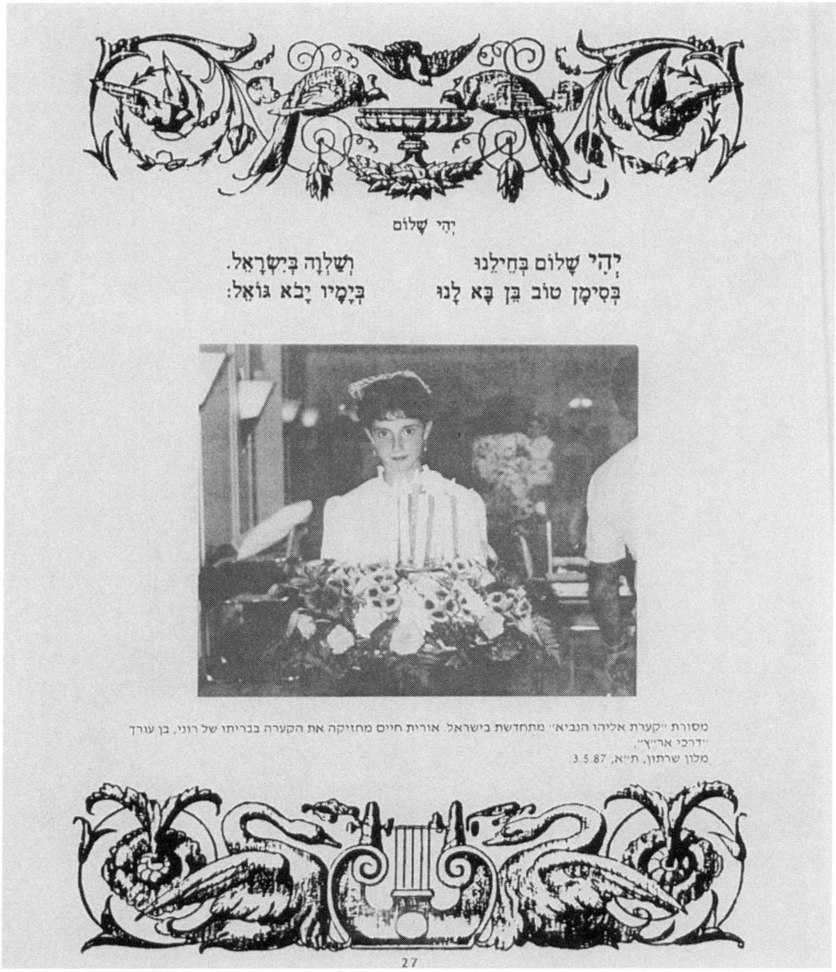
יְהִי שָׁלוֹם

יְהִי שָׁלוֹם בְּחֵילֵנוּ וְשַׁלְוָה בְּיִשְׂרָאֵל.
בְּסִימָן טוֹב בֵּן בָּא לָנוּ בְּיָמָיו יָבֹא גּוֹאֵל:

מסורת ״קערת אליהו הנביא״ מתחדשת בישראל. אורית חיים מחזיקה את הקערה בבריתו של רוני, בן עורך ״דרכי ארי״ץ״,
מלון שרתון, ת״א, 3.5.87.

27

Plate 19 Pizmon "Yehi Shalom." Courtesy Aleppo Heritage Center, Israel.

מזימרת אר"ץ

יְהִי שָׁלוֹם

סִימָן יְהוֹשֻׁעַ   מַקאם צַבָּא   לַאֲבִי הַבֵּן

יְהִי שָׁלוֹם בְּחֵילֵנוּ   וְשַׁלְוָה בְּיִשְׂרָאֵל.
בְּסִימָן טוֹב בֵּן בָּא לָנוּ   בְּיָמָיו יָבֹא גּוֹאֵל:

הַיֶּלֶד יְהִי רַעֲנָן   בְּצֵל שַׁדַּי יִתְלוֹנָן.
וּבַתּוֹרָה יִתְבּוֹנָן   יְאַלֵּף דָּת לְכָל־שׁוֹאֵל:

וּמְקוֹרוֹ יְהִי בָרוּךְ   וּמַן חַיָּיו יְהִי אָרוּךְ.
וְשֻׁלְחָנוֹ יְהִי עָרוּךְ   וְחָבְחוֹ לֹא יִתְגָּאֵל:

שְׁמוֹ יֵצֵא בְּכָל־עֵבֶר   אֲשֶׁר יִגְדַּל יְהִי גֶבֶר.
וּלְיִרְאֵי אֵל יְהִי חָבֵר   יְהִי בְדוֹרוֹ כִּשְׁמוּאֵל:

עֲדֵי זִקְנָה וְגַם שֵׂיבָה   יְהִי דָשֵׁן בְּכָל־טוֹבָה.
וְשָׁלוֹם לוֹ וְרֹב אַהֲבָה   אָמֵן כֵּן יֹאמַר הָאֵל:

הַנִּמּוֹל בְּתוֹךְ עַמּוֹ   יִחְיֶה לְאָבִיו וּלְאִמּוֹ.
וִיהִיֶה אֱלֹהָיו עִמּוֹ   וְעִם כָּל־בֵּית יִשְׂרָאֵל:

Plate 20 Joseph Saff. Courtesy Kay K. Shelemay

Plate 21 Cantor Isaac Cain. Courtesy Isaac and Ruth Cain

PRELUDE

Ramaḥ Evarai

At 8:30 A.M. on December 20, 1987, several hundred people gathered at a synagogue in Deal, New Jersey, to celebrate the bar mitzvah of Alan Nasar. That the day was a Sunday enabled family and friends to travel to New Jersey for the occasion; indeed, a young cantor from a Syrian synagogue in New York City, who studied Ḥalabi musical and liturgical practice with the bar mitzvah boy's grandfather, Moses Tawil, made a special trip to New Jersey to help perform the ritual. Because there were no other celebrants that day, the bar mitzvah boy was able to give a speech as well as chant additional portions of the Torah. The absence of special constraints necessary for the Sabbath also meant that videotaping the ceremony was possible. In the musical domain, the performance of the ritual on Sunday meant that the maqām was not "regulated" and that the ritual could include "any maqām" (Shelemay fieldnotes, 20 December 1987).

During the ceremony for the reading of the Torah (Five Books of Moses), it is traditional to call individuals up to the pulpit to pronounce blessings. Individuals called forth in this manner are honored either because of their relationship to the bar mitzvah celebrant or because of another occasion, such as an impending wedding or the recent birth of a child. As an individual comes forward, or as they descend, it is customary to sing a pizmon. If a new pizmon has not been composed for the occasion, as is generally the case in late twentieth century Brooklyn, a song would be selected from the collection that is set in the "maqām of the day." In the case of Alan Nasar's bar mitzvah, his extended family has been the recipient of a pizmon that was a particularly appropriate choice.

Pizmon "Ramaḥ Evarai" had been composed five years earlier for the bar mitzvah of Alan Nasar's cousin, Moses Tawil, on May 23, 1982. The young Moses was named after his grandfather, Moses Tawil, following Ḥalabi practice. This pizmon also marked a second occasion: the dedication of a newly copied scroll of the Five Books of Moses donated by the senior Moses Tawil to the local Syrian synagogue where Moses' bar mitzvah ceremony took place (see plate 17). Thus the song commemorates both a young boy's coming of age and the philanthropy of his grandfather, a respected community leader. "Ramaḥ Evarai" was even more of a family affair than most pizmonim: the composer was Louis Massry, the senior Moses' brother-in-law, a businessman who is both a Hebrew scholar and a player of the ʿūd. Because of the relatively recent genesis of "Ramaḥ Evarai" and the willingness of the family to discuss the song, it is possible to explore the "compositional process" in considerable detail.

The melody chosen by Louis Massry for "Ramaḥ Evarai" came from "The Wheat Song" ("Al-qamḥ"), composed in 1946 by Muḥammad ʿAbd al-Wahhāb (1910?–1991; Azzam 1990:129). Somewhat atypical is the long time lag between the initial circulation of the song from which the melody is borrowed and the date of pizmon composition, in this case approximately thirty-six years. Composer Louis Massry, like many in the Ḥalabi community, was familiar with "The Wheat Song" from recordings: "I have every record and tape of ʿAbd al-Wahhāb. As soon as a new one came out, I would buy it" (L. Massry, 22 October 1991). In fact, most are unaware that this song was originally composed for a film, not surprising given the many years between its release and the composition of the pizmon, as well as the limited circulation of Arab films abroad in comparison to the ready availability of records and cassettes.

"The Wheat Song" ("Al-qamḥ") was composed in 1946 near the end of a thirteen-year period when ʿAbd al-Wahhāb was active in the burgeoning Egyptian film industry. The song accompanies a scene in the movie *Lastu malakan* ("I am not an angel"), during which Egyptian peasants are "reaping the wheat" (Nabil Azzam, 16 September 1996; J. Saff, 19 December 1985). The composer has stated that "The Wheat Song" and others of its genre "should serve the general atmosphere of the film. They must be light in style and short in length" (Azzam 1990:114; see musical example 4.1 below on pp. 144–147).

Indeed, "The Wheat Song" is light and short by Arab standards; its form is an ughniyah, a modern genre characterized by a strophic structure with a refrain. The text is a poem in colloquial Arabic written by Husayn al-Sayyid, ʿAbd al-Wahhāb's lyricist for several films (ibid. 123).

ʿAbd al-Wahhāb was known for striking innovations in Arab musical style, particularly manifested in his film songs. There he stopped using the

EXAMPLE 4.2. Flute theme, Tchaikovsky, *The Nutcracker* ballet, Act 2. Source: Kalmus Orchestra Library score, vol. 2.

traditional small ensemble of Arab instruments, the takht, and used the firqah, combining traditional Egyptian and Western instruments. The original recording of "The Wheat Song" uses a firqah that includes the traditional qānūn (zither) and Egyptian percussion instruments (three tiran, or large frame drums), as well as six violins, a cello, bass, accordion, piano, piccolo and female choir (ibid. 129).[1]

"The Wheat Song" begins with an 8/4 rhythm (*ʿiqā masmudi kabir*) played in moderate tempo by three tiran. The rhythm is repeated three times, the first by the tiran, joined by the riqq on the third. During the fourth percussion cycle, a solo piccolo enters playing a transformation of the flute theme from the second act of Tchaikovsky's "Nutcracker Ballet" (see musical example 4.2). ʿAbd al-Wahhāb, who said that in his film songs "I broke the bonds of conventionality" (ibid. 114), frequently quoted from a wide variety of Western classical compositions. A duple rhythm with an accent on the second beat begins at measure 12; it is called *krakoviak* and establishes the meter used for the song proper (ibid. 167–68). The song itself diverges from its maqām classification (ʿajam) to clearly imply a C major harmony, notably through the use of large intervals, accidentals, and regular harmonic rhythm (ibid. 148). In this case the accidentals do not signify a modulation to another maqām but are a type of melodic ornamentation often used in both composed pieces and taqāsīm, rendering "Al-qamḥ" a "single-mode song" (ibid. 145). The nod to a Western musical vocabulary is further enhanced by another innovation heard in the original recording of "Al-qamḥ": the use of European singers borrowed from the Cairo Opera Company singing a high countermelody set in an overtly harmonic texture (ibid. 142–43).

"Ramaḥ Evarai" adheres to the longstanding tradition of Hebrew contrafacta by following precisely the rhyme scheme of the original Arabic text; the original "Wheat Song" melody is presented almost completely intact. However, the pizmon differs from the Arab original in other areas. In addition to dropping the instrumental introduction, the women's chorus is discarded, along with the countermelody sung by high sopranos. Although it might at first seem surprising that the Syrian pizmon "Ramaḥ Evarai" omits the original introduction with the modified "Nutcracker" melody, it is perhaps a predictable omission given the limited instrumental resources available in Brooklyn. Additionally, the irony of using the borrowed Tchaikovsky melody is lost on most Egyptian audiences, who simply assumed that the melody was ʿAbd al-Wahhāb's own (ibid. 152). Not surprisingly, "Ramaḥ Evarai"'s composer, Louis Massry, indicated that he, too, was unfamiliar with the flute melody in the original recording. Finally, "Ramaḥ Evarai" includes relatively fewer choral and instrumental interjections between solo phrases than does its Arab model, as well as fewer alternations of the soloist and male choir.

The Hebrew text of "Ramaḥ Evarai," like most pizmonim, has references to Jewish law and custom at its core. In this pizmon, what appears as the first word, *ramaḥ,* is three Hebrew letters that represent the number 248, symbolizing "two hundred forty-eight organs." Traditional Jewish thought believes that the body contains this many parts, which is equivalent to the number of positive commandments enumerated in the Five Books of Moses; the metaphorical meaning is that the whole of one's body is to be utilized in the service of God. The text contains numerous other explicit references to liturgical custom; for example, several references to the donning of the *tefillin* (phylacteries) for the first time by the bar mitzvah boy. These two black leather boxes, which contain scriptural passages, are attached by leather strips on the left arm and on the head during most morning prayer services (see plate 18).[2]

The song text also alludes to the story of the prophet Moses, including his encounter with the burning bush, a particularly appropriate theme given the name of the bar mitzvah boy and his grandfather. Finally, the many references to the "secrets of the Torah" revealed to Moses may be a veiled reference to mystical secrets of the Kabbalah as well as to the Torah scroll dedicated that day in honor of the senior Moses Tawil.

Along with the numerous references to Jewish ritual practice, literature, and folklore, one finds encoded in the "Ramaḥ Evarai" text the names of four generations of Tawil men. In line three of the Hebrew text one finds the following names: Abraham, at once the biblical patriarch, the father of the junior Moses, and the great-grandfather; and the name Moses, both the biblical prophet and the grandfather. The name "Hannah" in the text does not refer to a Tawil family matriarch, but to the city of Hannah, mentioned in Joshua 19:14.

The pizmon text thus incorporates explicitly sacred ideas and references. At the same time it links a deeply personal and local occasion to other such rituals in the past as well as to a broader stream of Jewish belief. In contrast, the pizmon melody references a world explicitly outside Jewish faith and observance but equally a part of Syrian Jewish life.

According to Louis Massry, he used the melody of "The Wheat Song" for "Ramaḥ Evarai" because it was a "catchy tune, not a deep song, but a light, catchy song a lot of people could sing." Indeed, the song is often played at parties because of its "excellent tempo," which is "beautiful for dancing" (J. Saff, 19 December 1985). Massry noted that he especially liked the "ah, ah" section and found the entire song "a kick" (L. Massry, 22 October 1991). The composer's concern that the pizmon melody be "catchy" is an aesthetic value echoed by others in his community. As one man noted: "The poem depends on the music that he's putting words to. It's the music that controls the words that are being said" (J. Saff, 23 October 1984).

Following the bar mitzvah service at which "Ramaḥ Evarai" was sung, the crowd moved to a brunch held in the adjacent hall. The decor featured a "country" motif, with duck print tablecloths, small chickens on the napkin rings, and souvenir vases and pitchers for guests to take home. The buffet featured the usual mixture of Western and Syrian specialties, ranging from omelets to a round Syrian pastry covered with sesame seeds.

There was no live music during the reception that Sunday morning, although taped music filled the hall throughout the event. A mixture of Western rock, Arab songs and instrumental music, Hebrew songs, and Latin salsa quickly moved people to dance. Entire families crowded the dance floor for the Israeli hora and Middle Eastern line dances; only couples danced to the Western popular songs. By 1 P.M., most of the guests had left, departing earlier than usual because of rainy weather and a big wedding to which many were invited later in the afternoon.

EXAMPLE 4. Ramaḥ Evarai

Example 4. *(continued)*

Example 4. *(continued)*

אַה הַא הַא הַא אַה הַא
רַ׳מַ׳ח אֵבָרַי יָעִידוּ אֵין בִּלְעָדוֹ   יָהּ רָם תְּבָרֵךְ, תְּבָרֵךְ, וּשְׁלַח לוֹ 2
אֶת בִּרְכַּת אַבְרָהָם, וּמשֶׁה בֶּן עַמְרָם   יָהּ רָם תְּבָרֵךְ, וּשְׁלַח לוֹ
לִכְבוֹד חָתָן בַּר מִצְוָה, יָשִׁירוּ אֶת הַשִּׁירָה, בְּעִיר צִיּוֹן הַנְּעִימָה, קִרְיַת חַנָּה 2
קָשְׁרֵם עַל יָדְךָ אַה הַא   וּלְאוֹת יְהִי לְךָ, אַה הַא אַה הַא
וּלְמשֶׁה עַבְדּוֹ, סוֹד תּוֹרָה גִּלָּה לוֹ,   יָהּ תְּבָרֵךְ, תָּרֵךְ, וּשְׁלַח לוֹ
אֶת בִּרְכַּת אַבְרָהָם, וּמשֶׁה בֶּן עַמְרָם,   יָהּ רָם תְּבָרֵךְ, וּשְׁלָח לוֹ
עֲנֵג כַּבֵּד הוֹרֶיךָ, וּשְׁמוֹר מִצְוֹת בּוֹרְאֶךָ   יַאֲרִיכוּ יָמֶיךָ, בִּרְכַּת הוֹרִים 2
אָבִי שִׂימָה עָלַי, אַה הַא אַה הַא   תְּפִלִּין בֵּין עֵינָי, אַה הַא אַה הַא
אֶהְגֶּה בַּתּוֹרָה, אֶשְׁמוֹר מִצְוֹתֶהָ   וְשָׂשׂ אָנֹכִי, עַל כֹּל מִמְרָתֶהָ
צִיּוֹן לָעַד תִּבְנֶה, אֵל רָם שׁוֹכֵן סְנֶה,   נָהֲגֵם בְּחֶסֶד, וּבְרַחֲמִים
תֵּן לְרָעֵב לַחְמְךָ, לְעָנִי וּלְאֶבְיוֹנֶךָ   ה׳ יִפְרוֹשׂ עָלֶיךָ, אוֹצָר הַטּוֹב
רִנָּה וְקוֹל שִׂמְחָה, יִשָּׁמַע בִּיהוּדָה   נָשִׁירָה וּנְהַלְלָה, לְשׁוֹכֵן עַל
אֵל בָּרֵךְ הַחֶבְרָה, אַה הַא אַה הַא   וּשְׁלַח גּוֹאֵל בִּמְהֵרָה, אַה הַא אַה הַא 2
וּלְמשֶׁה עַבְדּוֹ, סוֹד תּוֹרָה גִּלָּה לוֹ   יָהּ רָם תְּבָרֵךְ, תְּבָרֵךְ, וּשְׁלַח לוֹ
אֶת בִּרְכַּת אַבְרָהָם, וּמשֶׁה בֶּן עַמְרָם   יָהּ רָם תְּבָרֵךְ, וּשְׁלַח לוֹ.
אַה הַא הַא הַא אַה הַא

Ramaḥ Everai

Let my whole being testify that there is none other besides him Who dwells in the heaven above,

Bless and send him the blessing of Abraham, and Moses the son of Amram, yes bless and send him.

In honor of the Bar Mitzvah, let them sing the song in the glorious city of Zion, and the city of Hannah.

Bind the words of the Shema on your hand, ah ah ah ah,

and let it be for you a sign, ah ah ah ah,

To Moses his servant, the secrets of the Torah he revealed to him,

Yes, bless and send him.

Gladden the hearts of your parents and honor them, and observe the commandments of your Maker, and this precept will lengthen your days.

Father, place upon me, ah ah ah ah, the tefillin between my eyes, ah ah.

I will meditate upon the Torah and keep its commandments, and rejoice in all its words.

Zion will be rebuilt for ever, and whose presence was even in the burning bush, lead them in love and compassion.

Give of your food to the hungry, to the poor and needy, and the Lord shall spread His bounty of goodness on you.
Let them be heard in Judah, singing and rejoicing, songs and praise to him who dwells on high.
God, bless our congregation, ah ah ah ah, And send the redeemer speedily, ah ah ah ah.
And to Moses, his servant, the secrets of the Torah he revealed.
Who dwells in the heavens above, bless and send him the blessing of Abraham and Moses the son of Amram.
Exalted God, bless and send him.

Example 4.1. Al-qamḥ ("The Wheat Song") by ʿAbd al-Wahhāb (transcription and translation from Azzam 1990:481–84, 372–73).

EXAMPLE 4.1. *(continued)*

Al-qamḥ

Tonight is the celebration of the wheat
May God bless it and let it increase

Pearly and clustered on the stem
The existence of life comes from its existence
It never misses its coming time
May God bless it.

Pearly from the Master's craft
He rules His servants.
Our souls are between His hands
and our life in it.
His good news came into the world
Returning life to life.
The order tonight is his order
May God protect it.

Oh beautiful girl, you cared for your land
and one look from you revives it.
You watered this land from your honeyed looks
And the time of bounty has come.
May God bless it.

And the Nile—despite the distance
from family and homeland—
Comes running to him on time to water him
The bounty flowed from our hands
When the Nile flooded.
Oh, God, protect it for us.

Now the breeze knew his time was coming
so it shook his cluster from longing
Tonight is the night of the grain
May God bless it and let it increase.

FOUR

Lived Musical Genres

If any subject has consistently occupied modern musical scholarship, it is the notion of genre. The hegemony of classification according to genus or kind in the mental maps of Western musical repertories, and by extension, in the scholarly literature on these musical traditions, is all-pervasive. A "systematic" approach to Western music history and literature tends to emphasize the connections between composers, individual works, and genre, implying a clear and unambiguous relationship between the three (Poultney 1983). Additionally, notions of genre in Western music assume a correspondence between form and function. Recent discussion of musical genres has questioned these assumptions and moved increasingly to ground approaches to genre in domains of social experience (Kallberg 1988).[3] Particularly germane are studies of popular music (Middleton 1990:238) that draw on Prague semiology to approach musical structure in regard to its social function and to acknowledge the different kinds of meaning a given unit can produce according to the code that listeners apply (ibid. 241). These models, based on Roman Jakobson's theory of the communication process, take into account not just form but context (ibid.). Furthermore, these studies acknowledge that genres and styles can be divided, or crossed and layered, producing hybrids (ibid. 248). In this chapter, I adopt a definition of genre that emerged from a study of popular music: "A musical genre is a set of musical events (real or possible) whose course is governed by a definite set of socially accepted rules" (Fabbri 1982:52).[4]

While cross-cultural musical study has helped clarify indigenous systems of classification within different musical traditions, it has also raised new questions. The very process of definition and categorization demands that the scholar delineate beginnings and endings within and between musical events, a process that often conflicts with the variable length of music as performed. Even when indigenous notions of fixed forms are present, the social contexts of performance may in fact be quite porous, with the same song or instrumental form used in various settings. Furthermore, what may be regarded as a discrete musical genre may in fact share characteristics with others as well as cross into other domains of experience. These points are demonstrated in an examination of Suya vocal genres where a "piece" may last 15 hours and there is no easily accessible vocabulary to discover what performers are doing (Seeger 1979:373). Two Suya genres, the *akia* and the *ngere,* share structural and nominal characteristics but produce meanings that vary according to performance context. The Suya examples suggest that music cannot be analyzed "separately from other parts of a people's artistic, philosophical, and social life" (ibid. 374). Similarly, the Andean Mapuche *tayil* repertory as a whole is distinguished by aspects of structure and performance practice, but is also "an ideological category that allows performers to concomitantly traduce and adjust the boundaries of many other 'categories of meaning'" (Robertson 1979:405, 407).

In the case of the Syrian pizmon, we have on the surface a song form that appears to be reasonably well bounded. The songs are named and recognized as a corpus within the community that transmits them and are compiled in a collection within which they are numbered and organized with well-defined beginnings and ends. The very title of the collection in fact signals a widely appreciated unifying theme of praise of God, a reality acknowledged by individuals within the community who discuss the songs: "Like we say, 'shir ushvaḥah' [song and praise!]" (J. Kassin, 30 March 1989).

Yet upon closer examination, this clear image blurs. The content of the songs is in fact quite heterogeneous, and any notion of overriding formal parameters quickly evaporates. A few individuals attempt to classify pizmonim according to historical or social categories. A rare example of this approach took place when a research associate taught pizmonim to members of the NYU seminar. After first distinguishing between "Eastern pizmonim in Hebrew" ("Sephardic pizmonim") and those of "Ashkenazic Jews," he next delineated between "songs for the Sabbath" and "songs of Israel." Later the man noted that he teaches "religious pizmonim" but then remarked that "all pizmonim are religious" (Anon.). Beyond the regularity of a Hebrew text set to a borrowed melody, it is clear that musical form is in fact ultimately dependent on the melody which is borrowed; any similarities between pizmonim arise from shared characteristics of the repertories from which their melodies were taken. For that vast majority of pizmonim based on models from Arab music, it is the classical forms of the Arab world that provide the framework on which the Hebrew text is subsequently constructed. This is equally true of songs drawing from texted Arab songs as well as instrumental repertories. "Ṣur Yah El," discussed in the prelude to chapter 1, provides a salient example of a pizmon based on the formal structure of an instrumental piece. Similarly, "Attah El Kabbir" (prelude to chapter 2) is an Arab muwashshāḥ, while "Ani Ashir Lakh" (prelude to chapter 3) is a dawr. For the small group of pizmonim based on popular songs of European or American provenance, their strophic forms, sometimes with refrains, reflect common structures within Euro-American popular song.

More complex, too, than it initially appears is the relationship between three related song repertories within the Syrian Jewish tradition. All are united in a close and interactive relationship with Arab music:

> We're going to discuss Arabic music as applied in pizmonim, bakkashot, and petiḥot, which all consist of poems that are put to music as traditionally sung by the Syrian Jewish community. Now these songs can go back, not the songs, the method of applying Hebrew words to Arabic music goes back perhaps 1000 years. (J. Saff, 23 October 1984)

As we have seen in chapter 3, many Syrian men learned the pizmonim through singing the bakkashot. Indeed, the close relationship between the repertories is cemented through this learning process. The bakkashot are imprinted particularly deeply on the minds and experiences of the men who know and sing them because they were acquired as children, heard on the cusp of awakening from sleep in the early hours of Sabbath morning, and then sung throughout the night until dawn:

> So you want to know how the first one goes? The reason I am telling you the first one is because I remember my brother-in-law. He used to tell me when he was a child . . . he and his father dressed early in the morning on Saturday morning, about four in the morning, and he's still like half asleep and he would hear his father singing the first bakkashot song trying to wake him up to come with him. . . . (Sings first verse of song) That's the first song you sing. So you can imagine your synagogue is all empty and about ten, fifteen people start to sing this and as the time goes more and more and more people coming and joining in. So this is the first one, this is for Abraham, so it starts with "El" . . . ["El Mistatter," SUHV, p. 8]. Every one is all poetry and just praises God. Then it goes into another song, after you finish that it goes right into another song (he sings the first verse of the second song), and it goes into another song. But each song has about six or seven verses and every song is different. You just heard two of them, they may sound almost alike, but they're not. (I. Cabasso, 13 November 1984)

Secondarily, the close connection between father and son and the memories of waking early and attending the bakkashot ritual together clearly carry with them deep emotional connotations. The singing of bakkashot was a tradition not just passed from father to son, but experienced by the two on a weekly basis following a walk through the dark, cold winter night. The heightened nature of this experience, so unlike any other in the life of a young child, must have rendered these musical associations particularly strong and lasting.[5]

Yet while the bakkashot and pizmonim can be joined in memory, they can be distinctive in their textual content, liturgical settings and functions, and times of performance:

> The Hebrew word "bakkashot" means to plead, which translated usually means "humble prayer." And bakkashot are sung Saturday morning—very early in the morning. . . . We are asking the Almighty to accept our singing and our prayers until such time that we're actually to pray to God in our regular services. (J. Saff, 23 October 1984)

The texts of the bakkashot (SUHV, pp. 8–72) in general praise the Sabbath, which God is said to have made following the six days of Creation. The series of poetic songs are considered to be the oldest and most revered aspect of the Ḥalabi musical tradition. The bakkashot tradition began in Safed, Palestine, in the sixteenth century under kabbalistic influence stressing the importance of singing after midnight. Most of the texts were written by local poets, with supplementary hymns by the Safed mystics (Shiloah 1992:151). Individuals conversant with the tradition actively discuss this history and credit important rabbis with creating both texts and tunes: "The bakkashot are so holy, when they used to create them, they made the tune and the words together" (G. Shrem, 9 January 1986). The bakkashot melodies are in fact "extremely heterogeneous, containing artistic and popular idioms, the latest novelties, and archaic traditions that had long since disappeared from the surrounding culture" (Shiloah 1992:151).

Bakkashot are regarded as particularly esoteric and prestigious because of their distinctive melodic properties: "It's original, it's not copied from anything else, and that's more than you got with the other songs" (M. Kairey, 6 November 1984). The perpetuation of the bakkashot in community memory is a further a point of pride since "nothing came down to us today in the twentieth century so much intact as the bakkashot" (D. Tawil, 11 December 1984).

In contrast to the bakkashot, pizmonim carry less prestige and honor within the community not just because of their more recent composition, but because of the well-known transfer of their melodies from secular Arab songs:

> You see, it's a sin for the Jewish people to sing the Oriental singing. . . . So they took the melody and they put Hebrew words to them and they used the tunes. (G. Shrem, 9 January 1986)

Knowledgeable members of the community are aware that rabbinical injunctions sanction the use of borrowed secular melodies under certain conditions. One pizmon, no. 187, "Mi Zot," is the source of frequent comment, since its melody is taken from the Neapolitan song "Santa Lucia" (See Ajani 1980 and chapter 5 n. 9 below):

> You see a lot of people . . . were hesitant to use this [pizmon no. 187]. I say, "So long as it is in Hebrew, you could take "My Country Tis [of Thee]," which they have. . . . So long as it's in Hebrew you can say anything you want in these prayers. . . . The Rabbi says it. As long as it is in Hebrew that's all. Any melody. You can take from the Arabs. They're reluctant to use it, but they use it. (H. Kaire, 14 March 1985)[6]

Beyond their role in introducing young boys to the Arab musical system of maqāmāt, the structure of bakkashot performance also established a framework for exposing participants to yet another type of song. When the bakkashot are performed in their customary order, the transitions between songs in different maqāmāt are often bridged by short musical improvisations called petiḥot:

> Now, petiḥot, the word itself means "keys" or "openings."[7] Actually, it's an overture to the coming song. (J. Saff, 23 October 1984)

A group of petiḥot, their texts drawn primarily from the book of Psalms, are included in SUHV on pp. 97–106, immediately following the bakkashot. The petiḥot are brief and always serve to bridge maqāmāt:

> Sometimes when they finish one song, all of a sudden they have like a little Psalm of David or something. . . . Like we ended off (he sings), then they say this psalm, and they end off to go into the next song, which is not the same maqām as we've just finished. (M. Kairey, 6 November 1984)

The lengths of petiḥot are not prescribed and their musical forms are quite free, open to the musical skill of the singer. Petiḥot melodies are "improvised, highly melismatic, and constructed in a way that creates modulation from the maqām (mode) of the preceding song to that of the subsequent one" (Shiloah 1992:151). However, one cantor notes that they should always be done with "good taste," in order to preserve congenial relations among the regular group of singers on Saturday mornings. There is no doubt that the aesthetic and musical values of petiḥot are highly valued and appreciated by aficionados:

> [Petiḥa] is always solo, because it was always improvisation, there was no particular melody, there's no particular song that you would go into. It was just an improvisation, it's like taking a violin and just playing because, you know, you love it. (I. Cabasso, 13 November 1984)

The bakkashot and petiḥot therefore exist in a symbiotic relationship, necessitated by the fact that bakkashot are always performed in a set sequence with a need to move in a carefully prepared way from maqām to maqām. While they are technically different genres with distinctive textual and musical content, bakkashot and petiḥot are effectively welded together in musical practice and community memory:

> What I wanted to bring out also is that over the years the bakkashot melodies are not individual melodies, whereas you include one and then stop and then go into the next one. Here, every song sort of fits into the next song, either through the melody or through a sentence from the psalms or a sentence from the prayers, mostly from psalms, they would take a passage and just get into the maqām to go into the next bakkashot. We call it a petiḥah, an opening. (I. Cabasso, 13 November 1984)

While the petiḥot most often precede bakkashot, a petiḥah can also be used in the manner that one finds a vocal improvisation, the layālī, used before a pizmon (Y. Nahari, 16 January 1986). Conversely, it is possible to insert an entire pizmon between individual bakkashot. Occasionally, a particularly beloved bakkashah will also be taken out of context and sung on another occasion, along with pizmonim in the same maqām. Thus the seemingly distinctive identities of pizmonim, bakkashot, and petiḥot become quite interactive and even blurred in the contexts of musical performance.

Ḥalabi Jews who are conversant with these three types of song further suggest that the differences between them reside in their distinctive affective and aesthetic properties:

> Pizmon is like a happy, you know, it's a festive thing. But bakkashot is in a class by itself. A person that loves, like he sees a painting of art, this is the bakkashot. . . . Anybody that knows it would agree with me on that point. (M. Kairey, 6 November 1984)

The blurred boundaries between song types manifest themselves in all aspects of Ḥalabi musical experience, extending into the liturgical sphere as well. This is set forth clearly in oral testimonies. For example, a late cantor in the Syrian community recalled a moment when he was singing a *kedushah* prayer[8] during the Sabbath morning synagogue service and realized it "is a pizmon I know from the bakkashot. Is this how they apply the pizmonim to the prayers? This pizmon you'll find in the bakkashot.[9] . . . That's the pizmon that was the key to my being a ḥazzan [cantor]" (G. Shrem, 9 January 1986).

Other individuals acknowledge learning pizmonim independently and only later encountering a pizmon melody in a liturgical context. One young man remembers learning pizmon no. 186, "Mi Yesapper," from a friend and later recognizing it in the liturgy: "One of the cantors happened to use it, fit it in to one of the prayers, and I recognized it from that" (M. Arking, 14 January 1986). Such liturgical use of pizmon melodies is habitual, guided by an index specifying which pizmonim in the different maqāmāt may be used for individual Sabbath prayers (SUHV, p. 567).

Thus, the varied uses and transformations of the pizmonim are determined by factors external to any bounded or formal notion of genre. The conceptual map that guides singing the pizmonim is coterminous with closely related songs such as the bakkashot, as well as with the singing of liturgical prayers. Syrian Jews are well aware of these overlapping repertories and tend to accommodate them by embedding discussion of songs within the social contexts for which the songs are composed and within which they are performed:

> Look up in the dictionary the word pizmonim—you will not find it. I could not find it. Till I had somebody look it up for me and they found it in the Judaica Britannica *[Encyclopaedia Judaica]* where they said the word pizmon is of Greek origin and it's supposed to mean, oh, it's used primarily in Arab countries and it's just songs. They're poems, oh yes. Literally, the meaning . . . is poems that are set to music praying to the Almighty. OK? Now bakkashot, as I said, would be sung before prayer. Pizmonim, the Hebrew songs that are in this book, there's a lot of them. The book has how many pages? 600 pages—there's a lot of them. [They] would be

> sung on Saturday after synagogue, if one has a party home, or a bar mitzvah. When the child's bar mitzvahed they have special songs for him, at a circumcision they have special songs that they sing during the circumcision, at marriage, or marriage reception, they would sing certain songs and on Saturday night after Havdalah.[10] And of course, on holidays, all of our Jewish holidays have different songs. (J. Saff, 23 October 1984)

Pizmonim are performed on virtually all occasions:

> If you give birth to a girl, there's a song for a girl. If you bring a little boy . . . there's a song. There's a song for Hanukkah [Festival of Lights], there's a song for the seventh day of Pesaḥ [Passover], there's songs for Shavuot [Festival of Weeks], when the Torah was given. There's songs for Rosh Hashanah [The New Year], songs for Sukkot [Festival of Booths], there are songs for Shemini Atzeret [Eighth Day of Sukkot], there are songs for Simḥat Torah [Rejoicing of the Law]. We have a million songs . . . for each occasion. (M. Kairey, 6 November 1984)

The following discussion summarizes the various occasions on which pizmonim are sung: first, events that mirror the major passages of life and the rituals which mark their occurrence; second, important moments in the annual liturgical cycle; third, certain domestic gatherings; and fourth, special commemorative occasions of both individual and shared significance.

Pizmonim of Life Cycle Rituals

Pizmonim are most frequently composed for and performed at the rituals marking circumcisions, bar mitzvahs, and weddings. The pizmon "Ramaḥ Evarai" (discussed in the prelude to this chapter) illustrates graphically the strong melodic and textual associations that this song holds for the family of the bar mitzvah boy. Indeed, it should be noted that the melody chosen is perhaps most obviously meaningful to the grandfather of the celebrant, since it is one of his favorite songs and its text as well alludes to his prominence and generosity. In this manner, a pizmon both honors a young boy upon the occasion of his bar mitzvah and also overtly acknowledges and celebrates patriarchs, both within his own family and as linked to historical figures whose names they share.

An occasion that is a particularly important catalyst for pizmon composition as well as a continued context for pizmon performance is the birth of a child. The most prominent venue for pizmon performance is the circumcision ceremony for male infants.[11] Of particular interest is the practice of setting circumcision pizmonim in maqām ṣaba, a tradition that has its roots in Syrian Jewish liturgical practice. As explained in chapter 3, while biblical portions are all cantillated in maqām sīkāh, their textual content is associated with another maqām that is then used throughout the liturgy for that day and for any pizmonim sung. The reading of the portion Genesis 17:9–16, which discusses the circumcision of Abraham, is traditionally associated with maqām ṣaba:

> The portion of the week was when Abraham was circumcised, so there is a special tune for that week, where for circumcision we sing a certain song and the whole prayer for that Saturday morning is based around that. (M. Kairey, 6 November 1984)

One member of the Ḥalabi community speculated that maqām ṣaba may be used for the circumcision ceremony because it is so similar to the word "sabi," which means "baby boy" in Arabic. He cannot remember from whom he heard this oral tradition (M. Arking, 28 April 1988).

The circumcision ceremony at which pizmonim in maqām ṣaba figure so prominently is celebrated among Syrian Jews in a distinctive and highly elaborated manner, whether held in the synagogue or in a private home. In addition to the circumcision procedure itself and the singing of pizmonim, the Syrian brit mila is distinguished by folk traditions which associate the prophet Elijah with Jewish circumcision ceremonies. In Jewish folk practice, many ceremonial sayings and procedures have developed to help ward off evil spirits; the Kabbalists were particularly instrumental in introducing and modifying traditions of these sorts (Trachtenberg 1974:153–80). Moments of transition—birth, marriage, and death—were considered to be particularly vulnerable to demonic forces and therefore "it was in such moments that . . . we find a massing of all those superstitious devices which from time immemorial have been accredited with potency to counteract magic, curses, etc." (ibid. 168).

The Syrian custom of setting aside a chair for the prophet Elijah during the circumcision ceremony is an ancient one observed by many other Jews, connected with a legend that God had rewarded the prophet for his defense of the ceremony with the promise that he would be present at every circumcision (ibid. 171). This custom originated as a type of bribe to evil spirits. During the Middle Ages, individuals at the ceremony would rise and greet the unseen Elijah (ibid. 171). Among Syrian Jews, the Elijah tradition is further elaborated with the passing of an "Eliyahu Hanavi [Elijah the Prophet] tray," a multi-level brass tray with candles mounted on it. A sketch of such a tray can be seen in the lower right-hand corner of the cover of the Purim Pizmon Concert program reproduced in plate 5, with a second tray pictured in plate 19. The candles may represent a common folk practice of performing the circumcision in a well-lighted place, the reasons for which are debated (ibid. 172).

The Eliyahu Hanavi tray is traditionally carried by a single young woman from the celebrating family. A married woman who has not yet had a child, or a mother who has only given birth to girls but who still hopes to conceive a son, may also carry the tray (S. Schweky, December 1996). Participants are expected to "put in a dollar and take back a penny for good luck" (Shelemay fieldnotes, 31 January 1989); after making a donation, each one lights a candle. Both men and women may light candles, although more women than men participate in this ritual. In most cases, the trays are owned by synagogues, which lend them to congregants as needed.

Over the years, the proliferation of circumcision ceremonies has resulted in the development of a strong tradition of associated pizmonim:

> All those pizmonim they used to sing them in the shul. When there is a bris for Eliyahu Hanavi, they used to sing that through the bris. To the father of a boy, another song. The father of a girl, another song. That's how they made them, those songs. And then, the young community that loved the music, they add to it. (G. Haber, 31 January 1989)

As much as half an hour prior to the ceremony, the singing of pizmonim begins, led by a lay cantor or a knowledgeable member of the community. The number of songs performed depends on the time it takes to bring in the baby for the ceremony. A typical selection of pizmonim in maqām ṣaba includes no. 405, "Yehi Shalom" (see plate 19); no. 406, "Eʿrokh Mahalal"; no. 409, "Ahallel Ve'agilah"; no. 410, "Attah Ahuvi"; no. 411, "Mah Tov"; no. 412, "Mibbeten Yedid"; and no. 413, "Yaḥon El Ṣur."[12] All these songs are identified as songs for circumcision ("lamila") and refer within their texts to the birth of a son and/or the circumcision ceremony. Nos. 406 and 410 include the name of the prophet Elijah. So often are these seven pizmonim used for circumcision ceremonies that members of one family prepared a special sheet of selected songs titled "The Milah Group," "just to facilitate things for the people who were there" (M. Tawil, 6 November 1984). The sheet was quickly duplicated and passed to others in the community.

Other pizmonim as well are sometimes sung at circumcision ceremonies, including no. 125, "Ram Leḥasdakh" (M. Arking, 14 January 1986; Shele-

EXAMPLE 4.3. "Ram Leḥasdakh"

♩ = 120
Ram le - ḥas-dakh ram le - ḥas-dakh ye - kav - vu ye - kav - vu
Lo-me-dei ha - to - rah lo-me-dei ha - to - rah lakh yo - du lakh yo - du

may fieldnotes, 24 April 1988). Composed by Taboush, "Ram Leḥasdakh" is set in maqām rāst to a foreign melody credited as a "polka" but which borrows the tune of the traditional French round "Frère Jacques" (see musical example 4.3). The reason for the association of no. 125 with the circumcision ceremony is unclear, although its text does contain a possible veiled allusion to the redemption of the firstborn ("pidyon haben"), a ceremony prescribed in Numbers 18:16–17. The two pizmonim preceding no. 125 in SUHV also allude directly to the circumcision ritual and redemption of the firstborn. Occasionally, popular Israeli songs such as "Jerusalem of Gold" are sung at circumcision ceremonies as well (ibid.).

The main function of the pizmonim seems to be as a musical marker of the beginning of the circumcision ritual, employing melodies that establish an appropriate mood. Other than a greeting of welcome in Hebrew that is sometimes sung to the mohel as he assumes his place and prepares his instruments, little singing marks the rest of the ceremony. Traditionally, the baby is brought forward by the paternal grandmother if he is the firstborn son; a second grandson is carried by the maternal grandmother. The grandmother passes the baby to the father, who then gives him to the paternal grandfather, whose namesake he is and upon whose lap he is held during the ceremony. The circumcision itself is brief, with the completion of the medical procedure marked by the raising of a bloody cloth. Mandatory ritual texts read include the Shema, several prayers of blessing including the Sheheḥiyanu, and a rendition of the Kaddish. Following the ceremony, everyone present greets the family with congratulations and partakes of a festive buffet.

A small number of pizmonim have been written to celebrate the birth of girls, although "they are not as numerous as the songs for boys" (S. Catton, 30 October 1984). A naming ceremony for a baby girl ("Lezeved habbat," Dobrinsky 1986:3) is found on p. 540 of SUHV. Notable among pizmonim dedicated to newborn girls is no. 231, "Yeromem Ṣuri," composed by Moses Ashear in honor of the birth of his own twin granddaughters, Sally and Betty, fathered by his son Joseph. Ashear embeds the names of the twin girls in the third verse before the end of the song.

> **sa li** maʿani lekha akra, **beti** umeʿoni haḥesh yased bimherah.

It may be significant that Albert Ashear recalled this pizmon in the course of showing me family pictures, including one of Moses Ashear and his twin granddaughters; in this case, the photograph cued memories of the pizmon. It is further noteworthy that pizmon no. 231 is composed in maqām nahāwand, set to a "Fantasy Nahāwand" (A. Ashear, 19 July 1989). In part because they are not restricted to maqām ṣaba, pizmonim written for the birth of girls may be performed on other occasions. Indeed, one member of the community mentioned hearing an unnamed pizmon in honor of a baby girl sung at a wedding.

Many pizmonim have been composed to celebrate weddings. Like the circumcision and bar mitzvah pizmonim, these songs are sung when the groom is called forward in the synagogue the week prior to the wedding ceremony. An index in SUHV (p. 570) lists pizmonim in seven major maqāmāt appropriate for celebrating joyous occasions and weddings; usually a pizmon in the maqām of the week would be selected. One particularly well known wedding pizmon, "Melekh Raḥaman," is discussed in the prelude to chapter 6. According to one authority, marriage ceremonies and their pizmonim tend to be performed in maqām ʿajam (E. Labaton, 26 December 1984).

Pizmonim in the Liturgical Context

We have seen that pizmonim are associated with life cycle occasions and are performed in multiple contexts both at home and in the synagogue. A similar situation extends to pizmonim whose primary associations are to formal liturgical observances in the synagogue but which can also be sung in domestic settings.

Most frequently mentioned because of their importance are pizmonim sung on major holidays—including the pilgrimage festivals (Sukkot, Passover, Shavuot), Hanukkah, and Purim—collectively termed "*lamoʿadim*" (H. Kaire, 14 March 1985).[13] These pizmonim are arranged by number and incipit in a special index of SUHV (pp. 571–72). The performance of any of these songs is associated with one of the holidays:

> They're going to be saying the holidays. This one here? [Referring to pizmon no. 435, "Attah Marom," in maqām sīkāh] This is for the *moʿadim,* for all the holidays. It is for *bayom ṭovah,* a happy day, a *simḥa* [lit., joyful occasion]. *Yom ṭov* is the holiday, any holiday. It associates with the holiday. (H. Kaire, 14 March 1985)

Some songs are associated with specific holidays because of their textual content. For example, no. 361, "Mi Yemallel," is sung during Passover because it contains references to the ten plagues which were visited upon Egypt (ibid.). Songs that refer to the prophet Elijah, many of them set in maqām ṣaba and discussed above in their common use for the circumcision ceremonies, are also associated with Passover, during which prominent references are made to Elijah at the Seder (Passover eve home ritual and meal). For example, pizmon no. 380, "Yaḥish Mevasser," which mentions the prophet Elijah, was sung at the reception following the Sabbath morning service during Passover (Shelemay fieldnotes, 2 April 1988).

It must be noted that the holiday songs must be sung not just because they are appropriate to the day, but also to insure that they are passed on by those who remember them:

> This we do, improvise, that's all. Because it sounds good, because you see, then we review all this, the pizmonim that they never used before, gives the people a chance to know it. I know the [songs of the] composer, that Moses Ashear, see. And the people that came from Syria know [songs of] the other, Ḥakham Raphael Taboush. And one knows one and the one just doesn't know the other one. (H. Kaire, 14 March 1985)

The extent to which individual holiday pizmonim are remembered and the memories they evoke are surprising. An elderly woman who was born in Aleppo and immigrated to the United States at age 15 in 1923 was present during the singing of pizmonim at the 1988 Catskills Passover observance. She afterward remarked that she remembered the melody of the Passover pizmon no. 380, noting that it had been a popular song in the period before her own wedding more than sixty years earlier. Only later, she noted, was it set as a pizmon (Shelemay fieldnotes, 2 April 1988).

Holiday pizmonim are sung in the synagogue during the Sabbath ritual, alongside songs marking other special occasions:

> You know when [the pizmonim] are sung? We have it every Saturday. . . . Come one day to [synagogue] Shaare Zion, you'd be amazed. First of all, they have probably ten occasions for the day. There'd be a bat [daughter],

> there'd be a ben [son], a boy, a girl, two weddings, a guy is going to get married, a guy's engaged, a guy comes back from his honeymoon. . . . So for each and every time that a person goes to a synagogue, every time he goes up to the Torah, they sing a song for him. The next guy comes, it'll be a bat, a different song for a girl. (M. Kairey, 6 November 1984)

Pizmonim in the Home

The context that most directly connects liturgical and domestic pizmon performance is the Sebet, a festive Sabbath afternoon gathering of family and friends usually held in a private home. Sebets are generally held outside the home only when the guests are too numerous to be accommodated or when the hosts live beyond easy walking distance from the synagogue. In these cases, a Sebet may be held in a synagogue auditorium or in a local catering hall.

> When a groom is going to get married, they give him the honor by calling him up to the reading of the scrolls. They sing for him, and then they go home and they make a little party. They call that "Sebet." "Sebet" is in Arabic "Shabbat," the Sabbath. They invite all their close friends. Sometimes they have over a hundred people. And they have very nice food prepared for them and they spend about two or three hours singing in this book, this little book that we put out [SUHV]. They have all types of songs. They sing, sometimes they dance. They do the same thing when they have an engagement, when they have a bar mitzvah, or when they have a new child, whether it be a boy or girl. (S. Catton, 30 October 1984)

The Sebet is perhaps the most ubiquitous Syrian domestic observance in Brooklyn and the event most instrumental in the continued transmission of pizmonim. The observance evidently emerged in early twentieth century Brooklyn following the period of immigration (J. Kassin, 30 March 1989). The Sebet is not generally performed among Syrian Jews in Israel. Rather, they gather after the Sabbath morning service in the synagogue for a reception, the "oneg shabbat," which does not involve the prolonged singing of pizmonim (Y. Bozo, 14 March 1993). Another Israeli cantor was familiar with the term "Sebet" only as meaning "Sabbath" in Arabic and observed that in Israel, pizmonim and other songs are sung only at the "seʿudah shelishit," the traditional "third Sabbath meal" eaten at the close of the Sabbath day (S. Shemi, 21 March 1993).

Elsewhere in the New World, traditions of teaching and singing pizmonim after lunch on the Sabbath are known, if not as elaborate as those in Brooklyn. Cantor Isaac Cain of Mexico City teaches his grandchildren pizmonim after lunch on the Sabbath, but not as part of a formal Sebet. Cain's wife Ruth was born and raised in New York and is familiar with the Brooklyn Sebet tradition. When asked if they observe the Sebet in Mexico, she replied: "You're talking about a Sebet, where after lunch they sit around and everybody sings? No, we don't do it that way. . . . He [her husband, Isaac Cain] just goes into a room we have there and they sit around and he teaches each [grandson] separately" (R. Cain, 7 September 1992). Ruth Cain went on to note, however, that people would hold a Sebet in Mexico City if there's "an affair . . . before a wedding . . . or for any happy reason" (ibid.).

The late twentieth century Brooklyn Sebet is a festive event. In order to accommodate a large crowd of family and friends, families often clear their public rooms of furniture. One room, usually the living room, will then be set with long tables and folding chairs for the men. Plates of food and bottles of whiskey and beer are set out on each table, but family members or others go back and forth bearing additional dishes and drinks. The women remain in a separate room, usually the dining room where the table is filled with buffet dishes and chairs line the walls. As men enter the house, they greet the host family and then go directly to the long tables. With the exception of a few very young girls, women do not enter the room where the singing takes place.

Virtually without exception, the Sebet is opened with a rousing rendition of pizmon no. 238, "Yaḥid Ram." One man notes that

> It's the opening song that they usually sing for whenever they have happy occasions in the house. (H. Kaire, 17 February 1988)

According to another, "this is the opening music . . . and if you hear the music you'll see why—it's catchy, it's fast" (J. Saff, 4 December 1984).

"Yaḥid Ram" was composed by Rabbi Raphael Taboush, who has woven his own name into the text of the second stanza as the words *refa El,* which means "O God, heal." The melody is borrowed from an unidentified instrumental prelude undoubtedly popular in Taboush's time, set in maqām bayāti.[14]

This pizmon was likely written in honor of a man named Joseph, since the end of the third stanza reads "Have mercy upon me, speedily, for the sake of the House of Joseph, Your righteous one." The name of Joseph also appears in the Hebrew acrostic. The text of the song (see CD contents, track 9), with its references to raising the voice in praise and exultation, is an apt choice for leading off the Sebet (musical example 4.4, "Yaḥid Ram"). It also contains a more esoteric theme of personal and national redemption, alluding to the coming of the Messianic Age, when (in the words of the Alenu prayer) "the world will be set right by the rule of God." However, the more obvious references to singing together "as in the days of old," which explicitly bring the Syrian community into focus, also sets forth a hope for the future where "every one of them shall sing."

Pizmon "Yaḥid Ram" is almost always followed by no. 239, "Nora Varam," another Taboush pizmon which both incorporates the poet's name and hints at the shortest prayer in the Bible, *El na refa na lah,* "Oh God, pray heal her now" (Numbers 12:13). The text of "Nora Varam" calls on the "supreme, living God" to "heal my sickness and my pains." A subsequent line asking God to "Banish the son of Hagar," an apparent reference to Ishmael, the son of Abraham and Sarah's handmaid, is one of the few such references in the pizmonim to the progenitor of the Arabs.

The remaining pizmonim for the Sebet are chosen by the individuals leading it, with consideration for the preferences of the host family and the occasion at hand. The general order will be the customary Sabbath pizmonim, a few "heavies" (that is, musically demanding numbers), and then special songs for the day (M. Tawil, 2 April 1988). A pizmon that is almost always included at the Sebet is no. 246, "Maʿuzzi," set to a classical Arab love song, "Bi-iladhī askara." The Arab source tune is a *tawshiḥ* (another name for the muwashshāḥ) in maqām bayāti. "Maʿuzzi," transcribed with the original Arabic text in Shave 1988:15, is such a popular pizmon that one individual termed it the "high point" of the Sebet; singers will frequently try to outperform each other by singing the third verse an octave higher (D. Shasha, March 1988). "Maʿuzzi" is always sung near the end of the Sebet, providing a counterbalance to "Yaḥid Ram" at the beginning.

At traditional Sebets, such as the one described above, the crowded conditions and noisy conversation make it difficult for women outside the main room to hear the singing. Additionally, many more men than women frequent the Sebets, with women attending mainly the ones held in their own homes or those of close relatives or friends:

> It's been a recent custom that the women had attended the Sebets. . . . You see, when the Sebets first started, when I think they first came over . . . the men used to get together after shul and they would maybe make a Kiddush and have some maṣṣah [hors d'oeuvres] and they would sing. . . . At that time there were only men that attended these Sebets. It

Example 4.4. "Yaḥid Ram"

Example 4.4. *(continued)*

Example 4.4. *(continued)*

was just the women in the family that attended the Sebets. But how did they attend them? Not sitting down with the men in the room, singing pizmonim, not at all. The women were in back helping serve. . . . I think that many, many years ago they didn't have them catered the way they do today, even though today many of them still prepare their own. But I think once they do prepare it—once—they say never again. A Sebet used to be twenty, thirty, forty men, maybe fifty men, which I imagine years ago was a large Sebet. Today, *in shā' Allah* (Arabic, "if God wills") they [have] two and three hundred people at a Sebet. It's really something. (J. Kassin, 30 March 1989)

The Sebet has played a major role in Syrian life in Brooklyn, providing a regular locus for music-making associated with the major events of religious and family life:

> It is a very necessary part of our, you might say, socializing. When we have a Kiddush, I mean a happy occasion, or Shabbat or on a holiday, what can we do? We can't use instruments, we don't use any other electrified type of music. So what do you do really in a social affair? Outside of talking, talking, talking, talking to someone? We sing! And you come, we put the very nice table, we put the drinks, and we start singing the pizmonim. So we want . . . our younger people to grow into it, to be familiar with it, so that they do not feel estranged and feel "What kind of oddball would do it?" And, they have grown into it. So this is the way we train them. And it's come a long way. You'll be surprised, they all are very interested. And they still go for this in a big way. They like it very much. This is the way. (M. Tawil, 6 November 1984)

Thus the Sebet has preserved both pizmonim and community interaction:

> Some of the boys are beginning to learn because they realize when they come to a Sebet, that's how it originally starts. They come to the Sebet and they want to take part in it, how do they take part? Just to eat? It's meaningless. What is part of the festivity? The songs and to be part of that. When they become 13, 14, 15, they begin to take part. They do bring in a lot of the Hebrew songs, but you always find that after the Hebrew songs are finished, what comes next? The pizmonim. (S. Schweky, 27 January 1988)

It is clear that the Sebet has served primarily to transmit pizmonim among men. Women insure that the pizmonim continue to be performed by perpetuating the Sebet and other domestic occasions at which songs are traditionally sung. Of particular import is the fact that women prepare and serve the food at the Sebet, while men sing at this event. If men's domain is song, women's is a complementary one of cooking and food. Moreover, in Ḥalabi memory, as in life, food and song merge as closely linked modalities of experience:

> Everybody knows everything, what they do on holidays, they have certain foods on different holidays. On Purim, we make kibbeh, meatballs, with mushrooms. We always have that, they are best on Purim. And we used to sing, get drunk. Oh there's a lot of songs. We used to sing in my family. There's a lot of nice songs. I used to know them all. . . . Things are not the same like they should be. For Rosh Hashanah we used to make rice and sweet sauce, you can't make a sour sauce. Everything sweet, you know. And different songs. Every holiday has a song. Passover had their own songs, and . . . Shavuot, they have their own songs. And the funny part is on Saturday, when they sing the songs they bring in the melody that goes in with the time. (S. Cohen, 28 February 1985)

Historical evidence suggests that the strong connection between music and food may derive from precedents in pre-modern Aleppo. Not only was the availability and cost of food an "ever-present" concern, but

> on another level, food figured in culture as a pleasure, even an art, and was rich in symbolic meaning. One resident gave expression to these sentiments in a long poem praising the local cuisine and its delicious creations.[15] Themes associated with food ran through the popular lore, expressing appreciation of good eating as well as a keen consciousness of the symbolic and vital aspects of food. Eating was most immediately associated with home and family. The community had no restaurant culture; going out to eat was an unfamiliar practice. Food was also the cornerstone of hospitality and celebration. (A. Marcus 1989:227–28)

Through a close look at food and music, one arrives at both a conjunction of the sensorium and a shared semantic field for aesthetics: both the pizmonim and Syrian food should be "sweet," not sour. Indeed, *Sheer Ushbahah Hallel Ve-Zimrah* is dedicated to the memory of "the sweet singer of Israel" [Moses Ashear] and to the holy songs "which are sweeter even than honey and the honeycomb" (see figure 1.1). Songs sung in the various maqāmāt should be "sweetened" by the condiments of "improvisation," just as food can be sweetened with sugar. In this way the memory of song is reinforced and strengthened through those of food, with which it shares a system of associations. The linking of the senses, which is clearly present in the synesthesic and inter-sense modalities discussed in chapter 3, provides insight into ways in which song is connected to other basic sensory processes.

If song and food interact in practice and in memory, they are further inscribed and preserved in written community records in similar ways. In the past, "the art of cooking was . . . passed on from one generation of housewives to the next by oral transmission rather than by written recipes or cookbooks" (A. Marcus 1989:228). Yet, like the pizmonim, recipes have moved from the oral tradition to writing in the form of a Syrian cookbook published in Brooklyn. Just as SUHV contains blank pages at the back to accommodate the texts of new pizmonim to be performed, the women of the Syrian community have published a cookbook with blank pages at the end of each section (*Festival of Holidays: Recipe Book* 1987) so that "everyone can add her own recipes" (S. Schweky, 27 January 1988).

Pizmonim for Special Occasions

Pizmonim are also performed at a variety of special occasions, ranging from parties to informal get-togethers to public concerts. Since these events are not held on the Sabbath or holidays, instrumental accompaniment can be used. Additionally, there are clear linguistic shifts, with Hebrew texts sung at occasions with religious import and Arabic used at purely social get-togethers (J. Kassin, 30 March 1989).

Parties for occasions such as wedding anniversaries (as discussed in the prelude to chapter 3) often feature an ensemble of Arab musicians to accompany the pizmonim. With most of the melodies well known to Arab musicians, and the songs sung in their original Arabic versions, music-making at these events necessarily highlights its Arab roots. However, a predilection for classical Arab songs of earlier dates and the maintenance of the small takht ensemble differentiate New World Arab culture from that in the modern Middle East (D. Tawil, 11 December 1984).

Special musical evenings, held in conjunction with certain Jewish holidays, can also provide occasions on which pizmonim are sung. For example, "Id-el-Fur: The Purim Evening—Aleppian Style" was held March 22, 1988, at a Tel Aviv synagogue and included both the reading of the Megillah and "entertainment" by Cantor David Shiro with choir and orchestra. Special Purim pizmonim were performed, including "Mi Kamokha" in Arabic. The World Center for Aleppo Jews Traditional Culture organized this Purim evening, issued a special booklet with details of Purim traditions in Aleppo, and distributed a videotape of the event (M. Cohen 1988:24–25).

The establishment of institutions within the Syrian community has also led to a range of public occasions for which pizmonim are commissioned and performed. One such event was discussed in the prelude to chapter 1, the celebration of Charlie Serouya's service to the youth of Congregation Magen David, and the composition of the pizmon "Ṣur Yah El." Other such occasions marked in song include the dedication of Brooklyn's Ahi Ezer Congregation, for which pizmon no. 202, "Shiru Shirah Ḥadashah," was composed in autumn 1959. The melody for this pizmon was borrowed from "God Bless America," the anthem composed by Irving Berlin and popularized in an Armistice Day concert, November 11, 1938, by the singer Kate Smith (Bergreen 1990: 370–71).[16] As the song became enormously popular, sung across the country in schools, churches, at political rallies, and on national holidays (Barrett 1994:173), it no doubt became equally well known among Syrian Jews, who were heavily involved both as members of the United States Armed Forces and in war efforts at home.

Even for occasions when no new pizmonim are commissioned, songs will still be sung. A salient example is the pizmon concert in honor of Mickey Kairey, described in the prelude to chapter 1. In addition to the use of "Ṣur Yah El," the program for this event featured a series of pizmonim and bakkashot.

Conclusion

To return to issues raised at the beginning of this chapter, a genre can be defined as "a set of musical events (real or possible) whose course is governed by a definite set of socially accepted rules. . . . In particular a certain 'musical event' may be situated in the intersection of two or more genres, and therefore belong to each of these at the same time" (Fabbri 1982:52). The Syrian case study makes a strong case for an approach that privileges the social event over formal structure and indicates "that a form is *not* sufficient to define a genre" (ibid. 55). Indeed, during interviews, individual singers within the Syrian community demonstrate the manner in which the text of a given bakkashah or pizmon could be sung to the melody of another song in a different maqām.[17] In the case of Syrian Jewish musical practice, songs technically classified within different genres are performed together.

In the end, it is less the formal properties of the pizmonim that are meaningful than their connection to so many aspects of Syrian life.

> Some of the songs that they sing in holidays and happy occasions, it has to be an occasion for them to sing it. Like Passover they sing certain songs, and Hanukkah and all, like when there's a bris or there's a wedding or bar mitzvah, there's all these different songs they sing for those occasions. In the songs it's related to the event, whether it's a bris. In the bris . . . they mention Abraham and the sacrifice . . . so all that is in the song, you see. And then Passover, the way when they're crossing the Red Sea and all that. All that is related to the song. So they sing it and think of the holiday. And Shavuot when the Ten Commandments were given they sing their song. . . . And if you say something else, they jump on top of your head. You have to say the song for that day. So that's how critical they are. . . . Like, so now, before the holidays, a week before sometime, they start to sing it to get in the mood for the holiday. (H. Kaire, 17 February 1988)

The pizmonim thus are compound aural memories. They are at once a vital part of life as lived, connecting moments in the present to broader themes and historical memory. In this way, the individual life and single song are transposed into a different plane of meaning. Music enables this pivot between present and past, and between the mundane and the sacred:

> The way a person feels is important. He can only pray with all his soul when he feels good. Music is important to this. . . . All [songs] are imbued with feeling and respect for the Kabbalah. Psalms, like in the King David psalms, are always talking about singing. Music is good to uplift the soul. Mysticism and feeling of the soul, something you get through music. (S. Catton, 29 November 1991)

In the end, pizmonim exist for individuals in the community not as bracketed musical genres but as lived experience, absorbed into the fabric of everyday life:

> I never really thought totally consciously about them. They are just part of my life. On Saturday it's part of the Sabbath, the Sebet. On the holidays, it's part of the holidays. [So now that you mention it, my eyes are beginning to open.] . . . I love it! It's part of me! It's not that I'm thinking about it, that I want to perpetuate it, no!! I love it, it is part of my home, it's part of my customs, it's part of my food, it's part of my holiday, in other words, this is all combined together. I do not mentally separate it. (S. Schweky, 27 January 1988)

PRELUDE

Yeḥidah Hitnaʿari

On October 23, 1984, Joseph Saff arrived at a seminar room at New York University to discuss the Syrian musical tradition with eleven members of the NYU Ethnomusicology Seminar. During that first semester of our research we had invited several prominent members of the Ḥalabi community with strong musical interests to visit the class and to introduce us to aspects of the pizmon tradition they thought important for us to know (see plate 20).

Joseph Saff brought along with him his two adult sons, Eddie (Ezra) and Isaac (Yitzhak). He told us he wanted to discuss, in his own words, "Arabic music as applied in pizmonim, bakkashot, and petiḥot." In the course of his visit, he talked at length about and sang a pizmon that Cantor Moses Ashear had composed for him in honor of his bar mitzvah.[1] The English translation of this pizmon, "Yeḥidah Hitnaʿari," no. 291, contains references to the occasion at hand as well as allusions to the particular situation of the Saff (Ṣafadiyyah) family.

Yeḥidah Hitnaʿari

A song for the Bar Mitzvah celebration of the gracious student,
Joseph Ezra Saff (Ṣafadiyyah), 13 Adar 5693 (1933).

And it shall be for a token upon thy hand;
and for frontlets between thine eyes.

You, the one and only, stir yourself,
An end to your trouble, enough, enough.
Put on your strength and awake,
And come to me, to me.
Eat up my honey with my honeycomb,
In the garden of my fields, my fields.
Pasture my kids.

The God of my father, my help
Who rides the heavens, the heavens,

Let Him adorn me with my crown,
And [make like] suckling babes my enemies, my enemies.
He will continue to gather my scattered ones,
For they have lasted long, my days, my days,
And I await my salvation.
You, the one and only . . .

Rejoice with me, my mother,
My brothers and my sisters.
For on this day today I enter,
On the [first] day of the fourteenth of my years,
To serve Him with my prayer,
In my heart and on my lips,
With the community of my congregation.
You, the one and only . . .

A crown I shall put between my eyes,
And a sign I will bind upon my arm,
To the One who performed miracles,
For the people of Mordekhai, my uncle.
Set your eye upon me, Lord,
For I am left alone,
There is no one to set up my curtains.
You, the one and only . . .

Strengthen, O God, upright and feared,
The bars of my gates,
And I shall see the Tishbi running,
Flying, leaping upon the mountains.
He seeks a forceful vision,
For he will remove my flock
To the place of my abode,
You, the one and only . . .

Praised is the One who has kept me alive
and lengthened my days;
The One who has preserved me
that I may start my performance of commanded things.
He let me reach this time,
[A time] when He'll forgive my debts.
And so, [to Him,] I dedicate my life.
You, the one and only . . .

May you, my teacher, be blessed.
May there be great peace for your children.
May you rejoice in them and be kept alive.
Like this, too, your son-in-law.

Let not the blessing of a layman
be light in your eyes.
Peace to you, my gentlemen.
You, the one and only . . .

(Translated by Geoffrey Goldberg and James Robinson)

Joseph Saff's discussion of "Yeḥidah Hitnaʿari" is presented below, with numbers inserted to mark the corresponding place in the facsimile of the Hebrew text (figure 5.1).

> I would like to elaborate now on pizmonim. Why and how and when the poet is going to make a song. As I said, when one is bar mitzvahed, when one is married—whenever there's a happy occasion in the family—the poet would write words fitting a certain particular song, which is popular of the day. And very important, in that song—in the poem that he wrote—he would mention the name of the groom—oddly they don't mention some places the wife's name—the father, the uncle, the brother, at times, a sister. He would use those Hebrew words within the poem. . . . All Hebrew names have a meaning, Yitzhak means "to laugh." Yosef, Joseph, means "that which will increase." And Ezra, my father's name, means "to assist," and the like of it. . . .
>
> Most of us do have Hebrew names, [so] when he uses Hebrew poems, naturally the word then would have a double meaning. It would be the meaning of the word in the text of the poem and also, for the person that he's honoring in that song. . . .
>
> And when the occasion arose, they would write songs for the occasion, whatever it was. Just by accident, I have something with me. Just by accident. When I was thirteen years old, Mr. Ashear wrote a pizmon for me. Now, how is anybody going to know the words of these songs? Here's what he'd do. You can see how old this is, this is 1933. . . . I'm going to read the words to you. (1) *Vehayah Leʾot al Yadekhah, uletotafot ben enekha:* This is just a biblical saying about tefillin [phylacteries]—this is my Bar Mitzvah. The tefillin will be a sign on my arm and between my eyes.[2] (2) *Shir lebar miṣvah*—Song for the Bar Mitzvah; (3) *Lehatalmid*—To the student; (4) *Ha naʿim*—good looking! (5) *Yosef*—myself; (6) *Ezra*—My father's name; (7) *Ṣafadiyyah*—which is my former name. For business reasons we cut it down to Saff. (8) Abbreviation, "May God keep him alive." (9) *Adar*—He puts the date here.[3] (10) And he tells you the maqām of the song—*Bayāt(i) nawā.* (11) And he says, *Siman*—the signs of the song, *Yosef,* which are these words next to Yosef, *Ḥazak* is the next word, *Barukh umvorakh* (lit. "Joseph, strong, blessed, and blessed"). (12) And here he mentions "laḥan", he tells you the name of the Arabic song, that he got the music from to write the song. *Laḥan*—"oh the rose tree, your roots are on the water."

ב״ה

[1]והיה לאות על ידכה

ולטוטפת בין עיניך

[2]שיר לבר מצוה

[3]להתלמיד [4]הנעים [5]יוסף [6]עזרא [7]צפדייה הי״ו [8]י״ג [9]אדר ש׳ תרצ״ג

[10]ביאת נאווה

[11]סימן יוסף חזק ברוך ומבורך

[12]לחן יא סגרת אל אזהארי שרושך עלא אל מי

[13]יהידה התנערי	[14]די לצרותך די די	[15]לבשי עוזך ועורי	[16]ובואי עדי עדי
[17]אכלי דבשי עם יערי	בגן שדי שדי	[18]ורעי את גדיותי	יחידה וכו׳
[19]ואלהי אבי [20]עזרי	[21]רוכב שמי שמי	יכתירני בנזרי	וינוקון קמי קמי
[22]יוסף לקבוץ פזורי	כי ארכו ימי ימי	ומקוה [23]ישועותי	יחידה וכו׳
שמחי עמי [24]ילדתי	אחי וגם אחיותי	כי היום זה נכנסתי	ביום יד משנותי
[25]לעבדו בתפלתי	בלבי ובשפתי	עם עדת [26]קהלותי	יחידה וכו׳
פאר בין עיני אשים	ואות אקשור על ידי	[27]למי שעשה נסים	[28]לעם מרדכי דודי
בי אדוני עינך שים	הן נשארתי לבדי	אין מקים יריעותי	יחידה וכו׳
[29]חזק אל ישר נערץ	את בריחי שערי	ואחזה לתשבי רץ	עף לדלג על הרי
[30]וישאל חזון נמרץ	[31]כי ימשה את עדרי	לנוה משכנותי	יחידה וכו׳
ברוך שהחייני	והאריך ימותי	ואשר קימני	להתחיל במצותי
לזמן זה הגיעני	ובו יסלח חובותי	לכן אקדיש עתותי	יחידה וכו׳
ומבורך מורי תהיה	[32]רב שלום לבניך	בהם תשמח ותחיה	וכזה חתניך
ברכת הדיוט אל תהיה	נקלה בעיניך	[33]שלום לכם רבותי	

FIGURE 5.1. Facsimile of pizmon "Yeḥidah Hitnaʿari." Courtesy Joseph Saff.

Now he would print, perhaps two, three, or four hundred of these and of course he had a chorus with him. He would teach them the song the Saturday before I was bar mitzvahed. They would all learn that song—three or four people—and then he would pass this out in the synagogue to the two or three hundred people that were there. And when I go up to the Torah, they would sing this song.

By accident I have this [the original Hebrew text, figure 5.1]. I'm saving it. In my drawer at home I have one envelope—"Joe Saff personals"—this is one of the things I have in my personals.

Now, he had an art, he was such a poet—he had an art of writing poems that suited the person for whom the song was being written. Usually, it was always praise to the Almighty. The opening words of this song (13) *Yeḥidah Hitnaʿari*—"you are alone the one"—*hitnaʿari* is my mother—"the one who carried me." Now I must tell you a little bit of my history so you can see how smart, how wonderful this man was when he put [the] words.

My father died when I was seven—the oldest one was nine, and there were four beneath us—I'm not saying this for sympathy—I'm just trying to bring it up to a point. It was very hard for my mother—she bereaved something awful. Now the old Syrian Jewish custom to mourn was pretty much the way Catholics mourn, which has changed in my community now. It was common for a woman that was mourning to wear a black dress anywhere from six months to nine months to ten months. Black dress, black shoes, black hosiery. And not to go out to the street the first two or three months because she's supposed to be in mourning. This was pretty common. In my mother's case, this was because of the way she bereaved my father or kids or everything else, he was forty-two and she was maybe middle thirties. I don't know if my sons know this? But, she took it very hard. Where black is normally worn for nine months—my father died in 1927—they used to cover the sofas and club chairs in the living room also with black—for two to three months because that's a sign of mourning. Now mother did not remove the black covering on the sofa and club chairs until 1937—which is ten years after my father passed away.

This song was written in 1933. Instead of staying indoors for three months, my mother stayed home indoors for ten years. Never went into the street. She had friends, she had sisters—I used to shop for her or let's say holidays came around—the children needed clothing, they'd take us out, they bought us clothing, [she] just never went out of the house. One instance I remember—maybe the fifth or sixth year after my father passed away, my aunt was very seriously ill—her sister—and she wanted to go visit her. And how dare she go out into the street during the day? Now this is all in her mind, nobody's limiting her to this. So we went out 8 or 9 o'clock at night, winter night through a side street to go to my aunt's house, so nobody would see my mother in the street. You got that picture.

Now these are the words that Moses Ashear wrote for my Bar Mitzvah. *Yeḥidah Hitnaʿari*—I'll try not to crack up. "You're alone, my carrier—my mother who carried me. (14) *Dai,* which means "enough," *leṣarotekh*—your troubles, *dai, dai*—so he's repeating "dai" three times. (15) *Livshi uzzekh veʿuri*—"awaken your courage and wear it"—"wear," in other words, "bring back your courage." Don't forget this is poetry, it's not literal words. (16) *Uvo'i adai adai,* "and come to me"—in other words, "don't ignore me, be part of your family." (17) *Ikhli devashi im yari*—"it's about time you started to eat or taste honey and honeycomb," in other words, taste some sweetness in life rather than this bereavement, this constant wearing yourself down and crying and bitterly crying for years.

He was aware of all this so that's how he got this. (18) *Uri et gediyyotai,* "lead me as you would a group." The next stanza, (19) *v-elohei avi,* "and the Lord of my father Ezri." Now this is the first time the name is mentioned. My father's name was Ezra. But he uses (20) *Ezri,* which is significant of "Ezra."[4] (21) *Rokhev shemei shemei,* "who gave me my name." He's overriding my name.

And then he continues on, I mean I'm just trying to show you parts of the song—to show you how this great poet was able to take a situation and to write words which are really not praise to the—later on there are praises to the Almighty in this song. But he was able to take that song and to write words to it fitting our particular situation.

Now if you'll look at this here, you see my father Ezra—(22) *Yosef,* which means "to increase"—my name, Joseph is I. (23) *Yeshuotai* is my uncle Yeshuo. (24) He did not mention my mother's name, but he mentions *Yoladti,* "the one that gave birth to me." (25) *Leʿovdo* is my uncle, Ovadiah. (26) *Kehil,* I don't know why that's there, I really don't. The next, (27) *Nissim* is my uncle—Nassim. (28) *Mordekhai* is my uncle, Mordekhai. (29) *Ḥazak el yashar* is El Yashar, who used to be a very close friend of the family. (31) [*Yimsheh*] Moshe is my uncle, (30) [*Yishal*] Shaul is another close friend of the family and (32) *Shalom,* oh there it is, I've never noticed that Shalom, is my mother's maiden name. And the last words of the song are (33) *shalom lakhem rabbotai*—"peace be with you, my dear friends, my audience." That's the song.

When Rabbi Ashear composed a song for this fellow at his son's bar mitzvah, he used to get paid for this, of course. He didn't do this for nothing. The poet, he went to expense of printing—he took time to put words and he printed and he sang it and all—that was a source of income. . . . In our instance, we couldn't afford to engage him—nobody knows why he ever composed it for us. Maybe out of sentimental feelings.[5]

Joseph Saff visited our seminar once again, on December 4, 1984. He discussed the maqām system and briefly noted that "my song that I sang for you is bayāt." Joe provided little other information about the strophic Arab song from which it derived. He believes that Moses Ashear chose the melody from among Arab songs he knew, selecting a simple folk song "that was not very popular" (J. Saff, 10 September 1996).

Albert Ashear, the late son of Cantor Moses, remembered that his father had composed "Yeḥidah Hitnaʿari" because Joe's father had been a friend of his. Ashear also recalled the difficult family situation conveyed in the text:

> He passed away very early. She was a widow and she wore black for fifteen years, a long time. So we made up the song for her son. It told her Yeḥidah Hitnaʿari, "You the lonely one, put on your makeup, take off your mourning clothes and come to me." Very nice words in that. (A. Ashear, 19 July 1989)

While Saff remembers that "Yeḥidah Hitnaʿari" was sung in the years immediately after its composition, the song slowly fell out of use. Its neglect evidently rests with shortcomings in its melody, which is considered both difficult and lacking in interest. Even Joseph Saff, when asked to perform the song, replied:

> You don't mind if I don't sing the whole song? Because, I'll tell you why. After you sing the first stanza, the music is just repetitious down the line and you'll get bored with it. Honestly, I'm bored with it. I never sing the whole song. I usually sing the first, second, third, fifth, and last [verses]. (J. Saff, 4 December 1984)

When asked if the pizmon might lend itself to any sort of elaboration or improvisation, he replied,

> No, the music doesn't apply itself. The only thing I can possibly do there, were I to, would be improvise in between, when I finish a stanza. I am singing bayāt. So I can improvise in the maqām of bayāt, my own music that I will create as I go along. But there's no word there that can be taken to be repeated. . . . This music does not lend itself to it. (ibid.)

Perhaps not surprisingly, Joseph Saff's pizmon has virtually disappeared from the repertory. Only he carries it in active memory, performing it for our seminar on October 23, 1984, and at a subsequent evening "music session" on February 21, 1985. On the latter occasion, the pizmon was preceded by a petiḥah and layālī performed by Rabbi Shimon Alouf and accompanied by musical instruments. Otherwise, the pizmon is not performed within any liturgical or social context that might insure its continued transmission. In this instance, however, "Yeḥidah Hitnaʿari" has been performed for and documented by scholars, a new context that will insure that Joe Saff's pizmon will not be forgotten.

Example 5. Yeḥidah Hitnaʿari

Example 5. *(continued)*

יְחִידָה הִתְנַעֲרִי, דַּי לְצָרוֹתֵךְ דַּי דַּי, לִבְשִׁי עֻזֵּךְ וְעוּרִי,
וּבוֹאִי עֲדִי עֲדַי, אִכְלִי דִּבְשִׁי עִם יַעְרִי, בְּגַן שָׁדַי
שָׁדַי, וּרְעִי אֶת גְּדִיּוֹתַי: יחידה

וֵאלֹהֵי אָבִי עֶזְרִי, רוֹכֵב שְׁמֵי שָׁמַי, יַכְתִּירֵנִי בְּנִזְרִי,
וִינַקֵּון קָמַי קָמַי, יוֹסִיף לִקְבּוֹץ פְּזוּרַי, כִּי אָרְכוּ
יָמַי יָמַי, וּמְקַוֶּה יְשׁוּעוֹתַי: יחידה

שִׂמְחִי עִמִּי יוֹלַדְתִּי, אַחַי וְגַם אַחְיוֹתַי, כִּי הַיּוֹם זֶה
נִכְנַסְתִּי, בְּיוֹם יַ״ד מִשְׁנוֹתַי, לְעָבְדוֹ בִּתְפִלָּתִי,
בְּלִבִּי וּבִשְׂפָתַי, עִם עֲדַת קְהִלּוֹתַי: יחידה

פְּאֵר בֵּין עֵינַי אָשִׂים, וְאוֹת אֶקְשׁוֹר עַל יָדִי, לְמִי
שֶׁעָשָׂה נִסִּים, לְעַם מָרְדְּכַי דּוֹדִי, בִּי אֲדוֹנִי עֵינָךְ
שִׂים, הֵן נִשְׁאַרְתִּי לְבַדִּי, אֵין מֵקִים יְרִיעוֹתַי:
יחידה

חֲזָק אֵל יָשָׁר נֶעֱרָץ, אֶת בְּרִיחֵי שְׁעָרַי, וְאֶחֱזֶה לְתִשְׁבִּי
רָץ, עָף לְדַלֵּג עַל הָרַי, וְיִשְׁאַל חָזוֹן נִמְרָץ, כִּי
יִמְשֶׁה אֶת עֲדָרַי, לִנְוֵה מִשְׁכְּנוֹתַי: יחידה

בָּרוּךְ שֶׁהֶחֱיָנִי, וְהֶאֱרִיךְ יְמוֹתַי, וַאֲשֶׁר קִיְּמָנִי, לְהַתְחִיל
בְּמִצְוֹתַי, לִזְמַן זֶה הִגִּיעָנִי, וּבוֹ יִסְלַח חוֹבוֹתַי,
לָכֵן אַקְדִּישׁ עִתּוֹתַי: יחידה

וּמְבֹרָךְ מוֹרִי תִּהְיֶה, רֹב שָׁלוֹם לְבָנֶיךָ, בָּהֶם תִּשְׂמַח
וְתִחְיֶה, וְכָזֶה חֲתָנֶיךָ, בִּרְכַּת הֶדְיוֹט אַל תִּהְיֶה,
נְקַלָּה בְּעֵינֶיךָ, שָׁלוֹם לָכֶם רַבּוֹתַי: יחידה תם

FIVE

Individual Creativity, Collective Memory

While ethnomusicologists have always worked with and focused on individual musicians during the fieldwork process, they have tended to extrapolate to the broader level of the community in their published writings; longtime anthropological traditions supporting anonymity for subjects of research have no doubt reinforced this tendency in ethnomusicological circles. Only in recent years have ethnomusicologists begun to turn their attention to the musical experience on the level of the individual and actively to incorporate this perspective into their written publications.[6]

Indeed, it seems desirable to incorporate both individual and collective perspectives in the study of any musical tradition. Music-making necessarily draws both the individual and the group into consideration because musical knowledge, in order to be transmitted and maintained, must be shared, while musical innovations are often the outgrowth of individual initiative. The Syrian pizmon provides a particularly rich example of a form of musical expression that serves to mediate between the individual and a broader collectivity. To better define this relationship, the following discussion takes a close look at the manner in which individuals create, sustain, and perform pizmonim. It seeks to identify the processes—compositional and psychological—through which melodies were incorporated into the pizmon repertory, a process that both adopted them "whole" and rendered them "holy."

Commissioning and Composing

> To compose a pizmon is like constructing a house. He puts the wood, pours the pavement, then throws away the wood. I learned Arabic, replaced them with Hebrew words, and threw the Arabic away. (A. Ashear, 19 July 1989)

Several considerations come into play when someone decides to compose a pizmon:

> If you want a pizmon to be written, of course you have to tell the lyricist[7] what song you wanted him to use. Then, certainly you're gonna pick on a song that doesn't have any [Hebrew] lyrics to it because if anything's already been sung, no sense writing lyrics, you know, a duplicate set of lyrics to a song. (J. Saff, 4 December 1984)

The process of selecting a melody was an idiosyncratic one, depending on the period during which the pizmon was composed, and sometimes, serendipity. The shared characteristic of all melodies used in the tradition is that they were an integral part of the Syrian Jewish experience at the time they were borrowed. Whatever their geographical or ethnic origins, pre-existing connection to different repertories, or seemingly separate cultural domains, all these melodies were at once part of the Syrian Jewish world. While the continued use of Arab melodies underscores a deep and on-going aspect of the Ḥalabi musical experience and Syrian Jewish identity, the pizmon has always incorporated multiple streams of musical tradition. The use of European tunes in Aleppo testifies to the growing European presence in Syria and its impact on the ears of local inhabitants.[8] There is also little doubt that, in Aleppo, "The local musical tradition was shared by all groups; what particularities rural migrants, women, the upper class, or the various religious communities brought to their music was outweighed by the common musical culture that united them" (A. Marcus 1989:234). Similarly, the use of melodies from sources ranging from school songs to musical theater marks the increasing integration of Syrian Jews into the American urban environment.

Virtually all melodies past and present entered the pizmon tradition through the oral tradition. Just as Raphael Taboush learned melodies almost exclusively at Aleppo coffee houses, twentieth century Brooklyn composers have drawn on 78 RPM records, or later, cassettes. The common denominator in song acquisition is the course of everyday life. One colorful example was recalled by Albert Ashear, who witnessed his father Moses composing a pizmon after hearing a melody played by an organ grinder accompanying a dancing monkey outside his window on the Lower East Side of Manhattan. The melody of this pizmon (no. 187, "Mi Zot") is taken from the Neapolitan song "Santa Lucia."[9] Therefore, once the person decides on a melody—in the following case for a bar mitzvah pizmon—

> You go over to the person, he'll write a song for your son. What's the son's name—Zion—he'll write Zion, who his mother was, who his father was, who his brothers [were]. . . . And they'll make his own song up

> from an Arab song or something like that, just for this particular bar mitzvah boy or if there's a wedding or whatever. (M. Kairey, 6 November 1984)

The composer's responsibilities did not end with the selection of a melody and composition of the text. He also had to arrange for the copying and printing of the text as well as for training singers who were to lead the song during its first performance in the synagogue:

> Usually if you want to get married, . . . you would say "make us a song." So we prepared the song, printed [it] on paper, and gave it out on the day of the singing and the celebration of the marriage. They give out those papers to the congregation. Already he taught his choir, his friends how they sing it. They sing it and they introduce it two, three, four times for the people to hear it and they learn it. (A. Ashear, 19 July 1989)

The economic details of pizmon composition are a sensitive subject, even with regard to figures long dead. Some individuals apparently charged flat fees for composing pizmonim, while others refused to set a fixed rate and accepted a gratuity or gift instead. Specifics of financial arrangements are for the most part intensely private,[10] but it is clear that most early compositional efforts received little more than the costs they incurred in time and printing of the song for distribution in the synagogue. Earlier in the century, too, many pizmonim were composed voluntarily, often to celebrate a rite of passage such as a wedding or to acknowledge a close relationship between a composer and the family. A good example of voluntary composition, as seen in the prelude to this chapter, is "Yeḥidah Hitnaʿari," which Moses Ashear set on his own initiative and presented to the grieving Ṣafadiyyah (Saff) family. Only more recently has pizmon composition become an overtly commercial process. It is reported that songs have been composed for influential individuals in the hope of receiving a large gratuity; one anonymous source reported that a pizmon commissioned around 1990 cost more than a thousand dollars. In the words of another anonymous insider, today pizmon composition is "more like a business."

In a very real sense, all modern pizmon composers work in the shadow of the revered Raphael Taboush, seeking to emulate his genius and his ability to "hear an Arab melody and in one second . . . put Hebrew words into it" (M. Kairey, 6 November 1984). Modern pizmon composers compare their own compositional processes to those of Taboush and Ashear:

> Ḥakham Taboush, Rabbi Ashear, left only about sixty or seventy years ago. So it's like for me to open the radio in Egypt and to hear some great composer, small piece about twenty mintutes [long], to take it and put Hebrew words. That's exactly what they did. Now sixty, seventy years ago there was no sketching around. He put the Hebrew words, that's how the song fit. They took the original, they learned the original of the music, and after they knew how to sing it by heart. (Y. Nahari, 6 January 1986)

Only a few amateur musicians have composed pizmonim. These include Ezekiel H. Albeg, a Jew of Iraqi descent who lived for many years in Brooklyn and who served as cantor at the Ahi Ezer Synagogue before retiring to Los Angeles. In addition to no. 313, "Ṣur Yah El," Albeg composed No. 509c, "Ashir Na Shir Tikvah." The latter, a bar mitzvah pizmon set to a melody from *Fiddler on the Roof,* is the single pizmon transcribed in Western musical notation in SUHV (see musical example 5.1).[11] The businessman Louis Massry, who composed the pizmon "Ramaḥ Evarai," has composed other pizmonim as well. In one instance, Massry set a pizmon to a tune that Umm Kulthūm sang not for an occasion, but "just because it was a beautiful song" (L. Massry, 21 February 1985).

Otherwise, pizmon composition in late twentieth century Brooklyn is primarily the domain of professionals, primarily cantors from abroad serving on a full-time or part-time basis. Here the Syrian community reflects the increasing "professionalism" of the cantorate in the United States during the second half of the twentieth century (Slobin 1989:94–111). In particular, Cantor Raphael Elnadav[12] and Albert Cohen-Saban have been active in adding new songs to the repertory.

Albert Cohen-Saban discussed his compositional process in some detail:

> I take the melodies, the Oriental melodies, and I put them to words, Hebrew words, fitting whatever occasions I'm preparing for. Whether it's a baby boy, new baby girl, or a bar mitzvah, or a wedding, or whatever occasion. (A. Cohen-Saban, 10 January 1985)

At the time of his interview in 1985, Cohen-Saban had composed seven pizmonim. He provided considerable detail about these songs and is quite conversant with the musical sources of his melodies. Two are set to well-known melodies of Muḥammad ʿAbd al-Wahhāb. One, no. 204c, is set to an early song, "Yawm wa-Layla" (Day and night), drawn from ʿAbd al-Wahhāb's first film, *The White Rose* (1933; Azzam 1990:113–44). Another pizmon, no. 318e, set in bayātī kurd, was taken from the song "Inta ʿUmrī."

EXAMPLE 5.1. "Ashir Na Shir Tikvah" (SUHV, no. 509c).

A third song, no. 318g, was composed for the birth of a son to Ezra Betesh Ha-Levy. The original Arab song was composed by Muḥammad Al-Mawjī and popularized by singer ʿAbd al-Ḥalīm Ḥāfiẓ (A. Cohen-Saban, 10 January 1985). Cohen-Saban recounts the special challenge of a pizmon commission in honor of an impending birth:

> It has been a very, very hard job because I didn't know where to shoot. The lady is pregnant. . . . I have to make two songs and have to keep working on both the directions. . . . Sometimes she gives birth on a

> Thursday, and you have to sing the song on Saturday. So you must print and type and practice, it's a lot of work. You know, when a woman is pregnant, it's the hardest job. (A. Cohen-Saban, 10 January 1985)

Some melodies were requested by individuals who commissioned the songs, including that of Cohen-Saban's pizmon "Hineh Mah Tov," set to the melody of the song "Sunrise, Sunset" from the musical *Fiddler on the Roof*.[13] Other melodies were chosen by Cohen-Saban himself. In one instance, that of the most recent song he had composed, he borrowed a pre-existing melody from a song of an unidentified French Jewish singer for the beginning of the pizmon and then composed his own tune for the middle section. Cohen-Saban called this process "using a skeleton":

> The "skeleton" means just the opening of the song. I used just the opening. Then in the middle of the song I put my own music. Then I come back to the skeleton. In other words, I just use the theme. That's what I used from the song. Everything else is my own. (A. Cohen-Saban, 10 January 1985)

Composition of completely new melodies is rare in the pizmon tradition, although there are examples. While he has used famous Arab melodies for his own pizmonim, Raphael Elnadav has composed the entire melody and text of other songs, such as no. 237f, a pizmon in nahāwand kurd.

In general, most composers prefer to use tunes that are well known, even when they are asked to compose a new melody:

> So far I have been using tunes that are known tunes. In other words, those that the community are familiar with and [which] are easy to pick up. . . . I have to imagine the people singing it together, you know. (A. Cohen-Saban, 10 January 1985)

Cohen-Saban maintains the traditional practice of preparing sheets with the Hebrew text of the new pizmon and distributing it for the occasion, usually during a Sabbath morning synagogue service, at which it is first performed. Each sheet also contains the Hebrew date, the occasion commemorated by the song, and the name of the individual honored. It is noteworthy that songs are frequently dedicated not just to the newborn child or bar mitzvah boy, but to the father or grandfather of the celebrant.

Occasionally, individuals well versed in Hebrew and Jewish tradition are quietly called on to assist a pizmon composer. Cantor Gabriel Shrem recalled that once he

> helped compose something. So this [person] used to live a few doors away from me and used to need a little help. He came over and I gave him whatever help I could. But he always picked out the melody himself. I used to help him. He didn't have a good handwriting, I used to copy it down and make it clear. And sometimes he used to put too many words to fit into a song. (G. Shrem, 9 January 1986)

It may well be the case that collaboration is more common than generally acknowledged in pizmon composition. Indeed, the process for Arab song composition is described by knowledgeable Syrian Jews as a communal one:

> Let's say now, I sit down and I want to compose a song. I can't write it down cause I have nothing to write! I just have to memorize whatever music I will compose, and usually, the composer would have one or two instrumentalists with him as he's composing who will also listen to the composition as he's going about it. And this way, there's three people that are sitting in on the composition and when the time comes for the song to be completed, they can replay it and now they got the music—but they don't have the words. They would call in a lyricist, an Arabic lyricist. There were cheap lyricists and there were expensive lyricists. The cheap ones gave you junky words, the good ones gave you fantastic words. And they would then write words to the music which the singer now, the composer, would go back and apply these words to the music that he composed and now he's got a song. And they would make a recording of it—what is it, the 78 RPM's. The slow one, the very first one. (J. Saff, 23 October 1984)

The composer usually leaves evidence of his artistry by including his own name in the dedication at the beginning of the song. Frequently, as we have also seen, he further embeds his own name in an acrostic.[14]

In general, pizmon composition is considered to be a great challenge. There are technical demands in composing an esoteric Hebrew text to match the meter and rhyme scheme of an existing song:

> To fit, to rhyme . . . you have to be very much in control of the language. You have to know a lot of Hebrew lyrics. (A. Cohen-Saban, 10 January 1985)

Time constraints figure prominently in the busy lives of the few pizmon composers active today:

> It has a lot to do with personal feelings about the rhythm and melody. Then the mood of putting the words. It's a luck involved, it's not easy. And it's like in one day I could compose three lines. Then the mood is

> down again. I'm busy in my job, my business. And then at times I'm stuck with a certain word, certain rhyme, so it takes me two weeks or three weeks. Sometimes I do a line or two and I feel I'm not on the right track. Then I make another two lines and I compare. Sometimes I make two, three, four sets. And then I pick the best set. This is the truth. This is exactly what goes on. Until you keep reading it and singing it, and you do your best. (A. Cohen-Saban, 10 January 1985)

To date, no women have been active as pizmon composers. However, the increasing involvement of women in learning pizmonim in the late twentieth century has begun to draw women into musical activities. The daughters of Moses Tawil actively express their desire to have pizmonim composed for family occasions such as anniversaries and bar mitzvahs. One has even considered melodies she would like to have used in this way:

> Every once in a while I'll hear a song and I'll say, oh, gosh that would be great for a pizmon. . . . One day I'm going to take a little book along with me and every time I hear those songs I'm going to jot them down so that when the time comes that I really would love to get a pizmon written for some occasion or another. . . . I'm gonna pick the proper song. (J. Kassin, 30 March 1989)

However, she does not wish to follow through the entire process of distributing the pizmon to the wider community:

> [My son's] going to be bar mitzvah in another year and I was thinking that I would love for a pizmon to be written, but I certainly wouldn't hand it out. . . . I wouldn't give it away. If anything, if that pizmon is going to be written, I'd like it to be done in our family or by our family. (Ibid.)

The Individual as Improviser

While some in the Syrian community compose, not all creative activity involves the invention of new songs. A number of individuals introduce new elements into the repertory by adapting performance practice. In fact, close ethnographic interviewing and observation indicate that a surprising range of opportunities exists for individual innovation in several domains.

A fine line separates the acts of composition and improvisation. Indeed, within the Arab musical tradition, improvising in the various maqāmāt is considered highly creative. There have been so few studies of "compositional process" and "improvisation" outside Western music that it may well be that the existence of these processes as separate categories is a result of attitudes distilled from the Western classical tradition. If creative processes in Western music are primarily subsumed under the rubric of "composition," it is clear that Arab-influenced musics such as the pizmon tradition subsume creativity more readily under "improvisation."

Thus performing a melody in a new way is considered by many to be as creative a process as inventing an entirely new melody:

> I compose when I'm in the *tevah* [the reader's desk in the synagogue]. I'm composing when I'm in the synagogue. Or I'm composing when I'm officiating in a wedding. That's when I compose the music. Now it's not really music. I do read notes, not one hundred percent, but there're no notes in our music. I don't come with ready notes. . . . Everything's from my head. Of course, the way of the maqāmāt, but I compose very many in the synagogue. (Y. Nahari, 6 January 1986)

Several individuals discuss improvisation in considerable detail, connecting their understanding of these processes to precedents in the Arab musical tradition. Of course, improvisation is an integral part of forms such as the layālī and petiḥah. Sometimes singers will also insert layālī between the verses of a pizmon, a practice that can be heard in the accompanying recording of pizmon "Attah Ahuvi." An accomplished singer will also often vary the melody of subsequent verses of a pizmon, a process clearly evident in the rendition of pizmon "Yehi Shalom" on the compact disc. On occasion, the entire melody of a pizmon can be altered. Some bakkashot, such as no. 70, are in fact intended to be sung in the maqām of the day at hand or, if the singer prefers, in maqām sīkāh. During an interview, Hyman Kaire performed no. 70 in maqām nahāwand, borrowing the melody of pizmon no. 210, "Attah El Kabbir," to set the text of no. 70. While doing this, Kaire commented: "I'm trying to make it, I'm trying to compose" (H. Kaire, 17 February 1988). On another occasion, Kaire began to sing a pizmon (no. 132A, "Meʿammi Tasim") for which he could only remember the first verse. He proceeded to explain that he would improvise the rest:

> I only know the introduction and in the rest I'm lost, but I'll try to make [sing] it. (Sings first verse) See, now I don't know the next paragraph, so I improvise with "Mishamayim," the piece from the bakkashot [no. 52]. And I say two of them . . . I put the first on this part and the second part from "Mishamayim." Cause I don't know the rest. (Ibid.)

Kaire therefore adapted the melody from a bakkashah in maqām rāst to fill out the rest of a forgotten pizmon in the same mode. While some "old-timers don't approve of improvisation and say 'stick to the same song,'" the consistent involvement of the bakkashot in improvisational processes reflects an older, established practice that Hyman Kaire learned from his teacher Eliyahu Menaged, who used to be "a great improviser" (H. Kaire, 17 February 1988). Menaged would "throw together different verses, even in the Kaddish," recalls Kaire. Beyond this, Menaged was renowned for his ability to modulate between maqāmāt:

> He had a beautiful voice and when he used to say a petiḥah, he was a pro. He would finish one sentence in one maqām, and go into a different song altogether from the pizmonim, then go back to the next sentence, go into a different maqām, go into a different song. . . . So he would have this freedom, but he would end up the last word before the next song in the same maqām. (M. Kairey, 13 November 1984)

Thus improvisation can be and is used in several different ways within pizmon performance. Most prominent is the improvisatory introduction, whether a layālī or a petiḥah, which first and foremost establishes the maqām of the song to follow. But improvisation can also be applied within an individual pizmon, ranging from replacing its entire melody with that of another, elaborating an existing melodic line, or jumping up an octave during the final line of a song. Some changes can be quite subtle, including simplifying an elaborate melodic line. What is important, according to one man, is to either

> put in a little extra or leave some out but not change the whole tempo of a song. Little nuances . . . makes it a little sweeter. (M. Kairey, 12 December 1984)

In this way, the individual places his own mark upon the pizmon tradition, participating in a creative—or compositional way—in an acknowledged individual aspect of collective pizmon performance:

> In fact, that's nice because sometimes you could, like in your own way, make it a little sweeter, or do a little thing. It becomes a personal thing and makes it nice. (Ibid.)

Improvisation, usually done by an individual, is particularly important in establishing the mood appropriate to the song. Here individual style joins with a shared notion of traditional artistry and aesthetics. Individuals emphasize that they improvise because

> sometimes you know, it's how you feel in the mood. You want to bust out. You want to say something else. Because [otherwise] it's too repetitious . . . (H. Kaire, 17 February 1988)

Indeed, some individuals suggest that affect is the most important ingredient in a meaningful performance. In the words of one: "I sing out of emotion, I don't sing out of learning" (B. Zalta, 16 March 1990).

A colorful aspect of improvisation relates to the entry and reuse of pizmon melodies within the liturgy itself. As we have seen, the pizmonim selected and sung for a given Sabbath reinforce the maqām for that day and correspond to and reinforce the affect of the biblical reading. Not only are pizmonim sung during processional moments such as the calling forth of individuals to say a blessing over a portion of the Torah to be read,[15] but their melodies are often re-used to set liturgical prayer texts for the day. In this way, a cantor can improvise on a familiar melody, rendering a prayer in a melodic setting already well known within the congregation.

The re-use of familiar pizmon melodies in the liturgy has led in many cases to a further improvisatory process within the liturgy—the direct adoption of various melodies of whatever source into the prayer service, omitting the pizmon stage altogether. This process is increasingly popular and can incorporate familiar and beloved melodies of any origin. Often a new melody is introduced simply for the sake of variety (See Kligman 1997:274–75). In one case, Cantor Yehiel Nahari noted that a melody from an unidentified aria said to have been sung by Caruso is used within the Sabbath liturgy of a Brooklyn synagogue:

> When we are taking the Sefer Torah out, we sing two lines. And so far, for twenty-five years, the shul has been singing one melody. I don't know what, but it's a very nice melody. But I want to change it because after twenty-five years, it's not Arabic. . . . The piece was taken from someone and it's about time they change it. (Y. Nahari, 6 January 1986)

This process of direct borrowing is particularly prominent in the practice of Cantor Isaac Cain of Mexico City (see plate 21). Cain was born in 1925, two years after his parents emigrated from Aleppo to Mexico. As part of his early exposure to Syrian liturgical practices, he became aware that pizmon melodies often reappeared with liturgical prayer texts:

> When I was a child, seven, eight years old, I used to go with my father to the synagogue in Cordoba, in Colonia Roma.[16] I sat with my father and I

> prayed like everybody. I listened to Nishmat[17] from the ḥazzan, I liked it, I liked the melody. Listen, I hear the same songs that they sang, because they're all from the pizmonim. (I. Cain, 7 September 1992)

Cain's opportunity to serve as a cantor coincided with the movement of Syrian families from Colonia Rosa to the fashionable Polanco neighborhood. Confronted with the prospect of walking miles to their old synagogue, the growing community rented a house within which to hold their own High Holy Day prayers beginning in 1951. Isaac Cain was asked to lead the prayers for that holiday season, as well as for the subsequent Sabbaths. But he soon found that his musical knowledge was inadequate to the task:

> I tried to say Nishmat, I didn't know any tunes, nothing at all. So I was very embarrassed and I went to see my grandfather and he introduced me to Ḥakham Hayyim Tawil. The first parashah [portion] he did was "Lekh Lekha,"[18] about Abraham, in [maqām] ṣabā. (Ibid.)

Tawil taught Cain a large repertory of pizmonim and instructed him on how to set prayer texts to these melodies, focusing on the Nishmat of the Sabbath morning service. In this manner, Cain learned how to adapt well-known pizmon melodies, such as "Yaḥid Ram," to set the Kaddish prayer in the liturgy on the appropriate day for maqām bayātī.

Once he had a thorough grasp of the process through which he could adapt pizmon melodies for liturgical use, Cain began to innovate more freely, adapting other melodies he knew and liked directly into the liturgy, without the mediation of a pizmon. His philosophy was quite straightforward: it was an explicit effort at liturgical innovation, a way to make something "different," "always new," and "never the same." The melodies Cain borrowed were derived from different musical styles he loved, selections ranging from Arab music to Western popular music. As Cain's involvement with music outside the Arab sphere grew, he began to incorporate those tunes into his liturgical improvisations. He remembers that he

> started in 1951 to take piano lessons. I didn't know anything about music. So the teacher used to make me buy the latest classical records, from Mozart to Tchaikovsky to Mendelssohn, Schubert, different composers. So I bought all this music and I started to listen and I loved it immediately. (Ibid.)

Over the years, Cain developed an extensive list of melodies he would draw on for liturgical use, reflecting the full range of musical traditions that have been part of his life. In so doing, he always followed the tradition of matching the melodic content of the borrowed melody to that of the maqām for a particular Sabbath. Western melodies in major keys were generally used for maqām ʿajam, while those in minor mode were categorized as nahāwand. Cain maintains a small notebook in which he has listed melodies of various origins, all correlated for use in the appropriate maqām. For example, among the musical selections he uses to set the Kaddish prayer in maqām nahāwand are the

> "Moldau" from Smetana, it's like the hymn from Israel, "Ha-Tikvah."[19] I make it with this also. Concert "Coca Cola Grande" is a melody I listened from the radio. The [violin] concerto of Mendelssohn. The *Sonata Pathétique* of Beethoven. [If] it's beautiful, I make a Kaddish. (Ibid.)

The initial reception of many of these melodies in the synagogue is guarded, in part because the tunes are not of Arab provenance. "They listen, you see, the first time, maybe they don't know it. But when I repeat the melody once or twice, they learn it" (ibid.).

Cain notes that sometimes people do recognize the melodies:

> Last year, for example, I say the Kaddish for the first time with the Concerto no. 2 of Rachmaninov. I finished Nishmat, and one of the teachers from the yeshiva, I can't remember his name, he came to me and said: "Beautiful, you made Concerto No. 2 of Rachmaninov! I also know classical music!" He told me that. Maybe he's the only one who noticed it was Concerto no. 2 of Rachmaninov. (Ibid.)

While Isaac Cain's borrowings are unusual in their variety and wide range, they demonstrate the exposure and engagement of Jews in the Syrian diaspora to an eclectic array of musical traditions. An instructive example of an early melodic exposure of this type by Cain occurred in 1954, during a visit to New York City. There he heard and learned a then-popular song by Charlie Chaplin, known to Cain by the title "Candelikas."[20] Invited to lead the Sabbath afternoon Minḥah service, Cain used this song and "everybody sang with me, because this melody was so famous" (ibid.). Other melodies used to set the Kaddish prayer can be heard on the compact disc.

If the entire sound world of a particular cantor is a potential source for melodic borrowing, the precise melodies borrowed are very much a product of individual choice. Sometimes music ubiquitous in the local environment is not actively borrowed; this seems to be the case in Mexico, where various genres of Mexican music are evidently not used for pizmonim nor for liturgical purposes (S. Harari, 7 September 1992).[21]

Individuals within Songs

If individuals compose pizmonim and improvise as an integral part of their performance, they are also memorialized within the songs. Through composing new pizmonim with family names within, and by using melodies of varied origins that are intrinsically meaningful to the dedicatee, most songs are at the time of composition tied directly to an individual, and by extension, his entire family. While it is widely known that individuals are commemorated in many songs, the specifics of a particular song are generally only known by the composer, dedicatee, and close relatives. When discussing his own pizmon, Joseph Saff noted:

> Many other pizmonim fit this pattern and have names in them. But you have to speak to someone from the family to find out. (J. Saff, 2 July 1985)

Some songs contain personal names that can be readily identified, as is the case with "Yeḥidah Hitnaʿari," where the printed text highlights their presence. In other instances names can be difficult to decipher. Often the names themselves have multiple references and/or are disguised; in these cases only a member of the family can retrieve and interpret them.

For example, Albert Ashear discussed pizmon no. 355, "Beni Vegilakh," composed by his father Moses for Albert's own bar mitzvah more than sixty years earlier. This pizmon evoked powerful memories for Albert Ashear throughout his life, recalling his bar mitzvah, his relationship to his father, and their family legacy. The song carries a dedication:

שיר לבר מצוה

סימן משה יוסף כהן חזק   **לחן בין אל ג׳נאין ואנא מאשי**

יסדתיו ליום שמחת בני ידידי אמריך הי״ו
א׳ברהם מ׳שה ר׳ב י׳וסף כ׳הן

Albert Ashear noted that

> they're beautiful words. It's mine. See it says in here [second line] "for my dear son, Amerik." . . . My [Hebrew] name is [third line] *Avraham,* right? His name is *Moshe* and his father is *Rav Yosef* and we are *Kohanim* [descen-

> dants of the priestly class]. See [the acrostic] *Amerik* [spelled in Hebrew]: "Alef-Mem-Resh-Yud-Kaf." He doesn't miss a trick, see. (A. Ashear, 19 July 1989)

The first line of the penultimate stanza of the pizmon begins with the phrase *yosef dodi yesammaḥ bitto:*

יוֹסֵף דּוֹדִי יְשַׂמַּח בִּתּוֹ, כִּימֵי נְעוּרִים:
יִפְנֶה אֵלֶיהָ יְבַשְּׂרֶהָ, בִּדְרוֹרִים:
וְהוּא יַעֲבוֹר כְּנֵיַעֲבוֹר, יִמְשֶׁה עֲדָרִים:

The undisguised name "Yosef" is that of both Moses Ashear's father (the bar mitzvah boy's paternal grandfather) and Albert Ashear's brother (the grandfather's namesake). However, the next word, "dodi," is a veiled reference to David, a second brother of Albert Ashear, while "yesammaḥ" is a disguised reference to Samḥan, Moses Ashear's mother (the bar mitzvah boy's grandmother). The subsequent line of the pizmon text begins with the phrase *yifneh eleha,* which refers to Albert Ashear's brother Eli; the subsequent word *yevassereha* refers to Shaul, one of Cantor Ashear's brothers (the bar mitzvah boy's uncle).

In other instances, personal names are presented with correct spellings but are disguised in other ways, such as being divided. One of the most notable examples of such a division of a name is found in pizmon no. 322, "Mizzivakh Tanhir":

שֵׁם אֵל נוֹרָא יִנְצְרֵנִי, וּלְצִיּוֹן יְנַהֲלֵנִי,
בְּחֹדֶשׁ נִיסָן יַרְאֵנִי, נֵס כְּבִזְמַן הַקַּדְמוֹנִי,
עֲבוּר אַבְרָהָם עֶבֶד יָהּ:

This has given rise to a humorous anecdote told by members of the community in several versions:

> So now . . . you're going to laugh when I tell you. . . . You see on 322, this is for a bar mitzvah. The *talmid* (student), his name was Ṣion, and the father was Shemuel, and the family's name is Nasar. . . . Now look at the second verse where it says *shem el nora yinṣereni,* you see it? "Shem el" is "shemuel," that's the father. "Yinṣereni" is Nasar, the family name. *Ṣion* [same line] is the boy that's getting bar mitzvahed. Now he mentioned all the family. *Abraham* [two lines down] is probably his other son. Now he

> [Shemuel Nasar] goes over to the guy [composer Moses Ashear], and he says: "Where did you put my wife's name?" His wife's name was Sanyar, a Syrian name. He's looking all over the book, he doesn't see it. So [Ashear] says, "Over here, now, one, two, three, four, on the fourth line over here, I'm going to sing the song, just that part, where your wife's name is." So he goes like this. "*Beḥodesh nisan yar'eni*" [in the month Nisan he shows me]. He says, "I cut her off in the middle!" (M. Kairey, 12 December 1984)[22]

Of particular interest in the case of pizmon no. 322 is the manner in which the wife's complete name can be heard when sung, yet seen only with difficulty when reading the text. Given the paucity of references to women in the songs, and the fact that women do not generally read or sing the Hebrew pizmon texts, the placement of a woman's name in a manner that calls into play oral comprehension is doubly interesting. A woman is being referenced within the medium she occupies, the oral/aural tradition.

Apart from songs that are commissioned, many pizmonim are composed out of familial devotion or in celebration of other close relationships. This is true of many songs composed by Moses Ashear. Several pizmonim were composed for members of his own family, including, as we have seen, for the bar mitzvahs of his sons. David Ashear, the honoree in no. 261, "Havu Godel L'Elohenu," was born in 1903, ten years before his younger brother Albert (Amerik). Set in a series of maqāmat, pizmon no. 261 includes the bar mitzvah boy's name in the last line.

צבא:
קַבֵּל יָהּ תְּפִלּוֹתֵינוּ. וּמַלֵּא מִשְׁאֲלוֹתֵינוּ.
כִּימֵי שָׁאוּל מְשִׁיחֵנוּ. כְּקֶדֶם חַדֵּשׁ יָמֵינוּ:

עג'ם:
אַמְּצֵנוּ יָהּ צוּרֵנוּ. בִּרְכַּת יוֹסֵף בָּרְכֵנוּ.
בֶּן דָּוִד יִמְלוֹךְ עָלֵינוּ. אָז יִמָּלֵא שְׂחוֹק פִּינוּ: תם

Also incorporated is the name of the bar mitzvah boy's brother, Yosef (Joseph), in the phrase *birkat Yosef* in the third line. Yet another reference is to the name of *Shaul* [Charles] in the second line, the brother of Moses Ashear who was a qānūn virtuoso in his native Syria (A. Ashear, 19 July 1989).

In chapter 1, it was noted that songs were sometimes written as a gift by a pizmon teacher for his students. Raphael Taboush wrote songs for his students Moses Ashear (no. 168, "Melekh Raḥaman," discussed in the prelude to chapter 6), and Hayyim Tawil (no. 117, "Ḥai Hazzan"), discussed further below. Moses Ashear continued this tradition, writing a song for his young student and eventual successor, Naphtali Tawil.

The composition of pizmonim so full of names and family patriarchs provides a strong incentive for remembering and performing the songs:

> Now [that] this man passed away, his children and grandchildren say this song. They know that there is a song, the[ir] grandfather sang it. It became a well known song. There are so many grandfathers in here that he made songs and they continue to sing the songs. (Ibid.)

Individuals and Their Favorite Melodies

If individuals are embedded in the texts, their musical preferences are often encoded in the melodies. Generally, the channels of text and tune remain separate in that religious and familial memories are primarily text-bound, while music sustains a connection with the sound world of everyday life. Occasionally the two channels cross, as in the instance of pizmon no. 322, where the name of the woman Sanyar may be recognizable only when set to melody. Indeed, this example is ideally suited to such a dual presentation, with the Syrian name "Sanyar" rendered audible only when sung to a melody the woman named must have known with its original Arabic text.

The choice of melody derives first and foremost from an aesthetic decision: the desire to select a "catchy" melody that will be remembered easily, hence insuring the survival of the song's text. However, it is certain that the vast majority of melodies carry much more specific associations for the individuals who knew them and in fact requested that they be used. A salient example is pizmon no. 189, "Mifalot Elohim," composed by Moses Ashear in honor of the wedding of Samuel Aharon Franco. The melody, used at the request of the groom, was the anthem of his high school on the Lower East Side of Manhattan, H.S. 62, which burned down in 1929 and was subsequently reconstructed as Seward High School (H. Kaire, 14 March 1985). One of the unexpected aspects of borrowing the song was that its melody was a previous borrowing by H.S. 62 and was widely known as the Christmas carol, "O Tannenbaum" (see musical example 5.2).[23]

In cases such as pizmon no. 189, the strong contextual associations of the original melody and its ubiquitous presence during the American Christmas season have rendered the song controversial within the Syrian community. Here, the process of transforming intensely secular sounds of everyday life into the sacred is sorely tested, in part because of the overtly religious nature of the melody's non-Jewish associations. No. 189 and some other pizmonim

Example 5.2. "Mifalot Elohim"

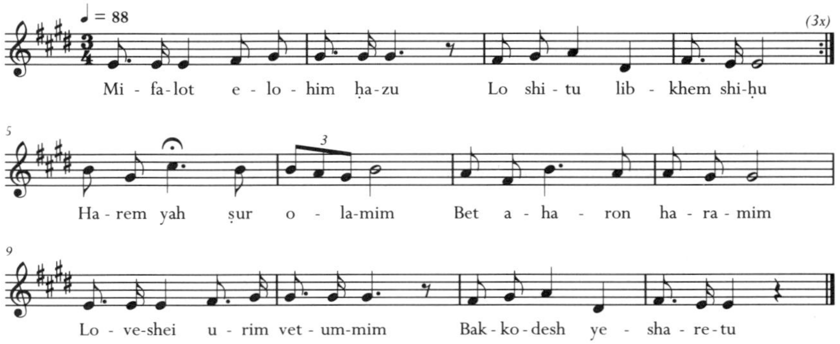

occupy a disputed space in Syrian musical tradition, one discussed by the men who sustain the songs:

> Lately they been saying how come Moses Ashear writes Christian songs? But there is in here, according to the Rabbis at the beginning of the book (SUHV) that it allowed that. So, this was an Italian song. Then you have the French song. He has all English songs, "My Country, 'Tis of Thee" is in here. He puts it into Hebrew. So, anytime he hears a song that's catchy, he would change it and put it into Hebrew. Once it's in Hebrew, it becomes holy. (A. Ashear, 19 July 1989)

Indeed, the stronger the association of a melody with memories outside the pizmon tradition, the more disputed the song may become. In contrast, one can take the example of the now obscure melody used to set pizmon no. 132a, "Meʿammi Tasim." The melody is said to derive from an Arab song famous during the World War I period, titled "Mother, Don't Cry Over Me." Its melody is today used to set the Keddushah prayer in maqām rāst, its strong secular associations long ago forgotten (M. Tawil, 21 August 1991).

Remembering—and Forgetting

The study of the pizmon tradition, by its very nature, limits inquiry to pizmonim that have survived and that can be deemed, by virtue of their survival, relatively successful. Yet while individuals speak openly about what comprises a "successful" pizmon, listening first for "the music" and then for "the words," it is rare that we have an opportunity to investigate a pizmon that has fallen out of use and been forgotten. The case of "Yeḥidah Hitnaʿari," discussed in the prelude to this chapter, is therefore all the more interesting because it provides such unusual insight. The criticism of this pizmon, not surprisingly, seems to rest on the fact that its melody was not "catchy" and could not be "picked up easily." However, even a beloved song does not always "translate" effectively into a pizmon. In order to be preserved, a pizmon has to be meaningful to individuals and the community at large:

> All the pizmonim are, you know, song[s] of religion in one way or another. What they do nowadays, it's all *shir ushevaḥah,* [song and praise] you made it to God. Also they mention the people about whom they write. Mmm, no, much more that I hear in the pizmon. (Anon.)

Ultimately pizmonim depend on individuals for their transmission. A close look at the pizmon repertories of several men provides insight into transmission patterns and the overall vitality of the pizmon tradition.[24] Four men reviewed an index of pizmonim contained in SUHV (1983) and marked the songs they knew; two additional repertory lists were collected as well.[25] Of four longtime Brooklyn residents who provided information on their repertory, only the late Gabriel Shrem was born abroad (around 1917 in Cairo, Egypt); he immigrated to the United States at age 13. The other three men (Meyer Kairey, Joseph Saff, and Moses Tawil) were born in the late 1910s or early 1920s to parents who had immigrated to the New World directly from Aleppo. Two additional repertory lists were gathered, one from a young Sephardic Jew born in Israel who moved to New York City shortly before the team project began in the mid 1980s (Menachem Mustacchi), and a second from a cantor born in Mexico City in 1925 (Isaac Cain). Since the bakkashot, petiḥot, and songs for Moṣa'ei Shabbat are included in the index, all the men supplied information about their knowledge of these repertories as well.

While individual repertories vary in size and content, initial informal estimates by the individuals involved proved on target, if not conservative:

> I guess that out of the 500 or so [pizmonim] that are in the book,[26] I know about 100. I have them listed and I'm sure that there must be about 40 or 50 known by others in the group. So that means there must be over 150 pizmonim that we know. (M. Tawil, 8 November 1984; see table 5.1).

The following totals emerged from the informal survey, showing that these admittedly knowledgeable individuals have repertories ranging from 61 songs to more than three times that number:[27]

TABLE 5.1. Summary of Individual Repertories

Maqām[a]	Total pizmonim[b]	Active transmission[c]	
rāst	69	34	[9]
māhūr	31	9	[11]
sasgar [sāz kār]	3	0	
ʿajam	54	16	[13]
lāmī	1	0	[1]
nahāwand	54	17	[6]
bayāt	99	26	[22]
muḥayyir bayāt	15	4	[5]
ḥusaynī	26	3	[10]
ʿushayrān	2	1	[1]
rahawa nawā	20	10	[6]
ṣabā	64	19	[12]
ʿawj	2	1	[0]
sīkāh	54	21	[6]
ḥijāz	62	17	[13]
misc.	4	4	
Total:	560	178	[115]

[a] Maqāmāt are listed in order of presentation in the fifth edition (1988) of SUHV.
[b] Total number of pizmonim included within each maqām.
[c] Number of pizmonim within maqām actively transmitted by two or more individuals surveyed. Number in brackets counts number of additional pizmonim transmitted by only one individual surveyed.

Isaac Cain	124
Meyer Kairey	80
Menachem Mustacchi	61
Joseph Saff	156
Gabriel Shrem	185
Moses Tawil	121

Given Gabriel Shrem's lifelong work as a cantor within the community and his active role in formal pedagogy, he commanded the largest repertory; he is said to have known "the whole book . . . which stands to reason, since he compiled it" (M. Arking and J. Mosseri, 14 January 1986). It should be noted that Shrem's total of 185 pizmonim includes sixteen bakkashot in the various maqāmāt. Joseph Saff's lifelong love of Arab music has resulted in a substantial repertory, with a particularly large number of pizmonim (47) in maqām bayāti. Similarly, lifelong involvement with Arab music has enhanced

Moses Tawil's repertory, as did exposure to the singing of his brother Naphtali and the scholarly involvement of his brother David with the pizmonim and Arab music. Meyer Kairey, a modest, revered teacher of pizmonim in the community, certainly understated here the number of pizmonim he knows. Finally, the extensive repertory of Isaac Cain of Mexico, and the considerable knowledge of young Menachem Mustacchi from Israel,[28] provide comparative insights into different transmission patterns in the various Syrian communities.

The repertory surveys confirm that transmission of bakkashot continues actively in Israel, since the youngest research associate, Menachem Mustacchi, already commands that entire repertory. Similarly, Meyer Kairey actively performs the entire repertory of bakkashot and petiḥot; in his repertory list, he even offered corrections to the SUHV index, noting that bakkashot nos. 30, 43, and 74 should be classified instead as petiḥot. Gabriel Shrem certainly knew all the bakkashot as well and discussed them in an interview on 9 January 1986. However, Joseph Saff and Moses Tawil, despite extensive pizmon repertories, do not know the entire bakkashot repertory, nor does Isaac Cain of Mexico. This most certainly reflects the reduced level of bakkashot performance in New York City and the discontinuation of that tradition in Mexico City.

Of the 560 songs in SUHV, we can confirm that no less than 178 are in the active repertory of at least two of the men from New York City; an additional 115 songs are in the repertory of at least one individual (see table 5.1). Seventy-seven of these remaining 115 songs were known only by Gabriel Shrem, which indicates that their transmission in New York since his death may in fact have ceased if others outside this small but knowledgeable group do not know the songs. It is noteworthy that Isaac Cain of Mexico shares 28 of the 77 pizmonim that only Shrem transmitted in New York City; Menachem Mustacchi shares 5 pizmonim with Shrem. This may indicate that aspects of Shrem's repertory—endangered in New York—are in fact more actively transmitted in Israel and Mexico.

There is broadly shared knowledge of a limited number of pizmonim. Songs such as no. 116, "Refa Ṣiri," by Raphael Taboush in maqām rāst, are known by all, in part because of their accessibility. According to Meyer Kairey, who selected this pizmon to teach to the New York University research team on 12 December 1984, no. 116 "is an easy one" (M. Kairey, 12 December 1984). "Refa Ṣiri" was also cited as the "first one in maqām rāst" (G. Shrem, 9 January 1986) and was described as "a very popular one" (M.

Arking and J. Mosseri, 14 January 1986). The melody of "Refa Ṣiri" is attributed to a Spanish song titled "Triste vida" ("A sad life"). While no version of a source song titled "Triste vida" has been found in oral or written sources, it appears that the melody was borrowed by Taboush from a song transmitted within the Judeo-Spanish tradition. The Hebrew pizmon is today widely circulated among Jerusalem cantors (E. Seroussi, personal communication, 19 January 1997), and a transcription of a rendition by a Jerusalem native with indirect ties to Taboush is published in an important anthology of Judeo-Spanish songs (Levy 1969:360).[29]

Other favorite pizmonim known by all were composed by Taboush. These include no. 124, "Ani Lishmakh," and no. 125, "Ram Leḥasdakh," both traditionally sung in honor of the birth of baby boys and both set to European melodies. No. 124 is set to an unidentified melody identified as a "polka," while no. 125, as noted in chapter 4, borrows the well-known French round "Frère Jacques." Although both of these pizmonim are catalogued under maqām rāst in SUHV, they are attributed instead by some to maqām girga (J. Mosseri, 14 January 1986), which may be a garbled reference to the Turkish makam *chargah* (E. Seroussi, 19 January 1997). In part because of the frequency of circumcision ceremonies for newborn infant boys, a number of pizmonim in maqām ṣabā traditionally used on this occasion are well known to many.

Most striking is the idiosyncratic nature of individual repertories. Each individual knows pizmonim with which no one else in the sample indicated familiarity; this was particularly the case of Isaac Cain of Mexico, who continues to transmit a number of Taboush pizmonim taught to him by Taboush's student, Hayyim Tawil. One is led to wonder whether Moses Ashear's activity as a composer of new pizmonim led him to be somewhat less instrumental in transmitting the songs of Taboush. Meyer Kairey, who studied in New York with Taboush's student Eliyahu Menaged, shares the knowledge of six Taboush pizmonim only with Cain. Gabriel Shrem, who learned pizmonim first as a child in Cairo in the decade immediately following Taboush's death in that city, shared twenty-five pizmonim only with Cain.

In several cases, it is clear that knowledge of a pizmon is limited to a single individual and that its transmission will almost certainly cease once that voice is stilled. A graphic example is provided by pizmon no. 291, "Yeḥidah Hitnaʿari," Joseph Saff's bar mitzvah pizmon. On the evening it was performed at a music session (21 February 1985), Joseph Saff was the only one who remembered the song, although Hyman Kaire followed haltingly, as did the instrumentalists. At the end of the rendition, one individual remarked that he had not heard the song in a long time (L. Massry, 21 February 1985).

Conclusion: Transmitting Pizmonim

The transmission of the pizmon repertory straddles the divide between individual and collective memory. On the one hand, it is necessary to have specialists and individuals who can actively teach and transmit pizmonim. Yet unless a song is accessible and amenable to group performance, it falls into disuse and is eventually forgotten. Songs that are more esoteric in text or that lack an easily grasped melody, such as "Yeḥidah Hitnaʿari," have an uncertain future; over the years they become more and more dependent on the memory of either a knowledgeable cantor or a devoted family member. No doubt those songs that are actively used (such as circumcision pizmonim) or which are re-borrowed for liturgical purposes have the longest lives of all, suggesting that only through shared performance in a variety of contexts does the larger repertory sustain itself. A song can be sustained in individual memory if it is attached to an important episode in the individual's life, such as Joe Saff's bar mitzvah pizmon. To achieve the same viability in collective memory, however, the song must be experienced often and repeatedly in the same liturgical, domestic, or social contexts.

Perhaps the most important moment at which individual and collective memories converge is during pizmon performance. As we have seen, pizmonim are almost always sung in group settings, whether in the synagogue, at life cycle rituals, or in social contexts. Many pizmonim are intended to be and are in fact best sung by groups: rousing hymns such as "Yaḥid Ram" and "Attah El Kabbir" provide good examples.

Yet at the same time, the pizmon remains a powerful venue for memorializing the individual. In addition to family names being encoded in song texts, songs continue to carry strong associations not just to the individuals for whom they were written, but to those who used to love and perform a given song:

> Last year we had a brit milah in the synagogue and we went to the person's house and he asked [me] to sing specific songs. I don't remember exactly which one in ṣabā, but the second [one] he asked me to sing [was] a bayāt song which he loved to hear from his father [who] was a good musician, [who] played the ʿūd. He used to hear him singing it and he asked me to sing it for him. (B. Zalta, 16 March 1990)

In general, melodies from outside the Arab tradition tend to reflect individual exposure, often of a highly idiosyncratic nature. As we have seen, Isaac Cain was introduced to Western art music through recordings recommended by an enthusiastic piano teacher; Cain has subsequently incorporated his favorite tunes into the liturgy. It is only through close ethnographic interviewing that one can identify the actual path through which a melody enters into Syrian Jewish musical experience. Sometimes this path is a most surprising one. For example, Benjamin Zalta, who has used the main theme from Mozart's Symphony no. 40 to set liturgical texts, first heard Mozart's melody in an *Arab* song:

> The interesting thing, the Arabic song was taken from a symphony. You know Fairuz? . . . The song goes (sings opening phrase of Mozart Symphony no. 40) . . . and I picked it up not from listening to Mozart, but I listened to the Arabic music first and when I came here in college, I had to take a music course. And it was introduced to me and Aha!! This is where they got it from. So I got the melody and put it in a Kaddish. In the prayers, in the Kaddish. (B. Zalta, 16 March 1990)[30]

The use of melodies from outside the Arab tradition can provide evidence of the involvement of Syrian Jews with a wider world of music. For example, pizmon no. 478, "Rabbat Sovʿah," borrows the melody of a Spanish song still known and sung in Brooklyn, "Mis Hermanos":

> "My brothers," in Spanish. They made it for Yom Kippur. Yeah. It's in ḥijāz and it's by Taboush. (J. Mosseri, 14 January 1986)

Without an attribution to a particular song, however, it can be difficult or impossible to identify the cultural origin of a source melody. This is because

> Some sound Western, but you know why you can't know? Because some of the Arabic ones sound Western because the Arabic themselves borrowed from Western people. (M. Arking, 14 January 1986)

The classification of Western melodies according to the maqām system further masks the identity of non-Arab melodies.

Finally, while Western melodies have been borrowed by Syrian pizmon composers living in the United States, a number of foreign melodies were earlier incorporated into pizmonim composed in Aleppo. As we have seen, there were ample opportunities for borrowings from other musical traditions well before the American period. Labels on approximately five percent of the pizmonim in the current compendium indicate that they are set to melodies of foreign origin. While some Western melodies may be subsumed under songs whose source melodies are termed "musika,"[31] the term "polka" appears to be an even more widely used generic term for a Western (possibly instrumental) melody of unknown origin. In the end, one can only be sure of the source of a borrowing when the attribution is given in Hebrew script, although there are certainly errors even in the most specific attributions.[32]

Whatever the motivation for pizmon transmission, all are keenly aware that they compose and perform for posterity. One reports that he feels

> a song like this lives forever. . . . And the family that has that song, every time they [sing it], also their children and grandchildren, and this is going to live for a long time. . . . This is their song. I mean, it has been done for this particular family. (A. Cohen-Saban, 10 January 1985)

Beyond the personal and familial aspects of pizmon transmission stand the power of religious belief and the knowledge that the act of composing and performing pizmonim ties the singer to a long historical continuum, as well as to the divine. Syrian Jews sing because

> this is what singers have done in the past, and it is what singers do in our own time. They take non-Jewish songs and introduce them to holiness by using their tunes to accompany songs sung to the Lord. (Kassin 1988:32–33)

PRELUDE

Melekh Raḥaman

"I was the seed of Aleppo and the fruit of America," recalled the late Albert (Amerik) Ashear.[1] Conceived in Aleppo, Albert was named Amerik by his mother in celebration of his birth in America shortly after her arrival in 1912. Albert Ashear's metaphor might easily be applied to the pizmon tradition as well: long rooted in Aleppo, the songs were brought to New York and nurtured there by Albert's father, Moses Ashear, cantor at Magen David Congregation until his death in 1940.

While Moses Ashear throughout his life composed pizmonim to honor others, he himself is memorialized in a pizmon composed in Aleppo by his mentor, Rabbi Raphael Taboush. As an expression of his affection for Ashear, Taboush composed the pizmon "Melekh Raḥaman," no. 168, upon the occasion of his student's wedding.[2] Over the course of the century of its life, Melekh Raḥaman has spread throughout the Syrian diaspora, where it is universally remembered and performed today.

The ubiquity of "Melekh Raḥaman" is such that the song is transcribed in Western musical notation and published in a book widely circulated within the Syrian community (Sutton 1979:[147]). Its melody is noted to have been borrowed from an Arab song of the period titled "Dām yā zamān." While nothing else is known about the provenance or original textual content of the Arab song, which is certainly more than a century old, Albert Ashear observed that the melody, formally categorized as maqām ʿajam, is in "C major."

The Hebrew text of "Melekh Raḥaman" employs familiar religious imagery, seeking God's protection for the people of Israel and portraying the Sabbath as Israel's bride and bridegroom. The text suggests that God, through the rebuilding of his city, will gain honor throughout the world.[3] The acrostic spells the name "Moshe," honoring the bridegroom, Moses Ashear.

The song further contains names of "the whole [Ashear] family." It incorporates to an unusual extent references to the bride, who is mentioned by name in the dedication above the song as "Ṣalaḥah, the daughter of Jacob Shamaʿa." Other family members are named as well: Yaʿakov, the bride's father; Avraham, the bride's brother, Albert's uncle;[4] Shaʾul and Shlomo, Moses' brothers, and Rinah, Moses' sister.

For Albert Ashear, the pizmon "Melekh Raḥaman" sustained multiple streams of memory. On the most immediate level, it served to record his father's relationship with Raphael Taboush, who "made up the song for him because he was getting married."

The song also memorializes generations of the Ashear family, moving Albert to reminisce about his own responsibility to say the mourner's Kaddish prayer for these deceased relatives. Remembering—and explaining—the names of family members in "Melekh Raḥaman" gave Albert Ashear great satisfaction, since he was able to give the ethnomusicologist "something new that you didn't know." Discussion of the song, which Albert was no longer able to sing because of a heart condition,[5] also evoked an overwhelming flood of poignant memories about his father. At one point, Albert exclaimed in a voice full with emotion,

> I tell you [since] he died 1940 there isn't a day that I haven't mentioned his name. Not a day, not a day—I'm telling you. I miss him.

Albert Ashear was aware and proud of the active transmission of "Melekh Raḥaman":

> Anyone that knows any song from pizmonim, that's the first one. Its a very well-known one. Very popular! It's easy to sing because it's C Major.

"Melekh Raḥaman" continues to be sung worldwide by Syrian Jews. It was sung at Congregation Shaare Zion in Brooklyn when a groom was called forth to the Torah the week before his wedding (Shelemay fieldnotes, 16 February 1985). "Melekh Raḥaman" was included as part of a concert of pizmonim presented on November 17, 1986, at a conference on "The Jews of Syria" held at the CUNY Graduate Center in New York City (Shelemay fieldnotes, 17 November 1986). The pizmon's melody is used to set the Kaddish prayer in the Sabbath morning service of Congregation Maguen David in Mexico City (Shelemay fieldnotes, 5 September 1992). "Melekh Raḥaman" is one of two pizmonim[6] known to everyone I interviewed in Mexico City, Israel, and Brooklyn. It has survived a century of intense change, continuing to be sung among Syrian Jews worldwide, wherever they live, and retaining its original association as a wedding pizmon. The song also carries within it the names and memories of Moses Ashear and his extended family, providing a genealogy of an Aleppo family that continues to be sung by its descendants. While Moses Ashear is known and loved for the many pizmonim he himself composed, his name is sung most frequently in the song within which he himself is memorialized:

> All over the Sephardic world where they know Arabic music they sing that. Children today all over, everybody singing these. After his death, it became . . . pretty much wanted all over. In Israel they sing these, all over. Even my father's song when he was married.

Example 6. Melekh Raḥaman

Example 6. *(continued)*

38
Rubato
bah ta - dir Ka - lat Mo - sheh hi vat ya - a - kov ish tam. Ho - du
43
na am e - mu - nah Be - kol Rin - nah
48
A tempo
La - el ga - dol ve - ne - e - lam Le - o - lam la - el ga - dol ve - ne - e - lam
53
Rubato
A tempo
Le - o - lam Hu - ro - i u - mo - shi - i be - khol id - dan uve -
56
Rubato
khol ze - man Me - ḥa - sa - dav eḥe - zeh no - am Hu ro - i
60
A tempo
u - mo - shi - i be - khol id - dan uve - khol ze - man Me -
63
ḥa - sa dav eḥe - zeh no - am Yut - tan li yah la - ad
68
bir - kat Av - ra - ham Av ha - e tan. Sha - ol esh - al me - el han - ne - e - man
73
Ki - mei sh - lo - mo ya - ir et ho - di ba a - gal

מֶלֶךְ רַחֲמָן. שְׁמוֹר נָא וּגְאַל נָא לְעַם לְךָ יְחַל. וּבְנֵה
צוּר לָעַד עִיר הַחֶמְדָּה. וּבָהּ כָּבוֹד יִנְחָל:

שִׁיר בְּחִבָּה. רְצֵה נָא עֵת אָשִׁירָה. מוּל הֶחָתָן. עִם
כַּלָּה נָאָה. עֵזֶר לוֹ בָאָה. וְיִשְׂמַח בָּהּ תָּדִיר כַּלַּת
מֹשֶׁה הִיא בַּת יַעֲקֹב אִישׁ תָּם:

הוֹדוּ נָא עַם אֱמוּנָה. בְּקוֹל רִנָּה לָאֵל גָּדוֹל וְנֶעְלָם.
לְעוֹלָם הוּא רוֹעִי וּמוֹשִׁיעִי בְּכָל־עִדָּן וּבְכָל־זְמָן.
מֵחֲסָדָיו אֶחֱזֶה נֹעַם. יִתֵּן לִי יָהּ לָעַד בִּרְכַּת
אַבְרָהָם. אָב הָאֵיתָן. שָׁאוֹל אֶשְׁאַל מֵאֵל הַנֶּאֱמָן.
כִּימֵי שְׁלֹמֹה יָאִיר אֶת הוֹדִי בַּעֲגָל: תַּם

Melekh Raḥaman

Merciful King, protect, pray thee, and redeem, a people that awaits You.
Oh Rock, rebuild forever the pleasant city; through it He will gain honor.

Pray accept, a song out of love, when I sing,
before the bridegroom, with beautiful bride,
a helpmate has [surely] come for him.
May he rejoice with her always,
the bride of Moses, the daughter of Jacob, an upright man.

Give thanks, faithful people, with the voice of rejoicing,
to God, He is great yet hidden.
He is, forever, my shepherd and deliverer, in every epoch and age.
From his mercies, I shall behold a beauty.
May the blessing of Abraham be granted me, Oh Lord, forever.
Constant Father. I shall surely ask of the Faithful One.
Let my glory shine, speedily, as in the days of Solomon.

SIX

Conclusion: A Community in Song

The previous chapters have provided an overview of the Syrian pizmon, focusing on the most recent century of its transmission. During this period Ḥalabi Jews migrated from their Middle Eastern "homeland" to various locales abroad, struggling all the while to preserve bonds of family, community, and tradition. Throughout this process, they continued to compose and sing pizmonim, nurturing a song repertory which assumed an increasingly important role as both a celebration of and an anchor for lives lived in changing times and in shifting geographic spaces. Indeed, the pizmonim can be said to both reflect and shape the experiences and sensibilities of the community that sustained it.

The following pages summarize what has been learned about the pizmonim, providing an opportunity to review some of the insights that the song texts and tunes provide into the Ḥalabi musical experience and world view. It is also an opportunity to learn from the pizmonim and to explore implications that transcend the case study at hand and that speak to broader issues concerning processes of memory. The panoply of personal testimonies, song melodies and texts, and processes of pedagogy and performance examined in the preceding chapters allow us to explore more fully here the three broad questions posed in the introduction:

- Why is music so frequently implicated in sustaining memory?
- What is remembered through music?
- How are memories transformed during musical performance into meaningful acts of commemoration?

The following pages, then, bring the primary concerns of this book full circle, providing an overview of what the Ḥalabi pizmonim tell us about music and memory, as well as the perspectives they provide of the Ḥalabi community itself. In this manner, we can begin to construct an "ethnomusicology of memory," providing detailed readings that enhance our understanding of a particular stream of expressive culture within one musical community while opening a door for further cross-disciplinary exploration of the role of memory in song.

Memories in Song

Music, particularly song, provides a medium that binds together disparate strands of experience, serving as a malleable form of cultural expression able to transcend the vagaries of time and place. Songs have been characterized as "compound aural memories" (Feder 1992:241), an apt description of their complex roles as carriers of both semantic memory (conceptual and factual knowledge) and procedural memory (skill and habitual knowledge) (Schacter 1996:17).[7]

Both the melody and the text of a pizmon can be said to be constructed purposefully to sustain memory. First, the melody is selected expressly to be meaningful to the individual for whom it is written. We have seen that some melodies are chosen by honorees for their own pizmonim, whether drawn from a favorite school song, such as the use of the H.S. 62 song, or from a beloved popular tune. In cases where a child or young man does not indicate a preference, or when the composition of the pizmon itself is planned as a surprise, the composer will select a melody known to the honoree or community. The use of tunes such as ʿAbd al-Wahhāb's popular instrumental piece "Country Girl" for the pizmon in honor of Charlie Serouya, or the borrowing of "God Bless America" to set a pizmon celebrating the construction of Ahi Ezer Synagogue, are examples of this process. Indeed, the inclusion of any melody in the pizmon repertory can be said to confirm that it was both memorable and meaningful at the time of its appropriation.

The choice of melody also implicitly references both individual memory and group recollection. While the individual—whether honoree or composer—was for the most part the conduit through which a particular melody entered into the pizmon repertory, it is certain that any tune so used was familiar to others in the community as well. In this way, melodies were purposefully chosen and pizmonim composed to mark important occasions as well as to sustain memory of them into the future.

There is ample evidence that the use of a "catchy" tune, one that could easily be retained, has long been given high priority within the Ḥalabi tradition. Stories told of pizmon composers such as Raphael Taboush borrowing tunes they heard performed only once in the oral tradition strongly suggest that they must have drawn on melodies that were readily learned. These conclusions, extracted from ethnographic observation and interviews, are borne out by psychological testing regarding other repertories, which show that "for [melody] to be effective in aiding recall it must be easily acquired" (Wallace 1994).

Following the period of migration from the Middle East to new homelands in the early twentieth century, it is certain that the only Arab songs that reached individuals in the Syrian diaspora were those popular enough to be distributed internationally through commercial recordings. The closely bounded nature of Syrian diaspora communities in the Americas, wherever their locations, had the further outcome that any given generational cohort of Syrian Jewish children, growing up in the same neighborhood amid extended family and attending the same schools and synagogues, shared a sound world. In a very direct way, then, pizmon melodies emerge from and continually reconstruct the particular time, place, and context of their entry into Syrian Jewish experience.

In this manner, easily remembered tunes from the popular domain became part of the traditional life of the Syrian community. The close and symbiotic relationship between what are often perceived by scholars as separate streams of "traditional" and "popular" music suggests that no such divide exists, but rather that pizmon melodies achieve the status of "tradition" only when they are memorable—that is, when they are both widely dispersed and "popular" enough not to be forgotten. Likewise, the same media—especially oral and aural technologies—shape transmission and prod memory within what have been mistakenly viewed as separate domains of musical culture.

If melodies were purposefully selected for re-use in Syrian pizmonim, the song texts were also carefully fashioned to incorporate multiple levels of signification. Most immediately, each pizmon speaks to an occasion that marks a milestone in individual and family life, whether a birth, bar mitzvah, or anniversary. In this way a song is linked to an individual, whose personal experience is purposefully embedded in the text. Names, genealogies, and some details of personal circumstance are intentionally incorporated. While in some cases these references are apparent and even highlighted in some way when written down, as can be seen in the facsimile of the pizmon text distributed for Joseph Saff's bar mitzvah reproduced in figure 5.1, often such textual allusions are veiled or disguised, often in ironic or humorous ways.

Pizmon texts further speak to the major shared occasions of the Jewish life cycle. Careful readings of the texts expose a dense intertextuality, with citations from and paraphrases of a range of Jewish liturgical and literary sources. In this manner the texts initiate and sustain a dialogue between the present occasion and others of its kind, as well as with different domains of Jewish thought, oral tradition, and written discourse.

Sung Reminiscences

If pizmon texts and tunes purposefully construct memory on multiple levels, their union also transcends their content and provides additional affective and emotional arousal. In some cases, the association of a maqām or specific songs with an occasion, such as the circumcision ceremony, may trigger a reminiscence of other such events of great significance. Strains of a familiar pizmon can transport a listener back to a single important moment in his or her own life, for example to a bar mitzvah ceremony or to the circumcision ceremony of a firstborn son named after a beloved grandparent. In this manner, the repeated singing of a pizmon serves to recall specific occasions in the individual life cycle and to bind that event to others of its kind, thereby enhancing its meaning.

Here music serves as a powerful cue for what psychologists term episodic or flashbulb memories, a type of "mental time travel" that allows an individual to relive something that happened in the past (Schacter 1995b:18, citing Tulving 1983:127). Yet while cognitive scientists have tended to discuss flashbulb memories more often in terms of traumatic events that are vividly remembered, it appears that music also has the capacity to enhance recall of overwhelmingly happy moments with strong emotional content.

Songs can further cue reminiscence of a more general sort, eliciting powerful memories of a long dead parent or of an experience of loss. The fact that songs continue to be sung in situations similar to those in which they were first performed reinforces and cues the highly charged process of reminiscence. Singing, for the performer as well as the listener, both arouses and recreates events and emotions experienced before.

Pizmonim are particularly powerful venues for a type of reminiscence termed "nostalgia." If nostalgia can be defined on a general level as "a wish to return to an idealized past," it also links an affect or emotional state with a particular range of semantic memories (Feder 1981:307, citing Kleiner 1970:473). Indeed, it has been suggested that nostalgia is an affect comprising both sensations and ideas, and that sensations of pleasure or discomfort stem from early childhood experience, while other ideas later become associated over time (Feder 1981:311–12). Nostalgia can be manifested in and worked through in musical form, a process traced by Stuart Feder in a discussion of the song "The Things Our Fathers Loved" by American composer Charles Ives. Specifically, Feder proposes that song formalizes and represents the affect of nostalgia:

> Through the medium of auditory form with its symbolic implications, the composer achieves an organized musical structure that in some way is expressive of an affect. It both represents and communicates nostalgia. *I suggest that it does so through an intrinsic morphology which mirrors the mental organization underlying the affect.* . . . The representation and communication of nostalgia are not achieved by mere self-expression in the activity of emoting. Rather, the crucial artistic activity is one of the creation of forms. . . . Here the individual tunes with their endless cognitive and affective connotations are intrinsic to a formal structure. (Feder 1981:329)

The Syrian pizmon may be interpreted similarly, but with the caveat that its formal structure is shaped by different cultural models and transmission processes. While Ives embedded quotations of many tunes in fragmentary form within a single song, which Feder argues is a structure that resembles closely the way recollections exist as free associations in memory itself (1981:318), pizmonim generally borrow and perpetuate full melodies from a single song, or at least substantial sections such as a complete chorus or verse. Additional melodic quotations or references within songs borrowed tend to be discarded; such an example is the omitted reference to Tchaikovsky's Chinese flute theme heard in the original introduction to "The Wheat Song," the Arab source for pizmon "Ramaḥ Evarai." One might want to attribute the use of a single, full Arab melody within a pizmon to exigencies of a transmission process exclusively within the oral tradition; in contrast, the songs of Ives are fully composed and notated. However, when multiple pizmonim are sung together, in changing combinations and orders, there is also present in the performance the close juxtaposition of a stream of melodies; it simply tends to occur *between* rather than *within* songs. The Arabic waṣlah (suite) form here may play a role as an orally transmitted framework that contains important elements of "free association" similar to that constituted within individual written songs in the Western tradition. Pizmon texts, which are of course transmitted largely in writing, contain multiple interwoven textual references and quotations much more similar to the processes of melodic fragmentation and transformation in Ives's [written] melodic settings. The spontaneous sequence of melodies in a live pizmon performance can therefore be interpreted as a real-time manifestation of memory. This fluidity is preserved in performances of pizmonim at occasions like the Sebet and within the Sabbath morning ritual (see Kligman 1997). Rubin (1995: 175–93) suggests that recall in oral traditions occurs in a linear fashion, moving from beginning to end. However, his theory is only partially applicable to a song tradition such as the pizmonim with orally transmitted melodies and written texts and does not explore cross-cultural differences.

The borrowing of whole melodies in the pizmon tradition and their reuse in situations where their original identity is also known—the process of contrafactum—further provides a fine example of a compositional device used to sustain memory cross-culturally. The widespread use of contrafacta over time and across geographic boundaries within so many musical traditions suggests that deep-seated cognitive factors underpin such procedures and resulting formal structures.

Psychological studies have shown that borrowing the melody of a strophic song to set a text can, in some situations, facilitate learning and recall. In a series of experiments using North Carolina ballads, the psychologist Wanda Wallace concluded that

> Text is better recalled when it is heard as a song rather than as speech, provided the music repeats so that it is easily learned. When [subjects] heard three verses of a text sung with the same melody, they had better recall than when the same text was spoken. . . . Furthermore, the experiments indicate that the melody contributes more than just rhythmical information. Music is a rich structure that chunks words and phrases, identifies line lengths, identifies stress patterns, and adds emphasis as well as focuses listeners on surface characteristics. The musical structure can assist in learning, in retrieving, and if necessary, in reconstructing a text. (Wallace 1994:1471)

Wallace further observes that melodies with simple symmetrical contours facilitate text recall, as does repetition of verses (ibid. 1481–82). The pizmon tradition, which emphasizes "catchy tunes" and repetitive strophic structures, possesses both these characteristics.

A recent study in cognitive ethnomusicology has suggested that musical genres such as the lament, which share formal and performative aspects across cultural boundaries, potentially provide ideal case studies in which to locate precultural levels of musical meaning (Tolbert 1992:18). The contrafactum, where processes of borrowing pre-existent melodies and reusing them with newly composed texts are well documented, would lend itself to such an approach. Moreover, one can only wonder at the potential utility of the contrafactum to cognitive scientists seeking to unravel the manner in which the brain constructs memory during retrieval. Recent studies have suggested that the brain brings together fragments of experience from different locations, "binding them to one another and to preexisting knowledge" (Schacter 1996:66). If indeed the brain uses different systems for retrieving written and spoken information (ibid.), the contrafactum's inscribed text and orally transmitted tune would lend itself to investigation as to the ways in which these traces of the past are brought together and connected.

In addition, contrafacta are often used within ritual contexts that seek to sustain the performance of sacred texts. Not only do contrafact procedures both characterize and serve to habituate religious practice, but they are often of signal importance in inculcating philosophical ideas concerning the manner in which transformation of sound can be equated with transformation of belief. Here the notion of transformation—conceptualized in the pizmon tradition as "making clear" the sparks of melody—can in fact be enacted and symbolized through re-performing a melody with a new, sacred text.

While a number of ethnomusicological studies have focused on iconicity of structure and experience in music, more recent work has proposed that musical meaning is at least partially iconic with the processes of perception and cognition:

> Crucial to this argument is that aesthetic feelings are associated with these primary structures, an iconicity of structure and experience that gains force because of the felt congruence between processes of perception and an experienced "reality." Musical experience is not only meaningful, but feelingfully meaningful because of its reliance on preconceptual structure. (Tolbert 1992:17)

In the case of the contrafactum, which unites text and tune, songs literally construct different levels of meaningful experience. Just as the song of Ives refers in its text to "tunes of long ago," thereby explicitly acknowledging the process underway in its music (Feder 1981:317), a pizmon always carries within itself the "echo" of its source melody, particularly in instances where the source melody in itself can still be recalled with its original text.

Memorializations

If a pizmon is a rich source for meaningful reminiscence, it also preserves the past and plays an important role as a "highly condensed form of knowledge" (Feder 1981:330). Here the strong tendency of the pizmonim to memorialize and commemorate emerges at its fullest. In their texts, pizmonim revisit aspects of Jewish law and observance valued by the Syrian community. They further memorialize everyone involved with their genesis and performance: they not only name the honoree and generations of his family, but metaphorically link these individuals with patriarchs of the past and the occasion at hand with similar events in Jewish history. For example, in pizmon "Ramaḥ Evarai" the bar mitzvah boy's name (Moses) and his grandfather's are linked to the biblical Moses; similarly, the presentation of a new Torah at a New Jersey synagogue is likened to the giving of the law at Mount Sinai. The composer, too, is memorialized within the medium in which he works, his name emerging in written versions of the song text, explicitly present in acrostics.

A survey of the repertory shows that the pizmonim memorialize the high points of Halabi life, the celebrations. They rarely mention the tragedies or grief. Given the surfeit of pizmonim for life cycle occasions of celebration, it is noteworthy that there are apparently no pizmonim marking death. There is no singing at Syrian Jewish funerals and no tradition of composing pizmonim in posthumous commemoration.

Indeed, one Syrian Jew noted antipathy in the community toward songs about death, saying "nobody likes those" (S. Catton, 9 October 1996). Catton went on to point out that one of the few texts about death in the Syrian tradition is found within the liturgy for the morning of the Day of Atonement, sung immediately before the reading of the Torah. This portion, "Hakkokhavim Asfu" (The stars gathered), tells of the death of Nadab and Abihu, the sons of Aaron (Alouf 1995:510–11).[8] Given the dearth of references to death in the pizmonim and liturgy, it is also interesting to note that "among the [Syrian] Jews . . . funerals tended to be much quieter [than Muslim funerals], prompting a local saying to liken a solemn and hasty affair to a Jewish funeral" (A. Marcus 1989:269–70).

Rather, pizmonim celebrate life and its continuities. They memorialize an individual through a musical record of his birth, bar mitzvah, or wedding, occasions that foreground procreation, community, and continuity. Here, too, music may stand to contribute to a broader conversation and perhaps even speak across the disciplines by providing data on memory as constituted through shared normative and expressive processes. If studies of memory in the cognitive sciences have tended to focus on distortion and trauma to achieve understanding of the general processes involved, music may provide insights into occasions of positive celebration and commemoration.

The Pizmonim as Social History

Through their role in commemoration, the pizmonim bind the past as constructed through memory to the historical past, a particularly complicated and contested relationship in Jewish tradition. Thus the pizmonim provide venues through which memory and history come together and reinvigorate each other.[9]

Perusal of *Sheer Ushbahah Hallel Ve-Zimrah* provides genealogies of important families; it at once commemorates and documents the occasions on which they celebrated births, comings of age, and other rites of passage. Song dedications provide dates from the historical past, along with a map of social networks in the community that maintain and transcend boundaries of kinship. In terms of music history, the names of borrowed melodies provide an anthology of the Syrian Jewish sound world since at least the late nineteenth century, opening windows on the pervasive power of Arab music along with the occasional entry of other sounds into Syrian Jewish lives. The consistent attempts to transcribe titles of source melodies both by pizmon composers and editors who later compiled pizmon collections provide a documentary record of this process.

Close readings of individual pizmon texts provide further accounts of shared events and occasions within their community at large. In some instances, individual songs provide narratives that shed light on family life and local events; a fine example is found in "Yeḥidah Hitnaʿari," the pizmon discussed in the prelude to chapter 5. Similarly, other songs can be read and heard in different ways: what appears on the surface to be a petition for God's mercy may on a deeper level refer to a specific historical situation.

One such example is no. 116, "Refa Ṣiri," a pizmon by Raphael Taboush; the transmission and melody of this song are discussed in chapter 5. The Hebrew text of "Refa Ṣiri," which is provided in English translation below, is to all appearances a straightforward prayer for healing, with a messianic reference based on Leviticus 25:10 embedded in the third stanza:[10]

> Heal my pain, oh faithful Lord,
> Because you are the master healer.
> Fortify the weakness of my mind(?)
> And give strength to my soul.
>
> Open the gate of mercy,
> Him who resides on high.
> On your servant bestow your kindness;
> There is no merciful one besides you.

> Living God, accept my prayer
> and hasten my succour.
> Quickly call for the liberation
> of the nation of the Lord.

Oral traditions about this pizmon link it to a theme not mentioned in the text, composer Raphel Taboush's loss of eyesight, suggesting that the songs can carry information not obvious on the surface:

> The words of this song is sort of like a prayer to God, asking him to heal his eyesight. And he's telling him that he knows that it's in God's power to give him back his eyesight and you know, it's like a prayer that he should. . . . And at the same time like, if you wouldn't know that, you could have like a different interpretation of the words like, when you, when you're singing it, just to, that God should give you strength in your religious duties like to, you know, give you power and strength. So like the words can be taken either way. . . . Like sort of a play on words. (M. Arking, 14 January 1986)

That this pizmon retains a strong association with healing is confirmed by the context in which it is performed: it is presently sung in Syrian synagogues when an individual who has recovered from an illness or surgery is called forth to the Torah: "Because his prayers were answered to be healed. . . . So they would sing the song for him" (ibid.).

Closer examination indicates that "Refa Ṣiri" is only one of several pizmonim that are connected through both their textual content and oral traditions to healing practices. As noted in chapter 4, pizmon "Yaḥid Ram" contains the phrase *refa El,* which means "O God, heal," in its second stanza; this is interpreted as a veiled reference to its composer, Raphael Taboush. Similarly, pizmon "Nora Varam" (no. 239), which was written by Taboush and is often sung after "Yaḥid Ram" at the Sebet, both contains Taboush's name and hints at the shortest prayer in the Bible, *El na refa na lah,* "O God, pray heal her now."

These pizmonim contain the residue of a belief that sung prayer can effect healing, an association that almost certainly emerges from deep cultural memories maintained by Syrian Jews long separated from Aleppo. In using the expression "cultural memories," I here follow the usage of Samuel A. Floyd, who defines cultural memories

> as a repository of meanings that comprise the subjective knowledge of a people, its immanent thoughts, its structures, and its practices; these thoughts, structures, and practices are transferred and understood uncon-

> sciously but become conscious and culturally objective in practice and perception. Cultural memory, obviously a subjective concept, seems to be connected with cultural *forms*—in the present case, music, where the "memory" drives the music and the music drives the memory. (Floyd 1995:8)

In the case of "Refa Ṣiri" and other pizmonim related to healing, seemingly vague cultural memories are deeply grounded in documented history, where an overlap can be confirmed to have existed between traditional medicine and official religion. Notably, "In addition to employing doctors, the Jews called in rabbis to pray at the bedside of the sick in order to help combat the work of evil spirits, and even hired Muslim holy men to apply their powers of divine intercession and exorcism" (A. Marcus 1989:267). While healing and charming are technically forbidden to Jews by biblical injunction (Deuteronomy 18:11), traditional healing practices, including the use of amulets, pleading with saints, and consulting astrologers, were widespread among Jews in premodern Aleppo (A. Marcus 1989:267). With an epidemic of plague and staggering casualties occuring roughly every decade, major changes in health care began only in the nineteenth century with the importation of European ideas and practices. Indeed, traditional medicine is known to have persisted among Syrian Jews until early in the twentieth century (ibid. 168).

That traditional healing practices remained in active memory following the period of immigration is made clear by literary references to them in SUHV. A sentence in Moses Ashear's introduction to that volume states "I have not made for myself [a name] like the name of the great men, those who work charms" (SUHV, p. 9). These references found in the writings of Ashear and others are part of a larger network of allusions to and quotation from mystical sources. Cantor Ashear also quotes a scholar of Kabbalah active in the Safed community during the sixteenth century, R. Moses Alshekh (SUHV, p. 10; see also Preschal 1972), while Rabbi Kassin's preface includes Kabbalistic imagery, directing the reader to "go now to that book and see for yourself the lovely statements and hidden words" (SUHV, p. 29).

"Refa Ṣiri," with its textual references to healing, sustains but a faint trace of the Ḥalabi community's complex historical engagement with folk beliefs about spirits and exorcism (Patai 1983). Moreover, this influence is still remembered and acknowledged by members of the Syrian community when they remark that the pizmonim are "imbued with feeling and respect for the Kabbalah" (S. Catton, 29 November 1991). A mystical connection is noted particularly in relation to the bakkashot (D. Tawil, 11 December 1984), an observation elucidated by musicologists who have traced the impact of the Zohar and the formative role of the Safed Kabbalists in relation to that repertory (Shiloah 1992:133). Kabbalistic beliefs and practices are still discussed by Syrian Jews in late twentieth century Brooklyn. One woman mentioned that "my father was learned of Torah and used to read Kabbalah" (Anon.), while others recalled that techniques such as writing Hebrew backward used to be practiced by scribes within the Brooklyn Ḥalabi community (H. Kaire, 17 February 1988).

Yet while some individual songs such as "Refa Ṣiri" shed light on largely discontinued historical practices and community memories rarely articulated, the pizmon repertory as a whole provides an idealized and even mythologized view of the Ḥalabi past. Pizmonim serve to inscribe and transmit a history that would not otherwise be remembered. In a very real sense, the pizmonim enable an individual in the present to re-sing, re-hear, and re-experience the past.

What sort of history do the pizmonim construct? Their record is necessarily incomplete and almost always valedictory. The history they sing is idealized and selective. The affirmation of life is the central message of the pizmonim. If stable environments can be celebrated through heterogeneous musical repertories, it is as if the rapidly shifting landscape of Syrian Jewish experience has been stabilized through perpetuating a unified vision through songs.

The songs are particularly eloquent in their modeling of a traditional, patriarchal society. Pizmonim were written for men, by men, and have historically been performed by men as well. Their texts compare Syrian fathers to the biblical patriarchs, after whom they are also named. Women are present only occasionally and when evident, appear as a result of unusual situations: here we can place the Saff bar mitzvah pizmon written to a mother in extended mourning, or a pizmon dedicated to the unexpected arrival of twin girls. Yet women are ever-present in the *lived* world of pizmon performance. In this case, the ethnographer is privy to a cultural dimension of pizmon transmission otherwise invisible within the song texts and largely absent from men's testimony about them.

The Arabic "Source"

It is ironic that this discussion of Arab influence on the musical life of Syrian Jews dates primarily to the years in which the Ḥalabi community has lived outside the Middle East and away from daily interaction with Arab culture. Indeed, the only period of Syrian Jewish history truly accessible to ethnomusicological inquiry, given the transmission of Syrian music as an oral tradition, is that during which the community has been separated from its Middle Eastern "homeland."

The long residency of Syrian Jews outside Syria and their separation from a living world of Arab music renders all the more striking the continued resonance of Arab musical thought and practice among them. As noted in chapter 2, in the records of their sixteenth-century Ottoman conquerors Arabic-speaking Jews were termed mustaʿriba. While the term certainly implies Arabic language use as the primary marker of this identity, the linguistic factor is acknowledged to have been but one part of a broader pattern of a composite cultural life aptly characterized as a "Judeo–Islamic symbiosis":

> The process of the acculturation of the Jews in the Arab Islamic world goes beyond the point of Arabization, a term that is perhaps too narrowly linguistic, and might better be designated as Islamicization. . . . What is intended here is not the adoption of the Islamic religion, but assimilation to Islamic modes of thought and patterns of behavior. (Lewis 1984:77)

The materials presented in the preceding pages suggest that a Judeo–Islamic symbiosis is still actively perpetuated by Syrian Jews, particularly those who today live in the Americas. If substantiation is needed for the existence of Judeo–Islamic cultural expression outside the linguistic realm, we need look no farther than the Ḥalabi musical tradition in Brooklyn. While their longstanding use of the Arabic language has declined markedly during their years in the Americas (S. Catton, 30 October 1984; M. Kairey, 12 December 1984), their distinctive musical life has not. Indeed, it may be suggested that perpetuation of the Ḥalabi musical culture, especially given the ubiquitous presence of musical activity in social and religious life, serves as a surrogate for Arabic language use and provides the main venue through which the community maintains continuity with its Middle Eastern past while keeping its equilibrium in an ever-changing American setting.

It is therefore not coincidental that many of the most striking statements concerning Ḥalabi music touch in some way on its symbiotic relationship to Arabic language. The observation of one community member that "before you could say it in Hebrew, you have to know it good in Arabic first" (G. Shrem, 9 January 1986) applies equally to the linguistic and musical domains of Ḥalabi culture. In order to function in the Syrian Jewish world of the past, men had to know both Arabic and Hebrew, since for centuries the Arabic language was often written by Jews in Hebrew script (Lewis 1984:78). Women, who were not active in Jewish ritual life or commerce, usually spoke Arabic at home (generally a local Judeo-Arabic dialect) and, with few exceptions, were not instructed in Hebrew. Boundaries between the pizmonim and the Arab songs from which they are derived are equally porous and in fact replicate the relationship of the languages in which a Hebrew surface encased an Arabic core.

Just as many Syrian Jews knew the Arabic script in which the Arabic language was originally written, they are familiar with many of the Arabic songs that were sources for the Hebrew-texted pizmonim, especially those composed during their lifetimes. Many individuals attach special importance to the original Arabic words, feeling that the manner of expressing sentiment "really touches you" when it is in Arabic (G. Haber, 31 January 1989). One recent immigrant to Brooklyn who was not involved with pizmon performance in his native Damascus recalled that

> The first time I was exposed to the [pizmon] book was when I came here. . . . However, I knew all the songs in Arabic. This music is taken from Arabic music. Whenever I hear them singing in the synagogue . . . it sounds very familiar to me. I know the song in Arabic, however, I don't know the words. They put words in Hebrew. (B. Zalta, 16 March 1990)

The original Arabic texts continue to predominate even among native residents of Brooklyn. At one music session, Moses Tawil acknowledged that it was the first time he had sung one pizmon (no. 331, "Melekh Hadur") in Hebrew (M. Tawil, 20 November 1984). He had earlier noted that

> until maybe about twenty years ago, I sang only Arabic. . . . And I still do sing a lot of Arabic in many of the songs, that we sing in pizmon[im], I sing them in Arabic, which is the authentic song. Which gives it the authentic flavor, because invariably, it could change in the translation. I'm not talking about the translation of the words, and passing the melody, but the authentic *makor,* the base (lit. "the source" [Hebrew]), is the Arabic and that's that. (M. Tawil, 6 November 1984)

It is therefore not surprising that when seeking to define the pizmon, most people struggled to articulate its essential doubleness: "A pizmon . . . it's an Arabic song, but it's a pizmon in Hebrew" (Y. Nahari, 16 January 1986). The symbiotic relationship of the Hebrew and Arabic texts is perhaps best explained metaphorically in a story about Cantor Moses Ashear:

> He [Ashear] had an Arabic song on a record. Somebody came in one day and he is listening to Arabic music. That needs an explanation. He told them: "It's the same like somebody wants to build, he builds and he puts wood, and he pours the pavement. . . . So the pavement will be hard and then he throws away the wood he's building, see? I, too, learned the Arabic. Once I put in the Hebrew music phonetically and everything, then I throw away the Arabic. It doesn't mean anything to me anymore. That's why I'm learning this first." He's learning the Arabic first. (A. Ashear, 19 July 1989)

The translation process in the musical domain involves much more than just substituting Hebrew for pre-existing Arabic text. Hebrew words are chosen that mimic to the greatest extent possible the original Arabic meter, rhyme scheme, alliteration, and assonance (See Kligman 1997:132–55). Thus a pizmon with a Hebrew text is intentionally set by a composer with

> the words [that] are exactly like he'll hear it in Arabic. He'll put the same words in Hebrew, that you'll think it's Arabic words. The song, the words. They're Hebrew words but in poetry they'll sound exactly like you're listening to an Arab song. (M. Kairey, 6 November 1984)

The structure of the pizmon is therefore congruent on both cognitive and cultural levels with the bifurcated Jewish/Arab identity that produced it, embodying its different streams while welding them into a unified whole. Song furthermore serves to give shape and sound to deeply held beliefs:

> This is what singers have done in the past, and it is what singers do in our own time. They take non-Jewish songs and introduce them to holiness by using their tune to accompany songs sung to the Lord. (Kassin 1964: 32–33)

The Pizmon and the Politics of Everyday Life

If the conceptual and affective doubleness of the Syrian pizmon is at once an expression of a dual Jewish and Arab identity, it may also serve to conceal that symbiosis. Only occasionally are political tensions between Jews and Arabs identified as a reason for cloaking Arabic songs in Hebrew texts:

> You know we take a song from the Arabic and make it Hebrew. Many of the melodies are from the Arabic. You know we have had business with the Arabs, so we do them in Hebrew. Those from Aleppo who love Hebrew, they love them in Hebrew, but they love the Arabic songs and translate them to Hebrew. (I. Abadi, 21 November 1984)

While the pizmonim are eloquent in so many ways, most of the songs, particularly those of recent composition, are silent about pressing contemporary issues. However, most pizmonim contain biblical references which may be interpreted metaphorically in their relationship to the present day. Injunctions to "rebuild the Sanctuary" pervade a great many pizmonim, such as "Ṣur Yah El," while the entreaty that "all of their enemies shall be destroyed" is incorporated into a seemingly "light" pizmon, "Ram Leḥasdakh." While the pizmonim appear to lack explicit references to current national and political issues, they speak deeply and emotionally of a desire to return from diaspora to the Jewish homeland.

One text of particular historical importance is no. 105, "Libbi Ve-Mizraḥ," attributed to Judah Halevi, a Hebrew poet and philosopher from Spain who died in Egypt on his way to the land of Israel around the year 1141. "Libbi Ve-Mizraḥ" is one of his most famous poetic works, from a collection known as *Shirei Ṣiyyon* (Poems of Zion) (*Encyclopaedia Hebraica* 1972:355–62). Halevi's poem is included in SUHV not among the pizmonim, but among the petiḥot, the poetic verses sung to improvised melodies before and between bakkashot and pizmonim.

"Libbi Ve-Mizraḥ" speaks directly to the political situation in Arab-ruled Spain during Halevi's period and the poet's desire to visit the remains of the Temple in Jerusalem:

> My heart is in the east, and I in uttermost west—
> How can I find savour in food? How shall it be sweet to me?
> How shall I render my vows and my bonds, while yet
> Zion lieth beneath the fetter of Edom, and I in Arab chains?
> A light thing would it seem to be to leave all the good things of Spain—
> Seeing how precious in mine eyes to behold the dust of the desolate
>   sanctuary.
>
> (Brody 1973:2)

"Libbi Ve-Mizraḥ" is both well known and frequently performed among present-day Ḥalabi Jews: Halevi himself is termed "our national poet" in SUHV (Kassin 1988:28). "Libbi Ve-Mizraḥ" is considered to be a text "with a lot of meaning to it" (H. Kaire, 17 February 1988). Individuals particularly emphasize its references to the Temple:

> Look at the words. . . . That's pertaining to the Wailing Wall. . . . I happen to like them. Maybe I'm sentimental. Some people say it . . . the people that understand, you know. (Ibid.)

After nearly a century of Arab–Jewish conflict in the Middle East, Syrian Jews continue to compose and sing pizmonim, but not to comment in musical discourse on the broader course of events. Rather, awareness of political and religious tensions surfaces in oral testimonies about the tradition and its place in individual lives. Of particular interest are the tales concerning the deleterious effects on historical figures who entered the world of Arab music and sought to transform it for Jewish use. Raphael Taboush is said to have gone blind as a result of being discovered surreptitiously listening to music in an Arab village. Moses Ashear is said to have died while trying to recall an Arab song that was the source of a pizmon. At the same time, the (dangerous) act of transforming and singing a foreign tune is on another level perceived as redemptive. This perspective, likely shaped by Kabbalistic doctrine, suggests that

> By singing of (foreign) tunes you cause God to take account of the nation whose song is sung, for having persecuted you. Consequently the ancient and contemporary poets borrowed the tunes of foreign (= Arabic) songs and composed for them holy words. (Divrê Mordekai, fol. 27b, translated in Fenton 1982:125 n. 6)[11]

If, as the literary scholar Ammiel Alcalay has pointed out, "the negation of the past" is a characteristic of the literary tradition among modern Arab Jews, resulting in the circumscribing of "a certain space and the relations within it" (1993:264), one may speculate that a similar tendency is present in the musical domain. Just as "what is not in this poem becomes another mode of description" (ibid.), textual ambiguity and the power of metaphor enable pizmon performance to give voice to the continued vitality of a shared identity that has survived conflict and transcended political realities. Syrian Jews do not sing about the dislocations, migrations, and violence that have marked their own and broader Middle Eastern history for the last century. Rather, they sing in spite of it.

In one of the few published statements by a member of the community concerning his own Judeo-Arab heritage, the author suggests that the Ḥalabi community consciously separates its cultural life from contemporary politics:

> Forty generations ago, goes the legend, my Syrian ancestors held two great devotions: Judaism and Arabic culture. When my father emigrated to the United States, he brought them with him and adapted as best he could. Though an exotic among his brethren of European background, he

> is dedicated to his religion, and he remains faithful to his Arabic upbringing, which he holds dear and separate from current politics of the Middle East. (Haddad 1985)

Today the Judeo–Islamic symbiosis in Syrian Jewish musical life remains powerful:

> At one time, I thought I was odd because I love Syrian music. When I first got married, I had to listen to rock and roll garbage, and to me Syrian music was beauty. A lot of my friends, to them it was alien, and then after a couple of years, I found that, interesting, they do like Syrian music. When we would have an affair, no one would even think of having a band or rock and roll, no, it was Syrian music. When it came to bar mitzvahs, or with a small party, it's Syrian music. When it came to engagements, it's always Syrian music. Anything in the house was always Syrian music. That's just synonymous with a happy occasion. So I was amazed at how many people actually do appreciate the Syrian music. (S. Schweky, 27 January 1988)

Many Syrian Jews may still be said without hyperbole to inhabit a sound world of Arab music, ranging from the businessman who keeps Arab music cassettes in his office so that while he is working he can listen to them "all day" (I. Cain, 7 September 1992) to the elderly woman who listens to tapes of Umm Kulthūm and ʿAbd al-Wahhāb before going to bed at night (S. Harari, 7 September 1992). However, pressures from the outside as well as the inevitable dynamics of change have led to modifications both in musical repertories and conceptualization of the tradition. Young people of the community still

> sing Arabic. Now especially the lighter songs, the ones with the timing and the beat. Those, yes, they learn to sing them and they sing them and they like to take part in it. And they dance to them. The dancing is very, very graceful and very enjoyable, this type of Oriental dancing. . . . This is very common, very popular. When there is a party, a bar mitzvah, engagement, the wedding, particularly if it's in a home, more often than not, we use Arabic music. And quite often, when it's in a ballroom, and it's a wedding or a bar mitzvah, they use the Western music, and after that, well, if they feel like it . . . they bring in the Arabic music. Or even when they have the disco, the disco people that cater to us, many of them and their repertoire, they have Arabic music. (M. Tawil, 6 November 1984)

Perhaps not surprisingly, along with the changing repertories, new technologies, and the increasing adaptation by Ḥalabi young people to their New

York setting, the strong historical ties of the Ḥalabi community to Aleppo have subtly weakened. If attachments to specific localities have long characterized the world view of many Middle Eastern peoples,[12] we begin to see hints that Syrian Jewish ties to Aleppo are slowly being supplanted by a connection to a delocalized and, perhaps, idealized "Oriental" past. As one woman explained as she described preparations for a family occasion:

> I'm busy now making the family tree and I want to blow up old pictures. . . . What I had planned to do, I bought a paisley wallpaper and I want to have an Oriental feeling. And I was going to superimpose a beige tree on it and you know, put each individual, a picture of them, calligraphy their dates. . . . I'm only going to do my immediate family. Now my cousin made a family tree going as far back as my father's father. (Anon.)

Through their performance of pizmonim, Syrian Jews bridge time and space. There is little doubt that the pizmonim represent the Syrian Jewish community at its best in its past; the songs provide moments in which they can "taste some of the sweetness of life" (J. Saff, 23 October 1984). At the same time the songs serve to anchor and validate the present while providing a pathway for the future through which the community may sustain its identity and exist at its fullest as a "community in song."

Embroidered Rag

POEM ON UMM KULTHUM

She had a black evening gown on
and her voice hammered steel nails
into the elbow leaning on the table
in the cafe on Struma Square.
"My eyes have gotten used to seeing you,
and if you don't come one day
I'll blot that day from my life."
I came with a sponge to rub out
a huge eagle drawn in chalk
on the edge of a cloud.
A embroidered rag that years later the cook at
the base at Be'er Ora hooked to his belt loop
fluttered under its wings.
I asked him for a couple of oranges
and on the cassette player her gown darkened again.
He shut his eyes to the steaming lunch and kept
  peeling potatoes.
Who's that singing, I started, Umm Kulthum?
He nodded.
For all he cared, I could have cleaned out the whole
  kitchen.[1]

NOTES

Epigraph and Anagraph

1. Poems by Ronny Someck (1989:19 ["Jasmine"], 1989:18 ["Embroidered Rag"]), translated by Ammiel Alcalay (1993:266, 265–66).

Introduction

1. While Syrian Jews living in Israel have received only limited scholarly attention from anthropologists and ethnomusicologists (see Zenner 1965; R. Katz 1968), published work on Syrian cultural life in the diaspora is also sparse (Zenner 1983, 1988; Ginsberg 1987; Zerubavel and Esses 1987). One recently completed Ph.D. dissertation provides an overview of Syrian biblical cantillation (Ya'ar 1996), while another documents the use of Arab *maqāmāt* in the Syrian Sabbath morning liturgy (Kligman 1997). Other notable contributions to date are non-scholarly "insider" writings about the Syrian communities in Brooklyn and Mexico City, which include Sutton 1979 and 1988, Chira 1994, and Ashkenazi 1982.

2. Discussion of the Syrian community and its multi-layered identity is found in chapter 2.

3. See Shelemay 1988 for a detailed account of the team research project that took place in 1984 and 1985.

4. Formal interviews, listed in alphabetical order in the references, were transcribed in full. When formal interviews are cited verbatim or paraphrased within the text, they are identified by the name of the individual interviewed and date. While only one individual requested anonymity when sitting for a formal interview, I have in some instances chosen not to attribute certain sensitive quotations from others. Many informal exchanges took place before, during, and after music sessions, which are listed in chronological order in the bibliography and are occasionally cited by name of interviewee and date. Additional attributions to different dates or to individuals not included in these lists make reference to information conveyed on other occasions, including through casual conversations or by telephone. Descriptions of events and other observations are cited directly from my fieldnotes.

5. See Tolbert 1990, a study of Karelian laments, "an essential part of remembrance feasts for the dead" (p. 80).

6. These include fields as diverse as history (Spence 1983), literature (Van Vleck

1991), cultural studies (J. Boyarin 1994), anthropology (Battaglia 1990), and even architecture (Bloomer and Moore 1977).

7. Meyer 1967 briefly touches on music and memory (pp. 46–47). See also Treitler 1974. Treitler's early work further sparked the interest of the psychologist David C. Rubin, whose own volume, *Memory in Oral Traditions* (1995), came to my attention after this book had been drafted.

8. A salient example is Mozart's Requiem, the commemorative role of which has been the subject of considerable speculation. See Wolff 1994.

9. Studies distinguish between short-term memory (STM) and long-term memory (LTM). STM generally refers to a system that retains information temporarily in a special status (Squire 1987:135). In contrast, LTM is a more stable, potentially permanent store. LTM, also termed secondary remembering, is thus defined as a process subsequent to and qualitatively different from primary remembering. To date, studies of musical memory have mainly focused on aspects of STM such as interval or melody retention. Yet much more relevant to ethnomusicological interests and open to ethnomusicological investigation is LTM, which is vulnerable to both unconscious and intentional transformations (Casey 1987:51).

10. The "preludes" also have an aesthetic intention described more fully below.

11. Fentress and Wickham (1992:ix) provide a similar perspective.

12. A term I prefer to use in regard to the pizmon, which is at once born of cross-cultural contact, and a fusion of the traditional and massified; I use hybrid in preference to syncretism, synthesis, or transculturation (see Kartomi 1981, Kartomi and Blum 1994). For a recent and insightful discussion of the tensions between tradition and modernity and the manner in which these are posited in cultural production, see Canclini 1995. Canclini's study, which focuses on the crossings of indigenous and colonial legacies within contemporary art and electronic cultures in Latin America, endorses the perspective that abrupt oppositions between the traditional and the modern do not work. He also uses the term "hybridization" to indicate "diverse, intercultural mixtures" (p. 31).

13. See particularly the special volume of *The World of Music,* "Ethnomusicology and Music Cognition," which includes Koskoff 1992 and Tolbert 1992, providing a useful overview of issues and current literature.

14. Most influential in ethnomusicology to date has been Dowling and Harwood 1986. A recent contribution approaching musical competence as a distinct cognitive domain is Brinner 1995. Of particular interest for this discussion, too, is the research of Wallace (1988, 1991) and Wallace and Rubin (1987), which examines constraints shaping memory processes in ballad transmission. It seems possible that much of the psychological literature unwittingly presents barriers to cultural analysts because it often takes experimental data from the pathological subject, while humanists tend to extrapolate from a shared norm. However, recent studies, such as Schacter 1995b, provide useful models for cultural analysts who seek to apply concepts such as memory distortion in a qualitative context.

Chapter One

1. The choir was conducted by Rabbi Shimon Alouf; the instrumentalists included Sam Answary (electric keyboard), Abe Tawil (qānūn), Ezra Ashkenazi (darābukkah), and Hakki Obadia (violin).

2. Indeed, it could also be said that the performance was of the "original" Arab music upon which the melody of Ṣur Yah El had been based, since the Arab source in fact was an instrumental piece. The compositional process is discussed below.

3. While bayātī is the most common spelling of the name, Syrian Jews in Brooklyn tend to refer simply to this maqām as bayāt. I will use bayātī in my narrative but will follow local usage in direct quotations.

4. C. Serouya, 15 July 1993. Shaul (Saul) means "borrowed" or "taken on loan."

5. I thank Virginia Danielson and Edwin Seroussi for this dating and the observation that the 1951 date renders a dedication to Nasser unlikely.

6. "Ṣur Yah El" was performed at L'Chaim: A Festival of Jewish Arts, on September 17, 1989, by Vita Israel, Hakki Obadia, George Bassil, and Joseph Zaroura under the rubric "Near Eastern Jewish Music and Song."

7. The 1983 edition is the first to use the lyre emblem on its cover; prior printings, the first in 1964, presented the title of the book, [Sefer] *Sheer Ushbahah Hallel Ve-Zimrah* (hereafter abbreviated SUHV) within a rectangular frame. Decorative representations of a violin are placed at each corner. It should be noted that the title of the edition draws on a phrase from the Sabbath morning liturgy that translates "Song and Praise, Praise and Song."

8. Hanoch Avenary traces this practice to a thirteenth-century mystical source (1979:186).

9. A statement contained in Rabbi Jacob S. Kassin's introduction to SUHV. The following discussion summarizes Rabbi Kassin's comments.

10. This explanation draws on the ideas of the Lurianic Kabbalah, which derives from the influence of Rabbi Isaac Luria (1534–1572), a kabbalist in Egypt and Safed. His work was transmitted and promulgated by his student R. Hayyim Vital, who lived for a time in Damascus. See Scholem 1970, esp. col. 596; Scholem 1941; and Blumenthal 1978, esp. pp. 159–68. Kabbalah is the term used for esoteric teachings of Judaism and Jewish mysticism dating from the twelfth century onward (Scholem 1970:489). For additional information see Scholem 1941 and Idel 1988.

11. The first edition of Najara's *Zemirot Israel* was printed at Safed; a second expanded edition with 346 poems appeared in Venice in 1599–1600 (Idelsohn 1929:362–63). See also Avenary 1979, Yahalom 1982, and Seroussi 1990.

12. Safed is a town in northern Israel very near the modern Syrian border. It should be noted that Najara was apparently born in Damascus (David 1972:798). For additional details, see also Seroussi 1990.

13. For an excellent summary of the relationship of paraliturgical song repertories to mystical practice, see Shiloah 1992, esp. pp. 131–56. Mystical speculations of Islamic Sufism further influenced Jewish beliefs about the redemptive function of music (Fenton 1982:125). I thank Mark Kligman for bringing this article to my attention and Ezra Barnea for an instructive conversation on this subject (10 March 1993).

14. For example, no. 10 in SUHV, which is not formally a pizmon but is included within a related group of paraliturgical hymns known as *bakkashot,* further discussed below. Bakkashot and pizmonim are referred to in the Syrian Brooklyn community by the page number on which they appear in SUHV. While it should be noted that each song is also preceded by a Hebrew number clearly visible in the book, I will follow community practice and refer to pizmonim by the page numbers on which the songs begin.

15. Only one member of the community with whom I worked mentioned compositional activity by another historical figure besides Taboush. Isaac Abadi (21 November 1984) took great pains to point out that two of the bakkashot (nos. 51 and 52) are attributed to Rabbi Mordekhai Abadi, whom he claimed to be his great grandfather. Abadi went on to emphasize that he had named his own son Mordekhai after this ancestor.

16. I thank Ezra Barnea and Edwin Seroussi, who independently directed me to this reference. Taboush's date of birth is not listed, although a photograph provides the date as 1873 (Shelemay fieldnotes, 12 September 1992).

17. Gracia Haber gave great emphasis to this point, noting afterward "that's how we are." See below for a discussion of Syrian Jewish naming traditions.

18. Ḥakham is a traditional title given to a learned man.

19. Taboush's picture hangs in the Sephardic Community Center in Brooklyn and is reproduced in plate 8. Another portrait is found in SUHV, p. 7.

20. Raphael was evidently escorted everywhere by his Uncle Yehudah, the mentally handicapped brother of his mother Seti. There are amusing stories about escapades of Raphael with Yehudah, including one recounting how Yehudah escorted Raphael to the public baths: "Yehudah took Raphael to the bath and he walked him naked outside. Raphael noticed that he was on the street, but Yehudah didn't. This is a joke they used to tell about Yehudah. There were so many" (G. Haber, 31 January 1989). The public bathhouses for centuries doubled as places of amusement and socializing, giving rise to a rich lore of popular sayings and stories centered on this social institution (A. Marcus 1989:231).

21. According to Hyman Kaire, he sang no. 8 ("El Mistatter") and no. 41 ("Uri Neṣurah") (14 March 1985). The melodies of the bakkashot are thought to have been newly composed. See chapter 4.

22. Moses Ashear's name is recorded in Hebrew and Arabic as "Ashkar." However the Anglicization "Ashear" is today used universally (S. Catton, 27 September 1996).

23. Not all individuals from Aleppo claimed Taboush as a mentor; there were evidently other paths for transmission of songs. An instructive example is the story of Isaac Abadi, an active teacher of pizmonim who was born in Aleppo and immigrated to the United States after lengthy stays in Lebanon and Israel. Abadi remembers: "I was ten years old when I began to study songs. I was in the orphanage school, Bet Yatomi, in Ḥalab [Aleppo; see chapter 2]. I did not have a father, my mother died. I was the first—I had a beautiful voice at age ten. At ten years I started. Often I had forty children I taught. We used to go if anybody has a *simḥa* [happy occasion], a bar mitzvah, or something, we used to go because they used to give [a] donation to the orphanage school. I

had my bar mitzvah in the orphanage school. They made cake, everything, they were like a father and mother. . . . About once a week we had some teacher and he came and taught us maqāmāt, this and that, and we learned. They graduated me first among the children at the school but I love to teach and I do not take money. I taught many boys in Israel. In 1928 I came to Israel from Syria (I. Abadi, 21 November 1984).

24. While Ashear is commonly said to have been orphaned, in fact only his father died in 1883, when Moses was six years old. Moses Ashear's mother survived and later immigrated with her sons to New York City, where she died in Brooklyn in 1921. Moses Ashear's eldest brother Joseph, after whom one of Moshe's sons was named, predeceased his mother in 1918 (A. Ashear, 19 July 1989). A brief biographical sketch of Moses Ashear, written by his grandson Allan J. Ashear, is found in the introduction to SUHV, pp. 11–13.

25. Another teacher remembered in the Brooklyn community was Ezra Mishan, who "didn't have a voice, [but] knew a lot, mostly from his head" (G. Shrem, 9 January 1986). Mishan, who died in 1985, is remembered fondly by pizmon aficionados of all ages (M. Arking, 14 January 1986).

26. Isaac Cabasso, a lay cantor and relative of Mickey Kairey who has been honored for decades of service at Brooklyn Synagogue Bet Torah, is said to have credited Menaged as instrumental in his own training. "Everyone who hears him [Cabasso] thinks that he was brought up in Syria, the way he conducts the services" (H. Kaire, 17 February 1988).

27. For a discussion of the traditional practice of *sharḥ,* the translation of Hebrew texts into Arabic, see Zenner 1965:74 and Kligman 1997:155–56.

28. For example, a biography of Isaac Shalom (1885–1968) appears on p. 14 of SUHV. While Shalom was a community leader and philanthropist who helped establish synagogues, yeshivot [religious schools], colleges, and youth centers, he played no direct musical role.

29. Shrem's life history is recounted in chapter 2.

30. Taboush himself no doubt drew on *Divre Mordekhai* (Aleppo, 1873), a collection of sixty-nine pizmonim assorted by maqām, compiled by Mordekhai Abadi; as well as a collection of bakkashot titled *Sefer Miqra Qodesh* (Livorno, 1883 [Seroussi 1993:118–19]), compiled after Abadi's death. See A. Marcus 1989:244 for the history of earlier Jewish religious writings in Aleppo, including rabbinic legal opinions (responsa) and scriptural commentaries, some of which were published by Hebrew presses in Livorno and Istanbul.

31. Sam Catton notes that the Brooklyn pizmon edition also borrows from Hayyim Shaul Aboud's *Sefer Shirei Zimrah Hashalem,* first published in 1931 in Jerusalem, still used actively today in Israel in its fourth edition (S. Catton, 23 October 1984).

32. When Shrem arrived in New York City with his family in 1928, he was refused admittance because of an eye infection, likely trachoma. See chapter 2 for further discussion. Shrem was blind when interviewed in 1986.

33. Albert Ashear remembered that he supplied the original pages from his father's book for reprinting in the community, which eventually resulted in the publication of SUHV (A. Ashear, 19 July 1989).

34. One error is said to be the placement of several unidentified ʿajam songs under maqām rast (J. Mosseri, 14 January 1986). The melody of pizmon no. 187 is incorrectly identified as "Opera Africa" when it is actually the Neapolitan song "Santa Lucia," further discussed in chapter 5 (ibid.). Finally, the first of the bakkashot, while attributed to Abraham Maimon, is acknowledged to have been composed by Abraham Maimyn, a Kabbalist who lived in sixteenth-century Safed (D. Tawil, 11 December 1984).

35. This passage quotes a bible commentary by R. Shalom b. Raphael Gabbai, which in turn quotes Deut. 4:9 and Mishnah Avot 3:8. The passage goes on to interpret the phrase "from his mishnah" as meaning "from the letters of his soul." I thank James Robinson for his translation and explanation of this passage.

36. "Bakkashot and Saturday Night Songs" (3 tapes) were produced and released by the Sephardic Archives of the Sephardic Community Center, 1987. I earlier made a field recording of Cabasso, Kaire, and Kairey singing the complete bakkashot at a session held at New York University on 12 June 1985. H. Kaire (14 March 1985) also recalled that he, Kairey, and Cabasso had recorded some bakkashot two years earlier.

37. The pizmon composed by Cantor Raphael Elnadav is dedicated to Ezra, son of Mordekhai Tawil.

38. The bakkashot are paraliturgical hymns of supplication sung in the early hours of Sabbath morning before prayers. The relationship of the bakkashot to the pizmonim is discussed in subsequent chapters.

39. For members of the community who trace their ancestry to Jews exiled from Spain, names are further marked: "Traditionally we were all from Aleppo, our ancestry goes as far back as 1503. Prior to that our forefathers were from Spain. We are known as Sephardic Jews, but . . . there's a manner in which a person may sign his name in Hebrew and at the end of the name you put two letters. One is the *samekh* and the second one is the *ṭet*. And the indication is: *Sefaradi Ṭahor*. '*Sefaradi*' means a 'Spaniard,' *ṭahor*, 'who was pure, who did not marry a Christian or who did not convert to Christian world,' that's a Safaradi Ṭahor. Now those would have been those individuals that escaped from Spain, gone through Europe, and ended up finally in the focal point of Aleppo" (D. Tawil, 11 December 1984). The abbreviation "samekh ṭet" is instead interpreted by some as meaning "Siman Ṭov," literally "a good omen" or "a blessing" (R. Alcalay 1963:1751).

40. The Sephardic tradition here deviates from that of the Ashkenazic Jews, who under no circumstances name children after living relatives. A study of traditional religion among Germanic Jews from the eleventh to the sixteenth centuries found that "the desire to bless a child with a richly endowed name was balanced by the fear that the soul of its previous owner would be transported into the body of the infant—a fear which stood in the way of naming children after living parents or after any living persons, and thus robbing them of their soul and their life. This dread led indeed in some cases to a superstitious refusal to adopt the name even of a dead ancestor, since this would oblige the soul to forsake its heavenly abode and re-enter the realm of the living" (Trachtenberg 1974:78).

41. "Syrian" refers to the Arabic language, either the Syrian dialect or in some cases a dialect of Judeo-Arabic.

42. See Ginsberg 1987 for a discussion of changes in the lives of Syrian women.

43. Indeed, Sheila's sister, Joyce Kassin, considers it important to teach children pizmonim in school in order that they transmit them to homes where the songs are not actively sung (J. Kassin, 30 March 1989).

Chapter Two

1. Vita Israel, born in Cairo in 1917 to Syrian parents and who immigrated to Brooklyn in 1956, was joined by violinist Hakki Obadia, an Iraqi-born Jewish musician who has been very active in both Syrian Jewish and Arab musical circles in the United States. The qānūnist was George Bassil, a Beirut native (b. 1933) who immigrated to the U.S. in 1975; and the percussionist, Joseph Zaroura (program for *L'Chaim: A Festival of Jewish Arts,* produced by the Jewish Community Center of Staten Island and Snug Harbor Cultural Center, Inc., 1989).

2. The musicians also performed "Eḥezeh Veno'am" (no. 213), "Ṣur Yah El" (no. 313, introduced by its Arabic title "Bint al-Balad" but sung in Hebrew), and "Ma'uzzi" (no. 246). They did not have time to perform a final number in maqām ḥijāz nor an announced encore "Fantasy Nahāwand."

3. A rendition from a commercial recording published in Brooklyn in 1979 is transcribed in this prelude (from *Pizmonim: Sephardic-Hebrew Songs* 1979). The other recordings compared include number 1/4538 (Syria, Ḥalab) of the National Sound Archive at the Jewish National and University Library, Jerusalem, performed in 1983 by a seventeen-year-old boy who has prayed at the "Great Synagogue Ades of Aleppo Jews" in Jerusalem all his life, and a rendition sung during an interview of Yaqov Bozo, carried out with the assistance of Ezra Barnea on 14 March 1993 in Jerusalem. A recording by Moses Tawil and ensemble, made on 11 December 1984, is included on the compact disc accompanying this book.

4. See Idelsohn 1923. The 1913 article appears as chapter 4, pp. 52–112. See also Schleifer 1986:103.

5. Bnai Brith (1991:24) estimated that 4,000 Jews lived in Syria in 1991, including 3,200 in Damascus, 600–700 in Aleppo, and 100–200 in Qamishli, a small town near the Turkish border. In 1992, *The New York Times* reported 4,500 Jewish citizens in Syria, numbers soon greatly reduced by a quiet emigration of Syrian Jews, primarily to New York, beginning in May 1992, after a Syrian government announcement that lifted a travel ban and permitted Jews to travel (Clyde Haberman, *The New York Times,* 3 May, 6 May, 23 May 1992). By late 1993, approximately 3,300 Syrian Jews had left the country, most settling in Brooklyn ("Jews' Exit from Syria Slows," *The Boston Globe,* 5 October 1993, and *The New York Times,* 30 December 1993).

6. Derived from the Arabic name for Aleppo, "Ḥalab" means "milk" or "he milked." The name is traced to the tradition that Abraham pastured his sheep on the mountain of Aleppo and distributed their milk to the poor on its slopes (Ashtor 1972:562).

7. Philips n.d.:457. The story used to illustrate this maxim was of a family said to have moved from Brooklyn to a New York City suburb a few miles away. Two years later, it is emphasized, their son married a non-Jew. While marriage within the community is highly preferred, in fact a significant number of Syrian Jews have married Jews of Ash-

kenazic descent. According to Zenner (1983:178), as many as twenty-five percent of the weddings in the late 1950s were to Ashkenazim. It is clear that even very close and traditional Syrian families "intermarry." In one family active in preserving traditional Ḥalabi culture, a sister married an Ashkenazic husband, as did both her daughter and niece (Anon.).

8. See Reyes Schramm 1975:7–8; Slobin 1993; and *Diaspora* 3/3 (1994), which contains a special section of five articles on diasporic musics, edited by Mark Slobin.

9. A notable example is Jocelyne Guilbault's recent study *Zouk: World Music in the West Indies* (1993). Based on extensive ethnographic interviews and observation, this book seeks to integrate a "micro and a macro analysis within the same research," capturing both local and international aspects of the music.

10. Reliable population figures are hard to come by. The Sephardic Community Center in Brooklyn estimates there to be approximately 35,000 Syrian Jews in the New York metropolitan area (M. Witkes, 24 June 1993), a figure also reported in *The New York Times* (30 December 1993). A 1991 publication of the Bnai Brith (p. 24) gives the number as 30,000 in Brooklyn, with 4,000–5,000 living year round in Deal, New Jersey.

11. It is notable that the large Syrian community in Israel is not mentioned. The World Center for Aleppo Jews Traditional Culture in Tel Aviv, Israel, estimates the number of Syrian Jews in Israel at 130,000, divided between 45,000 Ḥalabi Jews and an additional 85,000 of Shāmī (Damascus) heritage (M. Cohen, 23 March 1993). Although the broader Sephardic community in Israel is a source of influence on Syrians abroad, particularly through the circulation of cantors and rabbis, the Syrian community in Israel is less bounded and more integrated into a broader Sephardic network. See Zenner 1965:1, which discusses "trends toward assimilation and fusion among the Syrian Jews in Jerusalem." The World Center for Aleppo Jews Traditional Culture endorses this assessment, reporting a problem in identifying Syrian synagogues in Israel because of their "mixed membership" (M. Cohen, 23 March 1993).

12. The emphasis on physical proximity in Brooklyn evidently does not derive from a strong pre-migratory pattern. In eighteenth-century Aleppo "there was no neighborhood inhabited exclusively by a single group, whether Jews or carpenters or upper-class families or ashraf or Turkmen tribesmen. Even in quarters named after social groups the composition was inconsistent with the labels; these names tended to identify only one element in the locality and were even at the time anachronistic. The Jewish Quarter housed only a section of the Jewish community and was also inhabited by many Muslims" (A. Marcus 1989:317).

13. Other shared travels include groups of Syrian Jews who go to Puerto Rico or Florida for the Passover holiday escorted by lay cantor Mickey Kairey. One member of the community commented that "everyone on the plane feels safe with Mickey on board carrying the Sefer Torah" (Anon.). The extended Tawil family along with as many as two hundred others have celebrated Passover at the Concord Hotel in upstate New York since 1963.

14. This statement reflects the expectation that Syrian women marry young and give birth quickly; like their predecessors earlier in the century, they tend not to seek

employment outside the home (Zenner 1983:178) except in cases of financial necessity. Marriage of women at a young age was a common practice in Aleppo, a custom noted from at least the eighteenth century (A. Marcus 1989: 196, 256). While many women are involved in volunteer work within the community (Zenner 1983:178–79), Syrian women with professional training and full-time careers are still relatively unusual and tend to move away. A similar point is made by Zerubavel and Esses 1987:529, who suggest that it is acceptable for women to have professional involvement only before they have children or after the children are grown. A personal struggle of one Syrian woman who desired to both have a career and "not abandon" her community is traced in an autobiographical essay by Dianne O. Esses (1992:12–13).

15. An inscription on the oldest section of the Great Synagogue dates to the year 834 C.E. (Ashtor 1972:562). While Aleppo Jews have tended to read the date of the inscription as 345 C.E., scholars have accepted the later date. For a discussion of the inscription and varying interpretations, see Adler 1905:160–61. Also, Baron (1957: 104–5) argues that the Great Synagogue existed not later than the fifth century and may have been founded a century earlier.

16. By 1750, it is estimated that Aleppo included 80,000–90,000 Sunni Muslims, 20,000 Christians, and 3,000–4,000 Jews. There were also subdivisions within these communities, including four distinct churches among Christians (A. Marcus 1989:40). Different sectors of the Jewish community are discussed below.

17. "Our forefathers came from Spain. We are known as Sephardic Jews" (D. Tawil, 11 December 1984). Similar family histories were recounted by I. Cabasso (31 October and 13 November 1984) and Ruth Tawil Cain (7 September 1992). A few individuals describe the Ḥalabi Jews as "the oldest Jewish community in the world," uniting an "old identity" from the time of King David with a "new Sephardic identity" following the sixteenth-century Spanish influx (A. Sitt, 10 September 1992).

18. For details concerning the controversies surrounding privileged Jews of foreign origin, see A. Marcus 1991:46–47. Some tried to dissociate themselves from the common dhimmi and to win recognition as a separate social group. By 1806, their special privileges were abolished.

19. A few Syrian Jewish women in Brooklyn, including Gracia Haber (31 January 1989) and Sarah Tawil (30 March 1989), mentioned that their fathers used some Judeo-Spanish words.

20. Clyde Haberman, "Israel's Influx from Mideast Nears an End," *The New York Times,* 3 May 1992, estimates that Jews who by birth or background come from the Middle East and northern Africa account for nearly half of Israel's 4.1 million Jews. Of a total of 13.4 million Jews worldwide outside Israel, there are an estimated 1.3 million Sephardim. Díaz-Mas (1992) notes that Sephardic population figures are therefore particularly problematic because most "official data" generally come from Israel or Jewish institutions that use the term "Sephardi" in the broadest sense.

21. For additional perspectives, see Joel Brinkley, "For Jews from Arab Lands, New Views of Israel's Future," *The New York Times,* 23 July 1988. For an overview of "myths about civilized Western Ashkenazim and barbaric Eastern Sephardim," see Elazar 1989, who also discusses the modern ascription of Sephardic identity to groups such as Ye-

menite or Persian Jews who did not originate in Spain. The inclusive or exclusive use of the Sephardic rubric in the late twentieth century tends to emerge in political contexts.

22. See for example Moore (1981:387), who summarizes and questions these models in discussing East European Jewish immigrants and the manner in which their second generation achieved an "ethnic synthesis," which is too often overlooked (ibid. 404).

23. Eickelman 1981:273, citing Lynch (1960), who defines "imageability" as "that quality in a physical object which gives it a high probability of evoking a strong image in any given observer. It is the shape, color, or arrangement which facilitates the making of vividly identified, powerfully structured, highly useful mental images of the environment. . . . The concept of imageability does not necessarily connote something fixed, limited, precise, unified, or regularly ordered, although it may sometimes have these qualities" (pp. 9–10).

24. Examples include pizmonim nos. 132, 150, and 157, identified respectively as French, Italian, and German melodies. Equally interesting is the fact that tunes of Arab origin, whatever their original period or locale, are generally mentioned by incipit, Arabic if known, subsequent Hebrew text if not. This is particularly the case for Ḥalabi pizmonim composed in the twentieth century, drawn from the output of Egyptian composers, or secondarily, from new melodies encountered in the diaspora.

25. Late twentieth century Syrian Jewish men from one locale are often "married off" in other diaspora centers, an inversion of an older pattern of returning to Aleppo to take a bride.

26. An oral history recorded by Jacob (Jack) Shrem (born in Kilis, Turkey, in 1898) recalls that Kilis, a town of perhaps 45,000 inhabitants with about 300 Jewish families, was a miniature Ḥalab. It had ritual slaughterers, two synagogues, and a religious school. The Kilis Jews considered Aleppo to be "a mother city." They spoke "Aleppo Arabic" among themselves and Turkish with the local population (Sutton 1988:303–4).

27. Sophie's husband, whom she married at fifteen during his visit to her family in Mexico City, had established a business in New Orleans following a circuitous path leading from Aleppo to New York and then Puerto Rico. Following three years in New Orleans, the Ashkenazis moved to Ilton, Georgia, and after some years, back to Mexico. In 1936, they once again returned to the United States, moving from Birmingham, Alabama, to Atlanta, Georgia, and finally to Charlotte, North Carolina (Sutton 1988: 242–46).

28. This period resulted in an infusion of American melodies to Syrian experience and the pizmon tradition; see chapter 5.

29. The Bikur Holim is a Jewish community charitable organization formed to help the poor, sick, and unfortunate. The precedent for founding community organizations was set in Aleppo, where Ḥalabi Jews had a variety of institutions, including "a collectively organized system of poor relief," maintaining special funds to help poor families in times of need (A. Marcus 1989:216–17). Marcus observes that Jews in Aleppo used taxes rather than voluntary funds to support relief efforts, attributing their concern both to a long tradition of tight communal organization and a sense of insecurity as a minority group (ibid. 217).

30. See Sutton 1979, appendix VII, for a listing of Syrian synagogues and other

community organizations in the New York metropolitan area. A new Syrian congregation was founded in Manhattan in 1988 by "an energetic group of young Syrian professional people" (*Sephardic Highlights* 2(1), September 1988:3).

31. Syrian Jewish life in Mexico City falls somewhere between New York and Jerusalem Syrian life in terms of Ḥalabi/Shāmī relationships. Although the first Syrian synagogue founded in Mexico City, Monte Sinai, was a center for Damascus Jews (E. Goldfein, 2 September 1992), the Ḥalabi Maguen David Congregation is today more active. In Buenos Aires during the first decades after immigration, Damascene and Aleppine Jews each established their own institutions, "thus accentuating its separateness" (Mirelman 1990:194).

32. The Porat Yosef Yeshiva in Jerusalem was founded by Ḥalabis in 1920 and "since that time has been the official repository of Aleppoan 'authority' in the Holy city" (Sutton 1979:243). The yeshivahs were supported by donations forwarded from the Syrian diaspora, some of which were donated in return "for prayers for the recovery of the afflicted" (ibid. 48).

33. These include Raphael Elnadav, born in Jerusalem to Yemenite parents. Elnadav, who served as a cantor in Tel Aviv and Havana, Cuba, before arriving at Brooklyn's Congregation Shaare Zion (1959–1980), is "said to have a vast amount of knowledge of music" (J. Saff, 19 December 1985) and is characterized by some as "the greatest cantor the Sephardic people have in the whole world" (S. Catton, 30 October 1984). Yehiel Nahari, a Jerusalem-born cantor, was recruited and invited to begin serving in Brooklyn as a teenager: "A cantor of Ahi Ezer synagogue came to Israel and he was looking for young talent. To make a long story short, he met me, he did a cassette, and he brought me to this congregation. That's how I started, eleven, twelve years ago" (Y. Nahari, 6 January 1986).

34. Antebi's family also has other transnational ties: his wife was born in Mexico, his eldest daughter resides in Israel, and one daughter-in-law is from the United States (M. Antebi, 12 September 1992).

35. Zion and Avidani recorded under the Yedid imprint for Yeshivat Avidani in Jerusalem; Ben Hayyim's volumes, issued privately, are distributed by Renanot, the Institution for Jewish Music in Jerusalem; Elnadav 1980 is album JCL-501 on the Caytronics label.

36. See Stillman 1979:393–99 for documents relevant to the Damascus Affair.

37. Zalta demonstrated the "slight melodic differences." Unfortunately, this interview was not recorded.

38. Jews from Morocco were the first Sephardic migration to Argentina, and there was a large influx of Christians and Muslims from the Ottoman empire by 1890, at least ten years before Ottoman Jews arrived in Argentina. One Ḥalabi Jew wrote to his family that upon his arrival in Buenos Aires in 1904, he found many acquaintances from his hometown, who tended to live near each other in a single area of the city (Mirelman 1987:27). A process of chain migration shaped Syrian Jews' entry into Argentina, and "many already had relatives and friends there; they were assured of jobs until they could start their own businesses" (ibid. 29). In general, the Argentine Syrian community is said to protect "purity" (S. Shemi, 21 March 1993) and to have "more singing" than

in Mexico. However, the Argentine community presents a challenge for ethnographic investigation since it is said to be "fragmented into five to ten parts, and to have many members living outside Buenos Aires as well" (M. Antebi, 9 September 1992).

39. Syrian Jews went to Manchester in the late nineteenth century to trade in cotton and woolen cloth and ended up remaining there (Sutton 1979:5–6).

40. E. Barnea, who is of Persian descent, learned the bakkashot in Jerusalem in 1960 (10 March 1993). At a singing of the bakkashot at the Great Synagogue Ades of Aleppo Jews in central Jerusalem, Barnea participated actively and sang several solos (Shelemay fieldnotes, 14 March 1993).

41. A similar observation was made by B. Zalta (16 March 1990), who visited synagogues in Mexico not long after his arrival in New York City from Damascus: "They know a lot of pizmonim, they use a lot of them . . . they are interested. But to a lesser extent than the American Syrian community. I don't know for what reasons."

42. Bozo also refers to Mordekhai Abadi (Abadi 1873), discussed in chapter 1.

43. Jose Chacalo officiated at the original Maguen David synagogue, where he founded a choir (R. Betech, 8 September 1992; Askenazi 1982:208), but his own students do not seem to have succeeded him. Hayyim Tawil, a Taboush student who immigrated to Mexico in 1912, was discussed in chapter 1.

44. Of particular note are the many melodies from Western art music incorporated into liturgy by Isaac Cain, discussed in chapter 5. Cantor Shlomo Shemer is also credited with organizing Spanish music concerts within the community, although not with incorporating local Spanish melodies into pizmonim (R. Betech, 8 September 1992).

Chapter Three

1. According to one ethnomusicologist, at East Coast parties among Arab Americans, musicians mingle with the hosts and their guests; this situation did not pertain in other locales, where newer immigrant musicians sat separately and were treated as professionals (Rasmussen 1991:335 n. 7).

2. "A Yiddishe Mameh," with music by Jack Yellen and Lew Pollak, lyrics by Zelig/ Jack Yellen, was issued in both Yiddish (Crawford Music Co.) and English (Ager, Yellen and Bernstein Co.) in 1925. A bilingual edition of sheet music for the song had a photograph of Yossele Rosenblatt (Heskes 1992:257).

3. A record catalogue gives a dating of 1931. See Mulḥaq jadīd shahr fibrāyir sanah 1931 al-Ustādh Muḥammad ʿAbd al-Wahhāb al-Mūsīqār. Sharikah Bayḍāfūn al-Waṭanniyyah (Baidaphon National Record Company.) New Supplement for the month of February, 1931. The Musician al-Ustadh Muḥammad ʿAbd al-Wahhāb, 94031, 94033. However, F. Saḥḥab (1987:307) states that this song was first recorded in 1928. Dates and other documentary information concerning the songs of ʿAbd al-Wahhāb in the published literature are quite problematic, and I am grateful to Virginia Danielson, who provided these references.

4. I thank Virginia Danielson and Iman Roushdy Hammady for transliterating and translating "Aḥibb Ashūfak."

5. The transcription in this prelude does not contain instrumental interludes, which can be heard on the recording.

6. Moses Tawil is accompanied by Louis Massry and Joseph Catton on ʿūd, and Ezra Ashkenazi on darābukkah. The chorus, heard only in the dawr section of the song, is sung by Hyman Kaire, David Tawil, Menachem Mustacchi, Ralph Shasho Levy, Walter Serure, and Meyer Cohen.

7. For discussions of music in the modern Middle East, I have adopted the nomenclature used by Faruqi (1981:xvi) in distinguishing Mashriqi traditions ("pertaining to the East") from Maghribi music ("pertaining to the West," incorporating North Africa as far east as Libya). Two other major areas of the larger Middle East, Persia and Turkey, are generally viewed by scholars as having musical traditions distinctive enough to warrant separate classification and study.

8. The hohsh, a building with an inner courtyard, was the common residential architecture in Aleppo. According to Sutton, wealthy families occupied a private hohsh, while others housed two or three families (1988:39).

9. Continuing Turkish influence appears to be strongest among individuals not of Syrian descent who were raised in Israel and are now affiliated with the Syrian community in New York. One young cantor named several Turkish musicians whose talents he admires; this individual is also conversant with Iranian music (Y. Nahari, 6 January 1986). Another member of the New York Syrian community born in Turkey, but raised in Aleppo, seemed more heavily influenced by his long-term residency in Palestine from 1928 to 1946 (I. Abadi, 21 November 1984). However, a few American-born Syrian Jews expressed interest in or knowledge of Turkish music (M. Tawil, 6 November 1984).

10. Racy (1976:27) notes that there is an early Gramophone vocal recording of Shaykh Yūsuf al-Manyalāwī (d. 1911), a famous Egyptian singer said to have visited Aleppo before ʿAbd al-Wahhāb (Sutton 1988:44, where his name is given as Shaikh Yousef Il Milinawi). Sutton also mentions that he possesses a "scratchy phonograph recording of Shaikh Salameh [Salāmah Ḥijāzī, mentioned above] performing the death-scene of Shakespere's Romeo and Juliet, in an Arabic-opera version" (ibid.).

11. The qaṣīdah is a musical rendering of a classical Arabic poem of the same name (Faruqi 1981:260) "sung in an improvised recitative fashion without repetitions" (D. Tawil, 11 December 1984, mimeographed handout of definitions prepared for the New York University Ethnomusicology Seminar; also, Danielson 1987). The muwashshāḥ, the three-part vocal composition discussed in the prelude to chapter 2, a form dating from tenth-century Spain (Faruqi 1981:219), constitutes "the bulk of Arabic music in our days" (D. Tawil, 11 December 1984).

12. Rashid Sales, established in 1934 on Atlantic Avenue in Brooklyn, today carries the largest inventory of Arab recordings in the United States (see Dehmer 1984).

13. The mawwāl is "a song without a definite form or rhythm improvised on a type of verse having the same name, 'mawwāl.' Though originally light in character, it is now included in concerts of high artistic caliber. In fact it has gradually been replacing the qaṣīdah, and the text sung is of a more elevated language" (D. Tawil, 11 December 1984). Faruqi concurs that the mawwāl has moved from the world of folk music to art music (Faruqi 1981:179).

14. The ṭaqṭūqah is a precomposed, strophic, metered song, simpler and more

straightforward than the nineteenth-century dawr, which it resembled. Given its brevity and simplicity, the ṭaqṭūqah was especially well suited for the early recording era, where time limitations complicated the recording of longer and more heavily improvised forms. Most popular through the 1930s, the ṭaqṭūqah continued to be used through the 1970s (Danielson 1991:355–56). It is a form well known to Syrian Jews in Brooklyn (D. Tawil, 11 December 1984).

15. Saff remembers one song to have been "Ashkī li-min dhū al-hawā," also composed by Murād. From Saff's description of the song as distributed on two twelve-inch records with the picture of a gazelle on their red labels, the 78 RPM disks can be identified as those issued by Baidaphon in the early 1920s (Racy 1976:41). The Baidaphon Company was founded by Lebanese brothers who in 1907 first sold records in Beirut that were recorded and manufactured for them in Berlin; later they began to record elsewhere in the Middle East, eventually opening a branch in Egypt. By the 1920s, Baidaphon customers living in North and South America could order records by mail directly from the company's Berlin office (ibid. 40–41).

16. The reference here is to what are more often called "quarter tones," intervals smaller than those of the Western tempered scale.

17. The word dawzet probably derives from *dawzanah,* "tuning of a musical instrument" (Faruqi 1981:59). The verb is *dawzana,* "to tune." I thank Virginia Danielson for her confirmation of this etymology. ʿAbd al-Wahhāb credited Sāmī al-Shawwā with changing the style of Arab violin playing mainly by using slurs in the bowing (Azzam 1990:183 n. 5).

18. The recordings evidently have a further role as what may be termed "retrieval clues" (Schacter 1996:64), purposely used to prod the memory. An example is provided by Joseph Saff, who has saved his collection of Arab records even though he does not have a phonograph. He refuses to throw them out until he hears them once again "because they're going to bring back memories to me from 30, 40 years. Just sitting in my house" (J. Saff, 4 December 1984).

19. As noted in chapter 1, n. 38, the bakkashot are hymns of supplication sung in the early morning hours before the Sabbath prayers. They are performed only during the winter months, between the holidays of Sukkot and Passover. The bakkashot are set to Arab melodies of uncertain antiquity and provenance.

20. The Proceedings of the Congress were published as *Kitāb muʾtamar al-mūsīqá al-ʿarabiyyah* [Book of the Congress of Arab Music] (Cairo: al-Maṭbaʿah al-Amīriyyah bil-Qāhirah, 1933), as well as in a French translation titled *Recueil des Travaux du Congrès de Musique Arabe* (1934).

21. This maqām, likely *sāz kār* in Arabic, which subsumes only two pizmonim composed by Taboush, must have been current in nineteenth-century Aleppo. It is not included in Faruqi 1981.

22. Used for only two pizmonim, both attributed to Moses Ashear, maqām lami [lāmī] is not included in Faruqi 1981. According to David Tawil, it is a "sophisticated" Persian maqām not used in either Egypt or Syria, with a "gauzy, airy, light sound" (11 December 1984). I thank both Virginia Danielson and Edwin Seroussi for the information that lāmī is an Iraqi maqām. Tawil includes maqām lami within the "kurdy" family.

Only one other member of the Syrian community mentioned maqām lami during an interview (G. Shrem, 9 January 1986). In SUHV, maqām lami is interpolated between the maqām ʿajam songs of Taboush and those of Ashear (pp. 183–85).

23. This maqām is said to be a "new part of bayāt" within the last twenty years (D. Tawil, 11 December 1984; Y. Nahari, 16 January 1986).

24. Only two pizmonim, one each by Taboush and Ashear, are set in maqām ʿushayrān. Listed in Faruqi (1981:383), ʿushayrān was not mentioned in interviews.

25. This modal category, which includes songs from Taboush and Ashear, was not discussed in interviews. Rahawy and nawā are both included within the rāst family by D. Tawil (11 December 1984). Nawā is also said to be "similar to nahāwand" (Y. Nahari, 16 January 1986).

26. Not discussed in interviews, two songs by Raphael Taboush in maqām awj [ʿawj] are included in SUHV (pp. 430–31). See Faruqi 1981:24.

27. Maqām ʿirāq is said to date from the thirteenth century and also to be called *sīkāh tamm* (Faruqi 1981:112–13, 313). It was recognized as one of the "principal maqāmāt at the Cairo Conference" (S. Marcus 1989:333).

28. Among Syrian Jews, maqām kurd is associated with the young ʿAbd al-Wahhāb (J. Saff, 19 December 1985). It is characterized as the "weakest maqām" and one that is little used (D. Tawil, 11 December 1984). According to Faruqi, it is a contemporary melodic mode (1981:150).

29. According to J. Mosseri and M. Arking, songs considered by many people to be in maqām jihārkah are subsumed in SUHV under maqām ʿajam. Jihārkah melodies are said to be mainly of Western origin (J. Mosseri and M. Arking, 14 January 1986). Maqām jihārkah apparently dates from the fifteenth century and is still used in modern Arab practice (Faruqi 1981:125).

30. Kurd ("kurdy") is included by David Tawil among the major maqāmāt, bringing his total to eight (D. Tawil, 11 December 1984). For a further discussion drawing heavily on exegeses by David Tawil, see Kligman 1997:88–94. Many are also aware that each major maqām subsumes numerous others, "that each principal has its tributaries" (D. Tawil, 11 December 1984), and that "by changing a quarter note, you can get fifty to seventy maqāmāt" (J. Saff, 23 October 1984). Raphael Elnadav, a cantor who has served at Syrian synagogues in Brooklyn, is said to know "150 maqāmāt" (J. Saff, 4 December 1984).

31. The layālī is a solo vocal improvisation in free rhythm using the words *yā layl* ("oh night!") and/or *yā ʿayni* ("oh my eye!"), repeated with varying melodic passages. The taqsīm is the instrumental equivalent of the layālī (Faruqi 1981:156). The purpose of the layālī is said to be "like stretching out your muscles before jogging . . . or stretching your voice before you go into a musical rendition. It gives them a chance to stretch their vocal cords, reach the entire scale or scales in most instances, and now get into their first particular song" (D. Tawil, 11 December 1984).

32. Around 1850 in the Middle East, the violin replaced the *kamanjah,* an unfretted spike fiddle with two strings (El-Shawan 1981:145).

33. The five pairs of strings on the ʿūd are tuned (from top to bottom): C″, G′, D′, A, and G. These pitches are named as in the Arab *jadwal* ("gamut" or "scale"): C″ =

kirdan, G′ = nawā, D′ = dūkāh, A = ʿushayrān, and G = yakāh (Obadia 1969:8–9). I thank Mark Kligman for bringing Obadia's publication to my attention. For information on the Arab *jadwal,* see also Tawil 1984 and Faruqi 1981:116–17.

34. Mohamed Elakkad and Hakki Obadia are hired by both Arab and Jewish patrons. Obadia is credited, along with Eddie Kochak, with innovating a musical hybrid called "Ameraba" (Rasmussen 1991:302). Within the Ḥalabi community, he is praised as an artist with a "fine ear" and "delicate delivery" (M. Tawil, 6 November 1984). Obadia studied at the conservatory in Baghdad and received a university degree in music after coming to the United States in 1947 (Rasmussen 1991:331–32). Performances by Elakkad are also mentioned in Rasmussen 1991:260. In Mexico City, where there are few amateur instrumentalists in the Jewish community, local Arab musicians are hired for parties.

35. Ashkenazi remembers most vividly spending hours with the recording "Port Said," featuring Muḥammed el-Bakkar and his Oriental Ensemble. This record is discussed in Rasmussen 1992:81.

Chapter Four

1. The original 78 RPM recording has been reissued on a 1973 Cairophon cassette titled "Immortal Melodies." ʿAbd al-Wahhāb himself is the solo singer.

2. Rabinowitz 1972:898. The tefillin are worn in obediance to a biblical injunction to put "these words" of the law for "a sign upon thy hand and a frontlet between thine eyes."

3. Kallberg, in a discussion of Chopin's Nocturne in G Minor, notes that "while often construed as a concept inherent in musical compositions alone, genre is better perceived as a social phenomenon shared by composers and listeners alike. . . . The meaning of a term . . . is connected to the willingness of a particular community to use that word and not another; meaning sheds light on the characteristic uses of a particular term as opposed to others that are available. This is why definitions that consider only the term itself are of limited value: they fail to consider the community that employs the term. . . . Meanings, in short, must emerge from the context of the term" (1988:243).

4. I thank Charles Hamm for bringing Fabbri's work on genre to my attention.

5. It seems reasonable to speculate that the decline in bakkashot transmission and performance in the Syrian American diaspora may relate directly to its truncated performance context an hour or two before Sabbath morning services. In addition to singing only selected verses of individual songs, the absence of the close bonding of father and son in the midnight awakenings must have robbed the modern ritual of much of its emotional power and ability to implant itself in long-term memory. The lively maintenance of the bakkashot at the Ades Synagogue in Jerusalem, performed in a traditional manner in the early morning hours, is testimony to the close linkage of complete performance in maintaining transmission. This hypothesis is borne out in individual repertories discussed in chapter 5.

6. In the words of one cantor, "You take the unpureness, as we call it, and to pour it

to holiness of the Hebrew" (Y. Nahari, 6 January 1986). Chapter 1 presented rabbinical commentary on this point.

7. R. Alcalay 1963:2140, literally "opening" or "beginning." The term "key" (Hebrew *mafteaḥ*) also appears to be used interchangeably, as indicated by a request "to find the introduction to bayāt, the mafteḥot in bayāt" (H. Kaire, 14 March 1985). The poetic text is sometimes also preceded by a free improvisation on vocables or Arabic terms of endearment, called a layālī, discussed in chapter 3. In everyday practice, singers may refer to a petiḥah when they are technically performing a layālī.

8. The kedushah (sanctification) is the generic name for the prayer celebrating the sanctity of the Sabbaths, holidays, or God (Hoffman 1979:191). Hoffman identifies the kedushah as the most obvious example of the *merkavah* [Jewish mystical] influence on the liturgy (ibid. 61–62), an observation that renders even more interesting the frequent musical elaboration of this text.

9. Shrem was referring to no. 45, "Male Fi." "Male Fi" is performed by Shrem on his series of private recordings, amid pizmonim in maqām ʿajam (in SUHV, the pizmon is listed as ʿajam or rāst). Shrem introduces his performance of no. 45 on the tape in the following manner: "The next pizmon is found in the bakkashot, no. 45." Shrem, who at the end of each pizmon recording consistently repeats a given pizmon melody with the liturgical text it most frequently carries, sang the "Male Fi" tune to the Kaddish prayer. On some tapes (as in ʿajam examples) Shrem sings pizmonim with strong liturgical associations and then announces he will sing as many songs that are "only pizmonim" as the tape can fit; that is, pizmonim without strong liturgical associations. Interestingly, he includes "Melekh Raḥaman" (no. 168, discussed in the prelude to chapter 6) in the second group.

10. The concluding ceremony at the end of Sabbath that separates the day of rest from the week to follow.

11. The birth of a child may also be marked in the synagogue, usually by calling forth the father to participate in the reading of the Torah. This moment is traditionally accompanied by the singing of a pizmon (H. Kaire, 14 March 1985).

12. One individual mentioned that the mohel (who performs the circumcision) sometimes sings no. 413, "Yaḥon El Ṣur," softly while performing the circumcision, but that this song is difficult to hear (M. Arking, 28 April 1988).

13. The word *moʿed* means a "fixed time" (R. Alcalay 1963:1234). There are historical differences in the manner in which holidays are categorized, a subject discussed at some length in Hoffman 1979:91–114 passim.

14. The performance of "Yaḥid Ram" has changed in twentieth-century Brooklyn to include an extra syllable, so that the incipit is sung "yah yaḥid ram" (H. Kaire, 17 February 1988). While "the original old-timers say you're not supposed to say "yah yah" because of [invoking the name of] God, they may do it for balance" (ibid.).

15. This poem dates to the nineteenth century and has been published in Arabic. See A. Marcus 1989:371 n. 14.

16. The song was originally composed for Berlin's musical *Yip, Yip Yaphank,* which was first performed in New York on August 19, 1918 (Root 1980:579). In October

1938, Berlin revised the text and melody, resulting in "God Bless America" (see Bergreen 1990:368–72 for details for the song's revision).

17. H. Kaire (17 February 1988) demonstrated the manner in which the text of bakkashah no. 70, "Agaddelkha Elohai," set in maqām sīkāh, could also be sung to melodies in other maqāmāt, including those of "Attah El Kabbir," no. 210 (nahāwand) and "Mamlekhot Ha'areṣ," no. 326 (muḥayyir bayāt). In cases where "it can be difficult to fit the words," Kaire noted, "you try to inject a couple of words."

Chapter Five

1. The recording of "Yeḥidah Hitnaʿari" included on the compact disc is performed by Joseph Saff.

2. Saff here paraphrases Biblical passages (Exod. 13:1–10, 11–16; Deut. 6:4–9, 11:13–21) requiring Jews to wear the tefillin. See also Rabinowitz 1972:898.

3. Joseph Saff was born on the leap year day, February 29, in 1920. His bar mitzvah took place on the thirteenth day of Adar in 1933.

4. Note that in the facsimile Hebrew words representing personal names are set in larger letters.

5. Ashear's act may have grown out of empathy since his own father died when he was a young boy, see chapter 1.

6. Among recent work of this type, one can cite Judith Vander's *Songprints: The Musical Experience of Five Shoshone Women* (1988), which incorporates the statements and songs of five women through quotation, transcription, and reproduction of lengthy transcripts of conversations between the women and the ethnomusicologist, Vander. A Bulgarian couple who are musicians are the center of Timothy Rice's *May It Fill Your Soul* (1994). Virginia Danielson's *The Voice of Egypt: Umm Kulthūm, Arabic Song, and Egyptian Society in the Twentieth Century* (1997) is one of the first full-length biographies of a great female performer from outside the Western tradition. Recent studies of Ethiopian Christian chant also explicitly set forth an individual musician's map of that musical tradition (Shelemay, Jeffrey, and Monson 1993; Shelemay and Jeffrey 1993–97).

7. Attitudes toward and terminology describing the pizmon composer have shifted in late twentieth century New York, where Western notions of the individual conceiving a melody and then committing it to Western notation have begun to predominate; the term "lyricist" has likely entered the vocabulary from Western popular music and musical theater. These changes are reflected in the vocabularies of modern Sephardic musicians, one of whom termed Taboush a "word composer" (Y. Nahari, 6 January 1986). However, several musicians in the Syrian community do compose new melodies for pizmonim, including Raphael Elnadav: "Elnadav likes making up his own things. He's a musician, he makes up his own tunes, own words, own everything. That's the way he likes it" (J. Mosseri, 14 January 1986). Another individual identifies as composers only those who write both music and text. "You can find a lot of ḥazzanim in the community, most of whom never studied music. They just know the maqām and how to go, what's the scale [for] singing it. They don't read music, they never wrote music, they don't know the history of it. . . . Elnadav does and Elnadav is a composer, as simple

as that. He composed many songs, you know about that? . . . He wrote the music, and he wrote the words. That's what I meant by composer" (B. Zalta, 16 March 1990).

8. This in contradiction to A. Marcus's observation that although many new songs and musical pieces appeared on the local scene during the eighteenth century, Ḥalabi Jews "remained untouched by Western influences," and that "few residents ever had the opportunity to hear European music" (1989:234).

9. For unknown reasons, the source song has evidently been mistaken for an operatic aria, likely one from the opera *Aida,* and is identified in SUHV as "Opera Africa." The composer of "Santa Lucia," Teodoro Cottrau, was also a Neapolitan music publisher and a close friend of Bellini and other opera composers of his time (Ajani 1980:830). The mixing of operatic arias with other songs from the Neapolitan tradition is seen in song collections of that repertory; see *Neapolitan Songs,* described on the cover as "An outstanding collection of Neapolitan songs, as well as a number of the most beautiful arias from Italian Grand Opera and several Classic Songs" (1938), which contains "Santa Lucia" (pp. 82–83) as well as a number of operatic arias by Verdi, Donizetti, and others.

The melody of "Santa Lucia" is classified as maqām ʿajam, the usual category under which foreign melodies in a major key are subsumed. The text of pizmon no. 187 indicates that it was composed in honor of the birth of a baby girl. The text begins with a paraphrase of the Song of Songs 6:10: "Who is she that shines through like the dawn, tired. She is radiant and beautiful, the pleasing daughter of Zion."

10. In several cases I was asked not to discuss financial issues. I have respected those constraints and have only provided here information offered without such admonitions.

11. Albeg was also active in early projects documenting aspects of Syrian and Iraqi liturgical music and pizmonim. Between 1939 and 1941, he made field recordings of "Babylonian Jewish Music" with Sophie Lentschner Eisenberg, who worked under the supervision of director George Herzog at Columbia University's "Archives of Primitive Music"; the original tapes from these sessions are today deposited in the Archives of Traditional Music at Indiana University under accession numbers 54–238-F and 54–309-F. A record featuring Albeg, titled *Babylonian Biblical Chants,* was published by Folkways Records, in 1959.

12. Raphael Elnadav, who declined to participate in this study, was born in Jerusalem to Yemenite parents. He acquired the Sephardic musical tradition in Jerusalem and is particularly known as a connoisseur of the maqāmāt and Turkish music. Elnadav served as Chief Cantor at Shaare Zion Congregation in Brooklyn from 1959 to 1980 (Jacket notes, *Sephardic Prayer Songs for the High Holy Days: Raphael Yair Elnadav,* 1980). Several of Elnadav's songs are widely sung in the Syrian community, including "Romemu," no. 237d, in maqām nahāwand, composed for the bar mitzvah of Ezra Tawil to the melody of "Inta al-Ḥubb," a popular Arab song performed by Umm Kulthūm. Elnadav also composed a pizmon "El Al Shir" in 1984 for the bar mitzvah of Shaul Ashkenazi, son of Ezra Ashkenazi. The first two stanzas were taken from an unidentified melody suggested by Ezra Ashkenazi; the rest of the song was newly composed (E. Ashkenazi, 20 December 1984).

13. The music for *Fiddler on the Roof,* premiered in New York City in 1964, was

composed by Jerry Bock. (The vocal score was published in a piano reduction by Robert H. Noeltner [1964]). I thank Albert Cohen-Saban for supplying copies of the texts of his pizmonim, only three of which had appeared in SUHV (no. 318e, no. 204c, and no. 318g) at the time of our discussions.

14. In other instances, such as "Yeḥidah Hitnaʿari," the name of the honoree is in the acrostic.

15. Known in pan-Jewish tradition as the *aliyah,* this custom entails a literal "ascent" up the steps to the pulpit by an individual, who then says the blessings before and after a biblical portion is read aloud. In some cases, portions are re-read, enabling additional people to be called forward (L. Massry, 21 February 1985).

16. The Colonia Roma area was the neighborhood in central Mexico City where most Syrian Jews lived until about 1950. The Cordoba synagogue is still active in this area.

17. An important section of the Sabbath morning service, discussed in detail in Kligman 1997.

18. The portion at the beginning of Genesis 12:1, which translates: "Get thee out of thy country . . . to the land that I will show thee . . ." (*Jerusalem Bible,* p. 11). As noted in chapter 4, many of the prayers for the Sabbath on which this portion (which describes the circumcision of Abraham) is read are set in maqām ṣabā.

19. "Ha-Tikvah" (The Hope) became the Zionist national anthem in 1897. The text was written in 1878 by Naphtali Herz Imber (1856–1911) and published in a collection of his poems called *Barkai* (The Morning Star) in Jerusalem in 1886 (Idelsohn 1929:454). In 1948, "Ha-Tikvah" became the unofficial Israeli national anthem. The "Ha-Tikvah" melody is similar to those of several European folksongs of Slavic and Spanish origin; the Rumanian folk song "Carul cu boi" ("Cart and Oxen") is considered the main source (Bayer 1972; a comparative transcription of "Ha-Tikvah" and Smetana's theme is found in Idelsohn 1929:222–25, table XXVIII). A variant of this melody had earlier been used in the eighteenth century to set the "Leoni" Yigdal prayer, adapted by Meier Leon (d. 1800), a cantor in London who later served in Kingston, Jamaica (ibid. 220–21).

20. The song is published as "Eternally" and was composed for Chaplin's movie *Limelight.* With music by Chaplin and lyrics by Geoffrey Parsons, it was copyrighted in 1953 by Bourne Co., New York City. The song was reissued in a collector's edition titled *The Songs of Charlie Chaplin* (1992:32–33).

21. This point deserves further investigation. Rather, the young people know a lot of Spanish songs and "expensive Mexican singers" are brought in to sing these songs on special occasions.

22. Another version of this story, told by several individuals, has a somewhat more risqué punch line. After showing the father the way in which the wife's name is split between two words, the composer is reputed to have said, "I even spread her legs for you."

23. The melody is commonly attributed to Ernst Anschütz, a Leipzig schoolmaster, in 1824. In fact, Anschütz himself likely took and transformed the melody from the song "Es lebe doch," earlier published in 1799 (Keyte and Parrott 1992: 181).

24. The informal survey of repertories was suggested by a comment of Moses Tawil, who mentioned that he was going through the pizmon book listing by maqām all the songs he knew (8 November 1984).

25. Through a clerical error, only the printed key to the pizmonim organized by maqāmāt on pp. 553–64 was copied and distributed to the four individuals surveyed in this manner; additional new pizmonim found in typescript on pp. 564a–c were not included. Therefore, the number of pizmonim actively transmitted is certainly greater than the totals given here in light of the omission of many recently composed songs. As noted above, Moses Tawil compiled his own list and in fact included several of the newer songs in that context. Finally, I was able to compile a sixth repertory list from a collection of eleven cassettes recorded by Cantor Gabriel Shrem before his death in the late 1980s. This private collection, recorded for the use of students at Yeshiva University Cantorial Training Institute in New York City over the course of nearly a decade (G. Zetouni, 21 July 1992), contains a collection of the pizmonim in each maqām along with examples of an appropriate liturgical context in which each pizmon melody may be used. The purpose of the Shrem collection was therefore to supply enough model pizmonim for students to be able to set prayers in the maqām of the day; no doubt this list does not contain the totality of Gabriel Shrem's repertory. It should also be noted that the Shrem recordings incorporate selected bakkashot set in each maqām as well. I am grateful to Florence and Gabriel Zetouni, the daughter and grandson of Gabriel Shrem, who helped me obtain a copy of these tapes.

26. There are in fact 560 pizmonim in SUHV. See table 5.1 for a summary of the number of pizmonim in each maqām, as well as songs shown to be actively transmitted from the sample.

27. Others estimated their repertories informally. Isaac Abadi reported that there were "about 150 that I know well." He studied pizmonim both from an early age in Aleppo and later in Israel (I. Abadi, 21 November 1984).

28. Indeed, Mustacchi mentioned that he knows other pizmonim not included in the Brooklyn edition but actively sung in Israel (11 December 1984). Mustacchi is estimated to have been in his late twenties at the time the project was carried out.

29. I thank Edwin Seroussi for bringing Levy's edition of "Refa Ṣiri" to my attention and for providing information concerning its widespread modern transmission as part of the Judeo-Spanish repertory. Levy recorded the song from Shlomo Arieh ben Raphael Hayyim Ha-Kohen, a native of Jerusalem (b. 1921) and a member of the Sephardi synagogue Ohavei Tziyyon. The informant's father, Raphael Hayyim Ha-Kohen, was the editor of collections of pizmonim, including Taboush's book *Shir u-shevaḥah* (1905).

30. The Arabic song is "Ya Ana, Ya Ana," recorded by Fairuz *(The Very Best of Fairuz).*

31. According to members of the Syrian community, the designation "musika" can indicate either a European or a non-European song (J. Mosseri, 14 January 1986). A. Idelsohn noted that "musika" meant instrumental music of a military band (1923:99, cited in Seroussi 1993:120 n. 27).

32. For example, pizmon no. 220, "Melekh Ram," is said to borrow a melody from "March Chopin." We have been unable to trace this melody, which is apparently not correctly attributed to Chopin. I am grateful to Jeffrey Kallberg for his help in ruling out

a Chopin attribution. Edwin Seroussi has suggested that the attribution may be "March Suppan" in correspondence of 19 January 1997.

Chapter Six

1. All information about "Melekh Raḥaman" included here was provided by Albert Ashear on 19 July 1989 unless otherwise noted.

2. The precise date of composition is unknown, although Albert Ashear believed the wedding to have taken place before the turn of the century. Albert calculated the approximate date of composition from the age of his older brother, Joseph, who was the firstborn son *(bekhor)* and died at age 82. See chapter 1 for biographical details of Moses Ashear and his family.

3. I thank James Robinson for this interpretation.

4. Albert noted that his Hebrew name is Avraham: "Avraham is my uncle, my mother's brother. I was named Avraham also. So I was named after him."

5. The soloist heard on the compact disc recording is Isaac Cabasso.

6. The other, also composed by Raphael Taboush, was "Yaḥid Ram," no. 238. "Attah El Kabbir," no. 210, was also known by all but one research associate in all three cities. No doubt other pizmonim are also universally known, such as "Maʿuzzi," no. 246; however, I did not systematically question individuals about other songs.

7. Rubin (1995:94) suggests that multiple constraints operating in combination contribute to the stability of oral traditions in memory, including aspects of meaning, spatial and object imagery, rhyme, alliteration, and rhythm.

8. This portion can be heard on Raphael Yair Elnadav's recording *Sephardic Prayer Songs for the High Holy Days* (1980).

9. The exploration of remembrance as transmitted through music, and in particular, within song, also provides the ethnomusicologist with a potentially powerful tool for approaching and interpreting the historical past.

10. I thank Joshua Levisohn for his work on this translation and the related biblical reference.

11. I thank Mark Kligman for bringing this reference to my attention.

12. See discussion of this issue in chapter 2. Documents shedding light on Jewish communities in the Arab world during the Middle Ages suggest that, like their Muslim and Christian contemporaries, Jews held a strong attachment to their native cities (Goitein 1983:41). The historical tension in Islamic culture between attachment to home and the imperative to travel for various religious purposes has been explored in Eickelman and Piscatori 1990a. Of particular interest is the analysis of twentieth-century migration from the Middle Eastern home town for economic reasons, and the changing perception of the old center in relation to the new diasporic locale.

GLOSSARY

āhang (hank): passage sung to syllable "ah"

bakkashot: paraliturgical hymns in Hebrew sung in early Sabbath morning hours
bar mitzvah: male rite of passage at age thirteen
bashraf: instrumental piece
birkat hammazon: grace over meals
brit milah (bris): circumcision ceremony

daʿire: frame drum
darābukkah: hourglass drum
dawr: nineteenth-century Arab vocal form often with three sections
dawzet: hand position on stringed instruments
dhimma: pact establishing the treatment of non-Muslims, i.e., *dhimmis*
dīwān: collection of Arabic texts

Eikhah: Lamentations

fann: twentieth-century Arab art
firqah: large twentieth-century orchestra

ḥaflah: party
ḥakham: wise or learned man
Ḥalabī: of or from Aleppo (Ḥalab)
Hanukkah: Festival of Lights
Havdalah: concluding ceremony for Sabbath
ḥazzan (pl. ḥazzanim): cantor
ḥazzanut: art of cantorial performance

īqāʿ (pl. iqāʿāt): rhythm in Arab music; specific rhythmic patterns

jadwal: gamut or scale

Kabbalah: Jewish mystical writings
Kaddish: prayer of sanctification
khānah: internal section of Arab vocal and instrumental forms
klezmer: Yiddish term for instrumental ensemble

laḥan: tune
lawn: color or style
layālī: improvisatory vocal introduction

madhhab: opening section that may be repeated as refrain
maqām (pl. maqāmāt): Arab melodic system, melodic type; important maqāmāt are ʿajam, bayātī, hijāz, nahāwand, rāst, ṣabā, sīkāh.
mawwāl: improvised Arabic song form
maṣṣah: appetizer
Midrash: rabbinic literature of traditional stories
Mishlei: Proverbs
Moṣa'ei Shabbat: end of Sabbath
mūsīqā: music for entertainment; instrumental music
mustaʿriba: Arabic-speaking Jews in Ottoman empire
muwashshāḥ: classical Arabic vocal form known for rhythmic and melodic complexity

nāy: reed flute
nawbah: party
Nevi'im: Prophets
nekuddot: Hebrew vowels
Nishmat: section of Saturday morning prayers
nūbah: vocal-instrumental suite

paytan: poet
parashah: biblical portion
Pesaḥ: Passover
petiḥah: improvisatory vocal introduction with poetic Hebrew text
pidyon habben: redemption of the first born
piyyut: liturgical poetry
Purim: holiday celebrating deliverance of Jews from Persians

qaflah: cadence
qānūn: zither
qirā'ah: reading, pitched recitation of the Qur'an
qaṣīdah: classical Arabic poetic and song genre, usually without repetitions

riqq: frame drum
rīshah: eagle feather plectrum

salṭanah: mood of musical involvement
Sebet: festive Sabbath afternoon gathering
sefer: book
seliḥot: penitential hymns
Shabbat: Sabbath
Shāmī: of or from Damascus
Shavuot: Festival of Weeks, Harvest Festival
shir: song
shofar: ram's horn
shul: synagogue
Sukkot: Festival of Booths

taʿamim: biblical accents
takht: small, traditional Arab instrumental ensemble
Talmud: collection of commentaries on Jewish law and tradition
taqsīm (pl. taqāsīm): improvisatory instrumental introduction or piece
ṭaqṭūqah: precomposed, strophic song related to dawr
ṭarab: enchantment, entertainment; twentieth-century Arab art music
Tehillim: Psalms
tevah: reader's desk in Synagogue
tiran: large frame drums
Torah: The Law, The Five Books of Moses (Pentateuch)
turāth: heritage; traditional Arab music

ʿūd: lute
ughniyah: free-form contemporary song, often with refrain

waṣlah: vocal-instrumental suite
waṭan: homeland

yarmulke: skullcap
yeshivah: religious school

Zohar: book of Jewish mystical writing

CONTENTS OF THE COMPACT DISC

1	Ṣur Yah El	Translated by Geoffrey Goldberg and James Robinson Recorded 20 November 1984, Music session, Brooklyn, New York (for the text and translation, see the prelude to chapter 1)
2	Attah El Kabbir	Translated by James Robinson Recorded 11 December 1984, Music session, Brooklyn, New York (for the text and translation, see the prelude to chapter 2)
3	Ani Ashir Lakh	Translated by Geoffrey Goldberg and James Robinson Recorded 8 November 1984, Music session, Brooklyn, New York (for the text and translation, see the prelude to chapter 3)
4	Ramaḥ Evarai	Translated by Louis Massry Recorded 4 December 1984, Music session, Brooklyn, New York (for the text and translation, see the prelude to chapter 4)
5	Yehi Shalom	Translated by Joshua Levisohn Recorded 11 December 1984, Music session, Brooklyn, New York
6	Attah Ahuvi	Translated by Joshua Levisohn Recorded 11 December 1984, Music session, Brooklyn, New York
7	Mah Tov	Translated by Joshua Levisohn Recorded 11 December 1984, Music session, Brooklyn, New York
8	Ram Leḥasdakh	Translated by Joshua Levisohn Recorded 14 January 1986, Formal interview with Morris Arking and Joseph Mosseri, New York, New York
9	Yaḥid Ram	Translated by Geoffrey Goldberg and James Robinson

		Recorded 8 November 1984, Music session, Brooklyn, New York
10	Maʿuzzi	Translated by Joshua Levisohn Undated recording by Eliyahu Menaged, Brooklyn, New York, courtesy Hyman Kaire
11	Yeḥidah Hitnaʿari	Translated by Geoffrey Goldberg and James Robinson Recorded 21 February 1985, Music session, Brooklyn, New York (for the text and translation, see the prelude to chapter 5)
12	Ḥai Hazzan	Translated by Joshua Levisohn Recorded 13 November 1984, Music session, Brooklyn, New York
13	Ḥai Hazzan	Recorded by Isaac Cain, Mexico City
	Kaddish	Recorded by Isaac Cain, Mexico City. Renditions of the Kaddish prayer set to melodies of:
14		pizmon "Ḥai Hazzan"
15		S. Rachmaninov, Piano Concerto no. 2, Op. 18
16		J. Rodrigo, "Concierto de Aranjuez"
		Translation from Alouf (1995:15).
17	Melekh Raḥaman	Translated by Geoffrey Goldberg and James Robinson Recorded 4 December 1984, Music session, Brooklyn, New York (for the text and translation, see the prelude to chapter 6)

5. Yehi Shalom

יְהִי שָׁלוֹם בְּחֵילֵנוּ. וְשַׁלְוָה בְּיִשְׂרָאֵל.
בְּסִימָן טוֹב בֵּן בָּא לָנוּ. בְּיָמָיו יָבֹא הַגּוֹאֵל:
יהי שלום

הַיֶּלֶד יְהִי רַעֲנָן. בְּצֵל שַׁדַּי יִתְלוֹנָן.
וּבַתּוֹרָה אָז יִתְבּוֹנָן. יְאַלֵּף דָּת לְכָל-שׁוֹאֵל:
יהי שלום

וּמְקוֹרוֹ יְהִי בָרוּךְ. זְמַן חַיָּיו יְהִי אָרוּךְ.
וְשֻׁלְחָנוֹ יְהִי עָרוּךְ. וְזִבְחוֹ לֹא יִתְגָּאֵל:
יהי שלום

שְׁמוֹ יֵצֵא בְּכָל־עֵבֶר. אֲשֶׁר יִגְדַּל יְהִי גֶבֶר.
וּלְיִרְאֵי אֵל יְהִי חָבֵר. יְהִי בְדוֹרוֹ כִּשְׁמוּאֵל:
יהי שלום

עֲדֵי זִקְנָה וְגַם שֵׂיבָה. יְהִי דָשֵׁן בְּכָל־טוֹבָה.
וְשָׁלוֹם לוֹ וְרֹב אַהֲבָה. אָמֵן כֵּן יֹאמַר הָאֵל:
יהי שלום

הַנִּמּוֹל בְּתוֹךְ עַמּוֹ. יְחִיֶה לְאָבִיו וּלְאִמּוֹ.
וִיהִיֶה אֱלֹהָיו עִמּוֹ. וְעִם כָּל־בֵּית יִשְׂרָאֵל:
יהי שלום תם

To the father of the son:

May there be peace within our walls, tranquility in Israel.
In a favorable sign did a son come to us, in his days shall the redeemer arrive:

May the boy be refreshed, in the shadow of Shaddai will he lodge.
And the Torah he then will examine, he will teach the religion to all that ask:

May his fountain be blessed, his life span shall be lengthy.
May his table be ordered, and his offering shall not be defiled.

His name will go out in all directions, when he grows he will be a strong man.
And let him be a member of those that fear God, let him be in his generation like Shmuel.

Until old age and hoariness, he shall be plump with all manner of goodness.
And peace to him and much love, "Amen," so will say the Lord:

The circumcised in his nation will live for his father and mother.
And may his God be with him and with the whole House of Israel.

6. Attah Ahuvi

אַתָּה אֲהוּבִי, צוּרִי מִשְׂגַּבִּי,
כִּי אַתָּה נָתַתָּ, שִׂמְחָה בְלִבִּי,
בְּךָ אֶשְׁעַן:
בְּיוֹם הַמִּילָה, עֲבֵד הִלּוּלָא,
בְּשָׂשׂוֹן וּבְשִׂמְחָה, טוֹבָה כְפוּלָה,
שָׂמֵחַ עַל עַיִן:

רָץ קַל כַּצְּבִי, אֵלִיָּהוּ הַנָּבִיא,
בֹּא יָבֹא בִּמְהֵרָה, לְכַפֵּר חוֹבִי,
נִצָּב עַל עַיִן:

הַיֶּלֶד בְּנִי, כְּחוּט הַשָּׁנִי,
בְּסִימָן טוֹב כְּגַן רָטוֹב, לְנִמּוֹל בְּנִי,
מַחְמַד כָּל־עַיִן:

מַצְרֵף לַכֶּסֶף, יְהִי מְאַסֵּף,
לְזֶרַע אַבְרָהָם, בֵּן פּוֹרָת יוֹסֵף,
פּוֹרָת עַל עַיִן:

חֲזֵק אֶרֶץ טוֹבָה, הָעִיר הָרְחָבָה,
וּבֵית הַבְּחִירָה, מַרְגָּלִית טוֹבָה,
תִּרְאֶינָה עַיִן: תם

On the occasion of a circumcision and the weekly Torah portion of Lech Lecha:

You are my beloved, my Rock, my Refuge,
Because you gave happiness in my heart
Upon You shall I lean:

On the day of circumcision make a festive meal
In happiness and joy double goodness,
Place it before our eyes:

Run swiftly like the deer, Elijah the prophet,
He will surely come quickly to atone for my obligation,
Standing in front of all eyes:

The child, my son, like a scarlet thread,
Under a favorable sign like a fresh garden, the circumcision of my son,
the delight of all eyes.

A melting pot for silver shall be the gatherer
for the seed of Abraham, the fruitful bough of Joseph,
the fruitful bough by the spring.

Grab the good land, the spacious city
and the chosen temple, a fine pearl
the eye shall see.

7. Mah Tov

מַה טּוֹב מַה נָּעִים, דָּבָר בְּעִתּוֹ,
כָּל־אִישׁ יָשָׁר יָשִׂישׂ, עַל אִמְרָתוֹ,
כִּי תִגָּלֶה, תֵרָאֶה מַלְכוּתוֹ,
מַלְכוּת עוֹלָם, לְכָל־בָּאֵי־בְרִית:
אֵלִיָּהוּ, מְבַשֵּׂר הוּא, נִקְרָאֵהוּ, בָּעֵת הַהוּא,
לִהְיוֹת עוֹמֵד, עַל הַבְּרִית,
יוֹם הַמִּילָה, נֶצַח סֶלָה, נְהַלְּלָה, הִיא שְׁקוּלָה,
כְּקַבָּלַת לוּחוֹת בְּרִית:

רוֹנּוּ גַדְּלוּ, לַייָ אִתִּי,
יוֹם הַמִּילָה, אֵלָיו פִּי קָרָאתִי,
עֵת בְּחֶסֶד, כִּסֵּא הֲכִינוֹתִי,
לְאֵלִיָּהוּ מַלְאַךְ הַבְּרִית: אליהו

דּוֹרְשֵׁי אֵל חַי, צַדִּיק יְסוֹד עוֹלָם,
יִשְׂמְחוּ קְטַנָּם, עִם גְּדוֹלָם,
יַחַד יִשְׂאוּ, כַּנְּהָרוֹת קוֹלָם,
בְּהִגָּלוֹת נִגְלוֹת, אוֹת הַבְּרִית: אליהו

On the occasion of a circumcision:

How good, how pleasant, a matter in its proper time,
Every honest person shall rejoice upon his saying,
for it will be revealed, his kingship will be seen,
The kingdom of the world, to everyone who enters into the covenant.
Elijah, the newsbearer, we shall call him at this time
to be standing over the covenant (or the circumcision)
the day of the circumcision, forever, we shall praise, it is equal
to the receiving of the two tablets of the covenant (the Torah).

Rejoice, exalt the Lord with me,
the day of the circumcision to Him did my mouth call
at the time, with kindness did I prepare the chair
for Elijah, the angel of the covenant.

The seekers of the living God, the righteous one, the foundation of the world,
Their little ones will rejoice with their older ones,
Together they will lift up their voices like the rivers
As the sign of the covenant reveals itself.

8. Ram Leḥasdakh

רָם   לְחַסְדָּךְ יְקַוּוּ. לוֹמְדֵי הַתּוֹרָה לָךְ יוֹדוּ:
פְּדֵה   מַלְכִּי עַם נִדְווּ. וְכָל־אוֹיְבֵיהֶם יֹאבֵדוּ:
אֵל   מִטּוּבָךְ יִתְרַווּ. עַם נִבְחַר בְּשִׁמָךְ יָעִידוּ:   תם.

They eagerly await Your kindness, the students of the Torah thank you.
My king, redeem the sorrowful nation, and all of their enemies shall be destroyed.
God, from Your goodness they will be sated, the chosen nation will affirm Your name.

9. Yaḥid Ram

יָחִיד   רָם לְעוֹלָם. גַּלֵּה לְקֵץ נִטְמָן. כִּי בָא עֵת זְמַן
נֶאֱמָן. אֵל מַהֵר וּגְאַל לְעַם לֹא אַלְמָן:
וּגְאַל   נָא וּשְׁלַח נָא. מְבַשֵּׂר לִבְנֵי אַבְרָהָם. הָרֵם דִּגְלָם.
וּשְׁמַע לְקוֹלָם. בְּתוֹךְ עִירָם יָשִׁירוּ. כֻּלָּם. רִנָּה
יָרֹנּוּ תּוֹךְ אָהֳלָם. רְפָא אֵל צִירָם. הֵן עַתָּה כִּי
אַתָּה מֶלֶךְ רַחֲמָן נֶאֱמָן:
סִתְרִי   חַי אֵל שַׁדַּי. אוֹדֶה לְשִׁמְךָ יוֹמָם וָלַיְלָה. בְּבֵית
מְעוֹנֶךָ. כִּי בְךָ אֶשְׂמַח יָחִיד אֵל נוֹרָא נֶאֱזָר
בִּגְבוּרָה. אַתָּה הוּא אֲדוֹן כָּל־נִבְרָא. חָנֵּנִי בִּמְהֵרָה.
לְמַעַן בֵּית יוֹסֵף צַדִּיקֶךָ:
פְּנֵה   אֵלַי עֲנֵנִי. כִּי אַתָּה הוּא צוּר גּוֹאֲלִי. וּסְלַח נָא
לְמַעֲלִי. וּפְדֵנִי חַי לְעוֹלָם. רָם אֲהַלֶּלְךָ לָעַד בְּפִי
תָמִיד כִּימֵי עוֹלָם. אֵל נֶאֱלָם. קַבֵּץ נָא לְעַמָּךְ בְּהַר
קֹדֶשׁ חַי וְהַרְחֵב לָהֶם גְּבוּלָם. כֻּלָּם יוֹדוּךָ בִּנְוֵה
הָאוּלָם. נֶאֱמָן. שְׁעֵה נָא לְקוֹל מַהֲלָלָם. כִּי הֵם עַם
חָבִיב יְדִידֶיךָ:   הרם וכו׳   תם

Unique One, exalted forever,
reveal the hidden end.
For the time, a worthy time, has come.
Quickly, God, bring redemption, for a people not left widowed.

Pray, redeem them; and please send,
to the children of Abraham, a herald.

Raise their banner, and listen to their voice.
In their city, they, every one of them, shall sing.
In their tent, they will shout in exaltation.
Oh God, heal their agony; for surely, now, you are a merciful and reliable King.

My Place of Refuge, Living God, All-mighty.
I will give thanks to You, day and night, in the house of Your dwelling.
Unto You, alone, do I rejoice, awesome God, who are girded with power.
You are the Lord of all creation.
Have mercy upon me, speedily,
for the sake of the House of Joseph, Your righteous one.

Turn to me! Answer me!
For you are a Rock, you are my Redeemer.
Please forgive me for my unfaithfulness,
and redeem me, You who live forever.
Exalted One, I will praise you, forever, with my mouth; always, as in the days of old.
Hidden God,
gather Your people to the holy mountain of the Living God; enlarge for them their border.
They will all give thanks to you in the abode of the great hall,
Reliable One, have regard to the voice of their praise,
for they are a cherished people, Your beloved ones.

10. Maʿuzzi

מָעֻזִי אָז כָּלָה קֵץ עָזְבִי לָמָּה, עִמִּי עֲשֵׂה אוֹת לְטוֹבָה וְנֶחָמָה :
מָעֻזִי נָחַל גַּפְנִי גּוֹי אֵתָן צַעַד עַל שׁוּרִי וְהָרַג וְטָרַף:
מָעֻזִי אָז יָרַד דִּמְעִי עַל דָּמָם נִגְּרָה מִן עֵינִי נָהָר :
אָנָּא הָלַךְ דוֹדִי וְאָנָּא פָּנָה. בּוֹ אֶשְׂמַח שָׁלֹשׁ פְּעָמִים בַּשָּׁנָה:
תם

For the Festivals:

My Fortress of yore, the appointed time for the arrival of the Messiah has passed, why have you abandoned me?
My Fortress, the powerful enemy has inherited my vineyard, it has trampled upon my wall, it has killed and ripped apart:
My Fortress of yore, my tears fall upon the blood of the victims, from my eye did a river spill:
Where has my beloved gone, where has he turned, Him in whom I rejoice three times a year?

12 and 13. Ḥai Hazzan

חַי הַזָּן לַכֹּל תָּמִיד. אַתָּה הוּא אַתָּה הוּא. אֲדוֹן יָחִיד:
יָהּ אֵל גּוֹאֲלִי סְלַח מַעֲלִי. שָׂא אֶת גּוֹרָלִי. שָׂגְבוּ חֲסָדֶךָ
תָּדִיר:
יָאִירוּ בָּהִיר. יָעִידוּ לְךָ יוֹדוּ נֶאֱמָן. יָשִׁירוּ עֲדַת קְהָלִי
בְּתוֹךְ הֵיכָלִי. צַח אֵל גֶּאְדָּרִי זִמְרָתָם שְׁעֵה תָמִיד:
יה אל גואלי
מַלְכִּי שׁוּלְטָן לְעוֹלָם. צַוֵּה יָהּ חַסְדְּךָ יוֹמָם. עַל עַם
אַבְרָהָם. יָהּ אֵלִי מַלְכִּי. יָהּ אֵל רַחֲמָן דִּגְלָם
שָׂא נָא לְעוֹלָם צִדְקָךְ אַגִּיד: יה אל גואלי
חַזֵּק עֲדַת סְגֻלָּה. בָּרֵךְ חָתָן וְכַלָּה. שְׁנוֹת חַיִּים לָהֶם
תְּנָה. יַזְהִירוּ כְּאוֹר סַפִּיר: תם

Live, He who forever nourishes everything. You are He, You are He. The single Master:

O God, my redeemer, forgive my betrayal. Lift up my lot. Your kindness has always been sublime.

They will shine brightly, they will testify for you, they thank you faithfully.
My community shall sing inside my sanctuary.
My sublime Lord, their music shall always be pure.

My king is the ruler forever. Administer your kindness upon the nation of Abraham. O God, my king! O Lord the merciful, please raise their banner forever and I shall tell of your righteousness.

Strengthen the special community. Bless bride and groom. Grant them long years. They will glow like the light of a sapphire.

14, 15, 16. Kaddish

יִתְגַּדַּל וְיִתְקַדַּשׁ שְׁמֵיהּ רַבָּא: אמן בְּעַלְמָא דִּי בְרָא
כִרְעוּתֵהּ. וְיַמְלִיךְ מַלְכוּתֵהּ. וְיַצְמַח פּוּרְקָנֵהּ.
וִיקָרֵב מְשִׁיחֵהּ: אמן בְּחַיֵּיכוֹן וּבְיוֹמֵיכוֹן וּבְחַיֵּי דְכָל־בֵּית־
יִשְׂרָאֵל. בַּעֲגָלָא וּבִזְמַן קָרִיב. וְאִמְרוּ אָמֵן: אמן יְהֵא שְׁמֵהּ
רַבָּא מְבָרַךְ לְעָלַם לְעָלְמֵי עָלְמַיָּא. יִתְבָּרַךְ. וְיִשְׁתַּבַּח.
וְיִתְפָּאַר. וְיִתְרוֹמַם. וְיִתְנַשֵּׂא. וְיִתְהַדָּר. וְיִתְעַלֶּה. וְיִתְהַלָּל.
שְׁמֵהּ דְקוּדְשָׁא בְּרִיךְ הוּא: אמן לְעֵילָּא מִן כָּל־בִּרְכָתָא.
שִׁירָתָא. תִּשְׁבְּחָתָא וְנֶחָמָתָא. דַּאֲמִירָן בְּעָלְמָא וְאִמְרוּ
אָמֵן: אמן

Exalted and sanctified be His great Name (Amen). In the world which He created according to His will, and may He rule His kingdom, and may He bring forth His redemption, and hasten the coming of His Messiah (Amen). In your lifetime and in your days, and in the lifetime of the entire House of Israel, speedily and in the near future—and say Amen.

May His great Name be blessed forever and for all eternity. Blessed and praised, glorified, exalted and uplifted, honored and elevated and extolled be the Name of the Holy One, blessed is He (Amen); above all the blessings and hymns, praises and consolations which we utter in the world—and say Amen.

(Alouf 1995: 15)

REFERENCES

Bibliography

Abadi, Mordekhai. 1873. *Divre Mordekhai.* Aleppo.

Aboud, Hayyim Shaul, ed. 1931. *Sefer Shirei Zimrah Hashalem.* Jerusalem.

Adler, Elkan Nathan. 1905. *Jews in Many Lands.* Philadelphia: Jewish Publication Society.

Ajani, Stefano. 1980. "Teodoro Cottrau." *The New Grove Dictionary of Music and Musicians* 4:831–32.

Alcalay, Ammiel. 1993. *After Jews and Arabs: Remaking Levantine Culture.* Minneapolis: University of Minnesota Press.

Alcalay, Reuben. 1963. *The Complete Hebrew–English Dictionary.* Tel Aviv and Jerusalem: Massadah.

Alouf, Shimon H., ed. 1995. *Maḥzor Shelom Yerushalayim to Yom Kippur: Order of Prayers According to the Rite of Aram Soba (Aleppo),* translated by Isaac H. Catton. 2d rev. ed. Brooklyn: Sephardic Heritage Foundation.

Angel, Marc. 1982. *La America: The Sephardic Experience in the United States.* Philadelphia: Jewish Publication Society.

Appadurai, Arjun. 1991. "Global Ethnoscapes: Notes and Queries for a Transnational Anthropology." In *Recapturing Anthropology: Writing in the Present,* edited by Richard G. Fox, 191–210. Santa Fe: School of American Research Press.

Ashear, Allan J. 1988. Introduction to Shrem 1988, 11–13.

Ashear, Moses, ed. 1928. *Sefer Hallel ve-Zimrah.* 1928. Jerusalem.

Ashkenazi, Isaac Dabbah. 1982. *Esperanza y realidad: Raices de la comunidad judia de Alepo de Mexico.* Mexico City: Fundacion de la Sociedad de Beneficencia "Sedada y Marpe."

Ashtor, Eliyahu. 1972. "Aleppo." *Encyclopaedia Judaica* 2:562–66.

Avenary, Hanoch. 1979. "Gentile Songs as a Source of Inspiration for Israel Najara." In *Encounters of East and West in Music,* 186–93. Tel Aviv: Dept. of Musicology, Tel-Aviv University. Originally published in Hebrew in Fourth World Congress of Jewish Studies, *Papers* 2 (Jerusalem, 1968).

Azzam, Nabil Salim. 1990. "Muhammad ʿAbd al-Wahhab in Modern Egyptian Music." Ph.D. diss., University of California, Los Angeles.

Bahloul, Jöelle. 1996. *The Architecture of Memory: A Jewish–Muslim Household in Colonial Algeria, 1937–1962,* translated by Catherine Du Peloux Ménagé. Cambridge: Cambridge University Press. Originally published *La maison de mémoire: Ethnologie d'une demeure judéo-arabe en Algérie (1937–1961).* Paris: Editions Métalilié, 1992.

Baily, Samuel L. 1982. "Chain Migration of Italians to Argentina: Case Studies of the Agnonesi and the Sirolsei." *Studi Emigrazione* 19 (whole no. 65): 73–61.

Baron, Salo Wittmayer. 1957. *A Social and Religious History of the Jews,* 2d ed., vol. 3: *Heirs of Rome and Persia.*

Barrett, Mary Ellen. 1994. *Irving Berlin: A Daughter's Memoir.* New York: Simon and Schuster.

Barton, Josef J. 1975. *Peasants and Strangers: Italians, Rumanians, and Slovaks in an American City, 1890–1950.* Cambridge: Harvard University Press.

Battaglia, Debbora. 1990. *On the Bones of the Serpent: Person, Memory, and Mortality in Sabarl Island Society.* Chicago: University of Chicago Press.

Bayer, Bathja. 1972. "Ha-Tikvah." *Encyclopaedia Judaica* 7:1470–72.

Bergreen, Laurence. 1990. *As Thousands Cheer: The Life of Irving Berlin.* New York: Viking.

Bloomer, Kent C., and Charles W. Moore. 1977. *Body, Memory, and Architecture.* New Haven: Yale University Press.

Blumenthal, David R. 1978. *Understanding Jewish Mysticism: A Source Reader.* New York: Ktav.

Bnai Brith. 1991. *Jews of Syria: A Chronicle.* New York: Anti-Defamation League Publication.

Boyarin, Daniel, and Jonathan Boyarin. 1993. "Diaspora: Generation and the Ground of Jewish Identity." *Critical Inquiry* 19:693–725.

Boyarin, Jonathan. 1994. "Space, Time, and the Politics of Memory." In *Remapping Memory: The Politics of TimeSpace,* ed. Jonathan Boyarin. Minneapolis: University of Minnesota Press, pp. 1–37.

Briggs, John W. 1978. *An Italian Passage: Immigrants to Three American Cities, 1890–1930.* New Haven: Yale University Press.

Brinner, Benjamin. 1995. *Knowing Music, Making Music.* Chicago: University of Chicago Press.

Brody, Heinrich, ed. 1973. *Selected Poems of Jehudah Halevi,* translated by Nina Salaman. New York: Arno.

Canclini, Nestor Garcia. 1995. *Hybrid Cultures: Strategies for Entering and Leaving Modernity,* translated by Christopher L. Chiappari and Silvia L. Lopez. Minneapolis: University of Minnesota Press.

Casey, Edward S. 1987. *Remembering: A Phenomenological Study.* Bloomington: University of Indiana Press.

Chaplin, Charlie. 1992. *The Songs of Charlie Chaplin.* New York: Bourne Co.

Chira, Robert. 1994. *From Aleppo to America: The Story of Two Families.* New York: Rivercross Publishing.

Clifford, James. 1994. "Diasporas." *Cultural Anthropology* 9:302–38.

Cohen, Gillian. 1989. *Memory in the Real World.* Hillsdale, New Jersey: Lawrence Erlbaum.

Cohen, Judith R. 1990. "Musical Bridges: The Contrafact Tradition in Judeo-Spanish

Songs." In *Cultural Marginality in the Western Mediterranean,* ed. Frederick Gerson and Anthony Percival, 121–27. Toronto: New Aurora Editions.

Cohen, Moshe, ed. 1988. "Id-el-Fur: The Purim Evening—Aleppian Style." *Darchey "Eretz"* (Journal of the World Center for Aleppo Jews Traditional Culture) no. 4 (December): 24–25.

Cohon, A. Irma. 1986. "Idelsohn: The Founder and Builder of the Science of Jewish Music—A Creator of Jewish Song." *Yuval* 5:36–45.

Connerton, Paul. 1989. *How Societies Remember.* Cambridge: Cambridge University Press.

Danielson, Virginia. 1987. "The Qur'an and the Qasidah: Aspects of the Popularity of the Repertory Sung by Umm Kulthūm." *Asian Music* 19:26–46.

———. 1991. "Shaping Tradition in Arabic Song: The Career and Repertory of Umm Kulthūm." Ph.D. dissertation, University of Illinois, Urbana.

———. 1997. *The Voice of Egypt: Umm Kulthūm, Arabic Song, and Egyptian Society in the Twentieth Century.* Chicago: University of Chicago Press.

David, Abraham. 1972. "Najara, Israel Ben Moses." *Encyclopaedia Judaica* 12:798–99.

Dehmer, Alan. 1984. "On Freedom's Shores." In *Taking Root,* 47–53. Washington, D.C.: American-Arab Anti-Discrimination Committee Reports.

Días-Mas, Paloma. 1992. *Sephardim: The Jews from Spain,* translated by George K. Tucker. Chicago: University of Chicago Press.

Dobrinsky, Herbert C. 1986. *A Treasury of Sephardic Laws and Customs.* New York: Yeshiva University Press; Hoboken, N.J.: Ktav.

Dowling, W. Jay, and Dane L. Harwood. 1986. *Music Cognition.* Orlando, Fla.: Academic Press.

Eickelman, Dale F. 1981. *The Middle East. An Anthropological Approach.* Englewood Cliffs, N.J.: Prentice-Hall. (2d ed., 1989.)

———, and James Piscatori, eds. 1990a. *Muslim Travellers: Pilgrimage, Migration, and the Religious Imagination.* Berkeley and Los Angeles: University of California Press.

———, and James Piscatori. 1990b. "Social Theory in the Study of Muslim Societies." in Eickelman and Piscatori 1990a:3–25.

Elazar, Daniel J. 1989. *The Other Jews: The Sephardim Today.* New York: Basic Books.

El-Shawan (Castelo Branco), Salwa. 1981. "Al-Musika Al-ʿArabiyyah: A Category of Urban Music in Cairo, Egypt, 1927–1977." Ph.D. diss., Columbia University.

———. 1984. "Traditional Arab Music Ensembles in Egypt Since 1967: 'The Continuity of Traditional Within a Contemporary Framework.'" *Ethnomusicology* 28:271–88.

———. 1985. "Western Music and Its Practitioners in Egypt." *Asian Music* 17:144–53.

———. 1987. "Some Aspects of the Cassette Industry in Egypt." *The World of Music* 29:32–48.

Encyclopaedia Hebraica. 1972. "Judah Halevi." *Encyclopaedia Judaica* 10:355–62.

Erlmann, Veit. 1993. "The Politics and Aesthetics of Transnational Musics." *The World of Music* 35 (2) "The Politics and Aesthetics of World Music," 3–15.

Esses, Dianne O. 1992. "A Hunger for Syrian 'Exotica'." *The Melton Journal* 26:12–13.

Fabbri, Franco. 1982. "A Theory of Musical Genres: Two Applications." In *Popular Music Perspectives,* eds. David Horn and Philip Tagg, 52–81. Sweden: Göteborg & Exeter. Papers from the First International Conference on Popular Music Research, Amsterdam, June 1981.

Falck, Robert. 1979. "Parody and Contrafactum: A Terminological Clarification." *Musical Quarterly* 65:1–21.

———. 1980. "Contrafactum (1)." *The New Grove Dictionary of Music and Musicians,* 4:700–1.

Faruqi, Lois Ibsen al, compiler. 1981. *An Annotated Glossary of Arabic Musical Terms.* Westport, Conn.: Greenwood.

———. 1985. "Music, Musicians, and Muslim Law." *Asian Music* 17:3–36.

Feder, Stuart. 1981. "The Nostalgia of Charles Ives: An Essay in Affects and Music." *Annual of Psychoanalysis* 10:302–32.

———. 1989. "Calcium Light Night and Other Early Memories of Charles Ives." In *Fathers and Their Families,* eds. S. Cath., A. Gurwitt and L. Gunsberg, 307–26. Hillsdale, N.J.: The Analytic Press.

———. 1992. *Charles Ives: "My Father's Song," A Psychoanalytic Biography.* New Haven: Yale University Press.

Feld, Steven. 1990. *Sound and Sentiment: Birds, Weeping, Poetics and Song in Kaluli Expression.* Philadelphia: University of Pennsylvania Press, 2d ed.

Fenton, Paul. 1982. "A Jewish Sufi on the Influence of Music," *Yuval* 4:124–30.

Fentress, James, and Chris Wickham. 1992. *Social Memory.* Oxford: Blackwell.

Festival of Holidays: Recipe Book. 1987. Brooklyn: Sephardic Community Center.

Floyd, Samuel A., Jr. 1995. *The Power of Black Music: Interpreting its History from Africa to the United States.* New York: Oxford University Press.

Foucault, Michel. 1986. "Of Other Spaces," translated by Jay Miskowlec. *Diacritics* 16:22–27.

"From Our Songs." 1987. "*Darchey Eretz.*" (*Journal of the World Center for Aleppo Jews Traditional Culture*) 2 (June): 26. In Hebrew.

Garcia, Maria. 1984. "Middle Eastern Musical Instruments in Brooklyn." Paper prepared for the New York University Urban Ethnomusicology Seminar.

Gates, Henry Louis. 1988. *The Signifying Monkey: A Theory of African-American Literary Criticism.* New York: Oxford University Press.

Ginsberg, Faye. 1987. "When the Subject Is Women: Encounters with Syrian Jewish Women." *Journal of American Folklore* 100:540–47.

Goitein, S. D. 1983. *A Mediterranean Society,* vol. 4: *Daily Life*. Berkeley and Los Angeles: University of California Press.

Groesbeck, Rolf. 1984. "A Comparison of some Pizmonim with Arab Songs upon Which They Are Based: Renditions of Arab Composition by Moses Tawil and Muhammad ʿAbd al-Wahhāb." Paper prepared for the NYU Urban Ethnomusicology Seminar.

Gronow, Pekka. 1981. "The Record Industry Comes to the Orient." *Ethnomusicology* 25:251–84.

Guilbault, Jocelyne. 1993. *Zouk: World Music in the West Indies.* Chicago: University of Chicago Press.

Habermann, Abraham M. 1972. "Pizmon." *Encyclopaedia Judaica* 13:602–3.

Haddad, Heskel M. 1984. *Jews of Arab and Islamic Countries.* New York: Shengold.

Halbwachs, Maurice. 1992. *On Collective Memory,* edited and translated by Lewis A. Coser. Chicago: University of Chicago Press.

Heskes, Irene. 1992. *Yiddish American Popular Songs, 1895–1950: A Catalogue Based on the Lawrence Marwick Roster of Copyright Entries.* Washington, D.C.: Library of Congress.

Hitti, Philip K. 1951. *History of Syria, Including Lebanon and Palestine.* London: Macmillan.

Hoffman, Lawrence A. 1979. *The Canonization of the Synagogue Service.* Notre Dame, Ind.: University of Notre Dame Press.

Hooglund, Eric J. 1987. *Crossing the Waters: Arabic-Speaking Immigrants to the United States before 1940.* Washington, D.C.: Smithsonian Institution Press.

Hourani, Albert. 1991. *A History of the Arab Peoples.* Cambridge: The Belknap Press of Harvard University Press.

Idel, Moshe. 1988. *Kabbalah: New Perspectives.* New Haven: Yale University Press.

Idelsohn, Abraham Zvi. 1913. "Die Maqamen der arabischen Musik." *Sammelbände der internationale Musikgesellschaft* 15:1–63.

———. 1923. "Die arabische Musik." In *Hebräisch-Orientalischer Melodienschatz,* vol. 4: *Gesänge der Orientalischen Sefardim,* 52–112. Jerusalem-Berlin-Vienna: Benjamin Hart Verlag.

———. 1929. *Jewish Music in Its Historical Development.* New York: Schocken. Repr. New York: Holt, Rinehart and Winston, 1967.

The Jerusalem Bible. (The Holy Scriptures) 1969. Jerusalem: Koren.

Kallberg, Jeffrey. 1988. "The Rhetoric of Genre: Chopin's Nocturne in G Minor." *19th Century Music* 11:238–61.

Kartomi, Margaret J. 1981. "The Processes and Results of Musical Culture Contact: A Discussion of Terminology and Concepts." *Ethnomusicology* 25:227–49.

———, and Stephen Blum, eds. 1994. *Music-Cultures in Contact, Convergences and Collisions.* Basel, Switzerland: Gordon and Breach.

Kassin, Jacob S., Chief Rabbi. 1984. "Reaffirming Our Tradition." 3 June. Offset copy of proclamation.

———. 1988. Introduction to Shrem 1988, 28–33.

Katz, Israel J. 1988. "Contrafacta and the Judeo-Spanish *Romancero:* A Musicological View." In *Hispanic Studies in Honor of Joseph H. Silverman,* edited by Joseph V. Ricapito, 169–87. Newark, Del.: Juan de la Cuesta.

Katz, Ruth. 1968. "The Singing of Baqqashot by Aleppo Jews." *Acta Musicologica* 40:65–85.

Keyte, Hugh, and Andrew Parrott. 1992. *The New Oxford Book of Carols.* Oxford: Oxford University Press.

Kleiner, J. "On nostalgia." 1970. *Bull. Philadelphia Assn. Psychoanal.,* 10:11–30. (Also in *The World of Emotions,* edited by C. W. Socarides. New York: International Universities Press, 1977.)

Kligman, Mark Loren. 1997. "Modes of Prayer: Arabic Maqāmāt in the Sabbath Morning Liturgical Music of the Syrian Jews in Brooklyn." Ph.D. diss., New York University.

Koskoff, Ellen. 1992. Introduction. *The World of Music* 34 (3) Special Issue: "Ethnomusicology and Music Cognition," 3–6.

Langer, Lawrence L. 1991. *Holocaust Testimonies: The Ruins of Memory.* New Haven: Yale University Press.

Laniado, David. (1952)1980. *La-kedoshim asher be-ara"tz* ("On the Holy Men from Aram Tzuba [=Aleppo]"). Jerusalem.

Laskier, Michael M. 1992. *The Jews of Egypt, 1920–1970.* New York: New York University Press.

Levy, Isaac. 1969. *Antologia de liturgia judeo-española,* vol. 4. Jerusalem: Marán Book Mfg.

Lewis, Bernard. 1984. *The Jews of Islam.* Princeton, N.J.: Princeton University Press.

Lipsitz, George. 1990. *Time Passages: Collective Memory and American Popular Culture.* Minneapolis: University of Minnesota Press.

Longwood, William F. 1957. *Suez Story: Key to the Middle East.* New York: Greenberg.

Lynch, Kevin. 1960. *The Image of the City.* Cambridge: MIT Press.

MacDonald, John S., and Beatrice S. MacDonald. 1964. "Chain Migration, Ethnic Neighborhood Formation and Social Networks." *The Milbank Memorial Fund Quarterly* 42:82–95.

Marcus, Abraham. 1989. *The Middle East on the Eve of Modernity: Aleppo in the Eighteenth Century.* New York: Columbia University Press.

Marcus, Scott Lloyd. 1989. "Arab Music Theory in the Modern Period." 2 vols. Ph.D. diss., University of California, Los Angeles.

Meyer, Leonard. 1967. *Music, the Arts, and Ideas.* Chicago: University of Chicago Press.

Middleton, Richard. 1990. *Studying Popular Music.* Milton Keynes, England: Open University Press.

Mirelman, Victor A. 1987. "Sephardic Immigration to Argentina Prior to the Nazi Period." In *The Jewish Presence in Latin America,* edited by Judith Laiken Elkin and Gilbert W. Merkx, pp. 13–32. Boston: Allen and Unwin.

———. 1990. *Jewish Buenos Aires, 1890–1930.* Detroit: Wayne State University Press.

Moore, Deborah Dash. 1981. "Defining American Jewish Ethnicity." *Prospects* 6:387–410.

Naff, Alixa. 1985. *Becoming American. The Early Arab Immigrant Experience.* Carbondale and Edwardsville: Southern Illinois University Press.

Najara, Israel Ben Moses. 1587. *Zemirot Yisrael.* Safed.

Neapolitan Songs. 1938. New York: Amsco.

Nelson, Kristina. 1985. *The Art of Reciting the Qur'an.* Austin: University of Texas Press.

Noeltner, Robert H., arr. 1964. *Fiddler on the Roof.* New York: The New York Times Music Corporation [Sunbeam Music Division].

Nulman, Macy. 1977–78. "The Musical Service of the Syrian Synagogue: Its Structure and Design." *Journal of Jewish Music and Liturgy* 2:34–57.

Obadia, Hakki. 1969. *The Hakki Obadia Oud Method Book.* Brooklyn, N.Y.: Near East Music Associates.

Papo, Joseph M. 1987. *Sephardim in Twentieth Century America: In Search of Unity.* San Jose and Berkeley, Calif.: Pelé Yoetz Books and Judah L. Magnes Museum.

Patai, R. 1983. "Exorcism and Xenoglossia among the Safed Kabbalists." In *On Jewish Folklore,* 314–25. Detroit: Wayne State University Press. Originally in *Journal of American Folklore* 91 (1978): 823–33.

Philips, Dr. A. Th. n.d. *Pirkeh Avot,* "Ethics of the Fathers." In *Daily Prayers,* rev. ed. New York: Hebrew Publishing Co.

Poultney, David. 1983. *Studying Music History: Learning, Reasoning, and Writing about Music History and Literature.* Englewood Cliffs, N.J.: Prentice-Hall.

Powers, Harold S. 1981. "Introduction: Mode and Modality." In *Report of the Twelfth Congress of the International Musicological Society, Berkeley 1977,* edited by Daniel Heartz and Bonnie Wade, 501–3. Basel, Switzerland: Bärenreiter Kassel.

Preschal, Tovia. 1972. "Alshekh, Moses." *Encyclopaedia Judaica* 2:758–59.

Qureshi, Regula Burckhardt. 1981. "Islamic Music in an Indian Environment: The Shi-a Majlis." *Ethnomusicology* 25 (1): 41–72.

———. 1986. *Sufi Music of India and Pakistan: Sound, Context and Meaning in Qawwali.* Cambridge: Cambridge University Press.

Rabinowitz, Louis I. 1972. "Tefillin." *Encyclopaedia Judaica* 15:898–99.

Racy, A. Jihad. 1976. "Record Industry and Egyptian Traditional Music, 1904–1932." *Ethnomusicology* 20:23–48.

———. 1982. "Musical Aesthetics in Present-day Cairo." *Ethnomusicology* 26:391–406.

———. 1983. "The Waṣlah: A Compound Form Principle in Egyptian Music." *Arab Studies Quarterly* 5:396–403.

———. 1991. "Historical Worldviews of Early Ethnomusicologists: An 1991 East–West Encounter in Cairo, 1932." In *Ethnomusicology and Modern Music History,* edited by Stephen Blum, Philip V. Bohlman, and Daniel M. Neuman, 68–69. Urbana: University of Illinois Press.

Randel, Don M., ed. 1986. *The New Harvard Dictionary of Music.* Cambridge, MA: Belknap Press of Harvard University Press.

Rasmussen, Anne K. 1991. "Individuality and Social Change in the Music of Arab-Americans." Ph.D. diss., University of California, Los Angeles.

———. 1992. " 'An Evening in the Orient': The Middle Eastern Nightclub in America." *Asian Music* 23:61–88.

Recueil. 1934. *Recueil des Travaux du Congrès de Musique Arabe.* Cairo: Imprimerie nationale Boulac.

Reyes Schramm, Adelaida. 1975. "The Role of Music in the Interaction of Black Americans and Hispanos in New York City's East Harlem." Ph.D. diss., Columbia University.

Rice, Timothy. 1994. *May It Fill Your Soul.* Chicago: University of Chicago Press.

Robertson, Carol. 1979. " 'Pulling the Ancestors': Performance Practice and Praxis in Mapuche Ordering." *Ethnomusicology* 23:395–416.

Root, Deane L. 1980. "Irving Berlin." *The New Grove Dictionary of Music and Musicians* 2:578–79.

Rubin, David C. 1995. *Memory in Oral Traditions. The Cognitive Psychology of Epic, Ballads, and Counting-out Rhymes.* New York and Oxford: Oxford University Press.

Safran, William. 1991. "Diasporas in Modern Societies: Myths of Homeland and Return." *Diasporas* 1:83–99.

Saḥḥab, Fiktūr. 1987. *Al-Sab ʿah al-Kibār fī al-Mūsīqá al-ʿArabīyah al-Muʿāṣirah.* Beirut: Dār al-ʿIlm lil-Malāyīn.

Sanua, Victor. 1977. "Contemporary Studies of Sephardic Jews in the United States." In *A Coat of Many Colors: Jewish Subcommunities in the United States,* edited by Abraham D. Lavender, 281–88. Westport, Conn.: Greenwood.

Sauvaget, Jean. 1971. "Ḥalab." *Encyclopaedia of Islam,* new ed. Leiden: Brill; London: Luzac, 3:85–90.

Schacter, Daniel L. 1995a. "Implicit Memory: A New Frontier for Cognitive Neuroscience." In *The Cognitive Neurosciences,* edited by M. S. Gazzagnia, 815–24. Cambridge: MIT Press.

———. 1995b. *Memory Distortion: How Minds, Brains, and Societies Reconstruct the Past.* Cambridge: Harvard University Press.

———. 1996. *Searching for Memory: The Brain, the Mind, and the Past.* New York: Basic Books.

Scheindlin, Raymond P. 1991. *The Gazelle: Medieval Hebrew Poems on God, Israel, and the Soul.* Philadelphia: Jewish Publication Society.

Schimmel, Annemarie. 1989. *Islamic Names.* Edinburgh: Edinburgh University Press.

Schleifer, Eliyahu. 1986. "Idelsohn's Scholar[l]y and Literary Publications: An Annotated Bibliography." *Yuval* 5:53–180.

Scholem, Gershom. 1970. "Kabbalah." *Encyclopaedia Judaica*. Vol. 10, col. 489–653.

———. 1941. *Major Trends in Jewish Mysticism.* New York: Schocken.

Seeger, Anthony. 1979. "What Can We Learn When They Sing: Vocal Genres of the Suya Indians of Central Brazil." *Ethnomusicology* 23:373–94.

Sefer Miqra Qodesh. 1881. Leghorn.

Sephardic Archives. c. 1985. *Victory Bulletin: July 1942–September 1945.* Wartime newspapers of the Syrian Jewish Community in Brooklyn.

Seroussi, Edwin. 1990. "Rabbi Israel Najara: Moulder of Hebrew Sacred Singing after the Expulsion from Spain." *Asufot: Annual for Jewish Studies* 4:285–310. In Hebrew.

———. 1993. "On the Origin of the Custom of Chanting Baqqashot in Jerusalem in the Nineteenth Century." *Peʿamim: Studies in Oriental Jewry* 56:106–24. In Hebrew.

———, and Susana Weich-Shahak. 1990/91. "Judeo-Spanish Contrafacts and Musical Adaptations: The Oral Tradition." *Orbis Musicae.* Essays in Honor of Hanoch Avenary. [Tel Aviv University Dept. of Musicology] 10: 164–194.

Shave, Itzhak. 1988. "Of Aram-Zova's Songs: Mauzi." *Darchey "Eretz"* (Journal of the World Center for Aleppo Jews Traditional Culture) 4 (December):14–15. In Hebrew.

Shelemay, Kay Kaufman. 1988. "Together in the Field: Team Research among Syrian Jews in Brooklyn, New York." *Ethnomusicology* 32:369–84.

———. 1996a. "The Ethnomusicologist and the Transmission of Tradition." *The Journal of Musicology* 14:35–51.

———. 1996b. "Syrian *Pizmonim* in Brooklyn." *Peʿamim: Studies in Oriental Jewry* 67:96–110. In Hebrew.

———. and Peter Jeffrey. 1993–97. *Ethiopian Christian Chant: An Anthology.* 3 vols. Madison, Wisconsin: A-R Editions Inc.

———, ———, and Ingrid Monson. 1993. "Oral and Written Transmission in Ethiopian Christian Chant." *Early Music History* 12:55–117.

Shiloah, Amnon. 1992. *Jewish Musical Traditions.* Detroit: Wayne State University Press.

Shils, Edward. 1981. *Tradition.* Chicago: University of Chicago Press.

Shrem, Gabriel, ed. 1988. *Sheer Ushbahah Hallel Ve-Zimrah,* 5th ed. New York: The Sephardic Heritage Foundation Inc. and Magen David Publication Society. First ed., 1964.

Slobin, Mark. 1989. *Chosen Voices: The Story of the American Cantorate.* Urbana: University of Illinois Press.

———. 1993. *Subcultural Sounds: Micromusics of the West.* Hanover, N.H.: Wesleyan University Press, University Press of New England.

———, guest ed. 1994. "A Special Section on Diasporic Music." *Diaspora* 3 (3), pp. 243–304.

Soja, Edward W. 1995. "Heterotopologies: A Remembrance of Other Spaces in the Citadel-LA." In *Postmodern Cities and Spaces,* edited by Sophie Watson and Katherine Gibson, 13–34. Oxford: Blackwell.

Someck, Ronny. 1989. *Panther.* Tel Aviv: Zmora Bitan. In Hebrew.

Spence, Jonathan. 1983. *The Memory Palace of Matteo Ricci.* New York: Penguin.

Squire, Larry R. 1987. *Memory and Brain.* New York: Oxford University Press.

Stillman, Norman A. 1979. *The Jews of Arab Lands: A History and Sourcebook.* Philadelphia: Jewish Publication Society.

Sutton, Joseph A. D. 1979. *Magic Carpet: Aleppo-In-Flatbush: The Story of a Unique Ethnic Jewish Community.* New York: Thayer-Jacoby.

———. 1988. *Aleppo Chronicles: The Story of the Unique Sephardeem of the Ancient Near East—in Their Own Words.* New York: Thayer-Jacoby.

Taboush, Raphael Antebi. 1920/1921, *Sefer Shir Ushevaḥah,* edited by Raphael Hayyim Ha-Kohen. Jerusalem (1st ed., 1905).

Talbi, Haim. 1996. "Tradition and Change in Customs of Reading the Torah among the Jews of Aleppo." *Peʿamim:* Studies in Oriental Jewry 67:111–119.

Tawil, David. 1984. Definitions, summary of eight major maqāmāt, name of notes in Arabic music. Mimeographed handouts distributed to Urban Ethnomusicology Seminar, NYU, 11 December.

Tolbert, Elizabeth. 1990. "Women Cry with Words: Symbolization of Affect in the Karelian Lament." *Yearbook of Traditional Music* 22:80–105.

———. 1992. "Theories of Meaning and Music Cognition: An Ethnomusicological Approach." *The World of Music* 34(3):7–21.

Trachtenberg, Joshua. 1974. *Jewish Magic and Superstition: A Study in Folk Religion.* New York: Atheneum.

Treitler, Leo. 1974. "Homer and Gregory: The Transmission of Epic Poetry and Plainchant." *Musical Quarterly* 60:333–72.

Tulving, Endel. 1983. *Elements of Episodic Memory.* Oxford: Clarendon.

Van Vleck, Amelia E. 1991. *Memory and Re-Creation in Troubadour Lyric.* Berkeley and Los Angeles: University of California Press.

Vander, Judith. 1988. *Songprints: The Musical Experience of Five Shoshone Women.* Urbana: University of Illinois Press.

Wallace, Wanda. 1991. "Characteristics and Constraints in Ballads and Their Effects on Memory." *Discourse Processes* 14:181–202.

———. 1994. "Memory for Music: The Effect of Melody on Recall of Text." *Journal of Experimental Psychology: Learning, Memory, and Cognition* 20:1471–85.

———, and David C. Rubin. 1987. "Memory of a Ballad Singer." 257–62 In *Memory in Everyday Life.* Vol. 1 of *Practical Aspects of Memory: Current Research and Issues.* Eds. M. M. Gruneberg, P. E. Morris, and R. N. Sykes. Chichester: John Wiley & Sons.

Wolff, Christoph. 1994. *Mozart's Requiem.* Berkeley and Los Angeles: University of California Press.

Ya'ar, Avishai. 1996. "The Cantillation of the Bible: The Aleppo Tradition (Pentateuch)." Ph.D. diss., City University of New York.

Yahalom, Joseph. 1982. "R. Israel Najarah and the Revival of Hebrew Poetry in the East after the Expulsion from Spain." *Peʿamim: Studies in Oriental Jewry* 13:96–122. In Hebrew.

Yerushalmi, Yosef Hayim. 1989. *Zakhor: Jewish History and Jewish Memory,* 2d ed. New York: Schocken (1st ed., 1982).

———. 1988. "Réflexions sur l'oubli." In *Usages de l'oubli,* edited by Yosef H. Yerushalmi et al., 7–21. Paris: Editions du Seuil.

Young, Robert. 1978. *Analytical Concordance to the Bible.* 22d ed. Grand Rapids, Mich.: Eerdmans.

Zenner, Walter P. 1965. "Syrian Jewish Identification in Israel." Ph.D. diss., Columbia University.

———. 1982. "Jews in Late Ottoman Syria: External Relations." In *Jewish Societies in the Middle East,* edited by Shlomo Deshen and Walter P. Zenner, 155–86. Washington, D.C.: University Press of America.

———. 1983. "Syrian Jews in New York Twenty Years Ago." In *Fields of Offerings: Studies in Honor of Raphael Patai,* edited by Victor D. Sanua, 173–93. London and Toronto: Associated University Presses.

———. 1988. "The Cross-National Web of Syrian–Jewish Relations." In *Urban Life: Readings in Urban Anthropology,* edited by George Gmelch and Walter P. Zenner, 381–93. Prospect Heights, Ill.: Waveland.

Zerubavel, Yael. 1995. *Recovered Roots: Collective Memory and the Making of Israeli National Tradition.* Chicago: University of Chicago Press.

———, and Dianne Esses. 1987. "Reconstructions of the Past: Syrian Jewish Women and the Maintenance of Tradition." *Journal of American Folklore* 100:528–39.

Discography

Albeg, Ezekiel. 1959. *Babylonian Biblical Chants.* New York: Folkways, FR 8930.

Bakashot and Saturday Night Songs (3 cassettes). 1987. Brooklyn: Sephardic Community Center.

Ben Hayyim, Yigal. n.d. *Halleluyah Betzalzali Samaʿa: Sabbath Prayers According to the Jerusalem Tradition,* 6 cassettes. Jerusalem.

El-Bakkar, Muhammed and his Oriental Ensemble. n.d. *Port Said.* Audio Fidelity: (AFLP 1833, AFSD 5833).

Elnadav, Raphael Yair. 1980. *Sephardic Prayer Songs for the High Holy Days: Raphael Yair Elnadav.* 1980. New York: Caytronics Corp., TCL-501.

Fairuz. n.d. *The Very Best of Fairuz.* Beirut: Voix de l'Orient Series, A. Chahine & Fils; Digital Press Hellas, VDLCD 501.

Pizmonim: Sephardic-Hebrew Songs of the Middle East, vol. 1. 1979. Brooklyn: Magen David Publications Society.

Shelemay, Kay Kaufman, and Sarah Weiss, eds. 1985. *Pizmon: Syrian-Jewish Religious and Social Song.* Shanachie Records, Meadowlark 105.

Wahhāb, ʿAbd al-. 1973. *Immortal Melodies.* Beirut: Cairophon (TC-MCCO 122).

———. 1976. *Belly Dance.* Beirut: Cairophon (TC-MCCO 187).

Zion, Yehezkel, and Ephraim Avidani. n.d. *Nishmat Kol Hay: Saturday Sephardic Prayers,* 8 cassettes. Jerusalem: Yeshivat Avidani.

Formal Interviews

Abadi, Isaac. 21 November 1984

Arking, Morris. 14 January 1986 (with Mosseri)

Ashear, Albert. 19 July 1989

Barnea, Ezra. 10 March 1993

Betech, Ramon. 8 September 1992

Bozo, Yaqov. 14 March 1993

Cabasso, Isaac. 13 November 1984 (with Kairey)

Cain, Isaac, and Ruth Cain. 7 September 1992

Catton, Samuel. 30 October 1984

Cohen, Moshe. 23 March 1993

Cohen, Sophie. 28 February 1985

Haber, Gracia. 31 January 1989

Harari, Sadegh. 7 September 1992

Kaire, Hyman. 14 March 1985, 17 February 1988

Kairey, Mickey. 6 November 1984, 13 November 1984 (with Cabasso), 12 December 1984

Kassin, Joyce. 30 March 1989

Mosseri, Joseph. 14 January 1986 (with Arking)

Nahari, Yeziel. 6 January 1986, 16 January 1986 (by Monson)

Saff, Joseph. 23 October 1984, 4 December 1984, 19 December 1985 (by Weiss)

Schweky, Sheila. 27 January, 1988

Serouya, Charles. 15 July 1993
Shemi, Shaul. 21 March 1993
Shrem, Gabriel. 9 January 1986
Tawil, David. 11 December 1984, 10 May 1985 (by Foster)
Tawil, Moses. 6 November 1984, 21 August 1991
Tawil, Sarah. 30 March 1989
Yedid, Menachem. 23 March 1993
Zalta, Benjamin. 16 March 1990

Music Sessions

8 November 1984 **Moses Tawil and Ensemble.**
Moses Tawil, I. Cabasso, M. Kairey, H. Kaire, D. Tawil, Mac Tawil, S. Tawil, J. Saff, L. Massry, M. Massry, J. Catton, A. Tawil, E. Ashkenazi

13 November 1984 **Moses Tawil and Ensemble.**
Moses Tawil, H. Kaire, D. Tawil, Mac Tawil, I. Cabasso, M. Kaire, J. Saff, M. Mustacchi, J. Kassin, E. Patash, J. Catton, M. Massry, L. Massry

20 November 1984 **Moses Tawil and Ensemble.**
Moses Tawil, H. Kaire, Max Tawil, M. Mustacchi, D. Tawil, J. Saff, I. Cabasso, J. Setton, E. Patash, J. Catton, L. Massry

4 December 1984 **Moses Tawil and Ensemble.**
Moses Tawil, I. Cabasso, H. Kaire, D. Tawil, J. Saff, E. Setton, M. Levy, M. Cohen, S. Sabin, E. Ashkenazi, L. Massry

11 December 1984 **Moses Tawil and Ensemble.**
Moses Tawil, H. Kaire, D. Tawil, M. Mustacchi, R. Levy-Shasho, W. Serua, D. Esses, M. Cohen, L. Massry, J. Catton, E. Ashkenazi

10 January 1985 **Albert Cohen-Saban and Ensemble.**
A. Cohen-Saban, M. Elakkad, L. Massry

21 February 1985 **Shimon Alouf and Ensemble.**
S. Alouf, L. Massry, J. Saff, M. Mustacchi, H. Kaire, E. Setton

28 February 1985 **Shimon Alouf and Ensemble.**
S. Alouf, A. Shamah, E. Ashkenazi, D. Dweck, M. Mustacchi, E. Setton, H. Kaire

1 August 1985 **Eddie Erani and Ensemble.**
I. Askov, M. Mustacchi, E. Erani, H. Kaire, I. Zion

14 August 1985 **Eddie Erani and Ensemble.**
I. Askov, H. Kaire, M. Kairey, A. Bavey, D. Nizri, M. Mustacchi, E. Abadi

14 November 1985 **Moses Tawil and Ensemble.**
Moses Tawil, D. Tawil, H. Tawil, M. Mizrahi, H. Kaire, L. Massry, M. Massry, M. Schweky, Y. Nahari, E. Abadi, M. Cohen, Mac Tawil, D. Cohen, A. Cohen, J. Cohen, M. Shamah, J. Kassin

INDEX

Locators in *italics* refer to figures, examples, and song melodies and texts.

Abadi, Isaac, 117, 236nn. 15, 23, 253n.27
Abadi, Mordekhai, 236n.15, 237n.30, 244n.42
Abd al-Ḥalīm Ḥāfiṣ, 186
ʿAbd al-Wahhāb, Muḥammad, 108, 109, 110–11, 229
  additive approach of, 127
  "Aḥibb Ashūfak," 94–97, 112
  "Bint al-Balad" ("Country Girl"), 17–18, 213
  career of, 112–13
  instrumental works of, 54
  "Inta ʿUmrī," 111, 185
  oral traditions about, 112–13
  recordings of, 84, 97
  songs of, 93, 110, 115–16, 247n.28
  style innovations of, 136–37
  ʿūd playing of, 131, 246n.17
  "Wheat Song, The" ("Al-qamḥ"), 136–37, 139, *144–47,* 216
  "Yawm wa-Layla" (Day and Night"), 185
Aboud, Hayyim Shaul, 89; *Sefer Shirei Zimrah Hashalem,* 40, 237n.31
Ades Synagogue (Jerusalem), 59, 117, 244n.40, 248n.5
aesthetics
  Aleppo standards of, 105–6
  of Arab music, 12–13, 125–26, 133
  "catchy" as a value, 139, 162, 198, 199, 200, 213–14, 217
  favorite melodies, 198–99
  improvisation and, 191–92
  judgments of pizmonim, 177–78, 204
  listener involvement, 133–34
  petiḥot appreciation, 153
  popularity and, 199–200
  preference for vocal over instrumental music, 130
  "sweetness" as a value, 55, 168–69, 177, 191, 230
  of Syrian Jews, 124, 219, 229
"Agaddelkha Elohai," 250n.17
"Ahallel Veʾagilah," 157
āhang (also hank), 97
Ahi Ezer Synagogue (Brooklyn), 16, 170, 185, 213, 243n.33
"Aḥibb Ashūfak" (ʿAbd al-Wahhāb), 94–97
Aḥmad, Zakariya, 109
Albeg, Ezekiel H., 16–17, 185
Alcalay, Ammiel, 228, 233n.1; *After Jews and Arabs: Remaking Levantine Culture,* 3
Aleppo
  Arab/Jewish/Christian interactions, 71, 115, 183
  Arab sound recordings from, 43
  food and music in, 168
  musical life in, 106, 115
Aleppo Jewish community, 1, 4, 56, 82
  compared with Damascus community, 86
  diaspora of, 75–81, 104
  distinctive regional style of, 105–6
  European Jews in, 71
  European musical influence in, 183
  healing practices of, 222
  history of, 69–72
  links to Brooklyn community, 47
  migrants to Jerusalem, 59
  remnants of, 64
  Sephardic Jews in, 71–75
  Taboush circle, 29–34
aliyah, 252n.15
Alouf, Shimon, 84, 94, 235n.1

Alshekh, R. Moses, 222
"Ani Ashir Lakh"
  compared with Arab source, 94, 95–97
  composition of, 94
  difficulty of, 94–95
  form of, 96–97, 150
  maqāmāt in, 97
  melody of, 94, 95, *98–102*
  text of, 95–96, *103*
  transmission of, 94–95
"Ani Lishmakh" (Taboush), 203
"Anniversary Waltz," 93
Anschütz, Ernst, 252n.23
Answary, Sam, 235n.1
Anwar, Ḥasan, 94
Arab music and songs. *See also* Egyptian music and songs; maqām; *specific composers and songs*
  aesthetics of, 12–13, 125–26, 133
  collaborative composition in, 188
  history of, 119
  improvisation in, 126, 132, 189–93
  improvisatory introductions to, 12–13
  instrumental accompaniments for, 111, 137
  as living tradition, 108
  musical system of, 118–27
  musicians, 109–15
  musicians, status of, 127–29
  oral transmission of, 36–38, 52–53
  ornamentation in, 126, 127
  sacred *vs.* secular conception of, 119
  as sources for pizmonim, 1, 3–4, 5, 17–18, 48–50, 55, 59, 94–97, 104–34, 149–50, 152, 162–63, 169, 177–78, 183, 185, 186, 205, 207, 214, 216, 220, 223–26
  Syrian Jews' acquisition of knowledge of, 115–18
  ṭarab and turāth genres, 107–9
Arab peoples, Syrian Jews' interaction with, 71, 115, 183, 223–30
Arabic language, use of, 224–26
Arabic names, 48
Archives of Traditional Music, 251n.11
Argentinian community, 77, 80, 84, 86–87, 243nn. 31, 38
  anti-Semitic incidents against, 68
  formation of, 78
  size of, 65
Ashear, Albert, 84, 207–8, 237n.33
  bar mitzvah of, 195–96
  family migration of, 79
  reminiscences of father, 33, 34, 81, 159, 178, 183
Ashear, Charles (Shaul), 106, 131, 197
Ashear, David, 197
Ashear, family, 195–97
Ashear, Joseph, 79, 237n.24
Ashear, Moses, 60, 81, 89, 225–26
  "Beni Vegilakh," 195–96
  biography of, 40
  as cynosure, 184–85
  dedication of *Sheer Ushbahah Hallel ve-Zimrah* to, *39,* 40, 168
  "Havu Godel L'Elohenu," 197
  introduction to *Sheer Ushbahah Hallel ve-Zimrah,* 43, 222
  "Mi Zot," 152
  "Mifalot Elohim," 198–99
  "Mizzivakh Tanhir," 196–97
  oral traditions about, 33, 228
  pizmonim of, 47, 160, 183–85, 195–98, 246n.22, 247n.24
  Sefer Hallel ve-Zimrah, 38, 40
  son's reminiscences of, 33, 34, 81, 159, 178, 183
  students of, 34, 198
  as Taboush's student, 32, 33, 197, 207–8
  "Yeḥidah Hitnaʿari," 172–81, 184, 195, 199–200, 220
  "Yeromem Ṣuri," 159
Ashear, Shaul. *See* Ashear, Charles
Ashear family, 207–9
"Ashir Na Shir Tikvah" (Albeg), 185, *186*
"Ashkī li-min dhū al-hawā" (Murād), 246n.15
Ashkenazi, Ezra, 131–32, 235n.1, 245n.6, 251n.12
Ashkenazi, Shaul, 251n.12
Ashkenazi, Sophie Shafia, 80, 81
Ashkenazic Jews, 73; naming traditions of, 238n.40
Atlantic City community, 80
al-Aṭrash, Asmahān, 109–10
al-Aṭrash, Farīd, 109–10
"Attah Ahuvi," 157
  form of, 190
  text of, *260–61*
"Attah El Kabbir" (Taboush), 30, 250n.17, 254n.6
  composition of, 54–55
  dissemination of, 56–61, 83, 90
  form of, 55, 57, 150
  Idelsohn transcription of, 56–57

melody of, 55, 56–61, *62–63,* 190
performance of, 55, 204
text of, 55, 56–61, *61–62, 63*
"Attah Marom," 160
Australian community, 79
Autry, Gene, 16
Avenary, Hanoch, 235n.8
Avidani, Ephraim, 84

Bahloul, Jöelle, 9
Baidaphon Company, 246n.15
el-Bakkar, Muḥammed, 248n.35
bakkashot, 31, 119–20, 172, 236n.14, 246n.19
aesthetic and affective properties of, 153–54
childhood participation in, 116–18, 150–51
collections of, 38, 40
concert performance of, 170
improvisation in, 190–91
interpolation of pizmonim between, 118, 153
Jerusalem performances of, 82, 87–88, 117, 244n.40
maqām scheme of, 117
melodies of, 151–52
name references in, 46
nonliturgical performances of, 153
origin of tradition, 151
performance contexts for, 154
performance practice of, 117–18, 150–51
prestige of, 151–52
relationship to petiḥot, 152–54
relationship to pizmonim, 150–52, 153–54
relative importance in Israel, New York, and Mexico City, 87–88, 202, 248n.5
repertories of, 200, 202
sound recordings of, 44–45
texts of, 151
women's knowledge of, 52
bar mitzvah ceremony, 135, 138, 155. *See also* performance occasions and settings
Barnea, Ezra, 239n.3, 244n.40
bashraf, 17
Bassil, George, 235n.6, 239n.1
Beethoven, Ludwig van, *Pathétique* Sonata, 194
Ben Hayyim, Yigal, 84
Ben Suria, Yoab, 69–70
"Beni Vegilakh" (Ashear), 195–96
Bensonhurst. *See* Brooklyn community
Berlin, Irving, 170
"Bi-iladhī askara," 163
Bikel, Theodore, 54
Bikur Holim, 242n.29
"Bint al-Balad" ("Country Girl") ('Abd al-Wahhāb), 17–18, 213
Bock, Jerry, *Fiddler on the Roof,* 252n.13
borrowing. *See* quotation and borrowing; *specific genres*
Boyarin, Jonathan, 68
Bozo, Yaqov, 59, 89, 239n.3
Bradley Beach community, 65
Brazilian community, 78, 84; size of, 65
bris. *See* circumcision ceremonies; performance occasions and settings
Brooklyn, map of, *66*
Brooklyn community, 1–2, 80–82
Arab culture in, 224
bakkashot performance in, 118, 202
boundaries of, 67, 81–82
comparisons with Mexico City and Jerusalem communities, 86–89
dearth of professional female singers, 129
domestic music making, 116
enculturation of boys in, 15–16, 44, 55, 82, 161–63, 167–69
formation of, 81
hiring of outside instrumentalists, 131
instrumentalists in, 129–32
Kabbalah in, 223
as keepers of tradition, 83–84, 89
lack of contact with Muslim and Christian Syrians, 113–14
links to Aleppo community, 47
migration patterns of, 78–82
pizmon composition in, 184–89
pizmon repertories of, 200–204
prestige of, 42
Sebet tradition, 33, 95, 161–63, 167–69
size of, 65
Syrian minority status within Jewish community, 73
Taboush students in, 33, 34, 89
territoriality of, 75
transmission of "Ani Ashir Lakh" in, 94–95
transmission of "Attah El Kabbir" in, 54–55, 59–60, 61
transnational identification of, 65–67
value of Arab music to, 108–9
Buenos Aires. *See* Argentinian community

Cabasso, Isaac, 15, 237n.26, 241n.17, 254n.5
Cain, Isaac, 85, 162
borrowings of European art music, 192–94, 205–6, 244n.44
cassette recordings of, 44, 132
interaction with Brooklyn community, 84
marriage of, 82
pizmon repertory of, 200–204
as Tawil's student, 34, 59, 60–61
Cain, Ruth Tawil, 82, 84, 162, 241n.17
Cairo, Arab sound recordings from, 43, 107–9
Cairo community, 30, 56, 77, 78, 79–80
California community, size of, 65
Canadian community, 79
Canclini, Nestor Garcia, 234n.12
cantors (ḥazzanut)
amateur *vs.* professional, 128–29
circulating groups of, 82–84
interaction with congregation, 133, 192
Israeli musical practices of, 83, 87
knowledge of maqāmāt, 120–21, 124–25
pizmon compositions of, 185
training of, 35, 44
Caruso, Enrico, 192
cassettes. *See* sound recordings
Catskill Mountains, 61, 160, 240n.13
Catton, Joseph, 130, 245n.6
Catton, Sam, 80, 219
Central American communities, formation of, 78
Chacalo, Jose, 244n.43
chain migration, 77–78
Chaplin, Charlie, "Eternally," 194, 252n.20
Chopin, Frédéric, Nocturne in G Minor, 248n.3
circumcision ceremonies, 67, 125, 155–58, 203, 204. *See also* performance occasions and settings
classification, genre, 148–49, 170
Clifford, James, 68
"Coca Cola Grande," 194
Cohen, G., 8
Cohen, Meyer, 245n.6
Cohen, Sophie Kaire, 51, 52
Cohen-Saban, Albert, 79–80; pizmonim of, 185–87
commemoration. *See* memory and remembrance
Congregation Maguen David (Mexico City), 84, 208, 243n.31, 244n.43
Congregation Shaare Zion (Brooklyn), 118, 208, 243n.33
Congress of Arab Music (Cairo), 119, 121
Connerton, Paul, 9
contrafactum, 28–29
cognitive and ritual importance of, 218
pizmon tradition as, 29, 217–18
Cottrau, Teodoro, "Santa Lucia," 251n.9
cowboy songs, 16

daʿire, 132
Damascus community, 56, 82
"Attah El Kabbir" in, 60
compared with Aleppo community, 86
importance of cassette recordings, 85
persecution of, 86
remnants of, 64
darābukkah, 54, 129, 131
Darwīsh, Sayyid, 109
David, King, 69–70
dawr, 55, 96–97, 112, 150
Deal community, 16, 65, 135; differences from Brooklyn community, 89
dhimma pact, 70
diaspora, definition of, 68
dissemination, patterns of, 56–61
Divre Mordekhai, 237n.30
dīwān, 28, 124
Druze people, 109
dynamics, relation to mood in performance, 125

Egypt. *See also* Cairo
mass migration of Jews from, 79–80
recording industry of, 107–9
Egyptian music and songs. *See also* Arab music and songs
film music, 136, 185
as sources for pizmonim, 49, 84, 94–97
"Eḥezeh Veno'am," 239n.2
Eisenberg, Sophie Lentschner, 251n.11
"El Al Shir," 251n.12
"El Mistatter," 236n.21
Elakkad, Mohamed, 131, 248n.34
"Eli, Eli," 43
Elijah tradition, 156–57
Elnadav, Raphael, 60, 243n.33, 247n.30, 250n.7
career of, 251n.12
pizmonim of, 185, 187, 238n.37
recordings of, 85, 254n.8
enculturation, in Brooklyn community, 15–16, 44, 55, 82, 161–63, 167–69
Entebi, Meir, 84
"Eʿrokh Mahalal," 157

ethnomusicology
cognitive *vs.* cultural studies, 12, 13
focus on collective over individual experience, 182
lack of studies on memory, 6
musical *vs.* cultural studies, 13
European art music, borrowings of for liturgical use, 193–94, 205–6, 244n.44

Fairuz, xvii, 111, 253n.30
Fakhri, Sabah, 114
fann, 107
Farhi, Edward, 83–84
Feder, Stuart, 8, 215–16
Festival of Holidays: Recipe Book, 169
Fiddler on the Roof, 185, *186,* 187
firqah ensemble, 111; instrumentation of, 137
Flatbush. *See* Brooklyn community
Florida community, 65, 80
Floyd, Samuel A., 221–22
food, connections with music, 168–69
Forum (New York), 114
Foucault, Michel, 10
Franco, David E., 40
Franco, Samuel Aharon, 198
"Francos," 71
"Frère Jacques," 158–59, 203

Gates, Henry Louis, Jr., 2
genre, notion of, 148–49, 154, 170
"God Bless America," 170, 213
Gramophone Company, 107
Greek music, as sources for Jewish songs, 28
Guilbault, Jocelyne, 240n.9

"Ha-Tikvah," 194, 252n.19
Haber, Gracia Taboush, 116, 236n.17, 241n.19
family migration of, 78
recollections of Taboush, 30–31
"Ḥad Gadya," 51
Hadaya, Eliyahu Abraham, 48
"Ḥai Hazzan" (Taboush), 33, 197–98; text of, *265*
Halbwachs, Maurice, 9, 50
Halevi, Judah, "Libbi Ve-Mizraḥ," 227
Halleluyah Betzalzali Samaʿa, 84
Hamouwy, Grace, 30
handasah al-ṣawt, 119
Harari, Sadegh, 34–35, 80
"Havah Nagilah," 94
"Havu Godel L'Elohenu" (Ashear), 197
Hayyim ha-Kohen, Raphael, 38, 253n.29
Hayyim ha-Kohen, Shlomo Arieh ben Raphael, 253n.29
Heifetz, Jascha, 110
Herzog, George, 251n.11
"heterotopia," 10
Ḥijāzī, Salāmah, 106, 245n.10
"Hineh Mah Tov," 187
history, memory and, 25–27
Houston community, 78
Ḥusni, Dawud, 109
Husni, Mazal, *91*

Idelsohn, Abraham Zvi, 56–59, 253n.31
Imber, Naphtali Herz, "Ha-Tikvah," 252n.19
Immigration Quota Act, 77
improvisation
in Arab music, 126, 132, 189
in bakkashot, 190–91
of cantors, 125
composition *vs.,* 189–90
individual styles in, 191–92
of petiḥot, 152–53, 191
in pizmonim, 55–56, 133, 178
processes of, 189–95
viewed as sweetener, 55, 168, 191
India, Sufi people of, 6
insiders' maps, 90–91
instrumentalists, within Syrian Jewish communities, 129–30
"Inta al-Ḥubb," 251n.12
"Inta ʿUmrī" (ʿAbd al-Wahhāb), 185
īqāʿ (concept), 118–19
Islamic societies, minority communities within, 70
Israel. *See also* Jerusalem
changes to pizmon style in, 83, 87–88
differences from New World communities, 87
pizmon repertories in, 89
Syrian Jewish communities in, 82, 83, 85, 161, 240n.11
Israel, Vita, 54, 235n.6, 239n.1
Ives, Charles, 8; "The Things Our Fathers Loved," 216, 218

Jakobson, Roman, 148
Jerusalem community, 2, 40, 56, 77, 80
bakkashot performance in, 82, 87–88, 117, 202, 244n.40
comparisons with Brooklyn and Mexico City communities, 86–89

Jerusalem community (*continued*)
social mixing with other Sephardic Jews, 81–82
transmission of "Attah El Kabbir" in, 57, 59, 60
use of *Sheer Ushbahah Hallel Ve-Zimrah* collection, 42
"Jerusalem of Gold," 158
Jewish communities, importance of memory in, 10–11. *See also* Syrian Jews; *specific communities*
Jewish Community Center (Staten Island), 54
Jewish liturgical poetry, acrostics in, 45
Jewish music
borrowing tradition in, 27–28
prohibition against instruments in synagogue, 130
Jewish mysticism, 45, 222–23, 228, 249n.8
"Jews of Syria" conference, 208
Jolson, Al, 93
Jubal, story of, 26
Judeo-Spanish folksongs, 28, 203

Kabbalah, 222–23, 228, 235n.10
Kaddish, 61; text of, *266*
Kaire, Hyman, 45, 60, 117–18, 190–91, 236n.21, 245n.6
Kaire(y) family, 52
Kairey, Meyer (Mickey), 34, 89, 170, 240n.13
pizmon repertory of, 200–204
tribute to, 15, 18
Kaluli people (Papua New Guinea), gisalo song texts of, 6
kamanjah, 247n.32
Kassin, Jacob Saul, 40, 42–43, 222, 235n.9
Kassin, Joyce, 49, 51, 111, 189, 239n.43
kedushah, 249n.8
khānah (section), 17–18, 55
Kochak, Eddie, 248n.34

laḥan, 119
laments, 217; as commemoration, 6
ʿlamoʿadim, 159
Langer, Lawrence L., *Holocaust Testimonies: The Ruin of Memory,* 11
lawn (concept), 125
layālī (vocal improvisation), 12, 55, 126, 132–33, 153, 178, 190, 191, 247n.31, 249n.7
"L'Chaim: A Festival of Jewish Arts," 54, 61
Lebanese community, 80, 84
Leniado, David, 34–35
Leon, Meier, 252n.19
Levant
Arab/Jew relationships in, 3
Sephardic communities in, 29
Ha-Levy, Ezra Betesh, 186
Levy, Ralph Shasho, 245n.6
"Lezeved habbat," 158
"Libbi Ve-Mizraḥ" (Halevi), 227
Lipsitz, George, *Time Passages,* 9–10
Lower East Side. *See* Manhattan community
Luria, Isaac, 235n.10

Macon, Georgia, 80
madhhab (section), 96–97
Magen David Synagogue (67th Street, Bensonhurst), 16, 18, 33, 34, 37, 81, 170, 207
"Mah Tov," 157; text of, *262*
Maimon, Abraham, 238n.34
Maimyn, Abraham, 238n.34
"Male Fi," 249n.9
"Mamlekhot Ha'areṣ," 250n.17
Manchester community, 78, 87
Manhattan community, 33, 52, 80
"Attah El Kabbir" in, 59–60
bakkashot performance of, 117–18
broader community activities of, 67
differences from Brooklyn community, 89
formation of, 77–78, 81
al-Manyalāwī, Shaykh Yūsuf, 245n.10
Mapuche people (South America), tayil repertory of, 149
maqām (pl. maqāmāt)
affective associations of, 123–25, 168
ʿajam, 120, 247n.29, 249n.9; affect of, 124; correspondence to major scale, 137, 194, 207, 208, 251n.9; origin of, 49–50; uses of, 159
applied to non-Arab music, 126–27, 205
of bakkashot, 117
bayātī, 16, 17, 97, 120, 162, 163, 177, 178, 193, 204, 249n.7; popularity of, 122, 201; uses of, 123
bayātī kurd, 185
cantorial training in, 35
concept of, 118–27
concept of color and flavor in, 125–26, 127
geographic origins of, 49–50
girga, 203
ḥijāz, 120, 122, 123, 126; affect of, 124, 125; origin of, 49
ḥusaynī, 122

identification of, 121–22
ʿirāq, 247n.27
jihārkah, 247n.29
kurdy, 246n.22, 247nn. 28, 30
lāmī, 246n.22
learning techniques for, 122–23
liturgical use of, 123–25
"maqām of the day" practice, 123, 135, 159, 190, 192
modulation between, 122, 124–25, 132–33, 152–53, 191
muḥayyir bayāt, 247n.23, 250n.17
nahāwand, *56,* 57, 61, 97, 120, 126, 159, 190, 250n.17, 251n.12; correspondence to minor scale, 55–56, 194
nahāwand kurd, 187
nahāwand morasa, 97
perception of, 121–22
popularity of, 50
rāst, 120, 158, 190, 202–3; importance of, 123–24
rahawy nawā, 247n.25
sāz kār, 246n.21
ṣabā, 120, 121–22, 126, 193, 204; affect of, 124; origin of, 49; uses of, 125, 155–56, 157, 160, 203
in *Sheer Ushbahah Hallel Ve-Zimrah,* 120
sīkāh, 120, 160, 190, 250n.17; uses of, 123, 156
tables of, *121, 201*
use in pizmon classification, 40, 41, 44, 49–50
use in Sabbath services, 192
ʿushayrān, 247n.24
viewed as scales, 121
in waṣlah, 132–33
Mashriq region, 105
Massry, Louis, 79, 130, 245n.6
pizmonim of, 185
"Ramaḥ Evarai," 136, 138–39
Massry, Moses, 79, 131
"Maʿuzzi," 45, 163, 239n.2, 254n.6; text of, *264*
mawwāl, 109, 245n.13
"Meʿammi Tasim," 190, 199
"Melekh Hadur," text of, 225
"Melekh Raḥaman" (Taboush), 33, 159, 197, 249n.9
composition of, 207–8
melody of, *209–10*
popularity of, 207–9
text of, 207–8, *211*
"Melekh Ram," melody of, 253n.32
memory and remembrance
affective, 5
of Arab musicians, 109–15
artworks' reliance on, 7
celebratory, 214, 219
collective, 5, 8–10, 15–16, 45–53, 171, 204, 213–15, 218–19
commemorative, 218–19
cultural, 221–23
emotion and, 215–16
encoding processes of, 8
episodic (flashbulb), 215–18
familial, 5, 50–53, 150–51, 159, 195–98, 204–5, 206, 207–8, 220
food and, 168–69
formative processes of, 12
historical, 5, 11, 25–27
importance in Jewish communities, 10–11, 43
importance in Syrian Jews' culture, 8
individual, 8–10, 45–53, 150–51, 160, 171, 199–204, 208, 213–14
long-term, 234n.9
moment of constitution, 8
music and, 6, 8, 12, 25, 213–15, 217–18
of musical trends, 5
nostalgic, 215–16
oral transmission and, 216–17
pizmon repertories, 199–204
pizmon's role in, 4–5, 6–9, 10–12
popular culture and, 9–10
psychological aspects of, 6
reminiscences, 215–18
research on, 12
retrieval clues, 246n.18
role of family and religious life, 9, 117–18
selective, 223, 228
short-term, 234n.9
of singers, 45
sound recordings and, 44–45
spatial/geographic, 5, 48–50
tradition and, 25, 214
traumatic, 11
triggers for, 215
unconscious, 7–8
written transmission and, 38
Menaged, Eliyahu, 60, 89, 203
biography of, 34, 40
improvisational talent of, 191
sound recordings of, 45
as Taboush's student, 32
Mendelssohn, Felix, Violin Concerto, 194

Mexico City community, 2, 49, 80, 84, 109, 192–95
Aleppo and Damascus Jews in, 243n.31
anti-Semitic incidents against, 68
comparisons with Brooklyn and Jerusalem communities, 86–89
decline of bakkashot performance in, 88, 118, 202
decline of pizmon performance in, 89
domestic music making, 116
formation of, 77, 78
importance of cassette recordings, 44, 85
interaction with Brooklyn community, 82
lack of contact with Muslim Syrians, 114
pizmon repertory in, 202–4
popularity of Umm Kulthūm, 111
Sebet tradition, 162
size of, 65, 88–89, 192–93
Syrian minority status within Jewish community, 73
Taboush students in, 33–35
transmission of "Ani Ashir Lakh" in, 94–95
transmission of "Attah El Kabbir" in, 59, 60–61
use of *Sheer Ushbahah Hallel ve-Zimrah* collection, 42
use of synthesizers, 132
"Mi Kamokha," 169
"Mi Yemallel," 160
"Mi Yesapper," 48, 154
"Mi Zot" (Ashear), 152, 183
"Mibbeten Yedid," 157
"Mifalot Elohim" (Ashear), 198, *199*
migration patterns, 64–91, 109
American immigration data, 75, 77
chain migration, 77–78
Egyptian mass exodus, 79
"Mis Hermanos," 205
"Mishamayim," 190
Mishan, Ezra, 237n.25
"Mizzivakh Tanhir" (Ashear), 196–97
Moṣa'ei Shabbat, 40–41, 200
Mosseri, Joseph, 80
"Mother, Don't Cry Over Me," 199
Mozart, Wolfgang Amadeus, 205, 234n.8
Murād, Layla, 110
Murād, Zakī, 110, 112; "Ashkī li-min dhū al-hawā," 246n.15
mūsīqā, 119
Mustacchi, Menachem, 245n.6; pizmon repertory of, 200–204
musta'riba, 71, 224
muwashshāḥ, 108, 109, 150, 163, 245n.11; form of, 55
"My Country, 'Tis of Thee," 199

Nahari, Yehiel, 192, 243n.33
Najara, Israel, 28–29
names, derivations of, 47–48
Nasar, Alan, 135
Nasar family, Shemuel, 196–97
nāy, 130, 132
Neapolitan Songs, 251n.9
New Jersey shore, 65, 92. *See also* Bradley Beach; Deal
Nishmat Kol Hay, 84
"Nora Varam" (Taboush), 163, 221
nostalgia, 215–16
nūbah, 132
NYU Urban Ethnomusicology Seminar, 121, 149, 172

"O Tannenbaum," 198, *199*
Obadia, Hakki, 131, 235nn. 1, 6, 239n.1, 248n.34
oral transmission
of bakkashot, 116–18
of cooking arts, 169
within families, 50–53
generational reversal of, 52, 116
history and, 224
individual's role in, 200
past and present in, 26
processes of and occasions for, 36–38, 160, 161–63, 167–69, 204–6
role of circulating groups of cantors and rabbis, 82–84
role of memory in, 214, 216–17
Taboush, line of, 30–35
of texts, 8
ornamentation
in Arab music, 126, 127, 137
in pizmonim, 191
Ottoman empire, 71, 106
dissolution of, 75
map of, *76*

Pakistan, Sufi people of, 6
Panamanian community, 78, 80; size of, 65
Parsons, Geoffrey, 252n.20
Passover, 160, 171
performance occasions and settings
for Arab music, 37, 106
bar mitzvahs, 46, 135–39, 155, 171, 172, 183–84, 185, 189, 195–97, 251n.12

birth of girls, 155, 158–59, 223
birthday of Charlie Serouya, 16
births, 186–87, 203
circumcision ceremonies, 155–58, 171, 203, 204
coffeehouses, 106, 115, 183
concerts, 46, 106, 131, 169, 208
domestic, 35–36, 51–52, 115–16, 161–63, 167–69
festivals, 54, 61
genre and, 149, 170–71
Jewish holidays, 15, 60, 155, 159–60, 171
life cycle rituals, 35, 125, 155–59, 214–15, 218–19
liturgical (synagogue), 35–36, 37, 123, 150–51, 159–61, 192
parties, 35, 131, 155, 169
religious schools, 15–16, 37–38, 44, 82
special occasions, 169–70
tribute to Mickey Kairey, 15, 18, 170
wedding anniversaries, 92–94, 97, 132, 169
weddings, 155, 159, 171, 198–99, 207
youth services, 38
petiḥah (pl. petiḥot), 172
aesthetic and affective properties of, 153–54
collections of, 41, 227
function of, 152–53
improvisation of, 152–53, 190, 191
preceding pizmonim, 13, 133, 178
relationship to bakkashot, 152–54
repertories of, 200, 202
piyyutim, pizmon refrains in, 1
pizmon (pl. pizmonim). *See also* performance occasions and settings; text composition; *specific songs and composers*
aesthetic and affective properties of, 153–54
amateur composers of, 185
Arab melodic sources of, 1, 3–4, 5, 17–18, 48–50, 55, 59, 94–97, 104–34, 149–50, 152, 162–63, 169, 177–78, 183, 185, 186, 205, 207, 214, 216, 220, 223–26
cantorial training in, 35
as carrier of memories, 213–15
celebratory aspects of, 214, 219, 223
charts for appropriate use, 41, 123, 154, 159
collections of, 38–43
commemorative function of, 46, 47, 195–98, 204–5, 218–19
commissioning of, 46, 48–49, 170, 172, 177, 183–84
composer's responsibilities, 183–84
compositional processes in, 182–89
cultural meaning of, 3–12
definitions of, 1, 154–55
disputes over appropriate melodies, 198–99
encoding of memories in, 6, 7–8
in everyday life, 226–30
forms of, 55, 149–50, 216–17
genre classification difficulties, 149–50, 154, 170–71
healing contexts for, 220–23
as heterotopology, 10
historical constructions in, 223
historical roots of, 11, 27–28
as hybrid, 11–12, 25
importance in tradition and bringing communities together, 90–91
improvisation in, 55–56, 133, 178, 189–95
instrumental accompaniment of, 54, 92–93, 97, 169, 178
instrumental introductions to, 55, 97, 132–33, 178, 191
interpolated between bakkashot, 118, 153
lack of, at funerals, 219
in liturgical rituals, 123, 159–61, 192, 217
loss of, 29
maqām classification of, 41, 44, 49–50, 205
melodic sources for, 11, 27–28, 29, 49–50, 149–50, 152, 170, 183, 198–99, 203, 205, 213, 220 *(See also* Arab melodic sources, *above)*
melodies of, 4–5, 25, 48–50
melody selection process, 182–84, 187, 198, 213
memory processes and, 4–12, 25
origin myth for, 26–27
original melodies for, 187
ownership of, 46
patriarchal aspects of, 223
payment for, 46, 184
performance practice of, 132–34
performance settings for, 35–36, 95, 154–71, 204 (*See also under* performance occasions and settings)
performer/listener interaction, 133–34
performers for, 184
personal associations of, 45–46

pizmon (*continued*)
petiḥah introduction to, 13
popularity of, 4
preservation of, 44
references to time and place in, 48–50, 214
relationship to bakkashot, 150–52, 153–54
relative importance in Israel, New York, and Mexico City, 87–88
repertories of, 1, 49, 87–88, 89, 199–204
reused for liturgical prayers, 60–61, 192, 208, 217
rhythm of, 97, 118–19
ritual importance of, 218
sacred *vs.* secular performance distinctions, 95, 119, 154, 169
as social history, 220–23
as stabilizing factor, 223
status of, 152
suites of, 132
text content of, 5, 11, 25, 45–48, 124, 138–39, 159, 162–63, 174–77, 195–98, 207–8, 214, 219, 220–23, 227–28 (*See also under* text composition)
text copying and printing, 184, 187
text/melody perceptual dichotomy, 11–12, 36–37, 95, 119, 160, 225–26
tradition and, 206
transmission processes of, 2, 35–45, 82–85, 150
value in contemporary life, 228–30
viability factors in, 204–6
voluntary composition of, 184
women's performance of, 51, 116
written records on, 25
political concerns, 226–30
polkas, 203, 206
Pollak, Lew, "A Yiddishe Mameh," 244n.2
Porat Yosef Yeshiva (Jerusalem), 243n.32
Puerto Rico community, 78
Purim, 15, 157, 169

qānūn, 54, 129–30, 131, 137
qaraba (concept), 74
qaṣīdah, 108, 112, 245nn. 11, 13
quotation and borrowing
in ʿAbd al-Wahhāb's music, 127, 137
of European art music, 192–94, 205–6
of Ives, 215–16
in Jewish tradition, 28
in pizmonim, 216–17
Qur'ān recitation, 119, 123, 130

"Rabbat Sovʿah," 205
Rachmaninov, Sergei, Piano Concerto no. 2, 194
"Ram Leḥasdakh" (Taboush), 157–58, 203, 227; text of, *263*
"Ramaḥ Evarai," 155
compared with Arab source, 137–38
composition of, 135–36, 185
melody of, 136, 137, 138, *140–42,* 216
text of, 137, 138–39, *143–44,* 219
"Refa Ṣiri" (Taboush), 202–3, 253n.29; text of, 220–21, 222–23
register, relation to mood in performance, 125
remembrance. *See* memory and remembrance
rhythm
īqāʿ concept, 118–19, 137
krakoviak, 137–38
Rio de Janeiro. *See* Brazilian community
riqq, 130, 132, 137
Roman empire, 70
"Romemu Lo Bekol," 46
Rosenblatt, Yosele, 43
Rubin, David C., 8, 217

Sadat, Anwar, 112–13
Saff, Eddie (Ezra), 172
Saff, Isaac (Yitzhak), 172
Saff, Joseph, 46, 60, 214, 246n.18
on performance of "Attah El Kabbir," 56
on Syrian Jewish naming traditions, 48
pizmon repertory of, 200–204
pizmonim of, 195
seminar on Syrian musical traditions, 172–78
Saff family, 176–78, 184, 223
"Santa Lucia," 152, 183, 238n.34, 251n.9
al-Sayyid, Husayn, 136
scales
major, 137, 194, 207, 208
maqāmāt viewed as, 121, 194, 205, 207
minor, 56, 97, 194
Schachter, Daniel L., 7–8
Schweky, Sheila Tawil, 51, 52, 94
Seattle, Washington, 80
Sebet tradition, 33, 95, 161–63, 167–69, 217, 221
Sefer Hallel ve-Zimrah, 38, 40
Sefer Miqra Qodesh, 237n.30
Sefer Shir Ushevahah, 38, 253n.29
Sefer Shirei Zimrah Hashalem, 40, 237n.31
semiology, 148
Sephardic Archives, 1–2, 86; logo of, 90–91

Sephardic Community Center, 1, 15, 46, 86
Sephardic Jews
  definition of, 72–73
  expulsion from Spain, 71, 72
  history of, 72–73
  in Israel, 87
  Syrian Jews as, 68, 71–75, 104
Sephardic Prayer Songs for the High Holy Days, 85, 254n.8
Serouya, Charlie, 16–17, 36, 170, 213
Serure, Walter, 245n.6
Shaare Zion Congregation (Brooklyn), 251n.12
Shalom, Isaac, 40, 237n.28
Shamaʿa family, 208
al-Shawwā, Sāmī, 110, 246n.17
Sheer Ushbahah Hallel ve-Zimrah (SUHV), 1, 161
  blank pages in, 169
  classification scheme in, 40, 41–42, 123
  content of, 40–41
  criticisms of and corrections to, 41–42, 202
  dissemination of, 42, 84
  first edition of, 40–42
  indexes in, 41, 123, 154, 159, 200, 202
  individuals memorialized in, 36, 40
  introductory texts in, 27, 40, 42–43, 222
  maqāmāt included in, 120
  permissions issues, 41
  petiḥot in, 152, 227
  pizmonim appropriate for circumcision ceremonies, 157–58
  pizmonim appropriate for holidays, 159–60
  pizmonim appropriate for weddings, 159
  pizmonim included in, 94, 200
  preparation of, 38, 40
  punctuation in, 41–42
  references to healing in, 222
  social history in, 220
  subsequent editions of, 40, 42
  title page of, *39,* 43, 168
  value of, 42
Shemer, Shlomo, 59, 244n.44
Shemi, Shaul, 59
Sherman, Cheryl B., 54
Shirei Ṣiyyon, 227
Shiro, David, 169
"Shiru Shirah Ḥadashah," 170
Shrem, Gabriel, 17, 41, 187–88
  cassette recordings of, 44, 253n.25
  editorship of *Sheer Ushbahah Hallel Ve-Zimrah,* 38, 40–41
  family migration of, 79, 80
  on Syrian Jewish naming traditions, 47
  pizmon repertory of, 200–204
Shrem, Jacob (Jack), 242n.26
Shrem, Yosef Haim, 50
Sinai/Suez War, 79
Sitt, Albert, 78
Sitt family, 78
Smetana, Bedřich, "Moldau," 194
Smith, Kate, 170
Snug Harbor Cultural Center (Staten Island), 54
Soja, Edward, 10
Someck, Ronny, 233n.1
sound recordings
  of bakkashot, 88
  of cantors, 84–85
  as transmission sources for Arab songs, 37, 107–9, 111, 136, 183, 214
  transmission value of, 43–45, 84–85, 113–14, 120
Spain
  expulsion of Jews from, 71, 72
  medieval Arab musical life in, 119
  medieval Jewish community in, 27–28, 45, 227
Spanish music, as sources for Jewish songs, 28, 203, 205
Spence, Jonathan, 9
Sufi people, qawwali rituals of, 6
"Sunrise, Sunset," 187
Ṣur Yah El, 239n.2
  composition of, 16, 170, 185
  dedication to Serouya, 16, 36
  form of, 17–18, 150
  melody of, 17, *18–20*
  multiple levels of memory in, 18
  popularity of, 15, 18
  rhythm of, 17
  text of, 17, *20–24,* 227
  use as opening pizmon, 17–18
Suya people (Brazil), vocal genres of, 149
Synagogue Bet Torah, 237n.26
Synagogue Shaare Zion (Ocean Parkway), 16
synesthesia, 126, 168–69
synthesizers, 130, 132
Syria, establishment of, 75
Syrian Jews. *See also specific communities and topics*
  acquisition of knowledge of Arab music, 115–18
  antipathy toward songs of death, 219
  Arab culture and, 11, 104–34, 223–26
  broader community activities of, 67

Syrian Jews (*continued*)
 circulating groups of cantors and rabbis, 82–84
 circumcision traditions of, 155–58
 circumscribed social life of, 64
 community boundaries of, 67, 214, 220
 comparing communities, 85–89
 cousin marriages of, 67, 78
 diasporas of, 68–91
 economic activities of, 65–67, 70–71
 funeral customs, 219
 healing practices of, 221–23
 identity issues of, 72–75
 importance of memory in culture, 8
 instrumentalists in communities, 129–32
 interactions with Muslims, 3, 71, 73–74, 113–14, 115, 226–30
 intercommunity marriage, 82
 knowledge of maqāmāt, 118–27
 lack of contact with Muslim and Christian Syrians, 113–14
 lack of knowledge of īqāʿ, 118–19
 life cycle events of, 67, 74
 maqām concept applied to non-Arab music, 126–27
 marriage customs of, 67, 78, 82, 240n.14
 migration patterns of, 64–91
 minority status within Jewish community, 73
 mourning customs of, 176–77
 naming traditions of, 47–48, 135
 origins of, 69–72
 professional *vs.* amateur musicians, 127–29
 references to "saying" *vs.* "singing," 119–20
 relationship to Jewish diaspora, 68
 as Sephardic Jews, 68, 71–75, 104
 territorial concepts of, 74–75
 transnational networks of, 2, 44, 49, 64, 82–85

Taboush, Abraham, 30
Taboush, Isaac, 30
Taboush, Isaac (II), 30
Taboush, Joseph, 30, 115
Taboush, Raphael Antebi, 115
 "Ani Lishmakh," 203
 "Attah El Kabbir," 30, 54–63, 83, 90, 150, 190, 204, 250n.17, 254n.6
 children of, 32
 as cynosure, 184–85
 derivation of name, 48
 "Ḥai Hazzan," 33, 197–98
 lack of musical training, 128
 life of, 30–32
 "Melekh Raḥaman," 33, 159, 197, 207–11, 249n.9
 "Nora Varam," 163, 221
 oral traditions about, 30–31, 35, 213, 221, 228
 pizmonim of, 30, 31–32, 160, 183, 247n.24
 "Rabbat Sovʿah," 205
 "Ram Leḥasdakh," 157–58, 203, 227
 "Refa Ṣiri," 202–3, 220–23, 253n.29
 role of, 29
 Sefer Shir Ushevahah, 38, 253n.29
 as *Sheer Ushbahah Hallel ve-Zimrah* dedicatee, *39,* 40
 students of, 32, 33–35, 59, 83, 89, 197, 207–8
 voice of, 32
 "Yaḥid Ram," 30, 162–66, 193, 204, 221, 249n.14, 254n.6
Taboush, Seti (II), 30
Taboush, Seti Ades, 30
Taboush, Yehudah, 236n.20
takht ensemble, 111, 132, 169; instrumentation of, 129–30
taqsīm (pl. taqāsīm), 12, 55, 126, 131, 137, 247n.31
ṭaqṭūqah, 109, 245n.14
ṭarab, 107–8, 112, 133
Tawil, Abe, 235n.1
Tawil, Abraham, 80
Tawil, Alice, 92–97
Tawil, David, 34, 115–16, 119, 202, 245n.6, 247n.30; knowledge of maqāmāt, 121
Tawil, Ezra, 34, 238n.37, 251n.12
Tawil, Hayyim, 33–34, 60, 193, 244n.43; as Taboush's student, 32, 59, 197–98, 203
Tawil, Mordekhai, 238n.37
Tawil, Moses, 34, 44, 50–51, 55–56, 83, 89, 135–36, 225, 239n.3, 253n.24
 golden wedding anniversary of, 92–97, 132
 performances of, 94–97
 pizmon repertory of, 200–204, 253n.25
Tawil, Moses (II), 135
Tawil, Naphtali, 34, 40, 89, 198, 202
Tawil, Sarah, 50, 116, 129, 241n.19
Tawil family, 50–51, 80
tawshiḥ, 163
Tchaikovsky, Peter Ilyich, "Nutcracker Ballet," 137–38, 216
text composition, 182–89
 acrostics in, 17, 45, 55, 162, 188, 196, 207, 219

amateur composers of, 185
Arab-to-Hebrew correspondences and transformations, 95–96, 182, 188, 225–26
collaboration in, 187–88
commemorative importance of, 213, 218–19
content and allusion in, 5
holiday references in, 124
lack of women composers, 189
metaphor in, 227–28
multiple levels in, 214–15, 220–23, 226–30
occasions for, 155–60
payment for, 184
process of, 185–89
references to people in, 45–48, 138–39, 159, 162–63, 174, 177, 183–84, 195–98, 204, 207–8, 214, 219, 221
social history in, 220–23
time constraints of, 188–89
use of Hebrew, 27, 95, 169
voluntary, 184, 197
tiran, 137
tradition
importance of pizmonim in, 90, 206, 229–30
memory and, 214
time depth of, 25
transmission of, 25–27
transmission processes. *See* enculturation; oral transmission; sound recordings; written transmission
"Triste vida," 203
turāth, 108, 109, 112
Turkish music
in Aleppo, 106–7
as sources for pizmonim, 28, 49

ʿūd, 54, 129–31, 247n.33
ughniyah (pl. ughniyāt), 109, 136
ululations, 94
Umm Kulthūm, 93, 108, 109, 129, 185, 229, 251n.12
career of, 110–12
poem about, *231*
recordings of, 84, 111
"Uri Neṣurah," 236n.21

Victor Talking Machine Company, 107
violin, 54, 110, 129–30, 131
Vital, R. Hayyim, 235n.10

Wallace, Wanda, 217
Warda, 111, 114
waṣlah, 132
waṭan (concept), 74
"Wheat Song, The" ("Al-qamḥ") (ʿAbd al-Wahhāb), 136–37, 139, *144–47,* 216
Winston-Salem, North Carolina, 80
women
as cultural and musical carriers, 3–4, 35–36, 51–52, 167–69
knowledge of Arab music theory, 122
knowledge of Arabic, 225
musical participation of, 117, 118, 119, 129, 189
paucity of references to in pizmonim, 197, 223
as professional singers, 129
role at Sebet, 162, 163, 167–68
role in pizmon tradition, 27, 51, 116, 223
separation of, 4, 26, 27, 117, 162
status of, 240n.14
World Center for Traditional Aleppo Culture (Aleppo Heritage Society; Tel Aviv), 86, 169
written transmission, 38–43, 178; of texts, 216

"Ya Ana, Ya Ana," 253n.30
"Yaḥid Ram" (Taboush), 30, 193, 204, 254n.6
melody of, 162, *164–66*
text of, 162–63, 221, 249n.14, *263–64*
"Yaḥish Mevasser," 160
"Yaḥon El Ṣur," 157, 249n.12
"Yawm wa-Layla" (ʿAbd al-Wahhāb), 185
Yedid, Menachem, 59
"Yehi Shalom," 157, 190; text of, *259–60*
"Yeḥidah Hitnaʿari" (Ashear)
composition of, 174–77, 184, 252n.14
melody of, 177, 178, *179–80,* 199–200
text of, 172–74, *175, 181,* 195, 220
transmission of, 203–4
Yellen, Jack, "A Yiddishe Mameh," 244n.2
"Yeromem Ṣuri," 159
Yerushalmi, Yosef, 10–11
Yeshiva University, Cantorial School, 44
"A Yiddishe Mameh," 94, 244n.2

Zalta, Benjamin, 205, 244n.41
Zaroura, Joseph, 235n.6, 239n.1
Zemirot Israel, 28
Zerubavel, Yael, 11
Zion, Yehezkel, 84, 95